BEING HOLY IN THE WORLD

D1446281

Being Holy in the World

THEOLOGY AND CULTURE
IN THE THOUGHT OF
DAVID L. SCHINDLER

Edited by

Nicholas J. Healy Jr.
D. C. Schindler

William B. Eerdmans Publishing Company
Grand Rapids, Michigan / Cambridge, U.K.

Published 2011 by
Wm. B. Eerdmans Publishing Co.
2140 Oak Industrial Drive N.E., Grand Rapids, Michigan 49505 /
P.O. Box 163, Cambridge CB3 9PU U.K.

Printed in the United States of America

17 16 15 14 13 12 11   7 6 5 4 3 2 1

Library of Congress Cataloging-in-Publication Data

Being holy in the world: theology and culture in the thought of David L. Schindler /
    edited by Nicholas J. Healy Jr., D. C. Schindler.
        p.   cm.
    Includes index.
    ISBN 978-0-8028-6554-0 (pbk.: alk. paper)
    1. Schindler, David L., 1943- 2. Catholic Church — Doctrines.
    3. Christianity and culture.   I. Healy, Nicholas J.   II. Schindler, D. C.

BX1751.3.B445   2011
230'.2092 — dc22

                2011004301

www.eerdmans.com

Contents

Contents

Abbreviations

General

BM   *Beyond Mechanism: The Universe in Recent Physics and Catholic Thought,* ed. David L. Schindler (Washington, DC: The University Press of America, 1986)

CDVII   Joseph Ratzinger, "Commentary on Articles 11-22 of the Pastoral Constitution *Gaudium et Spes,*" in *Commentary on the Documents of Vatican II,* vol. 5, ed. Herbert Vorgrimler (New York: Herder and Herder, 1967-69)

CSA   *Catholicism and Secularization in America: Essays on Nature, Grace, and Culture,* ed. David L. Schindler (Huntington, IN: Our Sunday Visitor, 1990)

DS   H. Denzinger and A. Schönmetzer, *Enchiridion Symbolorum Definitionum et Declarationum de Rebus Fidei et Morum,* ed. 34 (Freiburg: Herder, 1967)

DT   Augustine, *De Trinitate*

EE   Claude Bruaire, *L'être et l'esprit* (Paris: PUF, 1983)

Gift   Kenneth L. Schmitz, *The Gift: Creation* (Milwaukee: Marquette University Press, 1982)

GL   Hans Urs von Balthasar, *The Glory of the Lord: A Theological Aesthetics* (San Francisco: Ignatius Press; New York: Crossroad, 1983-1991)

HW   David L. Schindler, *Heart of the World, Center of the Church:* Communio *Ecclesiology, Liberalism, and Liberation* (Grand Rapids: Eerdmans, 1996)

KB   Hans Urs von Balthasar, *The Theology of Karl Barth: Exposition and Interpretation* (San Francisco: Communio Books, Ignatius Press, 1992)

NM   Angelo Scola, *The Nuptial Mystery* (Grand Rapids: Eerdmans, 2005)
PG   J. Migne, *Patrologia Graeca*
TD   Hans Urs von Balthasar, *Theo-Drama: Theological Dramatic Theory,* vols. 1-5 (San Francisco: Ignatius Press, 1988-1998)
TL   Hans Urs von Balthasar, *Theo-Logic: Theological Logical Theory,* vols. 1-3 (San Francisco: Ignatius Press, 2000-2005)
UBLC   Hans Urs von Balthasar, *Unless You Become Like This Child* (San Francisco: Ignatius Press, 1991)
WPHD   *Wealth, Poverty, and Human Destiny,* ed. Doug Bandow and David L. Schindler (Wilmington, DE: ISI Books, 2003)
WR   Joseph Ratzinger and Marcello Pera, *Without Roots: The West, Relativism, Christianity, Islam* (New York: Basic Books, 2006)

Articles by David L. Schindler

"Catholicity and Theology"   "Catholicity and the State of Contemporary Theology: The Need for an Onto-Logic of Holiness," *Communio: International Catholic Review* 14 (1987): 426-450

"Christological Aesthetics"   "Christological Aesthetics and *Evangelium Vitae*: Toward a Definition of Liberalism," *Communio: International Catholic Review* 22 (1995): 193-224

"Christology and Imago Dei"   "Christology and the *Imago Dei*: Interpreting *Gaudium et Spes*," *Communio: International Catholic Review* 23 (1996): 156-184

"Christology and Public Theology"   "Christology, Public Theology, and Thomism: De Lubac, Balthasar, and Murray," in *The Future of Thomism*, ed. Deal W. Hudson and Dennis W. Moran (Notre Dame: University of Notre Dame Press, 1992)

"Church's 'Worldly' Mission"   "The Church's 'Worldly' Mission: Neoconservatism and American Culture," *Communio: International Catholic Review* 18 (1991): 365-397

"Creation and Nuptiality"   "Creation and Nuptiality: A Reflection on Feminism in Light of Schmemann's Liturgical Theology," *Communio: International Catholic Review* 28 (2001): 265-295

"Dramatic Nature of Life"   "The Dramatic Nature of Life in the Light of Love: Liberal Societies and the Foundations of Human Dignity," *Communio: International Catholic Review* 33 (2006): 183-202

"Homelessness"   "Homelessness and the Modern Condition: The Family, Community, and the Global Economy," *Communio: International Catholic Review* 27 (2000): 411-430

"Institution and Charism" "Institution and Charism: The Missions of the Son and the Spirit in Church and World," *Communio: International Catholic Review* 25 (1998): 253-273

"Is America Bourgeois?" "Is America Bourgeois?" *Communio: International Catholic Review* 14 (1987): 262-290

"Is Truth Ugly?" "Is Truth Ugly? Moralism and the Convertibility of Being and Love," *Communio: International Catholic Review* 27 (2000): 701-728

"Knowledge as Relationship" "God and the End of Intelligence: Knowledge as Relationship," *Communio: International Catholic Review* 26 (1999): 510-540

"Meaning and the Death of God" "On Meaning and the Death of God in the Academy," *Communio: International Catholic Review* 17 (1990): 192-206

"The Meaning of the Human" "The Meaning of the Human in a Technological Age: *Homo faber, Homo sapiens, Homo amans*," *Communio: International Catholic Review* 26 (1999): 80-103

"Modernity and Atheism" "Modernity, Postmodernity, and the Problem of Atheism," *Communio: International Catholic Review* 24 (1997): 563-579

"Person and Receptivity" "The Person: Philosophy, Theology, and Receptivity," *Communio: International Catholic Review* 21 (1994): 172-190

"Religion and Secularity" "Religion and Secularity in a Culture of Abstraction: On the Integrity of Space, Time, Matter, and Motion," in *The Strange New World of the Gospel,* ed. Carl E. Braaten and Robert W. Jenson (Grand Rapids: Eerdmans, 2002), 32-54; *Pro Ecclesia* 11 (2002): 76-94

"Religious Freedom and Liberalism" "Religious Freedom, Truth, and American Liberalism: Another Look at John Courtney Murray," *Communio: International Catholic Review* 21 (1994): 696-741

"Reply to Austriaco" "*Agere sequitur esse:* What Does It Mean? A Reply to Father Austriaco," *Communio: International Catholic Review* 32 (2005): 795-824

"Response to Joint Statement" "A Response to the Joint Statement, 'Production of Pluripotent Stem Cells by Oocyte Assisted Reprogramming,'" *Communio: International Catholic Review* 32 (2005): 369-380

"Significance of World and Culture" "The Significance of World and Culture for Moral Theology: *Veritatis Splendor* and the 'Nuptial-Sacramental' Nature of the Body," *Communio: International Catholic Review* 31 (2004): 111-143

Abbreviations

"Time in Eternity"   "Time in Eternity, Eternity in Time: On the Contemplative-Active Life," *Communio: International Catholic Review* 18 (1991): 53-68

"Toward a Culture of Life"   "Toward a Culture of Life: The Eucharist, the 'Restoration' of Creation, and the 'Worldly' Task of the Laity in Liberal Societies," *Communio: International Catholic Review* 29 (2002): 679-690

"Trinity, Creation, and the Academy"   "Trinity, Creation, and the Order of Intelligence in the Modern Academy," *Communio: International Catholic Review* 28 (2001): 406-428

"Truth, Freedom, and Relativism"   "Truth, Freedom, and Relativism in Western Democracies: Pope Benedict XVI's Contributions to *Without Roots*," *Communio: International Catholic Review* 32 (2005): 669-681

"*Veritatis Splendor* and Bioethics"   "*Veritatis Splendor* and the Foundations of Bioethics: Notes Toward an Assessment of Altered Nuclear Transfer (ANT) and Embryonic (Pluripotent) Stem Cell Research," *Communio: International Catholic Review* 32 (2005): 195-201

Introduction

The title of David Schindler's 1996 book, *Heart of the World, Center of the Church,* indicates the goal toward which the main thrust of his work, from his dissertation at the Claremont Graduate School in 1976, to his most recent writings on biotechnology, has aimed. The goal can be described succinctly: to think through the most urgent cultural problems to their deepest metaphysical roots, and to judge them at that level in the light of faith in the Trinitarian God of Jesus Christ and the concrete, sacramental, and ecclesial form that faith must necessarily take. What is unique about Schindler's view of the intersection of theology and culture is his relentless insistence on both the anthropological and metaphysical implications: the revelation of God in Jesus Christ not only reveals man to himself — as stated in what is no doubt the magisterial text most often cited by Schindler, *Gaudium et Spes,* 22[1] — but also reveals the meaning of *being* itself, and therefore the ultimate meaning of each and every thing in the universe without exception. According to Schindler, holiness is not limited to the spiritual order, strictly speaking, but runs analogously through the whole of being, unto its most rudimentary structures: space, time, matter, and motion: "In a word, holiness, with its call to share in the perfect love of the Father in the Son by the Spirit, is inclusive of the objective order of intelligence and of the meaning and truth of all created entities. Holiness is intended to comprehend the order of being in its entirety."[2] It may have been the unique threat to human life and human

---

1. "Christ, the final Adam, by the revelation of the mystery of the Father and his love, fully reveals man to himself and makes his supreme calling clear."
2. "Trinity, Creation, and the Academy," 412.

dignity posed by Anglo-American liberalism that opened this path for thinking, but increasingly Schindler's work has shown that the inseparability of a metaphysics of love and cultural engagement is itself rooted in the mystery of the Logos taking flesh and returning to the Father with all that the Father has made (cf. John 6:39).

Although Schindler is best known for the positions he has taken on a number of cultural issues — perhaps especially in the area of economics, and most recently in biotechnology — these positions are rooted in a profound theological and ontological vision that he has developed in an extensive body of work published over the past thirty-five years. Schindler and the "*communio* theology" that he represents have become regular reference points in Catholic intellectual discussions, and his thought has been the subject of many articles and dissertations. But in spite of his growing importance for contemporary debates, there has been to date no study devoted to presenting and developing his thought as a whole and in its foundations. As an attempt to fill this lacuna, the present book has a twofold purpose: on the one hand to show the unity of Schindler's thought in its development, and on the other hand to see the fruitfulness of this thought in relation to the particular areas of cultural concern he has addressed.

The essays are ordered thematically. The first three essays provide an orientation and overview of the main lines of Schindler's work. The next three essays explore the philosophical dimensions of Schindler's thought, with a particular focus on the theme of relationality. Finally, the third and largest section of the book takes up Schindler's contribution to various disputed questions on liberalism, economics, the nature of freedom, and the *imago trinitatis*. The last essay, "The Marian Dimension of Existence," provides a conclusion to the book by returning to the hidden center of Schindler's thought.

In the opening chapter, "Beauty and the Holiness of Mind," **D. C. Schindler** presents the conception of order or logos that unifies the wide-ranging themes of Schindler's philosophical and theological writings. "If Christianity is itself a logos," D. C. Schindler argues, "and indeed the ultimate form-giving logos of all worldly *logoi*, it bears simultaneously on the form and content of what individuals think and do, but also on the shape of the horizon in reference to which that thought and action understand themselves; it therefore has an essentially public or political dimension as well as a metaphysical and indeed a physical dimension." "To be truly Catholic, the mind must adopt and adapt itself to the form of holiness, not only in its moral activity, but first of all in its *logic*, i.e., in the conception of order that it presupposes in all of its deliberate acts, the conception that represents, as it were, the medium through which it engages all of its activities; and this logic of holiness requires the integration of the orders of the true and the good, an integration expressed by beauty."

Peter J. Casarella traces the development of Schindler's thought from his early essays on Whitehead and Aquinas through his engagement and common work with the theologians associated with the journal *Communio* — Henri de Lubac, Hans Urs von Balthasar, and Joseph Ratzinger — in an essay entitled "Trinity and Creation: David L. Schindler and the Catholic Tradition." Casarella shows that Schindler's thought represents a unique synthesis and retrieval of the tradition wherein Augustine, Aquinas, and von Balthasar are brought into conversation with Anglo-American sources such as Wendell Berry and Alasdair MacIntyre. The result is a renewed Christian humanism rooted in the analogy between God and creation that culminates in the mystery of Christ.

In "Theology and Culture," **Tracey Rowland** presents the sources and implications of Schindler's engagement with contemporary culture. "Schindler's achievement," Rowland suggests, "has been to take the theological insights of Balthasar, particularly his notion of there being a *logos* within every practice and culture, the account of the 'grace and nature' relationship of de Lubac, and the theological anthropology of John Paul II and Angelo Cardinal Scola, and apply them to an analysis of the culture of America, and more broadly, contemporary Western liberalism." Schindler's writings on culture have brought to light the essential difference between the hidden anthropology of liberal theory (and liberal institutions) and the Catholic tradition's understanding of the human person as constitutively related to God and others in Christ.

Schindler's theological engagement with culture entails a rethinking of philosophy, and philosophy's most basic objects, in the light of revelation. The next three essays address some aspect of this endeavor. **Nicholas J. Healy**'s essay, "*Praeambula fidei*: David L. Schindler and the Debate over 'Christian Philosophy,'" presents Schindler's contribution to the question of "Christian philosophy" against the backdrop of the unresolved debate of the 1930s between, inter alia, Gilson, Maritain, and Blondel. Can there be a philosophy that is intrinsically influenced by the revealed mysteries of God and yet distinct from theology? Schindler's affirmative answer to this question rests on two seminal insights: the first is that the "autonomy" that cannot be disregarded must nevertheless be interpreted specifically within the created order that receives its most ultimate meaning in Christ; the second is that "love tells us what it means to act in the highest and deepest sense — and thereby what it means most fully *to be*."[3]

In "'Constitutive Relations': Toward a Spiritual Reading of *Physis*," **Adrian J. Walker** interprets and develops Schindler's understanding of constitutive relationality as a privileged example of "Schindler's project of reconciling Christian novelty with classical metaphysics in what Balthasar calls a 'third way' of love that integrates what is best both in the ancients and in the moderns." "Just as Mary bears the incarnate Word without loss of her virginal integrity," Walker argues, "so, too, Christ enters into natures in a way that really 'affects' them without destroying their integrity. Christ really 'adds' something to nature and concepts, not by mutating their inner *logos*, or by mixing foreign elements into it, but by allowing it to bring him forth from out of themselves — from out of a depth that is both a new creation of his presence in it *and* the deepest truth they in some sense always already had."

The nature of science, and especially physics, has long been a focus of Schindler's interest, because he believes that the *meta*physical significance of Christianity, which the Fathers of the Church saw so clearly, will be lost to the extent that one fails to grasp its relevance even for the *physical* world. But a certain line of thinking in modern science, in denying that relevance, threatens to trivialize not only the Church but also the reality of the world itself. In "Beyond Mechanism: The Cosmological Significance of David L. Schindler's *Communio* Ontology," **Michael Hanby** develops the resources in Schindler's thought that allow for a recovery of a conception of nature at once more comprehensive and less reductive than the mechanism that shaped early modern science and that continues to inform assumptions about the nature of science, economics, and politics. Schindler's proposal is "more comprehensive because it includes *both* the mechanical manifestations of nature *and* those formal and qualitative features which mechanistic ontology regards as epiphenomenal, less reductive because it refuses to make the world less than the mystery it is by insisting that its reality conform to a defective concept of knowledge, allowing the forms of natural things to show forth of their own inner logic that the mystery of love constitutes them in their naturality."

The first four essays grouped in the third part of the book show the implications of Schindler's fundamental theological and metaphysical positions for important contemporary cultural and theological questions. In

---

3. "Person and Receptivity," 174.

"David L. Schindler and the Order of Modernity: Toward a Working Definition of Liberalism," **Larry S. Chapp** and **Rodney A. Howsare** present Schindler's account of liberalism's implicit understanding of the relationship between God and the world and human agency. At the heart of liberal anthropology is a conception of self as primitively constructive or creative. Thus relations are viewed preponderantly in terms of "doing" and "having," hence as manipulative in form if not also in content. "It is because the Western soul is so empty," Schindler writes, "that its patterns of thought and action are so mechanistic — and conversely. In a word, there is a direct link between a subjectivity (or will) become arbitrary and an objectivity (or reason) become 'techne.'"[4] Chapp and Howsare extend Schindler's argument with a reflection on what is to be done, given the spiritual poverty of liberal institutions and liberal ideology.

Stephen Long addresses Schindler's thought in the area of economics. In his essay, "A Balthasarian Theological Economics: Making Sense of David L. Schindler's Happy Baker," he develops the implications of Schindler's claim that "an economic system itself already embodies, indeed is also, a theology and an anthropology and a culture." A genuinely human and Christian economic order requires the following: "First, profit must be considered in terms of intrinsic goods and not simply as an index of human wills. Second, creativity must be considered as also a matter of receptivity. Third, the Catholic 'third way' beyond the either-or of capitalism/ socialism, which is represented in Catholic social teaching, cannot be rightly understood without the proper role for the Church in economics."

In "Freedom, Biologism, and the Body as Visible Order," **David S. Crawford** argues, on the basis of Schindler's theological and philosophical anthropology, that it is impossible to arrive at an adequate sense of either freedom or the body without seeing them as integrally related. The centerpiece of Schindler's anthropology is the idea that "human freedom is never its own source; it is never simply or purely spontaneous or self-originating. Rather, its 'originality' and genuine novelty is always first embedded within its origin in God and, in a real sense, all others." Crawford shows how this "being-given" that shapes freedom is expressed in the body, which possesses an inherently nuptial or familial form. "The body 'co-constitutes' freedom precisely as a visible order expressing not only the soul as form but also the order and destiny of the cosmos."

Antonio López elucidates the logic of gift that undergirds every as-

---

4. "Christological Aesthetics," 199.

pect of Schindler's work. As he elaborates in "*Donum Doni:* An Approach to a Theology of Gift," Schindler's metaphysics of creation finds its ultimate ground in a theology that considers the Triune God to be "an event of love." López shows how the Holy Spirit bears witness that "the necessity proper to the absolute spirit is a gratuitous and infinitely fruitful love. Without ever exhausting it, the 'gift of gift' reveals the mystery that the freedom of the absolute spirit, the Triune God, is nothing other than an indwelling whose form is that of a gratuitous and eternal giving of oneself."

The book's final essay illuminates the various levels of Schindler's thought in relation to the radiant mystery at the center of the Church's receptive heart. In "The Marian Dimension of Existence," **Stratford Caldecott** shows how the theology of Mary implicates not only the main teachings of Christianity (theology), but also our basic view of the world (ontology), and indeed our entire way of life (spirituality). "Mary, who is entirely creature (as distinct from her Son, who is both God and man) yet full of grace, represents and is the creation re-made, or the beginning and form of that re-making. . . . She becomes the Church, the fruit of the redemption, and the mother of all Christians in the order of grace, starting with John at the foot of the Cross. In her we see the proper relationship of nature and grace." It is only when we discover this Marian center of Schindler's thought that the whole matrix of his theological and philosophical work becomes evident: "The Marian fiat in which we can participate to the degree we ourselves become holy is the source of all spiritual maternity. It is this maternity to which we must look for a civilization of love and a culture of life."

It cannot be denied that modernity has brought with it great advances in the quality of life and in our understanding of the world, ourselves, and even aspects of the nature of God. But it is also impossible to deny that these advances have been accompanied at the same time by impoverishments in that understanding, as well as by new and sometimes severe problems in the way we live the call to holiness and inhabit the world. Many responses to the crisis in contemporary culture address the problems in isolated and partial ways. What distinguishes Schindler's response is that he aims to present a *comprehensive* critique, and indeed one that is specifically *theological*. In comparison with the typical responses that seek to preserve an optimism regarding the future of the West by balancing the achievements against the problems of modern culture, Schindler's approach, which sets into relief the way even the West's achievements participate in the most problematic features of modernity, may seem downright pessimistic. But, in fact, a fundamental theological critique such as this offers something more than optimism: it offers hope. Superficial diagnoses prompt essentially pragmatic solutions, which, as such, are not only bound to fail in the long run but will inevitably breed despair insofar as they neglect one of the greatest of all human needs, namely, the need for truth. Schindler's work, by contrast, is a relentless effort to reach the heart of the matter, to discover the unity beyond our cultural problems, to judge them in a comprehensive way, and thus to open the world to its foundations in the unconquerable love of God. If this dimension lies beyond any technical solution, by the very same token it touches the one sure basis of hope. The essays in the present book aim to reflect the various aspects of that hope in the thought of David L. Schindler, and so offer something of lasting value to the contemporary conversation.

NICHOLAS J. HEALY JR. and D. C. SCHINDLER

I

Beauty and the Holiness of Mind

D. C. Schindler

I. Introduction

The call to holiness comprehends the order of being in its entirety.[1] At the heart of David L. Schindler's exploration of the intersection of the theological and secular orders — being holy in the world — lies a particular interpretation of the nature of *logos,* in both its subjective dimension (as reason) and its objective dimension (as intelligible structure).[2] All thought and action are mediated by a particular conception of order. If the conception of order is inadequate, then no matter how sincere or well-meaning one might be in one's efforts to evangelize culture, those efforts will in profound and — therefore — subtle ways betray just what they seek to promote.[3] If the conception of order is inadequate, then the various institutions — the academy; economic, social, or political forms; the work of science and medicine — that are founded on that conception will foster a problematic mode of being regardless of the intentions, attitudes, and ideas of those who participate in the institutions.

To affirm this, of course, immediately raises the question, adequate according to what measure? And responding to this question returns us again to the center: the conception of order, the nature of *logos* must be adequate (both subjectively and objectively) to the love of the Father, as revealed in Jesus Christ, but must be adequate to that love in its most funda-

---

1. See "Trinity, Creation, and the Academy," 412.
2. See "Catholicity and Theology," 426-450.
3. Consider the way Schindler characterizes the positions of the various figures he intends to critique in his book, as examples of those who seek to be faithful to the mission of the Church, but who nevertheless follow a logic contrary to their aims: HW, 36.

mental reality, namely, to love understood simultaneously in terms of the drama of the Trinitarian life of God and in its ontological depths as expressing the ultimate meaning of being. The insistence on *logos* as central is, in short, precisely what allows the Christian claim to be genuinely comprehensive; or, in other words, it is indispensable for keeping those claims from becoming literally superficial — i.e., remaining on the surface of things — no matter how enthusiastically the claims may be lived out. If Christianity is itself a *logos,* and indeed the ultimate form-giving *logos* of all worldly *logoi,* it bears simultaneously on the form and content of what individuals think and do and also on the shape of the horizon in reference to which that thought and action understand themselves; it therefore has an essentially public or political dimension as well as a metaphysical and indeed a physical dimension. This latter dimension is perhaps the neuralgic center in Schindler's position: not because the physical aspect of reality is the most important (for of course it is not) but because, if we do not see that the Christian *logos* transforms what we commonly mean by time, space, matter, and motion, we will not in fact be receiving it as a *logos,* but rather as a moral inspiration or isolated and so inconsequential truth claim.

I wish to propose in the following essay that there is a unity to the wide-ranging themes in Schindler's work up to this point. His well-known criticisms of liberalism, of the Catholic Common Ground project, of stem cell research, of fragmentation in the academic disciplines, of neo-conservative politics and economics, of feminism, of the "American" style of religion, of secularism in the academy, of the neo-Thomist separation of grace and nature, of the objectivity claimed in "scientific" methodologies, of John Courtney Murray's conception of religious freedom, of traditional "substance" metaphysics, and so forth — for all of the integrity each of these themes possesses in its own right and the sets of problems and concerns that belong properly to each — arguably all turn on a single issue, namely, the failure to take seriously the implications of Christianity as a *logos.* Though there would be a number of ways of articulating this particular issue, and any number of ways of entering into the problematic it implies, I intend here to engage it in terms of the sanctity of the intellect, for two reasons: first, it allows us clearly to see the connection between Schindler's earliest work on theories of knowledge and the most recent criticisms of embryonic stem cell research, and, second, because inquiring into the relation between two terms that on their face seem to represent radically different orders — the order of the good (holiness) and the order of the true (mind) — brings us directly to the nub of the matter. I intend to show why beauty holds such significance for Schindler's Catholic critique of liberalism: the primacy of beauty is what ensures the integration of the orders of the true and the good, and therefore what makes clear and effective the comprehensive *logos*-character of Christianity, a comprehensiveness that liberalism systematically, if unwittingly, denies.

Schindler's thesis regarding the intellect can be stated in a straightforward way: to be truly Catholic, the mind must adopt and adapt itself to the form of holiness, not only in its moral activity, but first of all in its *logic*, i.e., in the conception of order that it presupposes in all of its deliberate acts, the conception that represents, as it were, the medium through which it engages all of its activities; and this logic of holiness requires the integration of the orders of the true and the good, an integration expressed by beauty. While it may seem to address a strictly "academic" issue, this thesis has deep and wide cultural implications. In order to feel its proper weight, it is best to view the thesis as the culmination of a particular line of inquiry, the development of a particular idea. To this end, instead of simply presenting the thesis, we will begin by gathering up the earliest threads of Schindler's reflection as it grew. We will first look at the critique of simple identity in his doctoral dissertation and show how this critique informs a theme underlying all of his work, namely, how to conceive a relation that avoids both assimilation (monism) and separation (dualism). Next, we will present the implications of this view of relation for the structure and operation of intellect with the aim of showing the significance of beauty. Finally, we will suggest how the holiness of mind illuminates other cultural questions and will consider some of its general implications. Along the way, we will try to point out a development of his thought that moves from the more abstract language of metaphysics to the concrete theological language of love, as well as the fundamental continuity that persists through all the developments.

II. Being in Relation

In the address to students that he gave when joining the Great Books faculty of the University of Notre Dame in 1979,[4] Schindler explained that his

---

4. Schindler, "On Coming to the Program," printed in *Programma,* a Notre Dame Program of Liberal Studies newsletter (February 1980): 5-7.

intellectual autobiography began with a question that arose after high school as he moved away from home for the first time and became aware of the difference between the values and ideas he had formed and those of other people with different backgrounds: How can we know whether the particular judgments we make, which seem to be determined to a great extent by the contingency of the particular circumstances into which each of us is born, are true in a way that transcends their particularity? In other words, are all judgments simply relative, are they simply the products of the unique historical situation in which each of us finds himself? This question matured into a more general question concerning the rationality of Christianity, to which a baptized Catholic is committed, as it were, from birth and thus before deliberately choosing it, and it eventually became the background question for Schindler's dissertation in the philosophy of religion: Can philosophy be *Christian*, and thus in some respect committed to particular truths prior to the final verification of those truths by critical reason, on reason's terms, without betraying its claim to universal rationality, which means of course betraying its claims to be philosophy at all in a rigorous sense?

The dissertation is called "Knowing as Synthesis: A Metaphysical Prolegomenon to Critical Christian Philosophy,"[5] and, as the title suggests, it engages the question at a general metaphysical level by addressing the specific issue of Christianity: What significance does *history*, and the ongoing movement of difference it entails, have for the identity that founds meaning? If it can be shown that real identities are always-already "shot through" with difference without this internal penetration compromising either their metaphysical integrity as identities or their intelligibility, so much so that the methodological failure to attend to the inherence of difference in identity necessarily implies a systematic falsification of reality, no matter how imperceptible that falsification may be in certain, relatively abstract contexts, then it follows that the *a priori* significance of history that is explicitly acknowledged in Christian faith — in, for example, the historically revealed dogmas that make an authoritative claim on the believer — is not in principle any less rational than the usually implicit *a priori* significance of history in all other philosophical thinking, without exception. It is, in other words, true that Christianity implies rational reflection within, and pervaded by, pre-critical commitments, but

---

5. Schindler, "Knowing as Synthesis: A Metaphysical Prolegomenon to Critical Christian Philosophy" (Claremont Graduate School, 1976).

the same can and must be said about all reflection, even the putatively most critical.[6]

If this is the case, then the commonly seen endeavor to "bracket out" Christianity from one's thinking or one's formation of and participation in cultural institutions (with the intention, of course, of reintroducing it at the appropriate moment, namely, when moral questions come to the fore) betrays at once a false understanding of Christianity and a false understanding of understanding. What is particularly remarkable here, though Schindler does not draw the inference himself in his dissertation, is that, precisely because of its explicitly embraced embeddedness within tradition and history, an embeddedness that arises from the movement of the Incarnation that founds meaning, and so does not in any sense compromise the universality of its scope, Christianity proves to be, not just one instance of pre-critical commitment among others intrinsic to rational thought, and therefore, as it were, "rationally justifiable" — which would seem to imply that Christianity is thus measured and judged by, i.e., "redeemed" by, a general idea that is more fundamental than it — but instead presents itself as the paradigm of rationality.

The principal metaphysical foundation of the argument he develops in the dissertation comes most directly from the "rediscovery" of the meaning of being as "super-formal" actuality in the existential Thomism of Étienne Gilson (and to a certain extent Frederick Wilhelmsen). In contrast to the identification of being and form in Aristotle, and, we might add, in Plato, albeit in a different sense, Aquinas affirms a new sense of being in the light of the doctrine of creation, namely, "existential" being — or, as Schindler writes it here, "be-ing," the act of "to be." The implications of this new sense of being are literally endless. If form, and the intelligible identity it specifies, accounts for the whole of reality, then whatever lies beyond identical form strictly speaking does not exist. It would follow in this case that difference is unreal. Now, one might argue that there is no need to affirm the reality of difference *qua* difference if it is true that all difference, all novelty and history, is ultimately the addition of some new form, and

---

6. It should be noted that Schindler developed this argument independently from MacIntyre, though it agrees in many ways with MacIntyre's notion of the rootedness of thought in tradition, even if it works out the position in a more systematic and explicitly metaphysical manner. On the other hand, Schindler cites Gadamer as an inspiration for the argument, as well as Bergson, Blondel, Čapek, Heidegger, Lonergan, Polanyi, Voegelin, and Whitehead. The main influences, however, are quite clearly Étienne Gilson and Frederick Wilhelmsen: see "Knowing as Synthesis," xxiii.

thus can be adequately accounted for at the formal level. But accepting this objection would, among other things, commit one to what Schindler calls here a purely "analytical" view of reality: all things would then be reducible to the sum of the formal identities that constitute them, identities, more-over, that have their being precisely in *not* being what is other than they, and therefore have their meaning in isolation from, or indeed in logical opposition to, everything else. If this is the case, then there is no concretely existing thing that is not better understood once it is boiled down to its ab-stract forms considered separately, which amounts indeed to saying that concrete things do not in fact ultimately exist as such, and there is in the end no universe, strictly speaking, insofar as a universe is a unified whole, but only an endless series of finite, isolated forms.[7] The result, in short, is chaos and fragmentation.

Schindler affirms, by contrast, that, if the primary sense of being is an act-uality that lies beyond the intelligible act designated by form, then it does not itself stand in logical opposition to the difference that is other than formal identity. It is not possible, in the present context, to follow the dissertation through its unfolding of the implications — and it ought to be noted that the dissertation is an extraordinarily powerful example of the faithful thinking through of the metaphysical foundations of cultural questions — but we can at least touch on some of the immediate conse-quences in view of ideas Schindler develops later. We will consider four.

In the first place, we see that this approach implies a sense of being that is inexorably concrete and inescapably analogical. If be-ing tran-scends identical act, it cannot itself be reduced to a formal identity that would distinguish it from difference. Be-ing cannot, that is, be identified with the synthesis of identity and difference without surrendering its act-ually synthetic (i.e., real) character.[8] Instead, it is, so to speak, as different as it is identical; it is simultaneously the ground of all identity and differ-ence. At the same time, and for the same reason, we must affirm that the meaning of being transcends time even while it is permeated through and through by history. It is the simultaneity of identity and difference, ac-cording to Schindler, that accounts for Aquinas's paradoxical assertion that *esse* is both what is most universal and what is most unique to each

---

7. The theme of the unity of the universe was a prevalent one in the decade after the dis-sertation: see BM, 1-12, and especially the paper given at the International Society of St. Thomas, December 28, 1981, entitled "Aquinas and Whitehead: A Dialogue on Existence, Value, and the Unity of the Universe."

8. "Knowing as Synthesis," 46.

thing.[9] The theme of analogy — which, as Schindler regularly cites from the Fourth Lateran Council, designates an ever greater difference *within* unity in the world's relation to God[10] — stems from the reality of supraformal being, as he developed this in the dissertation.

Second, this reality necessarily entails a method: in other words, we entirely misread its implications if we reduce it simply to a new content, a new idea, rather than recognizing how it also "trans-forms" the form or method of thinking. To see this as merely a new content would be in fact to identify being, i.e., to equate being with a particular identity or form, and thereby to undermine exactly what one means to affirm. This point, it seems to me, is one of the most critical, for it protects against what is no doubt one of the most common misunderstandings of Schindler's critique of "substance" metaphysics: the attribution of reality to difference in identity in a formal way, i.e., an identical way, which means taking difference to be another identity within identity, and thus to be always in competition with it. In order to avoid this attribution, it is necessary to think identity instead concretely, and therefore to allow difference to be inherent within identity in precisely a non-identical or non-formal way. Form, in other words, can be inwardly pervaded by what is different from it, form can exist historically, only if being is itself more than simple form. To put it yet another way, only concrete form can have an interiority — be able to relate to what is different in something other than an extrinsic way — and only the primacy of existential being allows us to understand form concretely. We may thus see the intelligible integrity of form as always subsistent within difference; identity and difference need not be opposed to one another in a dialectical way.

This point leads, then, to the third, namely, the intrinsic character of relation. We will see in a moment how fundamental it is, according to Schindler, to make distinctions in the proper way, that is, a way that preserves the inward character of relation. The "synthetic" view of being in his dissertation presents the crucial ground for this understanding. There are few things more constant in Schindler's work than the criticism of the extrinsicist understanding of relation, which affirms that things have their meaning most decisively in isolation from all other things, i.e., "outside" of them. If this is the case, then not only must relation be trivialized as failing

---

9. According to Aquinas, *esse* "is innermost in each thing and most fundamentally inherent in all things since it is formal in respect of everything." *Summa Theologiae*, I, q. 8, a. 1.

10. See, e.g., "Meaning and the Death of God," 192-206; here 203n.9.

to touch the core of being (relation, thus, as "merely accidental")[11] — which of course would imply that the core of being is an opaque and impenetrable (and ultimately unreal, because abstracted from the essentially synthetic character of real being) "nugget," an "atom" — but indeed by the same token all entities of whatever sort would stand in what one might call ontological competition with one another. The presence of one thing would precisely require the absence of the other, the insistence on "intrinsic" presence would then be the violent imposition of the other, and there would be in the end no such thing as interiority but only levels of other-excluding exteriority. If we understand being synthetically, by contrast, which means that the identity of identity subsists *within* and not *outside of* difference, then entities of whatever sort can effectively mutually inhere within one another without violence. According to Schindler, things thus have their most distinctive meaning only within relation. The existence of the mutual inherence of relation cannot be overstated if we wish to understand any other dimension of Schindler's thought.

The final point, which follows from this, is an acknowledgment of the "big picture" it generates: the drift of this thinking, which springs from the act-uality of being, is inevitably toward wholes, toward both integration and totality. If a formalistic understanding of being leads to the primacy of analysis in one's method — i.e., the isolation of parts from their context — Schindler's method is more properly "syn-thetic" (positing things together, as the Greek suggests). Thus, one begins with a whole that is greater than the sum of the parts, a whole that in fact sees the parts as interdependent, which means as intrinsically related to one another even in their difference, and one ends, as it were, always on the way to what is most ultimate. For, if being is act-uality and relation is therefore intrinsic, then parts require a sense of the whole in which they participate and which they co-constitute, and this means that there will be a certain restlessness in thought, that the endeavor to understand the most trivial of realities will betray an inner dynamism toward what is most ultimate and fundamental. In a word, "synthetic" thinking is always ordered to God intrinsically, i.e., as a function of its inner nature, and this ordering means that it possesses a positive relation to God *a priori*. We will return to this point shortly.

---

11. It must be added that a synthetic view of being does not in the least intend to remove the distinction between substance and accidents, but rather to relativize both, within their abiding asymmetrical difference, to a more fundamental actuality of being.

III. An Onto-logic of Creation

The topics that primarily occupied Schindler in the decade after his dissertation stemmed in a direct way from the critique of simple identity he elaborated there: in the first place, there was an attack on the separation of the orders of the true and the good, a separation evidenced in the fact-value distinction taken as axiomatic in the social sciences as well as in the tendency, in philosophy, to see the intellect and will as two separate faculties that operate extrinsically from one another.[12] Secondly, there was an exploration of the mechanistic cosmology implied in modern physics; inspiration for his criticism of this mechanism came not only from his own metaphysical reflections, but also from the work of the physicist David Bohm, who was developing an ontological interpretation of quantum mechanics that called into question many of the basic assumptions regarding the nature of matter that quantum physicists tended to take over from classical physics uncritically in spite of a willingness to challenge many of the ideas espoused by classical physics.[13] While they may not have agreed on the more explicitly theological implications of the critique of mechanism in physics, Schindler admired Bohm both for the metaphysical character of his physical reflection — i.e., the desire to think into the foundation of material reality in its ultimate nature — and for his recognition that theories in physics, however abstract they might initially seem, have profound and far-reaching cultural implications. Bohm's critique of a particular interpretation of Heisenberg's uncertainty principle, for example, is not to be separated from his critique of patterns of consumption in human culture. A similar thing might be said of Schindler's critique of simple identity.

But one might say that Schindler's work reached its first fruition in the series of articles he wrote at the end of the 1980s and the beginning of the

---

12. See Schindler, "History, Objectivity, and Moral Conversion," *The Thomist* 38 (1973): 569-588, and the presentation Schindler gave on August 15, 1980, at Louvain–La Neuve, Belgium, entitled "The Fact of Value and the Value of Fact: Another Look at the Convertibility of *Ens* and *Bonum*," Seminar on the Philosophical Mediation of Christian Values, sponsored by the World Union of Catholic Philosophical Societies.

13. In addition to personal correspondence between Bohm and Schindler, there is a published exchange: Schindler, "David Bohm on Contemporary Physics and the Overcoming of Fragmentation," *International Philosophical Quarterly* 22 (1982): 315-327, and Bohm, "Response to Schindler's Critique of My *Wholeness and the Implicate Order*," 329-339 in the same issue. See also the published papers from the conference organized by Schindler on the thought of David Bohm, which Bohm himself contributed to: BM.

1990s on neoconservatism, as represented principally by the work of Michael Novak, Richard John Neuhaus, and George Weigel. The immediate problem raised in these essays is the extent to which classical liberal institutions can be harmonized, in theory and practice, with Catholicism, and one of the most significant questions at issue here concerns the religious character of American culture: if it is true that America has a uniquely healthy religiosity, it would seem to suggest that Catholics ought to embrace in a basic way the liberal institutions on which America is founded, even if they ought to remain critical of later distortions of the logic of those institutions that one finds in certain limited arenas of the culture. Because it brings us to a core insight for Schindler, which bears on the issue of the Catholic *logos* and so the holy mind, it is worth dwelling on this issue for a moment. As Schindler has repeatedly observed, there is an obvious sense in which American culture is religiously healthy: there are few first-world countries on the planet with higher levels of church attendance, and the number of people who would call themselves atheists in the strict sense is a tiny minority. But, if we took statistics of this sort to be a sufficient barometer of religious health, we would essentially be identifying religion, on the one hand, with a weekly activity, and on the other hand with the acceptance of the simple proposition that a god of some sort exists, in abstraction from the question what content that proposition might hold, i.e., what the nature of that god might be. Notice the fragmentation here: what is taken to be determinative is an isolated activity and an isolated proposition, which in reality and precisely because of their abstraction from any larger context are strictly speaking not determinative of anything at all but themselves. In other words, for the weekly practice of church attendance to be determinative, we have to ask in what way it gives form to the whole, i.e., to the basic shape, the structures and patterns, of the whole of one's life, of which this particular activity is a part, and in turn how the whole of one's life gives shape to one's particular practice of worship. This means that the question of church attendance means nothing at all if one doesn't ask also about the *quality* of that practice or the nature of its *logos* — i.e., the theology to which it gives expression both in its most explicit forms (a creed, for instance) and in its most subtle forms (the aesthetics of the liturgy and the architecture, the nature of the drama of the rite, and so forth) — and at the same time about the quality of the life as a whole that lays itself before God in the act of worship. The mere fact of going to church has scarcely any more significance than where one goes to work or to school, and these latter facts may arguably be said to be *more* revealing about the religious character of one's life precisely because they come at the question from a less explicit perspective and thus express the deeper dimensions of that character more subtly. A man may tell his wife often that he loves her, may believe what he says, and may in fact bring her flowers without fail once a week — and yet at the same time he may exhibit a pattern of choices with regard to his career, for example, that trivialize his wife's significance in his life.

Likewise, the mere fact that one believes in the existence of God remains utterly empty if one does not ask, most obviously, how God is to be understood — i.e., whether the particular understanding is theologically adequate to the nature of God as Jesus Christ has revealed him and as the tradition has unfolded and differentiated that understanding both philosophically and theologically — and, less obviously, but, again, in some sense even more significantly, how the particular affirmation of the existence of God gives form to one's thinking as a whole, and how, in turn, the whole of one's mind comes to expression in one's assent to God's existence.

As we are beginning to see, it is impossible to raise the question of the religious health of a culture without raising the question of what it means to be religious and what cultural expression religion ought to take. But it is right here that we realize the critical significance of understanding Christianity as a *logos*. It is just this that makes Christianity comprehensive, or, we could say, truly catholic (*kata-holon,* in accordance with the whole): *logos,* as we said, is simultaneously subjective and objective, which means it indicates not only a discrete, explicit intelligible content, but also at the same time the implicit, because utterly pervasive, logic or form in which that content is expressed. Catholicly understood, form and content are inseparable; an inadequate content will inevitably generate an inadequate form, and vice versa. Schindler often observed, in relation to his debate with the neo-conservatives, that one thinks one agrees about the basic truths of faith (content) and disagrees only about the way to live those truths out existentially and institutionally (form), when in fact the disagreement regarding the latter invariably turns out in the end to presuppose a disagreement about the former. As we will see in a moment, the failure to see that there is an inseparable unity here is itself an expression of the lack of unity, i.e., of the fragmentation. Once again, as always, form and content reflect one another.

So what, then, according to Schindler is, so to speak, the *logic* of religion? The answer to this question cannot of course be adequately attempted in this limited context, but there are at least two basic dimensions to the answer that bear immediately on the issue at hand. The most fundamental truth of religion is that the being of the world cannot ultimately be accounted for simply in terms of itself[14] — world as eternal or self-created — but implies reference to a source beyond itself; in other words, the world is created. The two dimensions of the "logic" of religion stem directly from the created character of the world's being. In the first place, there is the "infinity" of God that follows upon a notion of God as Creator, and thus as one who transcends all worldly being as its source, and who therefore is most intimately within all worldly being as the *non-aliud,* to use the expression of Nicholas of Cusa that Hans Urs von Balthasar admired so much. A true conception of the transcendence of God necessarily entails a radical immanence, for a God who is ex-cluded from being, i.e., who "merely" transcends things in the sense of being apart from them, is a God who exists within the same order as created being so as to be able to be "juxtaposed" to it. This would be a God who is not truly transcendent but rather caught within the immanent ambit of the world. In other words, a Creator God is necessarily an infinite God, and an infinite God, by definition, must in some sense effectively bear on all things without exception, all the time: "A God who is truly God must affect everything. A God who in some significant sense is not everywhere and does not affect everything, and every aspect of everything, is not infinite but finite."[15] There is a certain parallel between a misunderstanding of the nature of transcendence, which would *exclude* God from the world and by that very fact *include* God within the world as one discrete entity among other created entities, and the understanding of religious health that is satisfied with the (discrete) affirmation of the existence of God and feels no need to ask deeper questions. If God is the Creator of the world, then his existence has effective, formal, final, and indeed in some sense material significance for everything in the world, and so the affirmation of God's existence must coincide with a particular way of thinking and speaking about, and dealing with, all other things. If God does not make at least implicitly a difference in the way one thinks about every-

14. To call this fundamental is clearly not to make it exclusive or even the ultimate truth of religion; we are looking at the truth of religion here from what might be called the relative abstraction of "natural theology," which therefore must be understood as inwardly and so implicitly and thoroughly ordered from the first to the revelation of God in Jesus Christ. In this respect, the notion of creation, and therefore of being as gift, must itself be embedded within the ultimate and explicitly personal gift of being in the Son's being begotten by the Father, and the reciprocal gift of self (and of the created world) he makes to the Father in the Holy Spirit.

15. HW, 195.

thing that is not God, if one assumes that God's existence is simply a "fact" that can be tidily captured in sociological data, empirically gathered, one is in fact denying God's existence. A fervent believer may be a practical atheist. God's existence is more than a fact; it is an all-embracing truth the significance of which the mind will never be able to catch up to. As such, there is an essential mystery to God's existence that will necessarily elude the positivistic methods of sociological data collection.

The second, more decisive dimension of the "logic" of religion follows immediately from this first: if worldly being is most fundamentally characterized as created, and therefore as gift, it means that receptivity lies at the innermost heart of reality — or, to put it another way, relation has an "absolute" primacy over substance, insofar as the gift of being in creation is not made to some "pre-existing" thing, but is a gift that is so radical it itself brings about the very receiver of the gift.[16] It is thus an absoluteness that does not exclude, but rather necessarily includes, the relative primacy of substance (in a way that is analogous, we might add, to the absoluteness of God's transcendence necessarily including the relativity of immanence). Now, if receptivity is absolute in this way, it must necessarily resonate in and into all other "levels" of being; the createdness of being implies a concrete mode of being that, as an ontological mode, makes itself felt everywhere.

Here we return to a theme from Schindler's dissertation, but from a somewhat different angle: the relationality of difference cannot be simply "tacked on" or made extrinsic to being in its innermost meaning, but must coincide with that meaning from top to bottom, not only because of the act-uality of being, but also more concretely because all worldly being is created, which is the ultimate reason for its act character. The implication of this point is crucial for an understanding of what Schindler would mean by a "religious" logic. Any pattern of life or form of thought that denies the significance of receptivity or indirectly undermines its primacy is therefore a secular logic; in other words, by effectively separating God's being from the being of everything else, then, no matter what one's intentions may be, this pattern is an implicit atheism. It is important to see that we may therefore have a mode of being — of thinking and acting — that excludes the significance of God by denying the created structure of being and therefore its primordial receptivity but that nevertheless coincides with a constant, enthusiastic, and sincere affirmation of the importance of God and one's devotion to him, and indeed with a heroic public witness to

---

16. See *Gift*, 34-63.

this importance. The point is that, unless one attends to the logic of that importance, not only in moral questions, which of course anyone would admit, but more subtly in the patterns and structures of culture, then one's witness to God reinforces a problematic secularism.

There have been other thinkers who have made similar arguments about the logical form of atheism that might co-exist with an explicit religiosity;[17] what is perhaps most unique about Schindler's approach to this question is his linking of this problematic specifically to the question of receptivity or the "from-another" character of being. It is important to grasp this particular ontological implication of religion in order to understand Schindler's critique of neoconservatism, and, indeed, to understand the connection between that particular critique and his assessment of other aspects of liberal culture. Without getting into the details of that particular debate, which will be treated at length in another chapter of this book,[18] we must nevertheless weigh the meaning of the question Schindler raises. Insofar as the neo-conservatives uncritically accept the statistics regarding church attendance and the like as a measure of religious health, insofar as they promote an economic theory that begins from the axiom that human beings are primordially self-interested agents (and thus order their loves around an individualistic center, regardless of how "morally" these loves may subsequently be regulated) or assume that human beings most originally image God in their creativity and productivity (and thus have their meaning most basically in outward action rather than first in their reception of being), insofar as they take political structures to be essentially neutral, to which Christians are subsequently called to give meaning by "filling in" the empty spaces with Christian substance, as it were, the neo-conservatives give expression to an atheistic logic.[19] A merely moral cri-

---

17. See, e.g., Michael J. Buckley, S.J., *At the Origins of Modern Atheism* (New Haven: Yale University Press, 1987).

18. See the essay by Larry Chapp and Rodney Howsare below.

19. On these three points, see "Is America Bourgeois?"; "Once Again: George Weigel, Catholicism and American Culture," in *Communio: International Catholic Review* 15 (1988): 92-120; "Catholicism, Public Theology, and Postmodernity: On Richard John Neuhaus's 'Catholic Moment,'" *The Thomist* 53 (1989): 107-143; "Church's 'Worldly' Mission"; "Christology and the Church's 'Worldly' Mission: Response to Michael Novak," *Communio: International Catholic Review* 19 (1992): 164-178; "Religious Freedom and Liberalism"; "'Civilization of Love': On Catholicism, Neoconservatism, and American Culture" (interview), *Catholic World Report* (October 1994): 42-49; "The Person: Philosophy, Theology, and Receptivity," *Communio: International Catholic Review* 21 (1994): 172-190; and "Economics and the Civilization of Love," *The Chesterton Review* (May-August 1994): 189-211.

tique of culture will always come up short; as we will see, the logic of liberal culture must be confronted by the Christian *logos,* and trans-formed by that *logos,* rather than simply be regulated by Christian moral teaching.

To appreciate the weight of this point, it is helpful to see how Schindler's argument against the neo-conservatives connects with a series of positions he articulates on other fronts. In every case, we see that what is at issue is never simply the particular problem being addressed, but always more fundamentally the pervasive mode of being that gives rise to the problem. These problems ought therefore to be interpreted as systematic expressions of a single pathology *(patho-logos),* namely, a kind of metaphysical atomism that makes relation secondary and therefore implicitly denies the created character of the world. We have, for example, the criticism of a merely moral critique of certain uses to which technology is put, a critique that fails to see that "technology" is a non-neutral *logos* that creatively and actively gives the natural world its meaning rather than receiving that meaning first as given;[20] we have the critique of John Courtney Murray's primarily juridical view of the state and, connected with this, his view of religious freedom, which gives primacy to the negative dimension of freedom over the ordering of that freedom from and therefore to God;[21] and we have the criticism of the sort of feminism that would seek to deny the "given" meaning of womanhood and therefore the radical significance of receptivity.[22] These criticisms all bear a connection to the earlier critiques of "objectivity" in scientific and scholarly method, which makes a determinative ideal of un-attached (i.e., non-receptive) observation and of the metaphysical presuppositions of mechanistic physics, which takes for granted that all relations are extrinsic and therefore best described in terms of effective force operating upon inert "stuff" (more on this below[23]). Once again, all of these things, whatever their differences, rest upon a similar *logos.*

IV. A Christo-logic of Love

Although the nature of Schindler's arguments remains largely the same from the early 1990s on, the perspective from which they are made begins to become both more concrete and more explicitly theological over the past

20. "The Meaning of the Human."
21. See HW, 60-65.
22. See "Creation and Nuptiality"; and HW, 237-274.
23. See also the chapter by Michael Hanby below.

decade or so: now, Schindler describes the *logos* of the world's order regularly as a *logos* of love, and he explicates the meaning of that term not only in the "natural" language of gift and creation, but also directly in terms of the theological doctrines of the Incarnation, the Trinity, Mary, the Church, the sacraments, and so forth. The *logos* of love, in other words, is taken to have a Eucharistic form, which itself can be properly understood only from within the Church's tradition as the concrete "extension" into time and space of the Son's redemptive act, which is at once the Son's expression of love from and to the Father, and of which Mary is the paradigmatic first recipient.[24] The subtle shift in perspective, which is perhaps better described as the deepening of the perspective Schindler had been developing from the outset, may be due in part to the increase of the importance for Schindler of the work of Hans Urs von Balthasar, with whom Schindler had collaborated for many years through *Communio,* but whose work Schindler began to see as fundamental just before the end of Balthasar's life in 1988, and also due to the more direct influence of the thought of John Paul II, occasioned by Schindler's move from the University of Notre Dame to the John Paul II Institute in Washington, D.C., in 1992. It is crucial to see that love in this perspective is very much a *logos* — i.e., that it designates not merely the order of the will. Love, for Schindler, reveals the meaning of being, and the meaning of love itself is ultimately revealed through the Church's principal dogmas. Christian dogma, he has often said, is simply the articulation of the various dimensions of the absolute meaning of love.

What significance does this "new" perspective have for Schindler's overall project? In fact, love provides a sort of "middle term" in the relation between the orders of nature and grace, which allows us to see that the structures of the world, even in their most rudimentary, physical dimensions, already have what we might call a "personal" significance, so that their explicit recapitulation in *human* being, and thus in what is properly personal, is not an arbitrary reconfiguration but rather a "new" meaning that nevertheless both unfolds and fulfills the meaning the world already has.[25] At the very same time, it allows us therefore to see that both the historical events in human existence and the historically revealed doctrines that lie at the foundations of Christianity have an ontological depth, a significance for the understanding of all being.

24. See Schindler, "Towards a Eucharistic Evangelization," *Communio: International Catholic Review* 19 (1992): 549-575.
25. See "Significance of World and Culture."

The new emphasis on the simultaneously personal and ontological meaning of the language of love serves to recast and, one might say, anchor and solidify many of the regular themes that were present in Schindler's work from the start. The term brings a compelling unity to the dimensions of Schindler's various critiques. The insistence, for example, on the intrinsic nature of relations may remain too distant and abstract if we see it as stemming from the supra-formal character of act-uality, which implies a synthetic meaning of being that makes difference co-incident with identity, but it is brought immediately close in the reality of love: a child comes to himself, both physically-developmentally and intellectually-personally, not in abstraction from all relations, but precisely as abiding *within* the presence of the love of his parents, and as being penetrated to the core by that love. This presence, if it is genuinely loving, does not at all compromise the child's identity, but is rather the abiding guardian of its integrity, and indeed its relative "independence" or "autonomy." The relations, then, are not extrinsic to or subsequent upon the substance, but intrinsic to it and constitutive of it in a way that sets it *substantially* free. The language of love at the same time connects the metaphysical issues such as the reciprocity of substance and relation directly with a variety of cultural themes.

Schindler often speaks about the importance of receiving, of a sense of contemplation. Now, one might initially suppose that what is being urged here is the multiplication of discrete activities that would explicitly be labeled as contemplative: i.e., an exhortation to spend more time in silence, in prayer, to build in more "leisurely" activities into one's schedule, or, on a more "political" level, to promote economic patterns that would allow keeping the Sabbath holy, and so forth. While all of these things have their merit, of course, the proposal acquires infinitely more depth the moment one connects it with love and thus at the same time with a logic of being. Contemplation as an expression of love is a receptivity that gives primacy to the other and receives one's self and thus all of the generous activities of the self from within the relationship to the other.[26] It is therefore a disposition of gratitude, an inclination to celebrate what is given before one makes or produces, an attitude that remains faithfully concrete, and so resists the temptation to reduce the variety of one's engagements with the other to the convenience of some technique or procedure. We will have understood the proposal properly when we thus see that the recovery of a sense of the contemplative concerns, in a certain respect, even more im-

26. See "Time in Eternity," 53-68.

portantly the manner of engaging activities that would normally *not* be thought of immediately as contemplative — for example, one's daily work, one's works of mercy, one's creative endeavors, and so forth. Affirming the contemplative dimension of not specifically contemplative activity reveals that the whole of one's life is formed in the logic of love and that one does not view one's life simply as a series of isolated happenings. Here we find an example of the decisive matter being subtle — indeed, too subtle to be registered by any poll or sociological data collection.

But in thinking through the implications of interpreting the whole of being in terms of love, it is especially important to avoid a reduction to the specifically human, which eventually means a reduction to explicitly spiritual *acts* and therefore once again a failure to understand love as ontological. Here, Schindler's interpretation of John Paul II's theology of the body arises right at the heart of this particular concern. The late pope developed this theology primarily in order to articulate the theological anthropology in which the Church's teaching in the area of sexual ethics has its roots. For Schindler, however, the significance of this anthropology resonates far beyond the sphere of sexuality and indeed beyond anthropology itself. In his theology, John Paul II speaks of the "nuptial meaning of the body," using the adjective "nuptial" not to describe a particular kind of activity, but to describe the meaning, i.e., the objective and intrinsic significance, of this particular instance of matter, this physical, corporeal entity.[27] To say that the body has a nuptial meaning is to say that it is ordered in its very structure, and therefore prior to any use to which it might be put or project into which it might be placed, to the mutual self-gift that occurs paradigmatically, though not exclusively, in marriage. This meaning may be "premoral," insofar as it exists prior to any deliberate and intentional use, but it nevertheless already has personal significance.

If this is in fact the meaning "built into" the body, the body is itself a physical manifestation of the general meaning of human life, and thus human beings will live that meaning only if they recapitulate in their properly spiritual acts the meaning already inscribed in their nature, and indeed do so in a way that bears an analogy to the reciprocal self-giving of spouses.[28] Schindler embraces this point articulated by the pope and draws out what

27. John Paul II, *Man and Woman He Created Them: A Theology of the Body*, 181-185.
28. It is important to see that the nuptial meaning of the body does not exclude the state of life defined by the evangelical counsels. Indeed, the gift of self in married life may be said to be an *image* of the reality of self-gift lived in the state of consecration: see John Paul II, *Man and Woman He Created Them: A Theology of the Body*, 419.

he sees as its further implications: what is said about *human* nature is in fact revelatory (in an analogous way) of the truth of nature more generally; what comes to expression in a particularly explicit way in this physical entity, namely, the human body, is the meaning implicit in all physical entities.[29] Notice, then, how the language of love once again both sharpens and deepens a regular theme in Schindler's thought: the general "relationality" of being comes to be seen in the more concrete form of reciprocal self-gift, and this form penetrates into the very physical roots of things.

The physics, then, passes once again to the supreme generality of metaphysics, and it is here that we see most dramatically that what is at issue is not simply a particular idea or even set of ideas, but in fact a particular way of thinking about all possible and actual ideas whatsoever. Schindler has often said that the fate of Western civilization turns on the nature of a distinction. If love reveals the meaning of being, and not simply a particular kind of human action, it is, to say it again, because it concerns a particular logic. Love is not simply a way of relating; rather, it expresses a particular structure of relation. If there is no aspect of the world, no matter how rudimentary, no matter how abstract, that is not created by a God who is love, and therefore there is no aspect of being that does not in some analogous way participate in the form of this love, then even the abstract forms of logical relations themselves are not ultimately indifferent to the truth of Christ. They must therefore in some respect be reconceived from a Christian perspective.[30] In this regard, Schindler's proposal bears a certain similarity to Hegel's rethinking of the logic of logic from a dialectical perspective that, to his mind, does more justice to the ultimate reality of *Geist* than traditional logic;[31] but they differ fundamentally in their point of departure, insofar as Schindler starts with the ultimate reality of love — Trinitarian love, understood Christologically and ecclesiologically — and therefore a more personal and positive notion of difference. This starting point leads Schindler to affirm that relations, within a created world, will have an analogously *spousal* character, which means that difference is always interpreted in the context of a prior unity, and that unity, properly

29. See "Significance of World and Culture," 111-142.

30. There is no room to go into detail here regarding the complexities of what it would mean to speak of a "Christian" transformation of logic, but we note that this transformation cannot entail any threat to the integrity of logic, and thus of reason; instead, it must represent the best way to safeguard that integrity. The complexity of this issue would have to be worked out with great care.

31. See, e.g., paragraphs 56-66 in Hegel's introduction to his *Phenomenology of Spirit*.

understood, is always fruitful, which means that it is always generative of further difference.

To call the relation analogously "spousal," in other words, implies that the terms of the relation are not indifferent or "neutral" with regard to one another, but are always already ordered to one another. This means, further, that they are in some sense positively related from the first, and this implies that their own individual meaning includes this positive relatedness without compromising the integrity of the individual identities. Precisely to the contrary, because positive relation is intrinsic to the identity in its foundations, the actualizing and perfecting of that relation liberates the identities into their unique individuality precisely in bringing them to closer union. In a good marriage, the spouses become more "independent" the greater their unity grows, and the child who has a fragile self-identity is not the one who grows up *inside* his parents' love but the one who grows up *outside* it. Schindler's basic critique of the traditional logic that founds intelligibility on the ultimacy of simple identity is similar to Hegel's. If A is what it is precisely as *not* being anything else (non-A), then either A's subsequent relation to anything other than itself will be an assimilation that compromises the identity of either itself or its other, or that relation will remain merely extrinsic to A; it will ultimately not mean anything. Schindler, like Hegel, objects to the lack of concreteness, the empty formalism, the inertness of meaning, that such a way of conceiving relations will necessarily imply. But while Hegel's response arguably concedes too much to the simplicity of simple identity, so that he yet thinks of relation in the negative and oppositional terms of dialectic and therefore is led to threaten the simplicity of simple identity by continually trumping it in terms of dialectical movement, Schindler's response embraces *both* simplicity and complexity at the outset. Nuptial meaning is a celebration of the positivity of difference, always within the embrace of unity.

If love reveals the meaning of being, it has significance not only for the "objective" dimension of the way things are — the orders described by metaphysics, logic, physics, and all the other sciences — but also for the subjective dimension of our access to reality. Abstract identity requires an abstracted mind to attain it; by contrast, the real order of being, in which identity and difference are reciprocally and intrinsically related, requires a loving attention precisely in order for the objectivity of things to make itself known. Anyone who has read Schindler's writings is aware of the central importance of the word "receptivity." It represents the keynote of his theory of knowledge. We must be careful not to interpret the word "subjectivistically" (as we will be inclined to do to the extent that we take for granted the notion of objectivity that Schindler intends to call into question) and take "receptivity" to be describing merely an affective disposition. Instead, for Schindler the term has a rigorously objective meaning; indeed, it is arguably the indispensable key to objectivity: receptivity implies a *priority* of the object to the subject, which means, first of all, that the object is always already in some respect present to the subject, at the very least in terms of the claims it makes on the subject, logically prior to the subject's deliberately relating to the object in its acts of intellect and will — and hence the union precedes and gives form to the difference, and the relation is intrinsic from the first — and, subsequently, that the most appropriate relation the subject can then engage with respect to the object is a welcoming "taking in" before it is a spontaneous creative or constructive "acting upon." If love is the meaning of being, our relation to being will be contemplative before it is analytic or technological, and this priority needs to be reflected *structurally* in the institutions that enshrine the intelligence. A lack of receptivity in one's manner of dealing with others and the world — to consider a concrete implication of this point — is an implicit expression of the rejection of God; it is a *practical* atheism, which may happen to coincide with a strong belief in God's power.

V. A Beautiful Mind

It is at this point that we can understand what Schindler means by speaking of holiness specifically in relation to the mind, and, more specifically, why beauty is the heart that gives life to this view of intelligence. We normally associate sanctity, of course, with the order of goodness and thus with the order of the will, and we normally understand the order of goodness and the will as relatively independent of (though of course regulated by) the orders of truth and the mind. This conventional view, it must be noted, does not exclude an insistence that in some respect the proper employment of the will requires a subordination of will to intellect, and thus goodness to truth. Nevertheless, to insist on this subordination still leaves in place a question that turns out to be decisive: Is the order of truth merely *regulatory* of the order of goodness, and to that extent understood as extrinsic to the volitional order *qua* volitional?[32] What may seem to be a

---

32. On the significance of the *internal* character of the relation between intellect and

fairly abstract question has infinite and pervasive implications: if, indeed, the intellect and will are extrinsically related, if we are led to think of the mind as operating in a space that is "neutral" with respect to the good, then we take for granted an instrumentalist, a formalist, notion of intelligence; we separate subjectivity and objectivity; we associate scientific objectivity with impersonal detachment; we believe passionate involvement — and thus also things like the "pre-critical" commitments of faith — intrude on vision and so compromise the free integrity of reason; we isolate public reason from what then becomes the private, subjective adherence of the will; we raise up the methods of modern science as a paradigm of rational universality and believe the realm of science is neutral with respect to metaphysical and religious questions; we claim that technology is "neutral" in itself, and becomes good or bad only in reference to the uses to which it is put; we become accustomed to a fragmented view of the academic curriculum — which is, incidentally, itself a reflection of the way a culture conceives of the "shape" of the mind — in the sense that we see the disciplines as isolated pieces of skills and information that can be "mastered" only by experts, even though they all share generally the same academic "method," mechanically applied; and, finally, along similar lines, we negotiate relations in the public order principally according to putatively "neutral" procedures, and we allow dialogue and engagement with the "other" only on the terms set by these procedures. In a word, when the orders of intellect and will are separated, "technique" of some form or another tends to substitute for the genuine operation of intelligence. But the objects of technique, no matter what one may "will" them to be — i.e., regardless of one's subjective intentions — are so many neutral, inert facts, and inert facts are not creatures of God. Absolutized technique secularizes the world.

To put it more sharply, Schindler's argument is that the systematic separation of the intellect from the will, and by implication the isolation of the true from the good and vice versa, is the secularization of the intelligence, and this is the case no matter how fervently this mind would wish, say, to affirm the existence and importance of God. The reason is that the affirmation implied here of the intellect as essentially an instrument, which can be used for good or ill without affecting its integrity as intelligence, and thus the insistence on its neutrality and thus initial indifference to-

will, see once again Schindler, "History, Objectivity, and Moral Conversion" (cited in note 12 above).

ward the moral order, entails the *logical* exclusion of God from the meaning of things. This is the argument that lies behind Schindler's constant suggestion that a university cannot genuinely be called Catholic if it simply takes over the conventional view of intelligence implicit in the typical ordering of the disciplines in the academy.[33] As we have repeated several times, if Christianity is a *logos*, it entails not only a distinctive way of *acting* but also a distinctive way of being and of thinking, and this of course bears directly on the form of a university insofar as a university is, at root, the cultural institutionalization of the thinking of being. Putting the matter in these terms at once allows us to see its urgency and why it is not something that concerns academics or intellectuals alone: the shape and order of a university is an institutionalized statement, however implicit, regarding the nature of Christianity.

It is not an accident that we do not think of beauty immediately when we think of academic institutions that are principally ordered to some pragmatic end: business schools, vo-tech programs, and the like. The instrumentalization of intelligence is in fact co-incident, according to Schindler, with the marginalization of beauty. As Schindler has explained in one of his most thorough treatments of the nature of the intelligence, "Faith, Reason, and the Mission of the Church,"[34] beauty, as it was classically understood, bears directly on the proper meaning of intelligence. The terms in which we have characterized what we might call the secularization of the intellectual life put us in a position to see its relevance directly. Beauty is central for at least three reasons: in the first place, as *id quod visum placet,* beauty represents precisely the integration of the orders of intellect and will; it represents an object that relates simultaneously to the mind and the appetite. To make beauty central, then, is to make the unity of the orders of truth and goodness in some sense prior to their distinctness and relative autonomy, and therefore to give their individual integrity the form of intrinsic unity with the other order. The importance of the thought of Hans Urs von Balthasar for Schindler has much to do with the primary place he gives to aesthetics in his "theological method."[35]

Secondly, the centrality of beauty entails a primacy of receptivity in the subject's relation to the object. As Schindler puts it, "The primacy of

33. See Schindler, "Catholicism and the Liberal Model of the Academy in America: Theodore Hesburgh's Idea of a Catholic University," *Catholic International* (May 2000): 179-190.

34. This manuscript was never published.

35. See GL 1:17-127.

beauty, then, makes *veritas,* primitively, into a matter of *splendor:* truth is not something the knower first *does* or *makes;* it is something the knower is first drawn into, by being drawn out of himself. Truth is the possession of the knower only as something that is always first received in and by the knower."[36] There is, in fact, a connection between the primacy of receptivity and the integration of the orders of truth and goodness implied in beauty. The reason both the mind and the will are engaged at once in the experience of beauty is that beauty calls on the subject in the core of his being.[37] This core cannot move as a whole unless it *is* moved, unless, that is, its movement is solicited from it by something that lies beyond it. As we all know, relationships that are merely a function of deliberate acts are invariably superficial: they remain extrinsic to the extent that they come about through the initiative of a being that is inwardly indifferent to the relation. We cannot move the whole of ourselves through our own act of will; we can move as a whole only insofar as we *are moved* and we participate willingly in that being moved. Beauty is just such a solicitation. To relate to an object *qua* beautiful is to move toward it as being moved by it. A thinking that is genuinely receptive — and therefore receptive toward and affirmative of the other in a fundamental disposition of contemplation, and which subsequently analyzes and manipulates *within* a contemplative always-already having welcomed and affirmed — is a thinking that occurs *within* the movement elicited by beauty.

Finally, the centrality of beauty implies a relating to the world principally as gift. Schindler draws the well-known distinction between the merely "given" — i.e., an essentially value-neutral *fact* — and *gift,* which is being as love.[38] There is nothing in the "given," as mere fact, that would of itself inspire a respect or modesty capable of restraining exploitation of whatever sort. Data are gathered "objectively" in order to be put to use in technological projects, or to accumulate information for the making of pragmatic decisions. Data, we might say, are essentially bourgeois: they represent nothing more than themselves, "they are what they are," and what they are is ultimately nothing more than useful. Data present the sort of objectivity that is, as it were, designed to be manipulated — which is, in-

---

36. "Faith, Reason, and the Mission of the Church" (unpublished manuscript), 32.

37. See Schindler, "Beauty, Transcendence, and the Face of the Other: Religion and Culture in America," *Communio: International Catholic Review* 26 (1999): 916-917; also, "Is Truth Ugly?" 701-728.

38. Schindler, "Beauty, Transcendence, and the Face of the Other: Religion and Culture in America," *Communio: International Catholic Review* 26 (1999): 916-917.

cidentally, why the use of statistics in sociology is "objective" in only the most superficial sense: it does indeed matter who is gathering the data, and who is funding its collection. By contrast, the "gift" is anything but bourgeois: it is the very nature of a gift to point beyond itself to a giver, and therefore to represent more, as it were, than it itself can contain. Notice the immediate connection, in this respect, between the notion of gift and the criticism of abstract identity we mentioned earlier.

Gift and beauty, moreover, go hand in hand: we speak of beauty as "gratuitous," meaning it exceeds rational calculation and projects of self-interest even while being luminous with intelligibility and the very meaning of self-fulfillment. To see the world, and thus all of the potential objects of the mind, as a beautiful gift is to approach what one intends to know, not first with the cold eye of critical distance, but with the warm and attentive disposition of welcoming wonder. Such a disposition, let it be noted, does not by any means exclude the rigorous work of intellectual analysis and the sort of "detachment" this work implies, but it nevertheless provides the original context of all of that work and so gives it a particular stamp from beginning to end — the stamp of gratitude, celebration, and service.

What, then, does beauty and its importance for the mind have to do with holiness? There are two responses to this question that we may offer in conclusion. Holiness indicates, among other things, a proper relationship to God. In what sense does the mind bear on a relationship to God *precisely as mind*? Schindler is fond of citing Aquinas's statement that the human intellect implicitly knows God in everything that it knows,[39] and points out that, while it is indeed true that the mind does not know God's essence in any direct manner in this world — so that it will remain true that God transcends whatever the mind is able to grasp — it is nevertheless also the case that it is impossible *not* to know God in some significant sense at every moment and in every context. The precise phrasing of Aquinas's statement is crucial: God is known implicitly in the things the mind knows. As Schindler interprets it, this means that we know God properly precisely in knowing all other things in a particular way, namely, as creatures, as gifts, and therefore as the beautiful bearers of God's presence.

In order to highlight the significance of this point, let us consider what

39. Aquinas, *De Veritate,* 22, 2, ad 1. See the section entitled "Aquinas and the Implicit Knowledge of God," in "Knowledge as Relationship," 519-525, and Schindler's preface to de Lubac's *The Discovery of God* (Grand Rapids: Eerdmans, 1996), ix-xi.

Schindler takes as contrasting alternatives, liberalism and mechanism, two patterns of thought that dominate modern Western culture:

> Liberalism displaces God by moving God to the margins or gaps of culture and consciousness: God is placed simply outside of the cosmos — of the discrete instances of being and meaning which make up our world; God influences the world, but only from outside and in terms of its movement rather than (also) from within and in terms of its internal structure or logic. Mechanism effects the same sort of displacement of God, as it were, to the outer reaches of the cosmos. But the term "mechanism" makes explicit the nature of the intelligibility which has typically resulted from this displacement which leaves God and God's mind external to the cosmos. The intelligibility is that of the machine. The intelligibility is that of discrete entities which are identifiable to one another simply in their externality; understanding of such entities can be thought of only in terms of control and manipulation.[40]

What is common to both of these is the presumption that the meaning of things is simply "contained" within those things themselves, in isolation from an organic relation to the cosmos and the other things in it, and therefore in abstraction from the transcendent order that makes them in fact an organic whole. Again, this is an essentially bourgeois *logos:* things of this sort are indifferent to what lies beyond them. One of the signs of this abstraction, we wish to argue, is the marginalization of beauty, insofar as beauty implies the unity of subject and object, the primacy of receptivity, and the sense of gift we have described above. To deny the significance of beauty in the operation of the mind is therefore to deny that the being of the world is rooted in God; it is also therefore to deny the fact of creation and the nature of God as Creator. Thus, it would be true to say that the holiness that is possessed without a sense of the organic relation implied in beauty, and therefore without an accompanying critique of the institutional forms of liberalism and mechanism, in a subtle but profound way obstructs the very following of Christ it seeks. It becomes a voluntaristic pursuit of goodness that undermines the ontological depth of goodness and empties out the Christian *form* of love.

The heart of Schindler's proposal, then, is, in his words, that "sanctity should provide the inner form of intellectual life."[41] Even before sanctity

40. HW, 193.

41. Schindler, "Sanctity and the Intellectual Life," *Communio: International Catholic Review* 20 (1993): 652.

bears on *what* the intellect should seek to know, it bears much more perva-sively on the *manner* in which it is meant to know all that it knows. As Schindler says elsewhere, God is present in the world as giving the things in the world the form of love,[42] or in other words, an *order* or *logic* of love, to which the mind must conform in order to understand what it is in real-ity. This order has implications for the order and methods of the academic curriculum, even in fields that do not directly concern the ultimate mean-ing of the world — even, and perhaps most tellingly, in the natural sci-ences, since nature, too, is after all created by God. The false logic of mech-anism is therefore, as it were, "unholy," even if it is put into the service of ostensibly good ends. If the world is created, and if its intelligibility in-cludes the relation creation implies, then we falsify the meaning of things by reducing them to objects of an abstract scientific method. To know them truly, we ourselves must participate in the relation that founds their being: "Only in love, by falling in love, can we truly *see* the meaning of be-ing which is love."[43] The intelligence, too, can — and must — "fall in love," which means it can and must con-form to the form of love, which bears the name of beauty. And this is its holiness.

---

42. HW, 197.
43. "Sanctity and the Intellectual Life," 668.

Trinity and Creation:
David L. Schindler and the Catholic Tradition

Peter J. Casarella

I. Metaphysics as Pilgrimage

David Schindler has maintained that a proper understanding of creation must consider the analogical relationship of the cosmos to its Creator and that this already theological relationship between God and the world needs to be further deepened in light of a Christocentric and Trinitarian understanding of reality itself. Taking the renewal of a Trinitarian *analogia entis* as his point of departure, Schindler then proceeds to demonstrate the narrowness of: (1) a mechanistic account of nature and the attendant consequences in diverse realms, including the realm of modern technology, (2) political liberalism and its many institutional variants (e.g., neo-liberal economics and the narrowing of the order of intelligence in the contemporary university), and (3) the "Murrayite" or liberal reading of the Second Vatican Council and those theological stances that depend upon it. In each of these instances, the reach of Schindler's critique seems limitless, but so too is its power to illuminate the legitimate gains of science, contemporary culture, and the everyday path whereby men, women, and children seek a home in the cosmos.

One can still get lost within the vast expanse of such an undertaking. It is no surprise that Schindler's works have met critics who think he went too far. The real expert on the pressing social and ethical questions of our day, so maintain the critics, is supposed to have technical command of the

---

I would like to express my gratitude to the editors of this volume as well as to Mr. Brendan Sammon for their able assistance in the research for this article.

particular domain of his scholarly inquiry. What scholar could legitimately claim to have mastered not only the plethora of philosophical and theological resources upon which Schindler draws but also each of the finite domains he has addressed (e.g., ethics, politics, biotechnology, history and literature, gender studies, etc.)?[1] Schindler's recourse to a language of metaphysics seems to his critics an evasion of the requisite technical mastery. Other detractors aim more squarely at the metaphysical dimension of the enterprise itself. Either way, Schindler's insistence that all participants in the debate recognize the metaphysical dimension of problems (*a fortiori* for problems that remain unresolved in the practical order) is indisputably central to his task. Both detractors and admirers of David Schindler should be able to agree on this modest point.

Precisely in this way we broach the new Catholic humanism represented by Schindler's thought. A Trinitarian ontology stands at the center of Schindler's commitment to a new humanism. Schindler's humanistic impulse is at once multidisciplinary and metaphysical. It is a path of criticism that leads to concrete proposals for reform. It is equally a spiritual exercise of a deeply personal *via purgativa* that passes ineluctably through the heart of the Christian tradition. Schindler's humanism envisages the human person as a perennial actor in an ever creative and evolving cosmos who cannot but engage the pressing social questions of our day.

Schindler's thought shows impressive unity, one that evolved over time. It arose out of engagements with diverse institutions with distinct physical and philosophical locations. If one limits one's view to mere cartography, David Schindler made an eastward trek across the United States. The path of his philosophical journey, I would submit, retains an equally American character in spite of Schindler's trenchant criticisms of U.S. culture, for he continued throughout to engage North American authors as diverse as A. N. Whitehead, Will Herberg, Kenneth Schmitz, Norris Clarke, and Frederick Wilhelmsen.[2] The stops on the way included: an early training in classics and philosophy at Gonzaga University in Seattle,

1. For Schindler's own analysis of this line of reasoning, see, for example, "Is America Bourgeois?" 278-282. The problem here is not the quantity of material that has to be mastered but the notion of knowing as a form of mastery over an object. Cf. D. C. Schindler, "Towards a Non-Possessive Concept of Knowledge: On the Relation between Reason and Love in Aquinas and Balthasar," *Modern Theology* 22 (2006): 596-598.

2. It should also be noted that Schindler lived twice in Austria: in 1974-1975 as a Fulbright Scholar and in 1985-1986 as the Director of the Innsbruck Program of the University of Notre Dame.

doctoral studies with John Cobb at the Center for Process Studies (Clare-mont), teaching at Mount St. Mary's College and The Program of Liberal Studies of the University of Notre Dame, editing for over thirty years the journal *Communio,* and a chair in metaphysics and fundamental theology at the Washington, D.C., session of the Pontifical John Paul II Institute for Studies of Marriage and the Family.

Throughout this pilgrimage one also notes the gradual but steady in-fluence of the thought of Hans Urs von Balthasar. The adjective "Baltha-sarian" is a crude label that the Swiss theologian would surely have found repulsive. On the other hand, Schindler's quest to refine his metaphysics evinces not only citations from Balthasar's works but a style of "kneeling theology" that Balthasar considered essential to his own project. The scope of Schindler's debt to Balthasar can be neither ignored nor exaggerated. One cannot assume that the translation of Balthasar's ideas into an Ameri-can key (albeit in a highly unmodern *and* socially critical way) is the *only* norm for interpreting Schindler's thought. The traces of other influences are palpably present in Schindler's writings, and the whole of his corpus could not really be interpreted without some attention to the fact that its germinating seeds were disseminated from places other than Balthasar's Basel.

In what follows I intend to follow the course of Schindler's thought from the publication of his early essay on actuality in Whitehead, Aristotle, and Aquinas to his engagements since the mid-1980s with Henri de Lubac, Hans Urs von Balthasar, Walter Kasper, Joseph Ratzinger, and others. I will not attempt to discuss every article he wrote in this period. I aim to do no more than to assess Schindler's own grasp of the Catholic tradition through an examination of his treatment of the Trinitarian *analogia entis.*[3]

Following this introductory section, the essay consists of four parts. Parts II and III lay out the development of a basic pattern of Trinitarian on-tology from its beginnings in Thomist metaphysics to its later elaboration in terms of a theological proposal influenced by the French and German theologians associated with *Communio.* Part IV examines the uses of Scrip-ture and tradition within Schindler's thought, paying special attention to

3. The term "trinitarian *analogia entis*" is borrowed here from Angela Franks, "Trini-tarian *Analogia Entis* in Hans Urs von Balthasar," *The Thomist* 62 (1998): 533-559. This form of reflection is increasingly seen as a resource for Protestant theology and can hardly be lim-ited to Balthasar or even the theologians associated with the review *Communio.* See, for ex-ample, Colin E. Gunton, *The One, the Three and the Many: God, Creation and the Culture of Modernity* (Cambridge: Cambridge University Press, 1993).

the parallels with the medieval Augustinian tradition. By way of conclusion, I will show in the final part that Schindler's account of being shares with St. Bonaventure and other medieval Augustinians rootedness in a much broader Catholic and Biblical tradition. The *Auseinandersetzung* of Schindler's path with the Christian tradition of a Trinitarian *analogia entis* brings into relief Schindler's distinct approach to catholicity as well as the uniqueness of his metaphysically oriented Catholic humanism.

II. A Philosophy of Creative Actuality

Trinitarian Christocentrism is not to be found in the earliest works of David Schindler. Instead we find a self-professed "existential Thomism" in dialogue with the thought of the process thinker A. N. Whitehead and the physicist David Bohm.[4]

Whitehead's thought represents in Schindler's earliest writings a substantial challenge and unavoidable horizon of understanding. When Whitehead conceives of creativity as an Ultimate, Schindler avers, he has reworked Spinoza's "monistic substance" into a new, more organic form.[5] Whitehead, Schindler continues, "resolves the problem of universals by transforming Aristotle's essentialistic universe into a radically dynamic universe."[6] To that end, Whitehead provides a key to understanding abiding metaphysical problems in a modern key. But Whitehead's metaphysics cannot stand on its own.[7] While Whitehead and St. Thomas Aquinas both locate the source of actuality in an indeterminate process, Whitehead's principle of creativity as an ultimate fails to actualize the sources of the process. Whitehead and his followers seemed satisfied, according to Schindler, with an elucidating explanation of the "whatness" of actual enti-

4. Cf. David L. Schindler, "Whitehead's Challenge to Thomism on God and Creation: The Metaphysical Issues," *International Philosophical Quarterly* 19 (1979): 295n.5: "The interpretation offered reflects my understanding of what is commonly referred to as existential Thomism. In this interpretation, for which I take sole responsibility. [sic] I am principally indebted to the writings of Joseph de Finance, Etienne Gilson, Joseph Owens, and Frederick D. Wilhelmsen."

5. David L. Schindler, "Creativity as Ultimate: Reflections on Actuality in Whitehead, Aristotle, and Aquinas," *International Philosophical Quarterly* 13 (1973): 162.

6. Schindler, "Creativity as Ultimate," 167.

7. Cf. David L. Schindler, "Whitehead's Inability to Affirm a Universe of Value," *Process Studies* 13 (1983): 117-130.

ties without posing the question of their "isness."[8] Whitehead's creativity as an ultimate is in this respect wholly inadequate. For Schindler, St. Thomas's metaphysics of God as *ipsum esse subsistens* is a principle that actualizes actual entities in a manner very much akin to that of process metaphysics while still offering a solution to the metaphysical question of the ground of actual entities.

This resolution in favor of St. Thomas hardly allows Thomists to ignore Whitehead's challenge. This challenge is treated six years later in an article on the metaphysics of creation.[9] Here the discussion focuses on the God of religious experience. The principal contribution of the God of Whitehead's process philosophy for Thomists, Schindler says, is to offer "an account of the nature of actuality which clearly affirms our (ontological) experience of the world in all its manysidedness, and our (religious) experience of a lover-God who is intimately involved with, affected by, the world."[10] While duly noting the insurmountable metaphysical differences between Whitehead's sense of God's mutable, consequent nature and the fully transcendent Creator of Thomist thought as well as the fundamental differences on actuality and potentiality, Schindler takes Whitehead's question regarding the primordial creativity of God with utter seriousness. Thomistic *esse* cannot be misconstrued as a static form hovering above all its instantiations in the world or as just another thing, even the highest thing on the great chain of being. St. Thomas's statement in *Summa contra Gentiles* that a God who is absolutely simple must be *totus ubique* ("as a whole everywhere") confirms this point, according to Schindler.[11] Whitehead's principle of creativity reminds Thomists of the folly of an approach that makes God so flatly transcendent as to call into question his actualization of all existing beings and of one that subdivides the indivisible divine being.

What challenge does Thomism present to Christian thinkers influenced by Whitehead's process metaphysics? Schindler notes several, but I will concentrate on just two. One differentiating characteristic between the two schools concerns the distinction between essence and existence. For

---

8. Schindler, "Creatively as Ultimate," 170.

9. Schindler, "Whitehead's Challenge to Thomism on God and Creation," 285-299.

10. Schindler, "Whitehead's Challenge to Thomism on God and Creation," 295.

11. Thomas Aquinas, *Summa contra Gentiles*, III, ch. 68, n. 9: "Non est autem aestimandum Deum sic esse ubique quod per locorum spatia dividatur, quasi una pars eius sit hic et alia alibi, *sed totus ubique est*." Italics added. The passage is cited by Schindler in support of this thesis in "David Bohm on Contemporary Physics and the Overcoming of Fragmentation," *International Philosophy Quarterly* 22 (1982): 325n.3.

Whitehead, Schindler claims, the difference is at best what scholastic theologians would call a "formal" one.[12] For existential Thomists, the difference is generally assumed to be "real." Likewise, the radical priority of *esse* to essence cannot be affirmed by process thought because of their in principle denial of the asymmetrical relation between existential act and potentiality. Potentiality for Whitehead is rather correlative to actuality, and "the Category of the Ultimate" is not only not immune to development but also, by virtue of the principle of process, must be co-determined by the self-creativity of actual entities. Creativity for Whitehead is not a form or an essence. But Whitehead's creativity is also not the act of existence from which every existing thing derives its existence. Existential Thomism therefore adds an important qualification to the notion of *esse* that a process thinker can in some fashion already affirm (albeit in the guise of the creativity of "the Category of the Ultimate"). For a Thomist, Schindler states, "*esse* must subsist."[13] Schindler seems to say that *esse* for a Thomist is the act that both instantiates and actualizes (i.e., lends being to) each actual entity. The indeterminacy of Whitehead's God is also indirectly acknowledged by Thomism inasmuch as there is no direct intuition except by God of *esse* as such. *Esse* for existential Thomists is wholly transcendent *and* subsists in the actual existence of entities. Thus construed, the Thomist can be seen as teaching the process thinker how it is that a principle of creativity actually exists in each actual entity, a point which Whitehead seeks to affirm through a different mode but cannot fully justify on the basis of his impoverished metaphysics of being.

Nothing in the early writings suggests an antipathy to a Trinitarian *analogia entis*. On the contrary, the Thomist sources cited by Schindler remain open to this development. For example, in his 1979 article Schindler notes his debt to "the writings of Joseph de Finance, Etienne Gilson, Joseph Owens, and Frederick D. Wilhelmsen."[14] Elsewhere he also acknowledges a debt to the philosophy of Kenneth Schmitz, particularly the seminal chapter on "the ontological drama" in his Aquinas Lecture, *The Gift: Creation;* Michael Polanyi is also a formative influence at this stage. In the late 1970s Christian personalism and Thomist metaphysics were already flowing together into a single stream in Schindler's thought.[15] This stream, in

---

12. Schindler, "Whitehead's Challenge to Thomism on God and Creation," 297.

13. Schindler, "Whitehead's Challenge to Thomism on God and Creation," 298.

14. Schindler, "Whitehead's Challenge to Thomism on God and Creation," 295n.5.

15. Schindler's thought is hardly out of step with the developments in Anglo-American Thomism from this period, although it cannot properly be classified as neo-Thomist since it

fact, is not diverted when he begins in his later writings to engage Trinity and Christology. Thomism just flows into a wider river.

The mention of the American Thomist Fritz Wilhelmsen (1923-1996) is particularly illuminating in this regard.[16] In the 1962 essay *The Metaphysics of Love,* Wilhelmsen made a case for a post-Heideggerian retrieval of the Christian tradition of Trinitarian metaphysics based upon the thought of Richard of St. Victor, Ramón Lull, and Xavier Zubiri.[17] Wilhelmsen follows a philosophical path illuminated by a rich Christian tradition that assumes that the Trinitarian revelation discloses an ecstatic structure of existence in reality and in the human person. The "we" of divine love illuminates the existential reality of the person and the personal structure of existence. A philosopher who follows Zubiri in explicating the *rationes entis* of this illumination can still remain loyal to the exigencies of reason, Wilhelmsen claims.[18] But the notion of being as act needs to be scrutinized in the light of the contemporary demands of historical existence. Zubiri, Wilhelmsen notes, cites a metaphor used by St. Bonaventure, according to which being can be understood either statically by comparison to the water contained within a reservoir or in an active sense as the flow of running water that fills and overflows a reservoir.[19] Like Schindler, Wilhelmsen enjoins Thomists to rediscover "the open and dynamic character of the act of existence."[20] When Gilson identified a tendency of Cajetan to limit existence to a final term in a process of change or as the

---

seeks to go back to a Thomism more original than the modern trends associated with neo-Thomism. A parallel to Schindler's existential Thomism can be found in what Maritain termed the "existential existentialism" of St. Thomas. In the 1971 edition of his survey of recent developments among Thomists, historian James C. Livingston noted the "Thomistic existentialism" of Jacques Maritain and especially Maritain's attempt to vindicate the insights of modern existentialists like Kierkegaard through Thomist wisdom. James C. Livingston, *Modern Christian Thought: From the Enlightenment to Vatican II* (New York: Macmillan, 1971), 395-398.

16. Frederick Daniel Wilhelmsen was an American who received his doctorate from the University of Madrid. For about thirty years he taught philosophy in Irving, Texas, and in Rome for the University of Dallas.

17. The book appeared in English in 1962. Below I am citing from the Spanish edition of 1964: *La Metafísica de Amor* (Madrid: Rialp, 1964).

18. Wilhelmsen, *La Metafísica de Amor,* 84.

19. Wilhelmsen, *La Metafísica de Amor,* 87. More recently, Javier Prades has noted the importance of Zubiri's reading of the active character of *energeia* for renewal in Trinitarian theology: "From the Economic to the Immanent Trinity: Remarks on a Principle of Renewal in Trinitarian Theology," *Communio: International Catholic Review* 27 (2000): 590n.68.

20. Wilhelmsen, *La Metafísica de Amor,* 100.

mere crown in the static order of being, he set forth a challenge to rediscover the original dynamic meaning of St. Thomas's philosophy of act. Following Chesterton, Wilhelmsen states plainly the significance of the Trinity for Thomism:

> The ecstatic and corporate structure of Catholic culture does not just re-
> flect the structure of being. It also reflects that the structure of being is an
> analogue of the interior life of the one Lord who is in himself a society.[21]

In spite of the grandness of the claim, Wilhelmsen nonetheless shows the
possibility of making a connection between a Thomist metaphysics of being renewed by the Trinitarian revelation of divine love and a philosophy
of history.[22]

There is a final point that needs to be made about Schindler's early
metaphysics, one that is rather critical in light of the later developments. In
some of the early essays, Schindler alludes to the shortcomings of Thomism. Schindler is inclined to the position that contemporary Thomism can
rediscover itself or reclaim resources hidden within its own past by engaging contemporaries such as Whitehead and Bohm. But in at least one text
he also seems to take the critique of Thomism from the side of modern
thought as seriously as he takes the critique of modern thought from the
side of Thomism.

In the 1979 article on Whitehead's challenge to Thomism, Schindler
notes that even with Whitehead's deficiencies there is "the correlative issue
for the Thomist" of how, if one asserts the priority of existential act, "one
can account adequately for the principle of 'otherness' necessary to ground
the possibility of a plurality."[23] Three years later the challenge to Thomism
seems even more pointed. Here he says that the organismic order rightly
defended by Bohm could potentially lead to a Thomist embrace of panen-
theism. He explains:

> The universe, when viewed in terms of an organismic order rooted fi-
> nally in esse, should properly be understood as a plurality of acting
> wholes which are in some significance sense "within" an Acting Whole.

---

21. Wilhelmsen, *La Metafísica de Amor,* 177. Wilhelmsen's Catholic triumphalism in this
passage and throughout can be explained only partly by his effort to parry the compelling
Trinitarian ontology of the Protestant theologian Paul Tillich.

22. Wilhelmsen, *La Metafísica de Amor,* 106.

23. Wilhelmsen, *La Metafísica de Amor,* 299.

How such a conception is to be worked out in positive terms, and in a way which does not eliminate the wholeness of esse precisely as esse (Esse), is of course an extraordinarily difficult and delicate issue.[24]

I do not want to assume that the challenge of plurality in an organismic universe represents precisely the challenge Schindler will take up again in his later writings, yet it is nonetheless striking that Schindler has identified a sense of otherness in the order of creation that is internal to the agency of Being. The implied message seems clear: Thomists must collaborate with thinkers such as Whitehead and Bohm if they want to refute the ontological blindness of modern Cartesianism. The result of such collaboration could lead to surprising results for Thomists, and the fear of the unexpected is no excuse for remaining disengaged from contemporary developments. Schindler sees in the new "organismic conception of a universe" the only fully adequate response to modern mechanism.[25] In making this bold claim, Schindler has pointed to the challenge of creaturely otherness left unanswered by existential Thomism, one that will require the reclaiming of both new and old resources in order to be addressed properly.[26]

III. The Turn to the Trinitarian *analogia entis*

God's Trinitarian communion of love was never thematized in the writings that we have so far addressed. This theme, however, becomes the Ariadne's thread to Schindler's writings beginning as early as 1987. This is not to suggest that a Trinitarian theology of God and the world was somehow "added" to a preexisting metaphysical system. One cannot deny that the metaphysics of creative actuality that Schindler defended in his early works is revised after the mid 1980s. Rather than seeing this revision as a reversal of or retreat from positions previously held, one can discern lines of continuity. In laying out the new points of departure, the new, more explicitly theological points of departure will be presented as complements

24. Schindler, "David Bohm on Contemporary Physics" 326.

25. Schindler, "David Bohm on Contemporary Physics," 327.

26. The question of the paradoxical "otherness" of essence vis-à-vis existence is thematized by Wilhelmsen, *La Metafísica de Amor*, 104. He maintains that the otherness of essence is not by virtue of its opposition to existence but by virtue of the paradoxical situation whereby essence is that which structures being from within existence itself.

to the early metaphysics. In other words, the already visible bud of a Trinitarian ontology has begun to blossom.

A good indicator of the Trinitarian thinking in Schindler's mature thought can be found in the concluding chapters of his book of 1996, *Heart of the World, Center of the Church*. Here the Thomist analogy of being has been supplemented by Hans Urs von Balthasar's understanding of an analogy of love.[27] In other words, there is a unity in difference of *esse* and *essentia* and of imparticipable *esse ipsum subsistens* and participating creaturely beings. Such unity and difference are now to be understood in terms of the revelation of love. Without in any way weakening his Thomist insistence upon the primacy of actuality, he has nonetheless recast in a new language the terms with which the relationship of God and the world is to be understood. Second, and even more fundamentally, the concrete form of the analogy of love now has a face:

> Something extraordinary happens when we approach nature first concretely, when we understand its divine imaging first in terms of the God who has revealed himself historically to be the Trinitarian love *(communio personarum)* become incarnate in Jesus of Nazareth. What happens is that we are now disposed to see love as constitutive of all of creation, as affecting intrinsically every fiber of every being in the cosmos. . . . *In Jesus Christ:* that is, all of these essential characteristics of Mary, the Church, and the communion of saints — given the latter realities' incorporation (through adoption, by grace) into Jesus Christ — themselves become further historical revelations of the meaning of divine love. These characteristics therefore unfold further the meaning of divine love as imaged in nature: they themselves become, as it were, the analogical *"figure"* or *"shape" in terms of which all of created being, including even physical being, is to be understood!*[28]

Here we see the full extent to which Schindler's vision of the relationship between God and the world has now become co-determined by the concrete revelation of Jesus Christ.[29]

---

27. HW, 305.

28. HW, 316.

29. This is not to say that Schindler has left behind the task of a proper metaphysics of creation in favor of a Barthian prioritizing of revelation. Following the line of interpretation initiated by Balthasar, he registers both agreement and disagreement with Barth in HW, 300n.17.

Roughly speaking, Schindler's supplementation of existential Thomism takes place in three stages. It is not a matter of gradually shifting away from one position in order to embrace an opposed one. In some ways, the shift in terms and concepts is really only a reclaiming of the original resources that Schindler from the outset indicated were needed to make existential Thomism more viable to the contemporary world. On another level, the adoption of the theological style of the French and German theologians of *Communio* becomes more and more evident over time. For Schindler, this development underscores that the relationship of God and the world is disclosed through the concrete revelation of Jesus Christ as the incarnate Son.

The first stage is the full-fledged adoption of a Trinitarian ontology, a development that has already taken place by 1987.[30] On the surface the two essays published in successive issues of *Communio* that year deal with very different topics, but the new accents in fundamental theology are the same. In the first, Schindler criticizes the "bourgeois ontology" of George Weigel. Here Schindler defends a view of being and selfhood that he distills from the elaboration of "Catholic-creedal Christianity" in Joseph Ratzinger's *Introduction to Christianity*.[31] Schindler embeds certain aspects of cultural analysis (e.g., Christopher Dawson's distinction between the extroversion of secularized Christian selves and the introversion of truly Catholic selves) in his fundamental claims; however, his basic point is that the doctrine of the *homoousion* claimed by Nicaea and Chalcedon can be translated into terms that have a direct bearing upon human existence as such.[32] In this view, the order of being, albeit inadequately, expresses the unique relationship in the Trinity of the Father to the Son, and even moral and social implications can be drawn from this relationship. The second essay responds to the fragmentation of the science of theology into a conglomerate of subdisciplines and simultaneously addresses the externalized notion of relation in a modern mechanistic account of the world. Here the doctrinal foundation is fourfold: God, Christ, Church, and creation.[33] Christ himself, he says, is a relational unity. Creation, too, is equally relational, as

30. "Is America Bourgeois?" 262-290; "Catholicity and Theology," 426-450.

31. While the influence of the theologian Ratzinger is indeed formative, Schindler's reason for choosing this starting point is here due to the fact that Weigel was responding to Ratzinger's charge that Catholic Christianity in America is in some ways marked by a bourgeois disorder. Cf. George Weigel, "Is America Bourgeois?" *Crisis* 4 (1986): 5-10.

32. Schindler, "Is America Bourgeois?" 268.

33. "Catholicity and Theology," 428-434.

Maximus the Confessor demonstrated when he interpreted Christ as the one "uniting created nature with the Uncreated through charity."[34] By taking Christ as the relationality par excellence of the entire created order, Schindler then goes on to argue for an "analogy established in grace, from above."[35] Whether one is considering the functional specialties within theological science or nature itself, Schindler maintains that the content and the form of the world need to be treated "from *within* the graced community of being."[36] Schindler then takes "onto-logic of holiness" to refer to a basic anthropological template stamped with a Marian watermark and visible in the created order. Holiness is thereby construed as a form of reflection and not merely a choice of action. Holiness is an intentional act whereby a believer orients his or her whole life to the Word of salvation, but it is not in the first instance the choice to enlist in a voluntary association. This difference becomes critical for Schindler's increasingly sharp criticisms in later years of the voluntarism lurking behind the otherwise vibrant forms of participation in North American religiosity.[37] Practical proposals that advocate a more scientific theology and a more liberating praxis can be judged both positively and negatively based upon "the onto-logic of holiness."

Schindler undertakes within the decade that follows (1987-1997) a second, even more concretely Christological step. A decisive movement in this direction can be found in his 1992 article "Christology, Public Theology, and Thomism," which contrasts the work of Henri de Lubac and Hans Urs von Balthasar, in which the ordering of nature is intrinsic and from its beginning toward the God of Jesus Christ, with the theology of John Courtney Murray, who seems to imply an extrinsic ordering of nature to grace.[38] The book already mentioned, *Heart of the World, Center of the Church*, appears in 1996. Here the following programmatic statement can be found:

---

34. "Catholicity and Theology," 430, 450 (citing *Ambigua*, PG 91, 1307c-1308c).

35. "Catholicity and Theology," 434-435. Schindler frequently appeals here to what Balthasar calls "katalogy." See Hans Urs von Balthasar, TL, vol. 2, as well as Schindler, "Christology and Public Theology," 250n.4; "Christology and Imago Dei," 178n.38.

36. "Catholicity and Theology," 440. Italics added.

37. See, for example, "The Religious Sense and American Culture," *Communio: International Catholic Review* 25 (1998): 679-699, which was reprinted in *A Generative Thought: An Introduction to the Works of Luigi Giussani*, ed. Elisa Buzzi (Montreal: McGill-Queen's University Press, 2003), 84-102.

38. "Christology and Public Theology," 247-264.

Man, and all of creation through man, is somehow made in the "image" of God. This image is of God conceived not abstractly but concretely: of the God revealed historically in Jesus Christ and in the Church that is Christ's body. And the "imaging" is to be understood in terms of an analogical relation that is intrinsic.[39]

Moreover, that same year he writes an article on how to interpret the theology of the *imago Dei* in *Gaudium et Spes*. Both the texts widen the aims of a Trinitarian ontology while tacitly elaborating the theology of *communio* that had been endorsed at the Roman Synod of Bishops of 1985.[40] Accordingly, Schindler highlights those interpretations of the decree of the Council that offer a Christocentric as opposed to a "merely theistic" approach to theological anthropology. He duly notes that neither paragraph 12 (on the image of God) nor the pivotal references to the rightful autonomy of earthly affairs (in paragraphs 36 and 59) have fully integrated either Christocentric anthropology or a fully realistic notion of sinfulness. He claims that the basic pattern for theological anthropology in *Gaudium et Spes* and more broadly can be gleaned from paragraph 22 on how the mystery of man becomes clear in the mystery of the Word made flesh. Although Schindler's focus is on the proper interpretation of conciliar and post-conciliar texts, two further substantive points are made. The first concerns the methodological distinction Schindler makes in retrieving the proper interpretation of paragraph 22. The Christocentrism of the passage, he notes, is not just moral but ontological.[41] As was discussed above vis-à-vis holiness, the orientation of the person to Christ extends beyond an independent domain of "moral intentions." He states: "Only if we understand man as first receptive — *from* God — can we understand properly the extent to which he is called to adore God; only if we understand man as called to adore God can we understand radically enough the true nature of man's socialness, the seriousness of his fall from grace, and the depth of his need for forgiveness."[42] The second concerns the clarification provided by Pope John Paul II regarding the Trinitarian character of the Christocentric anthropology in *Gaudium et Spes*.[43] In his early pontifical writings (e.g., *Redemptor hominis,* the Wednesday discourses on the theology of the

39. HW, 13-14.
40. "Christology and Imago Dei," 156-184.
41. "Christology and Imago Dei," 171-175.
42. "Christology and Imago Dei," 172-173.
43. "Christology and Imago Dei," 170.

body, and even the letter to families), the Pope insists that "man most fully images God as a *communio personarum*."[44] Schindler's engagement of questions regarding marriage, family, and gender takes this point as absolutely basic. God's most fundamental revelation in Jesus Christ is echoed — however imperfectly — in the intrinsically relational and receptive unity of the human person.

Finally, we see an even more synthetic appraisal of Trinitarian Christocentrism in Schindler's most recent work. The specific questions that Schindler has engaged in the decade running from 1997 to the present are far too numerous to detail; however, he elaborates the original proposal regarding a Trinitarian *analogia entis* in a twofold manner. The first concerns the new application of his theological theory of analogy to the order of knowing; it is articulated as a program in the essay "Trinity, Creation, and the Order of Intelligence in the Modern Academy."[45] The second concerns the further broadening of the scope of the project to illuminate social and political matters, the revival of the transcendental of beauty, and the perceived need to respond to the challenge of postmodernism.[46]

In the fall 2001 issue of *Communio*, Schindler made a concrete proposal that originated with the gathering of the members of the Arkwood Foundation. The wide-ranging proposal concerns the order of intelligence in the modern academy.[47] Its culminating point is the identification of the

---

44. "Christology and Imago Dei," 170.

45. "Trinity, Creation, and the Academy," 406-428. Two related essays came out in the preceding years: "Knowledge as Relationship," 510-540, and "The Catholic Academy and the Order of Intelligence: The Dying of the Light," *Communio: International Catholic Review* 26 (1999): 722-745. The question of the order of intelligence is not a new one for Schindler. His doctoral thesis written under John Cobb at Claremont was entitled "Knowing as Synthesis: A Metaphysical Prolegomenon to a Critical Christian Philosophy."

46. The summary given below is based mainly upon these three essays: "Modernity and Atheism"; "Homelessness," 411-430; and "Is Truth Ugly?" 701-728.

47. The proposal is based upon the guiding principles of the Arkwood Foundation, an initiative established in 1994 "for the purpose of studying the implications of the call to holiness for the order of intelligence" ("Trinity, Creation, and the Academy," 406n.2). It is revealing that the Arkwood proposal for a renewal of the modern academy took shape just two years after Schindler left the University of Notre Dame for the John Paul II Institute. Likewise, Schindler says the proposal came from discussions that took place annually at a farm in rural New Hampshire. Such detachment from an institutional place for the sake of its renewal finds parallels in the life of Balthasar as well as countless monastic figures of renewal. One thinks, too, of the nineteenth-century Catholic convert Orestes Brownson and his attachment to the utopian community of Brook Farm.

mechanistic order of the modern world ("with its primacy of simply [static] identity and of [external] power") as akin to an Adamic relationship to the world through mastery, power, and a functionalization of what is real.[48] Schindler is not claiming that modernity or the modern academy is the first or only sinner in the epochal history of the world. On the contrary, the proposal aims to reintegrate "modernity's concern for the [natural] integrity of creaturely identity and power" with "premodernity's defense of the primacy of the creature's relation to God."[49] The task of integration entails a rediscovery of the "sacramental-symbolic" character of the cosmos (reflecting a strong Eastern Orthodox influence mediated by Alexander Schmemann) and an understanding of holiness as an attribute predicable of all creaturely beings.[50] Grounded in a Trinitarian and Christological order, the intelligence being proposed for the contemporary academy does not simply meld human subjectivity into a cosmic frame but highlights creaturely receptivity to a personal mode of radical alterity as constitutive of personal being and knowing. Following Balthasar, the implicitly known *and* epiphanic smile that a mother imparts to a newborn becomes paradigmatically inscribed into the creature's mode of existence.[51] In this light, the task of the academy cannot be narrowly focused on educational, vocational, or even moral and political outcomes. The *raison d'être* of the academy is to make it genuinely possible to be saved by beauty.

From this vantage point, the second development in Schindler's thought since 1997 can be quickly sketched. Schindler's judgment regarding the "energetic" nihilism of the so-called postmoderns is emphatically *not* one of dismissal.[52] Beyond the common cause of laying bare the flaccid timidity of much in modernity that passes itself off as progressive and world-changing, Schindler can claim *with the postmoderns* that the absence of a transcendental signifier "God" is all-determinative for the interpretation of reality. The difference between Schindler and Derrida lies *not* in the filling up of space left vacant by the secular departure of God with

48. "Trinity, Creation, and the Academy," 424, citing Genesis 3:5-6, 22.

49. "Trinity, Creation, and the Academy," 428.

50. On Schmemann, see "Creation and Nuptiality," 701-728.

51. "Trinity, Creation, and the Academy," 414-415.

52. On the phrase "energetic nihilism," see David L. Schindler, "The Significance of Hans Urs von Balthasar in the Contemporary Cultural Situation," in *Glory, Grace, and Culture: The Work of Hans Urs von Balthasar*, ed. Ed Block, Jr. (Mahwah, NJ: Paulist Press, 2005), 30.

pious affirmations of faith. The difference lies precisely in the perception of whether that which is signified in God's self-revelation can or cannot disclose a real fullness of meaning. For Derrida the claim for fullness is the inevitable beginning of the play of signifiers. Theological fullness by definition belies the representation of any one thing. Hence, fullness is inextricably intertwined with emptiness, absence, an endless tracing of the semiotic labyrinth. With Balthasar, Schindler points to the representation of the mission of Christ in the life of Mary, St. Francis, and St. Ignatius of Loyola. The witness of sanctity does not fill the void left by the end of metaphysics. It expresses the fullness of being in a hitherto undiscovered place. It is the Marian form of the Church itself.[53]

As a consequence, when Schindler writes about the Catholic social teachings, he considers the implications of an expanding global economy on the family. Yet his proposal says little about either global markets or what is usually understood by "family values." Instead he proposes (agreeing in certain ways with both Wendell Berry and feminist philosopher Virginia Held) that the power of a mother to empower others is a paradigm for a more relational communion not only within the seemingly private domain of the nuclear family but for politics and economics as well. The "monoculture" of global networks (a process of homogenization that is only accelerated through the new electronic media) radically compresses time and space and precludes any consideration of a form of social existence based upon a true economy of communion. Families that are hard-wired to the internet no longer have time to experience either the local or the global village. The family as a domestic church (understood as a form of relationality that transforms modern homelessness) offers to the world an interior view of creaturely relationality. One cannot then *ipso facto* translate a Catholic/catholic sense of maternal affection into a paradigm for a global economy.[54] Nor can one reduce the multidimensional and socially productive witness of a family that shares love into a formula that produces discrete moral values. According to Schindler, Christian hope for social renewal lies in the domestic witness to cruciform, loving, social solidarity.[55]

"Is truth ugly?" — the question posed by Friedrich Nietzsche — seems to pose a sharp rebuke to any proposal that takes the recovery of wonder

53. Schindler, "The Significance of Hans Urs von Balthasar," 34.

54. Schindler writes: "John Paul II himself affirms a distinction between economic systems and cultural systems (cf. *Centesimus Annus*, 39, 36). What I am denying is that his distinction is to be read as an extrinsic relation between the two." "Homelessness," 426n.22.

55. "Homelessness," 430.

and beauty as seriously as does Schindler. But Schindler himself poses Nietzsche's question in order to sharpen his response to the current cultural climate. If the revelation of beauty is critical to a new program for theology, the Church, and the world, then the form of beauty's self-disclosure must pass through the crucible of Nietzschean criticism. Nietzsche, in fact, praises Christianity for being consistent "in conceiving the good man as ugly."[56] No theological aesthetics, Schindler argues, can abandon this genuine insight for the sake of recovering the glory of the Lord.

The article in which Schindler develops his response to Nietzsche's challenge represents Schindler's fullest response to those critics who claim that Pope John Paul II's espousal of the nuptial mystery is based upon a Romantic theology of the body.[57] In terms of the integration of metaphysics and theology, however, the most important development here seems to be the clarifying reflection upon the relationship of form and event, which itself is a return to the earliest concerns of Schindler's own thought. Schindler says that Nietzsche and his followers replace the appearance of *Gestalt* (form) with the happening of *Ereignis* (event). Schindler by no means intends to resist altogether the post-Nietzschean deconstruction of classical form as a lifeless abstraction. Postmodernity brings to the fore the critical issues regarding space, time, and the fragmentation of daily existence that need to be addressed from within an analogical grasp of the nuptial mystery. In *The Birth of Tragedy*, Schindler states, Nietzsche himself considers order (scil. Apollo) and event (scil. Dionysus) as a fruitful tension.[58] The postmodern unmasking of this tension is in Schindler's view a healthy antidote to the artificial masks inherent in modern culture. Schindler's solution is to bring to light the postmodern *disjunction* between form and event as the theological problem *par excellence*. Once again, for Schindler, Balthasar strikes the right balance. For Balthasar, a sheer actualism obscures the polarities of being. Being for Balthasar is not overcome by event. Balthasar roots his vision in a Thomistic vision of the good (and hence love and beauty) as the highest act of being.[59] Form can thus be seen as an always-already self-transcending reality, and this reas-

---

56. Nietzsche, *The Will to Power*, trans. W. Kaufmann and R. Hollingdale (New York: Random House, 1987), n. 88, as cited in "Is Truth Ugly?" 701n.1.

57. "Is Truth Ugly?" 702n.4.

58. "Is Truth Ugly?" 708.

59. "Is Truth Ugly?" 717. It is precisely on this point that Balthasar in TL, vol. 2, distinguishes his own project from that proposal in Jean-Luc Marion's *Dieu sans L'Être*, but it is not possible here to explore this fascinating *Auseinandersetzung*.

sertion of the transcendental of beauty can be made without denying to a beautiful form its capacity for self-identity. Schindler concludes by noting that a child is granted access to freedom to play within the sheltering embrace of a home.[60] Much can be learned from this simple insight. To impose a preordained view of beauty upon individuals is indeed a violation of personal freedom. Postmodernism shows how the cause of liberal progress created dogmatisms regarding the unreality of genuine love precisely in the name of upholding the venerable principle that human freedom has its own integrity. In the end, Schindler concludes, the seriousness of metaphysical questioning after postmodernism remains a variant of child's play: "Existence as play: this, finally, is the answer to the charge that truth and goodness are ugly."[61] Play maintains the proper balance between the perfection of classical form and the striving for infinite freedom of individuals today. The Christian appropriation of play involves the recognition that the same child who played at the feet of the Virgin Mary also caused her boundless grief at the foot of the cross.

Looking back at the stages of development of Schindler's thought, we can now pose the question: How does the mystery of the Holy Trinity irradiate being? Reality, in sum, is interpreted in the light of the revelation of Jesus Christ, a thesis that only underscores what the Council called "the rightful autonomy of earthly affairs."[62] Although his polemics are usually reserved for various forms of tacit extrinsicism, Schindler pays due attention throughout to the shortcomings of an integralism that fails to distinguish between nature and grace. He can even cite with approbation Karl Rahner on this point:

> God establishes the creature and its difference from himself. But by the very fact that God establishes the creature and its difference from itself, the creature is a genuine reality different from God, and not a mere appearance behind which God and his own reality hide.[63]

60. "Is Truth Ugly?" 727.

61. "Is Truth Ugly?" 728.

62. The issue of how to interpret *Gaudium et Spes* was addressed in "Christology and Imago Dei," but an even more synthetic presentation of the necessity of affirming the autonomy of nature within a Christocentric and ecclesial theology can be found in the essay co-authored with Nicholas J. Healy, "For the Life of the World: Hans Urs von Balthasar on the Church as Eucharist," in *The Cambridge Companion to von Balthasar,* ed. David Moss and Edward T. Oakes, S.J. (Cambridge: Cambridge University Press, 2004), 51-63.

63. Karl Rahner, *Foundations of Christian Faith: An Introduction to the Idea of Christianity* (New York: Seabury, 1978), 78-79, as cited in "Christology and Imago Dei," 160.

Schindler shows no interest in bringing nature closer to God or in using theological principles to circumvent physical or moral laws of the natural order. The distance and unconfusedness implied by the hypostatic union is both greater and more distinct than any opposedness that can be imagined in the realm of creatures alone. In other words, for Schindler, radical relationality and liberating receptivity are much more fundamental than nearness to God in the order of nature. Any sense of a sudden intervention of a *Deus ex machina* into the integral reality of the natural is formally excluded by the Christological and Trinitarian *analogia entis*. Without ignoring the genuinely Thomistic insights developed in this period, one still cannot help but notice residues in Schindler's mature thought of the account of nature derived from both Whitehead and Bohm.[64]

IV. Scripture, Tradition, and the Onto-Logic of Trinitarian Belief

Schindler's earliest academic training was in classics and philosophy, after which he studied theology, including process thought. With such a background, it is no wonder that Schindler often leaves his readers only brief references to the Scriptural foundations of his thought. The citations from Scripture increase slightly as he begins to cite with greater frequency the theologians of *Communio* (especially Henri de Lubac, Hans Urs von Balthasar, Walter Kasper, and Joseph Ratzinger) since these theologians tend to take very seriously the concreteness of the revealed Word. More often than not, Schindler hinges his theological metaphysics on just a few passages from the New Testament, e.g., John 1:1-3; 17:13-23; Colossians 1:15-20; Ephesians 1:3-10; 5:21-33; Galatians 2:20; Romans 8:23; 1 Corinthians 6:15-17; 10:16ff.; 15:28; Hebrews 1:2; and 1 John 4:10.[65]

The repetition of archetypal texts should not be taken as a canon within a canon. But this method is illustrative of Schindler's approach to Scripture and tradition. His preference for an ordering of schemata over detailed exegesis seems plain, for example, in the 1987 essay on the onto-logic of holiness.[66] In order to illustrate a point about the relational charac-

---

64. On the Thomism of Schindler's mature period, see "Christology and Public Theology" as well as the exchange with Norris Clarke in *Communio: International Catholic Review* (Fall 1993, Spring 1994).

65. These passages are all cited in HW, 1-40. They are, I believe, the key texts to which he returns in many of his writings.

66. "Catholicity and Theology," 431-434.

ter of created beings, he groups together three sets of texts. The first set affirms Christ as the firstborn of creation and thereby shows that all created entities have their being in and through him.[67] The second set points to the simultaneity of the "already" and the "not yet" in the revelation of Christ as the form of creation.[68] Simultaneity is used here in the specific sense of unity in difference. In fact, Schindler underscores the divine origin of the simultaneity to ward off upsetting the balance in either direction. Simultaneity is, he says, "neither some vague, abstract and impersonal relation, nor does it come 'from below.'"[69] The third set consists simply of the *homoousion* of the Nicene confession of faith, which in a note is buttressed by the repeated citation (with a changed emphasis) of John 17:21: "May they be one, Father, *even as (kathōs)* you and I are one."[70] The groupings are meant to be heuristic, and it would be misguided to read them as exegetical tools. On the other hand, they illustrate how Schindler uses a fairly limited number of texts of Scripture to find patterns that point to a source of his metaphysical principles. In sum, Schindler reads Scripture as a prismatic refraction of iconic appearances. Exegesis functions in his own texts like iconography in the sense that a mystery that transcends all understanding shines through each distinct image.

The apparent leanness of Schindler's Scriptural reasoning helps to focus the issue at hand. The texts from Scripture and the tradition just adumbrated deal with the spiritually palpable reality of the body of Christ. In the light of Christian faith, the Word made flesh integrates reality itself. In its sending forth from the Father, condescension, dwelling in our midst, iconicity, nuptiality, paschal mystery, spiritual fruitfulness, divine com-passion, and resurrection from among the dead, Christ's body joins time and eternity. Schindler focuses on the enfleshment of the Word, what the poet Péguy calls "in-carnal-ation *(encharnellement)*." The radical incarnateness of Christ's body is thus a starting point for both metaphysical reflection and genuine dialogue.[71] The incarnate body is joined to the second Person of the Trinity

---

67. "Catholicity and Theology," 431. He cites John 1:1-3; Col. 1:15-18; 3:11; Eph. 1:23; Heb. 1:3; cf. also Acts 17:28-29; Wis. 1:7.

68. Here he writes: "cf., e.g., Eph. 1:10; 4:13-16; 3:19; Rm. 8:22; cf. also in this connection the subjunctive mood in Jn. 17:21: 'That they all *may* ('ōsi') be one even as you and I are one'" ("Catholicity and Theology," 430).

69. "Catholicity and Theology," 433.

70. "Catholicity and Theology," 433n.8.

71. On the notion in Péguy, see Charles Péguy, *The Portal of the Mystery of Hope*, trans. David Louis Schindler, Jr. (Grand Rapids: Eerdmans, 1996), 58; and Michelle Borras, "At the

through a *sacrum commercium*. This connubiality of the human flesh and a human life with the triune, divine life points to the conjunction of radical Christocentrism with a Trinitarian ontology.[72] The sharing of the divine persons as a starting point for interpreting reality as a whole is thus inseparable from the revelation of the Word made flesh. Believers have no insight into the mystery of Trinitarian *perichoresis* except through the epiphany of Christ's face.

Schindler's fusing of Scriptural exegesis, theological reflection, and metaphysics is radical in the sense that it serves as a counterweight to the theological fragmentation he consistently decries. By the same token, Schindler's Scripturally based Trinitarian ontology also fits into a broad pattern of Augustinian thinking in the Catholic tradition. Schindler is aware that he is bringing Augustinian thought into his synthesis and is mainly concerned to acknowledge his dependency on this source while avoiding common stereotypes.[73] Balthasar, Schindler says, overcomes the putative (i.e., exaggerated) disjunction between a Thomist emphasis on objective truth and Bonaventure's Augustinian emphasis on a spirituality of love. In light of what was said above about the heuristic value of postmodernism, overcoming this Thomist/Augustinian divide remains for Schindler a purely modern as opposed to a genuinely scholastic problem.

To attain an even better sense of Schindler's Augustinianism, we can examine a text of Bonaventure that Schindler himself cites as a source for his own notion that "all things carry an openness *from within their being* which will *never* be explicable in *any other way* than in terms of the relation to God — and to each other in God — given by God in Jesus Christ."[74] In his *Disputed Questions on the Mystery of the Trinity*, question 1, article II, Bonaventure assumes that natural reason *can* prove the existence of God but *not* the existence of a triune God.[75] For Bonaventure, faith alone illuminates the mind with this revealed truth. Having distinguished between reason and revelation in this fashion, Bonaventure then seeks to prove the

Center of Life: Poetry as Trinitarian Conversation in the *Mysteries* of Charles Péguy," *Anthropotes* 19/1 (2003): 113-144, and (second part) *Anthropotes* 19/2 (2003): 353-385. See also "Is Truth Ugly?" 704-705 on incarnation and the flesh of the cosmos.

72. The Mariological theme in Schindler's thought cannot be developed here with the adequacy it deserves. It is, however, treated in this volume by Stratford Caldecott.

73. "Catholicity and Theology," 436n.13 and "Is Truth Ugly?" 719n.27.

74. "Catholicity and Theology," 436.

75. St. Bonaventure, *Disputed Questions on the Mystery of the Trinity*, trans. Zachary Hayes, O.F.M. (St. Bonaventure, NY: The Franciscan Institute, 1979), 122-137.

fittingness of what is revealed in the light of what natural reason can attain on its own. In modern terms, Bonaventure thematizes God's gift of a Trinitarian self-revelation. On the basis of this utterly gratuitous and most generous offering, how can human reason be put to work to show the beautiful symmetry of what faith knows as a given and what reason can achieve through its own powers? Bonaventure's mode of reasoning on the basis of reason's illuminated *pulchritudo* (beauty) and *convenientia* (fittingness) draws directly upon the style of theology he had encountered in St. Anselm and Richard of St. Victor.

In this article, Bonaventure hints at several ways in which creatures carry within their being a fundamental openness to the God of Jesus Christ. One way has to do with the kind of reasoning that a believer undergoes when thinking about the Trinity. In an objection, Bonaventure notes that scientific principles can be readily known when the principles of demonstration are self-evident to the intellect.[76] Because of the presence of unbelievers, so the objection runs, the truth of the Trinity cannot be as readily accessible as scientific knowledge. In his reply, Bonaventure argues that knowledge of faith is infused with piety.[77] As such, the truth "that the Highest Father should have an Only-begotten whom He loves as Himself, and whom He gives for the salvation of man," is not just a matter of dry speculation.[78] When the mind is filled with piety (i.e., Schindler's "ontologic of holiness"), then the acceptance of faith can be achieved just as readily as the mastery of a scientific principle.

The article in Bonaventure's *Disputed Questions* also addresses the attractiveness of beauty in the created realm and the natural sense of the whole that is completed by the vision of faith. Regarding beauty, Bonaventure maintains a parallelism between the book of creation, the book of Scripture, and the book of life.[79] The book of creation becomes largely illegible after the fall. In principle, however, its contents include both the vestige of the Trinity in all creatures and a more expressive image of the Trinity in the intellectual creature. With respect to the latter, Bonaventure cites the dual triads of St. Augustine: (1) memory, intelligence, and will, and (2) mind, knowledge, and love.[80] He notes, and per-

---

76. St. Bonaventure, *Disputed Questions*, q. 1, a. 2, obj. 8, p. 126, citing Aristotle, *I Post.* c. 2 and IV *Metaph.* text. 8 (III, c. 3).

77. He cites as a support Titus 1:1.

78. St. Bonaventure, *Disputed Questions*, ad 8, p. 135. See also ad 4, p. 134.

79. St. Bonaventure, *Disputed Questions*, resp., 128-131.

80. St. Bonaventure, *Disputed Questions*, 129.

haps thereby anticipates, the nuptial analogy that the Bishop of Hippo otherwise repudiated, that "mind [is] like a parent, knowledge like an offspring, and love like a bond proceeding from both and joining them together."[81] Whereas these analogies become obscured by original sin, the book of Scripture in a twofold way (Old and New Testaments) gives ample witness, including through the establishment of the sacraments, of the Triune revelation. Finally, the book of life, Bonaventure continues, "gives incontestable witness to the eternal Trinity to those who see God in heaven with 'unveiled faces.'"[82] Given the simultaneity of already and not yet, one might then ask about the usefulness of the eternal witness for the wayfarers on earth. Here Bonaventure introduces the notion of an innate (as opposed to an infused) light of reason that is given to "Christians, Jews, and Saracens, and even heretics."[83] While not quite going as far as Richard of St. Victor in claiming that one can thereby prove by necessary reasons that God is Triune, Bonaventure still sees a basic correlation between the two lights. What is revealed perfects what is known by natural reason. With respect to the Trinity, this means for Bonaventure that "to think the first principle in the highest and most reverent way" always already introduces the idea "that God can and does wish to produce one equal to and consubstantial with himself." Bonaventure thus opens the door to a new approach to Trinitarian reasoning even as he rightly maintains with typically Augustinian caution that a path predicated upon a gift from above should never be confused with the unholy idea that one can use reason alone to attain the disclosure of God as Father, Son, and Holy Spirit. In sum, the essential building blocks for a Trinitarian reconstruction of the *analogia entis* are already in place in Bonaventure's theology.

Other parallels can be drawn between Schindler and Bonaventure beyond this brief article. Both theologians, for example, defend the beauty of Christ, a Trinitarian interpretation of the human person as *imago Dei,* the essential correlation of theology and holiness, and the very notion of Trinitarian fruitfulness. In general, Schindler's reconstructed synthesis of Scripture, tradition, and philosophical reasoning follows an Augustinian pattern of reasoning. Schindler's Trinitarian *analogia entis* is written in the light of the analogy of faith that Bonaventure practiced in an exemplary fashion.[84]

81. St. Bonaventure, *Disputed Questions,* 129.
82. St. Bonaventure, *Disputed Questions,* 130.
83. St. Bonaventure, *Disputed Questions,* 131.
84. Cf. Gottlieb Söhngen, "Bonaventura als Klassiker der *analogia fidei*," *Wissenschaft und Weisheit* 2 (1935): 97-111.

V. Conclusion

What, then, is the genuine scope and hence catholicity of Schindler's humanism? In 1994 Schindler heaped praise upon the fine study of Balthasar's theology of divine immutability by the Jesuit Gerard O'Hanlon. Schindler concludes that essay by saying that O'Hanlon

> operates with presuppositions different from those we have become accustomed to take as traditional. These presuppositions do not so much depart from the tradition as they lift up from the tradition elements which have heretofore not received sufficient emphasis.[85]

These remarks reveal much about Schindler's own understanding of the Catholic tradition. From his very first publication, it was clear to Schindler that the Catholic tradition was not an archive or a towering monument to be admired from below. Whether the subject was Whitehead's God, Bohm's holism, or Michael Novak's view of American culture, Schindler put the resources of the Catholic tradition to work. Even though he repeatedly eschews the voluntarist strand of American pragmatism and the secular religiosity it spawned, there is still a very practical dimension to Schindler's metaphysical enterprise.[86] The presuppositions Schindler drew from the tradition alarm certain traditionalists precisely because they are not the customary ones. I have shown, *inter alia,* how Schindler lifts up certain Augustinian elements from the tradition. Schindler was the first to recognize that Augustinianism never replaced Thomism in his intellectual journey. The movement is rather that of a supplement, for Thomistic metaphysics remains an equally constant feature of his mature writings.[87] Schindler's thought is no more easily pigeon-holed into the tired assumptions of a school debate between Augustinians and Thomists than was the thought of his theological mentors, namely, de Lubac and Balthasar. Schindler's new humanism is rooted in a Catholic pattern of Trinitarian thought that is paleo-Thomist, neo-Augustinian, and deeply indebted to

85. *The Thomist* 58 (1994): 341.

86. In fact, Schindler conceives of the self "primarily in terms of being as distinct from doing and having." See "Is America Bourgeois?" 271.

87. Aside from the brief remark in "Is Truth Ugly?" 719n.27, see, for example, "Norris Clark on Person, Being, and St. Thomas," *Communio: International Catholic Review* 20 (1993): 580-592, and "The Person: Philosophy, Theology, and Receptivity," *Communio: International Catholic Review* 21 (1994): 172-190.

the European theologians who advocated a return to Scriptural and Patristic sources. The synthesis still occurs in a distinctively North American idiom, one that, for example, brings Balthasar into conversation with Wendell Berry, Luigi Giussani with Alasdair MacIntyre. Rather than seeing David L. Schindler solely as the harbinger of *Communio* on American soil, one can also see him as a Catholic who insightfully engages Anglo-American sources. Schindler's originality derives in part from the critical exchanges he undertook with process thought, contemporary philosophy of physics, and neoconservatism in the United States. True originality, of course, is not to be mistaken for recent vintage. True originality sounds the depths to listen for the echoes of actual creativity reverberating within a tradition. Such originality, I think, pervades Schindler's project.

Theology and Culture

Tracey Rowland

The territory known as the theology of culture is of relatively recent interest in Catholic scholarship. It is still regarded as of questionable legitimacy by some strict-observance Thomists. It arose as a response to questions raised by European Romantic and Existentialist scholars about the significance of culture for self-formation or, to put the question in more traditional language, the relationship of history to ontology, and by the need to understand the dynamics of evangelization in the West's increasingly anti-Christian culture. It is better received by Continental theologians who work within a milieu where Rousseau, Herder, Nietzsche, Heidegger, and Sartre, among others, are regarded as having asked important questions, even if their responses failed to square with Christian revelation. It also owes much of its theological ballast to the work of mid-twentieth-century European theologians, above all to the *Ressourcement* scholars, Henri de Lubac, S.J., and Hans Urs von Balthasar, and to their contemporary "students," Angelo Cardinal Scola, Marc Cardinal Ouellet, Fr. Aidan Nichols, O.P., and David L. Schindler. It is less at home in the United States where the great Catholic universities and liberal arts colleges were decidedly neo-Thomist before the Second Vatican Council and often divided between neo-Thomist and transcendental-Thomist orientations after the Council. For the neo-Thomists, de Lubac was an enemy of the faith, a dangerous anti-Thomist hiding behind the Patristics to mask a modernist agenda. Balthasar was just incomprehensible. What does Mozart or Goethe have to do with theology? Where are the syllogisms? What's the system? If culture is so important, why didn't St. Thomas address it? Paradoxically, for the transcendental Thomists, de Lubac was too anti-modern and became progressively more so as the centrifugal theological tendencies of the post-Conciliar era unwound.

David L. Schindler's achievement has been to take the theological insights of Balthasar, particularly his notion of there being a *logos* within every practice and culture, the critique of the extrinsicist accounts of the "grace and nature" relationship of de Lubac, and the theological anthropology of John Paul II and Angelo Cardinal Scola, and apply them to an analysis of the culture of America and, more broadly, contemporary Western liberalism. This has placed his work in tension with the project of the American Catholic neoconservatives or otherwise self-described "Whig Thomists" who tend to work within a neo-Thomist framework and who regard the U.S. constitutional order, its foundational philosophy, and the kind of political and economic culture that flows from it as something like an ideal to be emulated by other countries throughout the world, and something fundamentally favorable to a "Catholic moment." His work is also, of course, taking a different trajectory from the projects of those even more liberally oriented theologians influenced by the theology of Karl Rahner and other transcendental Thomists.[1] Any account of the theology of culture within the works of David L. Schindler must therefore begin with a rehearsal of de Lubac's critique of extrinsicist approaches to nature and grace. Two excellent sources that cover this are Schindler's essay "Grace and the Form of Nature and Culture" and an address delivered by de Lubac on a lecture tour of the United States in 1968.[2]

I. De Lubac and Neo-Thomism

The neo-Thomist hostility to de Lubac derives, in part, from his argument that the Thomism of Cajetan (1469-1534) and Suárez (1548-1617) and its influence on the Leonine and "neo" Thomism of the nineteenth and early twentieth centuries unwittingly fostered the secularization of Western culture.[3]

---

1. For comparisons of the Balthasarian and Rahnerian projects, see R. Williams, "Balthasar and Rahner," in *The Analogy of Beauty*, ed. J. Riches (Edinburgh: T&T Clark, 1986); and K. Kilby, "Balthasar and Karl Rahner," in *The Cambridge Companion to Hans Urs von Balthasar*, ed. E. T. Oakes and D. Moss (Cambridge: Cambridge University Press, 2004), 256-269.

2. See CSA; and Henri de Lubac, "Nature and Grace," in *The Word in History: The St. Xavier Symposium*, ed. T. Patrick Burke (London: Collins, 1968). See also D. L. Schindler, "Introduction to the 1998 Edition," in Henri de Lubac, *The Mystery of the Supernatural* (New York: Herder and Herder, 1998).

3. For the most important works on the opposition to the *Ressourcement* project, see the following: R. Garrigou-Lagrange, "La théologie nouvelle: où va-t-elle?" in *La synthèse thomiste* (Paris: Desclèe de Brouwer, 1946), 699-725; J. Guillet, *La théologie catholique en*

Diplomatically speaking, this is a little like accusing Osama bin Laden of promoting the Americanization of Islamic culture, but it is nonetheless de Lubac's claim that the account of the grace-nature relationship to be found in the works of the leading theologians of the Counter-Reformation era and those who followed them, extending into the twentieth century, had paved the way for secularism. In this judgment he was supported by the French historian of ideas Étienne Gilson.[4] Gilson complained of the tendency for people to "conjure up a Thomism after the manner of the Schools, a sort of dull rationalism which panders to the kind of deism that most of them, deep down, really prefer to teach."[5] He further described the commentary of Cajetan as "in every respect the consummate example of a *corruptorium Thomae*."[6] From this perspective, Baroque-era Thomism did not darn lacunae within the Thomist tradition, but contributed to the unraveling of the classical Thomist synthesis — a process that began in the fourteenth century but reached its zenith in the twentieth, by which time the theological components of the thought of St. Thomas had been decoupled from the philosophical and placed into separate boxes or disciplines. At its most extreme, Thomism became Aristotle with a Christian icing, and the specific difference of Christianity and the splendor of its revelation was submerged beneath mountains of apologetic works, all emphasizing the rationality of Christianity and its congruence with the classical traditions as if the Incarnation was not so radical an irruption in human history.

Whether or not one accepts this genealogy in large measure depends on what one makes of the idea of "pure nature" in the works of St. Thomas. The pro–de Lubac side argues that when St. Thomas referred to this concept he was merely referring to an intellectual abstraction — not a really existing "pure nature"; and further, that this tendency to think dualistically in terms of a supernatural order of grace and a natural "secular" order was

---

France de 1914 à 1960 (Paris: Médiasèvres, 1988); M-M. Labourdette, "La théologie et ses sources," *Revue Thomiste* 46 (1946); J. Daniélou, "Les orientations présentes de la pensée religieuse," *Etudes* 249 (1946): 5-21; A. Nichols, "Thomism and the Nouvelle Theologie," *The Thomist* 64 (2000): 12; F. Kerr, *After Aquinas: Versions of Thomism* (Oxford: Blackwell, 2002), 134-149; J. Milbank, *The Suspended Middle: Henri de Lubac and the Debate Concerning the Supernatural* (Grand Rapids: Eerdmans, 2005). See also a series of articles by P. J. Donnelly in *Theological Studies* 8 (1947): 483-491; 9 (1948): 213-249, 554-560.

4. Henri de Lubac, *Letters of Étienne Gilson to Henri de Lubac with Commentary by Henri de Lubac* (San Francisco: Ignatius Press, 1988).

5. *Letters of Étienne Gilson to Henri de Lubac*, 23-24.

6. *Letters of Étienne Gilson to Henri de Lubac*, 24.

not classical or paleo-Thomist, but a revisionist Baroque Thomism developed to defend the intrinsic goodness of a post-lapsarian humanity against Reformist tendencies to emphasize its depravity. Similar dualist trajectories were followed by those trying to defend the Catholic faith in the late nineteenth century with reference to various so-called Enlightenment standards of rationality, and in the twentieth century by those trying to defend the Catholic faith within the tradition of political liberalism. The analogues to sixteenth-century "pure nature" are eighteenth-century "pure reason" and twentieth-century "autonomous secularity." Although the motivations behind the various projects were good, as so often happens in the history of ideas, distortions arise because of a lopsided emphasis on one particular element of a tradition or because, in seeking to defeat an intellectual opponent, one ends by taking on board some of the opponents' characteristics — in this instance the Protestant affinity for dualisms. In each of these three instances, in the sixteenth, nineteenth, and twentieth centuries respectively, the project was to provide a Catholic response to an illegitimate critique of some aspect of the Catholic tradition. In each instance, however, the end result was the fostering of some dualism: nature and grace in separate boxes, faith and reason in separate boxes, the sacred and the secular as two distinct ontological entities.

Against extrinsicist readings of Aquinas, de Lubac argued that the division of all that exists into a two-tiered natural and supernatural order had the effect of marginalizing the supernatural as "an artificial and arbitrary superstructure"; and "while theologians were striving to protect the supernatural from all contamination, it became isolated from the life of the mind, and from social life, and the field was left open for the invasion of secularism."[7] This sharp dichotomy between the sacred (the order of grace) and the secular (the order of nature) was embraced by Catholic scholars who wanted to find common ground with non-Catholics on the territory of "pure nature." The hope was that the two could work together on the basis of shared understandings about what constitutes human nature, while more contentious theological propositions could be relegated to the territory of private belief.[8] However, in his commentary on *Gaudium et Spes,* and in apparent support for de Lubac's reading, Joseph Ratzinger referred to the idea that it is possible to construct "a rational philosophical picture of man intelligible to all and on which all men of goodwill can agree, to which can be

7. De Lubac, "Nature and Grace," 32-33.
8. See CDVII, 115-164 at 119.

added the Christian doctrines as a sort of crowning conclusion," as a "fiction," and he rhetorically asked why a reasonable and perfectly free human being should be burdened with the story of Christ, which might appear to be a rather unintelligible addition to a picture that was already quite complete in itself.[9] De Lubac concluded that the cumulative effect of this strategy is a conception of Christian progress according to which progress is realized in a "total secularization that would banish God not only from social life but from culture and even from the relationships of private life."[10]

The strength of de Lubac's conclusions and Ratzinger's reservations became much more evident in the final quarter of the twentieth century. Social divisions began to be understood in terms of radically different conceptions of human dignity and fulfillment. At the turn of the twenty-first century, the field of human nature is now the chief intellectual and cultural battleground. Social life, including all the significant public institutions, the courts, the universities, and the legislatures, are now, to use Alasdair MacIntyre's description, "sites of civil war" between proponents of hostile traditions with their own irreconcilable accounts of rationality, virtue, justice, human nature, and human dignity. For theists, human life is something divinely endowed, while for liberals and Nietzscheans our lives have the value that we choose to give them — *we* endow them with meaning. Moreover, the theist camp is itself internally divided. Militant Islamic thought does not place the same value on human life as that of creedal Christian thought, and Muslims in general do not see themselves as standing in the same position vis-à-vis the divine as Christians see their place in the life of the Trinity. These sociological observations are now commonplace.[11]

Schindler's important conclusion of principle can be summarized in his statement that "nature is never neutral with respect to religious form and the activities in and through which we extend nature into a culture are likewise never without a religious form."[12] In effect this principle means that *cultural forms are never theologically neutral.* They may be more or less open to the work of grace and the promotion of virtue. As a consequence, the Christian faith will find it more or less easy to flourish within different

9. CDVII, 120.

10. CDVII, 33.

11. This is the central thesis of the works of A. MacIntyre; see, in particular, his *Whose Justice? Which Rationality?* (London: Duckworth, 1988); and *Three Rival Versions of Moral Enquiry* (London: Duckworth, 1990). See also C. Taylor, *Sources of the Self: The Making of the Modern Identity* (Cambridge: Cambridge University Press, 1989).

12. CSA, 15.

cultural orders. The pastoral significance of this judgment is that the problematic is not, How do we accommodate Christianity to contemporary cultural practices? but, How do we assess contemporary cultural practices against Christian benchmarks? In Schindler's language, the need for cultural discernment is integral to the recuperation of nature itself and not something coming after that recuperation.[13] In Ratzinger's parlance, "faith, worship and ethos are interwoven as a single reality."[14] Those who believe that Western culture can be redeemed by ethics alone, and that liturgical and cultural questions are for dilettantes, fail to appreciate that nature itself is not impervious to culture, nor to culturally mediated grace and evil.

Following the Second Vatican Council, the dominant interpretation of *Gaudium et Spes,* the Constitution on the Church and the Modern World, was that the spirit of the times, or the ethos of the institutions of liberal modernity, was favorable to Christianity. Accordingly, much intellectual effort went into the project of accommodating the liturgical and other cultural practices of the Church to the culture of modernity and of reading down earlier magisterial criticisms of the liberal tradition to a very narrow section of that tradition, for some, to merely the expressions of that tradition in France in the years 1789-1794. This interpretation, however, was never universally accepted. One of its significant critics was Joseph Cardinal Ratzinger.[15] As early as 1966 he was critical of the treatment of the themes of freedom and conscience in *Gaudium et Spes,* describing the treatment of freedom as one of the least satisfactory in the whole document, and in his works of social commentary he never confused the City of God with some particular political order.[16] In his essay on the place of Christianity in a pluralist democracy, he explicitly endorsed the argument of the German scholar Robert Spaemann that the Church must not withdraw to the margins of society, representing merely a social need of some

13. "Significance of World and Culture," 111-143.

14. J. Ratzinger, *Deus Caritas Est.* For David L. Schindler's commentary on this encyclical see "Benedict's *Deus Caritas Est — God Is Love:* The Way of Love in the Church's Mission to the World," *Houston Catholic Worker* 26.3 (2006).

15. CDVII, 115-164.

16. For the criticisms of the treatment of freedom and conscience see CDVII, 136. Ratzinger notes: "In its essential kernel the objectivism of *Gaudium et spes* is certainly right and not vulnerable to critical thought. What is unsatisfactory is simply the way the concrete form of the claim of conscience is dealt with, the inadequate view of the facts of experience and the insufficient account taken of the limits of conscience." He also notes that, while much is made of Aquinas's thesis of the obligatory force of an erroneous conscience, this thesis is "nullified by the fact that Aquinas is convinced that error is culpable."

persons, but must understand herself as "the place of an absolute public validity surpassing the state under the legitimizing claim of God."[17] Here Ratzinger was not endorsing some form of theocracy but merely arguing that "the state must recognize that a basic framework of values with a Christian foundation is the precondition for its existence." Thus, Ratzinger's approach to the liberal tradition was much more nuanced than the whole-hearted embrace typical of many Catholic leaders in the 1960s and 1970s. In relation to the specific issue of the interpretation of *Gaudium et Spes,* he later endorsed the position of John Paul II (which was also implicit in many of Ratzinger's earlier commentaries) that this document needs to be read through the Christocentric lens of paragraph 22 — a paragraph that appears to have been taken word by word from de Lubac's *Catholicism.* For both John Paul II and Benedict XVI, *Gaudium et Spes* is not about baptizing liberal modernity. Rather, it is about the presentation of the Catholic belief that the deepest longings of the human heart (which may in some sense include archetypically liberal goods, such as personal freedom) can be fulfilled only by participation in the life of the Trinity. The complete inadequacy of various contemporary non-Christian humanisms to meet these aspirations was addressed by de Lubac in his *The Drama of Atheistic Humanism,* which can often be read as an intellectual backdrop to the thought of both Pontiffs. It is thus one thing to acknowledge that the Catholic faith may converge with the liberal tradition at some points — for example, the two may meet at the point of holding that religious tolerance is to be preferred to religious terrorism — but another to read *Gaudium et Spes* as a Conciliar endorsement of liberalism, or of a statement by the Church Fathers that there is something lacking in the Catholic tradition that only the liberal tradition can provide. It was rather, on the de Lubac and Ratzinger reading, more the case that while there are some legitimate aspirations that liberals and Catholics share, these aspirations can find their fulfillment only with Christian revelation.

II. Liberalism and the American Dream

David L. Schindler has also adopted this Lubacian hermeneutic for *Gaudium et Spes* and for his understanding of the significance of the Incar-

---

17. J. Ratzinger, "A Christian Orientation in a Pluralist Democracy?" in *Church, Ecumenism and Politics* (Slough: St. Paul's, 1988), 218.

nation for ethics and evangelization. In the words of fellow Communio scholar Angelo Cardinal Scola, "Christ did not leave the Father when he became man to bring all creation to fulfillment; and neither does the Christian need to leave his centre in Christ in order to mediate him to the world, to understand his relation to the world, to build a bridge between revelation and nature, philosophy and theology" — "the claim of Christ is total and it admits no exceptions."[18] This has had a deep impact on Schindler's understanding of the relation between the Catholic faith and the liberal tradition. Unlike many other American Catholic scholars of his generation, Schindler eschews the position that while European liberalism may be toxic to the faith, American liberalism is not merely a benign strain of this tradition but actually provides a culture in which the faith can flourish. The "American liberalism is different and good" position was very popular after the Second World War, when the great liberal democracies were seen to have saved the world from fascism. It received much of its defense from the works of the French Thomist Jacques Maritain and later the American Jesuit John Courtney Murray.[19] It is now, however, less fashionable with the youngest generation of Catholic scholars for whom the definitive political experiences were not the rise of fascism or the Cold War, but the problem of the spiritually degrading effects of Hollywood pop idol culture, liberal Catholicism, and market-obsessed materialism. For this latest generation, the globalized culture of America is part of the problem, and so-called Catholic conservatives find themselves agreeing with so-called left-wing communitarians on this point, even while they eschew any association with Marxism and liberation theology and even while remaining critical of welfare socialism.

18. A. Scola, "'Claim of Christ,' 'Claim of the World': On the Trinitarian Encyclicals of John Paul II," *Communio: International Catholic Review* 18 (1991): 322-331. See Colossians 1:15-20. See also Hans Urs von Balthasar, *The Word and Redemption: Essays in Theology,* vol. 2 (New York: Herder and Herder, 1965), 67-68: "Man, therefore, in investigating the relationship between nature and supernature, has no need to abandon the standpoint of faith, to set himself up as the mediator between God and the world, between revelation and reason, or to cast himself in the role of judge *over* that relationship. All that is necessary is for him to understand 'the one mediator between God and man, the man Jesus Christ'" (1 Tim. 2:5), and to believe him in whom "were all things created in heaven and on earth . . . all by him and in him" (Col. 1:16).

19. Ratzinger/Pope Benedict XVI has acknowledged that American liberalism is a different and perhaps more benign strain of liberalism than the European variant, but still treats it as problematic. See WR, 69-74. See also David L. Schindler's commentary on Pope Benedict's contribution to this work: "Truth, Freedom, and Relativism," 669-681.

Schindler is not opposed to many elements of a political culture that might look or sound liberal to those unschooled in the history of political theory.[20] For example, he is in favor of a constitution that recognizes limits on the authority of the state and the church. He would agree with Peter Lawler's statement that "constitutionalism really is possible without Liberalism because we are really citizens [or subjects] of two cities, with duties to both."[21] However, he does believe that at its deepest ontological levels liberalism *as a tradition* is hostile to theism and, in his words, "invites us into a con game."[22] It invites us to dialogue within the putatively open and pluralistic market of religions, while from the start of the game it has loaded the terms of that dialogue with a liberal theory of religion.[23] Schindler argues that, despite his honorable intentions, John Courtney Murray, S.J., has disposed Catholics to be victims of this con game.

Specifically, Schindler regards Murray's defense of the American political settlement as flawed with respect to two central premises: (1) that the religion clauses of the First Amendment are "articles of peace," and (2) that religious freedom is best understood first in its negative meaning, as immunity from coercion, and thus first as a formal notion empty of positive content.[24] Schindler believes that Murray's distinction between liberal political structures, which the Church can accept, and a liberal ideology, which it must repudiate, fails to apprehend just how the structures them-

20. For material that recognizes a distinction between liberalism as a political tradition and constitutionalism, see the works of Robert P. Kraynak, especially his *Christian Faith and Modern Democracy: God and Politics in a Fallen World* (Notre Dame: University of Notre Dame Press, 2001). Kraynak rejects the Actonian reading of Aquinas as the "first Whig," that is, as the father of the liberal tradition. He states that, "though intriguing, Acton's interpretation is misleading because Thomas defends power sharing and political participation, not as a right of the people to parliamentary consent nor as a means for protecting personal rights and liberties, but as the prudent application of natural law whose ends are best realized in a stable constitutional order dedicated to peace, virtue and Christian piety" (p. 98).

21. See Lawler's endorsement on the back cover of *Christian Faith and Modern Democracy: God and Politics in a Fallen World* (Notre Dame: University of Notre Dame Press, 2001).

22. For an account of the elements of an intellectual tradition see MacIntyre, *Three Rival Versions of Moral Enquiry,* and *Whose Justice? Which Rationality?* chap. 17, "Liberalism Transformed into a Tradition."

23. HW, 44.

24. Schindler argues that Pope Benedict XVI does *not* adopt the primarily juridical interpretation of freedom in *Dignitatis Humanae* (The Conciliar decree on religious freedom) that has prevailed among Catholics in Western democracies, especially the United States: see "Truth, Freedom, and Relativism," 669-681 at 678.

selves carry within them an atheistic logic, or what he calls a preference for the form of power over the form of love. In the language of William T. Cavanaugh, the liberal tradition is based on a theological presumption of original violence, rather than original peace, and hence it presupposes what Schindler calls the form of power as the norm of all action and relationships.[25] Further, Schindler argues that John Paul II's reading of *Gaudium et Spes,* which gave hermeneutical priority to paragraph 22, leads to a different understanding of the relationship between freedom and truth than that fostered by Murray. Murray was working within a neo-Thomist nature and grace framework. However, if one operates within a framework more typical of de Lubac, which Schindler argues we must do if we give *Gaudium et Spes,* 22, the emphasis that John Paul II and Benedict XVI have given it, then one arrives at a different understanding not only of nature and grace but of truth and freedom as well.[26] This is because the immediacy of nature's positive relation to God is such that the question of religious truth is implicated from the start in any discussion of the meaning of freedom. Schindler concludes that the difference between de Lubac's organic-paradoxical theology and Murray's dualistic theology "bears significant consequences for how one conceives the (supposed) constitutional indifference of the state relative to the substantive indifference of society, in the matter of religious truth."[27] Moreover, Schindler rejects the idea that the United States Constitution is pluralistic in matters of religion. He argues that the U.S. Constitution does not mean to render private all judgments regarding religious truth. Rather, "Protestant definitions and premises determined the original content of the clauses and their elaboration is now controlled by liberal individualism."[28]

Schindler juxtaposes the conclusions of Murray and de Lubac in the following summary:

25. W. T. Cavanaugh, *Theopolitical Imagination* (Edinburgh: T&T Clark, 2002).

26. Romanus Cessario believes that it is possible to adopt the Christocentrism of paragraph 22 of *Gaudium et Spes* without accepting de Lubac's account of the nature of grace, but he has not explained how. Paul McPartlan makes the point that paragraph 22 is taken almost word for word from de Lubac's work *Catholicisme.* See P. McPartlan, "The Legacy of Vatican II in the Pontificate of John Paul II," *New Catholic Encyclopaedia: Jubilee Volume* (Washington, DC: The Catholic University of America Press, 2001), 63-70; and "The Eucharist, the Church and Evangelization: The Influence of Henri de Lubac," *Communio: International Catholic Review* 23 (1996): 776-785.

27. HW, 53.

28. HW, 56.

According to Murray: faith and grace do not determine the structures and processes of civil society: these are determined by reason, in the light of the lessons of experience. . . . [The Church] does not aim to alter the finality of the state, but to enable the state to achieve its own finality as determined by its own nature. Conversely, for de Lubac, the state occupies no special "secular" space beyond the operation of the law of the relations between nature and grace. It is from within that grace seizes nature. . . . It is from within that faith transforms reason, that the Church influences the state.

For Murray, grace's influence on nature takes the form of assisting nature to realize its own finality; the ends proper to grace and nature otherwise remain each in its own sphere. For de Lubac, on the contrary, grace's influence takes the form of directing nature from within to serve the end given in grace; the ends proper to grace and nature remain distinct, even as the natural end is placed within, internally subordinated to, the supernatural end. For Murray then, the result is an insistence on a dualism between citizen and believer, and on the sharpness of the distinction between eternal (ultimate) end and temporal (penultimate) ends. For de Lubac, on the contrary, the call to sanctity "comprehends" the call to citizenship and all the worldly tasks implied by citizenship. The eternal end "comprehends" the temporal ends.[29]

Schindler concludes with the observation that "the apparently subtle difference between de Lubac and Murray on the relation between secular and sacred thus leads in the end to two different conceptions of the civilization towards which Christians should be working: one, a civilization wherein citizenship is to be suffused with sanctity; the other, a civilization wherein sanctity is always something to be (privately/hiddenly) added to citizenship."[30] This, in a nutshell, is the basis of Schindler's opposition to the project of the American Catholic neo-conservatives. They follow Murray; he follows de Lubac.[31]

Schindler acknowledges that there are different strains of liberalism and suggests that atheism can take "hard" and "soft" forms: it can be reso-

29. HW, 79.
30. HW, 80.
31. For another contemporary critique of John Courtney Murray's Thomist defense of the American settlement that concurs with the major premises of Schindler, see M. J. Schuck, "John Courtney Murray's Problematic Interpretation of Leo XIII and the American Founders," *The Thomist* 55.4 (1991): 595-613.

lutely theoretical, or it can be a practical kind of atheism that pushes God to the margins of a culture. Accordingly, he divides the liberal tradition into three primary stances vis-à-vis Christianity: (1) direct opposition, (2) a "hard dichotomy" of the secular and sacred, or (3) a "soft dichotomy" of the same. These divisions correspond to Alasdair MacIntyre's categories of radical, liberal, and conservative liberalisms. Within these divisions, Schindler locates the problem with John Courtney Murray's defense of the American political framework with the third type of dualism. Murray conflated the sacred-secular distinction typical of neo-scholastic thought into a Church-State distinction typical of the theology of the Reformers, and included within this political theory was an understanding of the Church and the State as purely juridical entities. The Catholic neo-conservatives who follow this trajectory are thus "conservative liberals." For Schindler, the state is more than and distinct from a purely juridical entity. It has itself a moral purpose. He therefore endorses the judgment of Robert Jenson that American liberalism and American conservatism are but "the atheist and superstitious branches of the same capitulation before a dead [mechanistic] universe."[32] Like Kraynak, Schindler's position is: "constitutionalism, Yes, liberalism, No."

In addition to his critique of John Courtney Murray's defense of Americanism, Schindler also takes on board critical insights from Tocqueville, who recognized a tension in American culture between the goods of individualism and equality. Individualism, and the Romantic tradition's notion of individuality, insists that each person should autonomously work out his or her own views on important questions of truth and goodness, but the principle of equality then immediately levels out all such views. Mass opinion becomes the tyrannical tradition of those who have no tradition, and democratic relativism is its dogma. Schindler reminds proponents of Americanism that Tocqueville claimed that he knew of "no country, in which, speaking generally, there is less independence of mind and true freedom of discussion as in America."[33]

Further, Schindler's critique of the culture of America includes a concern about the cultural manifestations of the Puritan aversion to sacramentality. Here he argues that "in the absence of a strong sense of the ef-

32. R. W. Jenson, *America's Theologian* (Oxford: Oxford University Press, 1988), 34; as quoted in Schindler, "Religion and Secularity," 81.

33. A. de Tocqueville, *Democracy in America*, vol. 1, part 11, chap. 7; quoted by Schindler, "Grace and the Form of Nature and Culture," in CSA, nn. 22, 28. See also "Truth, Freedom, and Relativism," 679.

fective (Petrine) presence of God in history and any permanently abiding Marian response from the side of the creature (two elements which are strong in Catholic cultures), covenantal freedom tends to become simply contractual in nature," and this contractual kind of freedom reinforces "individually conceived rights and the Cartesianized-technological rationalization of worldly order."[34] Catholics who fail to consider these cultural manifestations of Puritan theology run the risk of becoming Catholic in denominational allegiance, but Protestant in practice.

III. Plundering the Idioms of the Liberal Tradition

As a consequence of the above judgments, Schindler endorses Alasdair MacIntyre's argument that "only by either the circumvention or the subversion of Liberal modes of debate can the rationality specific to traditions of enquiry re-establish itself sufficiently to challenge the cultural and political hegemony of Liberalism effectively."[35] In other words, we need to start challenging the liberal parameters and language of debate, rather than focusing our intellectual efforts on transposing Catholic values and principles into the language of liberalism so that we can engage proponents of the liberal tradition on their own turf. The point is that strategically *there is no point* in playing a game in which the rules are rigged. Christians never win playing liberal games on liberal turf using liberal language. At best, all that can be achieved is a kind of holding position — a form of shadow boxing so as to avoid total marginalization from the public sphere. This provides the non-liberal troops with time to regroup, or, theologically speaking, re-evangelize, a decadent Puritan culture.

Moreover, the underlying philosophical presuppositions behind the strategy of transposing Catholic thought into the idioms of the liberal tradition have received very little scholarly attention in Catholic circles.[36] In the 1960s and 1970s the conventional wisdom was that adopting the idioms of the liberal tradition was just another example of the Patristic practice of plundering the spoils of the Egyptians. However, there was very little consideration of the question of the principles to be employed

---

34. "Dramatic Nature of Life," 1-20 at 16.

35. MacIntyre, *Whose Justice, Which Rationality?* 400; cf. CSA, 29.

36. An exception is the article by John Allen, Jr., "Language Becomes Catholic Battle-ground," *National Catholic Reporter,* December 26, 2003.

when working out whether or not some element of a rival tradition is worth plundering. At the peak of the post-Conciliar enthusiasm for this project, Balthasar warned that when engaging in such an exercise one should never adopt anything merely for the sake of putting a "garland" on a Catholic idea.[37] In other words, there needs to be some real substantial value or something more than a rhetorical value in adopting an element from a rival tradition. In his 1958 work *The Lord of History: Reflections on the Inner Meaning of History,* Jean Daniélou observed that the transposition of the faith from the Semitic into the Greco-Latin tradition was an operation of "extreme delicacy and difficulty."[38] It took centuries to complete, and, even then, the earliest Christian heresies can be regarded for the most part "as a sort of revenge taken by the Greek language for the efforts made to force it to describe new things."[39] Daniélou was not saying that the transposition was a mistake, merely that this whole territory of cultural and linguistic transpositions is, in his words, extremely delicate and difficult. More recently, Francis Cardinal George of Chicago has drawn attention to the debate in linguistic philosophy between the proponents of expressivist and instrumentalist theories of language. The expressivists hold that language is always embedded in a culture and takes its meaning from that culture. Cardinal George notes that when one reads speeches made by John XXIII at the time of the Second Vatican Council one gets the impression that the Pope was assuming an instrumentalist view of language. Fergus Kerr has also observed that the instrumentalist view was implicit in the thought of Karl Rahner.[40] However, the expressivist view is now the more widely accepted in academic circles.[41] Cardinal George concludes that "cultural forms and linguistic expressions are, in fact, not distinguished from the thoughts and message they carry as accidents are distinguished from substance in classical philosophy" (as John XXIII, Karl Rahner, and many other Catholic leaders in the 1960s and 1970s supposed). Rather, "a change in form inevitably entails also some change in content. A change in words changes in

37. Hans Urs von Balthasar, "On the Tasks of Catholic Philosophy in Our Time," *Communio: International Catholic Review* 20 (1993): 147-172.

38. J. Daniélou, *The Lord of History: Reflections on the Inner Meaning of History* (London: Longmans, 1958), 57.

39. Daniélou, *The Lord of History,* 57.

40. F. Kerr, *Theology after Wittgenstein* (Oxford: Basil Blackwell, 1986), 11.

41. See the entry on the Sapir-Wharf hypothesis in the *Cambridge Encyclopedia of Language* (Cambridge: Cambridge University Press, 1987).

some fashion the way we think."[42] This position has been highly developed by Michael Polanyi in his account of how the meaning of language (including, of course, theological and philosophical concepts) is tacitly acquired within the institutional cultures in which people live and work.[43] It is also supported by linguistic philosophers with reference to what is called the "Sapir-Whorf hypothesis."

Thus, both Schindler and MacIntyre agree that, by allowing proponents of the liberal tradition to define the rules of public debate and even to choose the language in which the debate is undertaken, Catholic intellectuals inadvertently give the proponents of a hostile tradition an advantage. Moreover, the more one does so, the more one entrenches the view that the liberal accounts of rationality, of politics, of virtue, of human nature, and of justice are the only, or definitive, accounts. This position in turn affects the way in which both Schindler and MacIntyre approach the human rights sub-discipline within the liberal tradition. Though their stances may differ on some aspects of the issue, they are in agreement that in public life the strategy of transposing the Church's teaching into the human rights idioms is counter-productive.[44] In this context Schindler makes the following points:

(i) A "right" as conventionally understood — as understood in the liberal tradition which has been a dominant force in America — is a claim which the self has on the other. The supposition is that the direction of obligation is from the other toward the self. The form or logic of the liberal understanding of rights, in other words, is self-centered. That logic

---

42. F. E. George, *Inculturation and Ecclesial Communion: Culture and Church in the Teaching of Pope John Paul II* (Rome: Urbaniana University Press, 1990), 47.

43. M. Polanyi, "Faith and Reason," *Communio: International Catholic Review* 28 (2001): 860-874; *Personal Knowledge: Towards a Post-Critical Philosophy* (Chicago: University of Chicago Press, 1962); *The Tacit Dimension* (Gloucester, MA: Peter Smith, 1983).

44. MacIntyre, for example, eschews the whole natural rights tradition but seems to accept the idea of common law rights, which is consistent with other aspects of his political philosophy, his understanding of how traditions develop, and his British background, where the common law system, unlike the continental civil law system, considers rights within the context of an ensemble of legal relationships, not from the perspective of one individual. In other words, MacIntyre's work (as well as the criticisms of the rights rhetoric in the work of Robert P. Kraynak) embodies a mostly implicit, though sometimes explicit, distinction between common law rights and so-called natural rights, which is a distinction that merits further investigation. See A. MacIntyre, "Rights, Practices and Marxism: Reply to Six Critics," *Analyse und Kritik* 7 (1982): 234-248; "Community, Law and the Idiom and Rhetoric of Rights," *Listening* 26.2 (1991): 96-100.

presupposes a primitive externality of relation between the self and the other, which in turn makes the self the center of relation. A right in this context, then, merely expresses the kind of obligation which results from this self-centricity of relation — that is, an obligation first of others to *me*.[45]

For this reason, "opponents of abortion who would make their case in terms of conventional 'rights' language fail to see that this language leaves intact the deeper logic which is precisely what has made American culture open to legalized abortion in the first place."[46] Moreover, "as Western liberal democracies succeed in making their liberally conceived rights pervasive in their cultures, these democracies will tend *of their inner logic,* to back ever more completely into totalitarianisms of the strong over the weak (and indeed thereby also into ever-purer dictatorships of relativism)."[47] Nonetheless, Schindler qualifies these statements by saying that he is not trying to say that human beings do not have legal entitlements, merely that the liberal interpretation of rights "serve[s] both as a sign and as a cause of the *ontological absence* in the self of God and others."[48]

The adoption of this stance in turn means that Schindler's account of natural law differs markedly from that of the scholars associated with the New Natural Law project who have sought to present natural law in terms conducive to its adoption by the liberal tradition, in part by theoretically severing natural law from its relationship to the eternal law and other theological presuppositions.[49] In other words, the "virtue" of the New Natural Law project is that it purports to offer a theory of natural law and natural right that can be applied within the general parameters of liberal juris-

---

45. CSA, 17-18.
46. CSA, 18.
47. "Dramatic Nature of Life," 13.
48. "Dramatic Nature of Life," 12.
49. This is not to say that the scholars associated with this school themselves deny the existence of the *lex aeterna,* merely that they argue that it is possible to present a theory of natural law without theoretical reliance on theological presuppositions. This assumes a neo-Thomist account of nature and grace, something that is explicitly accepted by Germain Grisez. See his account of natural law in the *New Catholic Encyclopaedia.* For other critiques of the New Natural Law project see the following: R. Hittinger, *The First Grace: Rediscovering the Natural Law in a Post-Christian World* (Wilmington, DE: Intercollegiate Studies Institute, 2003); E. Fortin, "The New Rights Theory and Natural Law," *Review of Politics* 44 (1982): 485-495; and N. Biggar, *The Revival of Natural Law: Philosophical, Theological and Ethical Responses to the Finnis-Grisez School* (Ashgate: Aldershot, 2000).

prudence. It transposes Catholic teaching into a language that allows Catholic jurists to play in the liberal game. Schindler, like MacIntyre, recognizes the good will driving this project, but believes that it is ultimately counter-productive. Thus he states:

> (ii) The common ground for which the Christian seeks in his natural law argument, therefore, is and can only be within the concrete history of the dialogue partners. Indeed, what needs to be underscored here is that the demand for a neutral form of natural law argument, for a form of natural law which would seek a common ground outside of the history of the dialogue partners, is as a matter of principle a demand for a liberal form of natural law argument. It is a demand for exactly the sort of abstraction of form which is characteristic of Cartesianism.[50]

> (iii) There is and can be — in the concrete historical order which is ours — no nature or natural laws which are neutral of religious form.[51]

Strategically speaking, Schindler occupies the same position as de Lubac, who argued that "Christian faith is not piecemeal; and any effort to 'adapt' this or that element in it to non-believing interlocutors in order to justify it to them runs the risk not only of remaining barren, but of producing the opposite effect."[52] To assume the "garlands" of the liberal tradition, to suggest that there can be rationality without God, without a certain *logos* embedded in creation, is, in effect, to try to convert pagans by withholding the very medicine they need to take. Alternatively, it might be argued that the better metaphor is that the strategy is to administer the medicine hidden within a mixture designed to appeal to the liberal palate, but the problem remains that Christianity is not ultimately a form of rationalism, but the revelation of a Person, belief in whom actually changes perceptions of what is reasonable.

50. CSA, 23.
51. CSA, 24.
52. Henri de Lubac, *Brief Catechesis on Nature and Grace,* 130. See also D. L. Schindler, "On the Catholic Common Ground Project: The Christological Foundations of Dialogue," *Communio: International Catholic Review* 23 (1996): 823-851. This position also converges with that of the "Christocentric moralists" such as Servais Pinckaers, O.P., who takes the view that "if the demand for the autonomy of ethics leads us to restrict to reason alone the task of solving ethical problems, then in the final analysis the Church and faith itself will *no* longer have much of a role in the moral life, they will merely represent one opinion among others, and will, moreover, always be viewed with suspicion as being an authoritative imposition." S. Pinckaers, *Morality: The Catholic View* (South Bend: St. Augustine's Press, 2001), 49.

IV. Creedal and Secular Rationality

Thus, underlying these critiques of liberalism, there is not only Schindler's adoption of de Lubac's criticisms of extrinsicist accounts of nature and grace, but also an analogous opposition to extrinsicist accounts of faith and reason. While Schindler's juxtaposition of faith and reason could legitimately be classified as Thomist, it is the Thomism of Étienne Gilson and Ferdinand Ulrich.[53] Indeed, Schindler has himself described his position (which he believes is also that to be found in John Paul II's encyclical *Fides et Ratio*) as a "Thomism developed in light of the theological anthropology of *Gaudium et spes*," meaning a Thomism that embodies the Christology and more broadly Trinitarian theology of paragraphs 22-25.[54] In other words, there is a most non-Kantian emphasis on the relationship between Trinitarian theology and anthropology, on the effect of faith on the intellect, on the epistemic importance of the example of saints, and on the circular relationship of faith and reason, leading Schindler to draw distinctions between what he calls "creedal rationality" and "secular rationality," evocative of Gilson's distinctions between Christian and non-Christian philosophy.

According to Schindler, secular rationality has as its hallmark the principle of simple identity. Its features come to expression in the manner in which causal activity is understood primarily in terms of effectivity; in the manner in which epistemological primacy is accorded to negation, doubt, and control over affirmation, faith, and openness; and in the manner in which meaning is derived by breaking the action or question into ever smaller bits for an analysis of the simplest conceptual units or by the addition of differences.[55] In contrast, "creedal" rationality has as its hallmark the principle of identities already in relation. Its features come to expression in several different ways: causal activity understood first as forceful gives way to activity that is from within and to effective activity now understood to be creative and generous rather than self-assertive; the primacy of negation, doubt, and control gives way to a primacy of affirmation, receptivity, and responsiveness.[56] Schindler is not arguing that these two logics are mutually exclusive or that the first is to be rejected altogether, but rather that for the fortunes of Christianity it is crucial which

53. A. Del Noce, "Thomism and the Critique of Rationalism: Gilson and Shestov," *Communio: International Catholic Review* 25 (1998): 732-745.

54. "Knowledge as Relationship," 510-540.

55. CSA, 173.

56. CSA, 173.

logic is accorded primacy.[57] This is because the presupposition of the principle of simple identity as a first principle forces inclusion by way of dualistic addition, whereas the presupposition of the principle of relation leads to inclusion by way of integration.[58] Schindler further argues that there needs to be a recognition that all "logics" are guided at the outset by some presupposed truth. For a secularized "Cartesian" logic, the truth is the principle of simple identity; for the "creedal Christian" logic, the truth is the principle of Trinitarian processions. From this he concludes that the appropriate question is "not whether one will weight intellectual enquiry in advance but *how* one will do so."[59]

In taking this position, Schindler is very much in accord with the spirit of Cardinal Ratzinger's Guadalajara speech of 1996 in which Ratzinger explicitly rejects the Kantian notion of pure reason and states that "neo-scholastic rationalism failed in its attempts to reconstruct the *praeambula fidei* with wholly independent reasoning, with pure rational certainty."[60] Ratzinger acknowledges that "there is, and must be, a human reason *in* faith"; but he also asserts that "every human reason is conditioned by an historical standpoint, so that reason pure and simple does not exist."[61] What is reasonable will depend on one's theological presuppositions, and, conversely, the character of one's theology will be related to the understanding of reason operative within it. To quote David C. Schindler, "if the 'revelational' dimension of Christianity remains simply extrinsic to reason, theology will not possess the capacity to see Christianity as an organic *whole . . .* it will inevitably collapse into mere history, fideism, biblical positivism, moralism, or a program of social justice and political action."[62]

David C. Schindler's colleague, Michael Hanby, suggests that this typically Kantian project to philosophize without a mediator represents a neo-Pelagian attempt to "smuggle Stoic cosmology into Christian thought." Hence, "at issue within the culture of modernity is the Trinity itself and specifically whether nature, the meaning of human nature, and human agency are understood to occur within Christ's mediation of the love and

57. CSA, 173.
58. CSA, 174.
59. CSA, 177.
60. J. Ratzinger, "The Current Situation of Faith and Theology," *L'Osservatore Romano* 45-46 (November 1996): 7.
61. CDVII, 120.
62. D. C. Schindler, "Surprised by Truth: The Drama of Reason in Fundamental Theology," *Communio: International Catholic Review* 31 (2004): 587-612 at 589.

delight shared as *donum* between the Father and the Son, or beyond it."[63] Here Hanby's work serves to strengthen David L. Schindler's point that the question is not whether one will weight intellectual inquiry in advance, but *how* one will do so. The mysteries of the Trinity and the Incarnation profoundly influence our perception of the real and the reasonable.

A problem that this insight highlights is the use of the word "autonomy" in *Fides et ratio* and other magisterial documents. In popular usage, "autonomy" often implies a relationship of complete separation. The use of this word in *Gaudium et Spes* is one of the factors that fostered the "accommodation to modernity" interpretation of that document. Both scholars and plain persons reading the word "autonomy" often assume that the Conciliar fathers were of the view that theology had nothing to do with politics, economics, art, literature, and the sciences — that such realms of culture lay outside the fields of grace and did not need to be redeemed. In the 2006 Harman Lecture, delivered at the John Paul II Institute in Melbourne, Kenneth L. Schmitz used the metaphor of a fence with a gate (rather than two separate paddocks with no connecting gates) to describe the relationship between faith and reason, and he suggested that the word "integrity" might be less open to misinterpretation than "autonomy."

V. The Form of the Machine and the Form of Love

The logic of secular rationality is related to what Schindler calls "the form of the machine." Schindler follows Balthasar, who in turn followed the French writer Georges Bernanos, in holding that the form of contemporary Western culture is the form of the machine.[64] He defines "form" as a pattern of intelligibility or a logic *(logos)*. Every practice is taken to have its own ontologic, which is inclusive of a spirituality.[65] The link between the form of secular rationality and its various manifestations within the liberal tradition, and the form of the machine, is externality of relations and the preoccupation with power.[66] For example, Schindler notes that sexual relations hol-

---

63. M. Hanby, *Augustine and Modernity* (London: Routledge, 2004), 73.

64. UBLC; Hans Urs von Balthasar, *Bernanos: An Ecclesial Existence* (San Francisco: Ignatius Press, 1988); see also E. I. Watkin, *A Philosophy of Form* (London: Sheed & Ward, 1950).

65. CSA, 14.

66. CSA, 18. See also S. Oliver, "Motion According to Aquinas and Newton," *Modern Theology* 17.2 (2001): 163-199.

lowed out into their material shell by ethical frameworks that marginalize or bracket theological truths become lustful manipulation. Political relations extracted from sacred bonds of brotherhood in Christ and indifferent to principles of the common good and social solidarity become brutal power. Market relations hollowed out into their material shell become hedonistic consumerism, and the music and architecture governed by the laws of such market relations become noise and harsh ugliness.[67]

Metaphysically speaking, Schindler characterizes the problem as a double dualism:

> The tendency is to separate form, that is, the meaning which gives the shape to a culture's institutions and patterns of life, from love; and this separation presupposes a more basic separation of nature from God; so that form, abstracted from love, becomes externalized, manipulative and forceful; while love, abstracted from form, becomes blind and empty of order.[68]

Here Schindler argues that it is crucial to understand that

> The difference between the visible-material world and the human personal world cannot be rightly conceived in dualistic terms, as though the non-living world could be adequately conceived on its own in exhaustively mechanical terms, to which organic acts like form and finality, and a movement shaped by the internal movements of form and finality, are then added. . . . On the contrary, the Incarnation of the Son of God implies a genuine . . . community established (freely) by God in Jesus Christ that reaches all the way down through the "flesh" of the entire created cosmos.[69]

67. CSA, 19.

68. "Christological Aesthetics," 201.

69. Schindler, "Freedom and the 'Nuptial-Sacramental' Nature of the Body: *Veritatis Splendor* and the Significance of World and Culture for Moral Theology," conference paper draft, 11. The final redaction of this paper appeared as "Significance of World and Culture"; the same ideas were expressed in more compact form over pp. 134-142. Cf. M. Hanby, "Creation without Creationism: Towards a Theological Critique of Darwinism," *Communio: International Catholic Review* 30 (2003): 654-694 at 687: "[The divine] action of creating is intrinsic to immanent processes and their effects: in the novelty of their coming into existence and their enduring actuality. Or rather, since God's action and God's being are the same, we might say the 'action of creation' transcends the distinction between what is intrinsic and what is extrinsic. Creation, which is really the presence of God in things, is at once utterly distinct from those things, irreducible to them, and is not neatly separable from them, since

Conversely, *Veritatis splendor* (paragraph 48) expressly rejects the idea that human nature, including the human body, is merely a presupposition or preamble, materially necessary for freedom to make its choice, yet extrinsic to the person, the subject, and the human act. If this were so their functions would not be able to constitute reference points for moral decisions, because the finalities of their inclinations would be merely "physical" goods, called by some "premoral." In reflecting on paragraph 48, Schindler makes the point that both cultural determinist and cultural relativist accounts of the role of culture in human development presuppose the absorption of the soul/freedom into the body/culture. Schindler acknowledges that culture does influence human development — "the historical differentiation may be a legitimate development of the authentic meaning of the *humanum,* or it may be a distortion: in neither case will the *humanum* be left in an unaltered state of static identity."[70] Nonetheless, Schindler rejects cultural determinism and cultural relativism and offers instead a notion of a mutual-asymmetrical openness of nature and freedom, and thus culture whose normativity (the normativity of nature, freedom, and culture) is grounded in the nuptial mystery. This is the anthropological contribution of John Paul II, a combination of his Lublin lectures on praxis and culture and intransitivity and his Wednesday audience lectures on the theology of the body and exegesis of the book of Genesis.[71] It also builds on the work of Angelo Cardinal Scola and, before Scola, Matthias J. Scheeben, who also influenced Hans Urs von Balthasar. Within this anthropology, the criterion for cultural discernment is given immanently; it lies within the nuptial-sacramental origin and destiny of the human body. Conversely, mechanistic notions of space, time, physics, biology, and political and economic institutions all fail to take account of the fact that the human body in its original structure is made for loving relationships.[72] In short, Schindler argues for an ontology developed in the light of the nuptial mystery, the essential element of which is the idea that someone first relates to us and sets our free-

---

it would compromise divine transcendence to delineate, in Pelagian fashion, the respective contributions of creature and creator in the being of the creature or in its immanent causal processes." Also cf. St. Thomas Aquinas, *Summa Theologiae,* I, q. 8, a. 1: "God is in all things; not, indeed, as part of their essence, nor as an accident, but as an agent is present to that upon which it works."

70. Schindler, "Freedom and the 'Nuptial-Sacramental' Nature of the Body," 17.

71. K. Wojtyla, *Person and Community: Selected Essays,* trans. T. Sandok (New York: Peter Lang, 1993); John Paul II, *Man and Woman He Created Them: A Theology of the Body.*

72. "Is Truth Ugly?" 701-728.

dom into motion.[73] This theme is also amplified in Hanby's *Augustine and Modernity,* where he distinguishes between a liberal (Pelagian-Kantian) notion of freedom and a Christian (Trinitarian) notion of freedom:

> In the one, *voluntas* is the site of our erotic participation in an anterior gift, and it is at once self-moved and moved by the beauty of that gift. Here will, whether human or divine, is constituted in a relation of love for the beloved and its freedom is established as dispossession. In the other, will names an inviolable power, and freedom consists in demonstrating this inviolability through the double negation both of itself and of created beauty.[74]

Thus, normatively, Schindler asserts that God affects all our meanings all the time by giving them the form or logic of love; consequently, "what an authentic Christian creationism requires is that the meaning whose identity has been assumed to be that proper to the machine be transformed into a meaning whose identity is rather that proper to love."[75] Such a meaning that finds its *logos* or form in love will be one that maintains its identity (in the theological idiom, its "legitimate autonomy" or, Schmitz would suggest, "legitimate integrity"), but nonetheless does so only from within relation.[76] The same position was expressed in the following passage of Joseph Cardinal Ratzinger in his work *The End of Time:*

> The act of being on the part of God that affects being is an *act of freedom.* . . . The *exitus,* or better, the free creative act of God, does in fact aim at *reditus,* but this does not mean that created being is revoked. Rather, it means that the coming-into-its-own of the creature as an autonomous creature answers back in freedom to the love of God, accepts its creation as a command to love, so that a dialogue of love begins — that entirely new unity that only love can create. In it the being of the other is not absorbed, not annulled, but rather becomes wholly what it is precisely in giving itself.[77]

---

73. D. L. Schindler, "Which Ontology Is Necessary for an Adequate Anthropology?" *Anthropotes* 15.2 (1999): 423-426; Scola, NM, especially chap. 5; Hans Urs von Balthasar, *Word and Redemption: Essays in Theology,* vol. 2 (New York: Herder & Herder, 1965), 76-86; M. J. Scheeben, *The Mysteries of Christianity* (London: B. Herder, 1946).

74. Hanby, *Augustine and Modernity,* 125.

75. "Meaning and the Death of God," 200.

76. "Meaning and the Death of God," 201. See also Schmitz, *Gift.*

77. J. Ratzinger, *The End of Time* (Mahwah, NJ: Paulist Press, 2004), 20-21.

This in turn relates to the Pauline theme that practices that would be truly Christian require transformation, a putting on of a new form, the form of Christ.[78] Here perfection is seen as a transformation from within rather than as a super-addition, such as a "topping up" with grace. Corresponding to the distinction between secular and creedal forms of *rationality*, Schindler thus speaks of a distinction between a Cartesian and a Marian-ecclesial form of *relationality*. For the former (the Cartesian), relationality is defined by reference to power; for the second (the Marian-ecclesial form), the key components are gift and receptivity. Moreover, Schindler argues, following Balthasar and Luigi Giussani, that a kind of "moralism" arises when one attempts to understand human practices outside of an ontology rooted in the nuptial mystery.[79] Under these conditions the practices of Christian life are reduced to duties that are performed because one is obliged for various reasons to do so. Balthasar's relative, Peter Henrici S.J., described the mentality as a kind of Christian Pharisaism.[80] Christian existence becomes viewed as a meritorious achievement that God commands and by virtue of which one is able to please him. We end up as Kantians or Jansenists or both together, and it should therefore be no surprise when Nietzscheans and many others find Christianity unattractive. Balthasar observed that those who suffer from the spiritual pathology of a Kantian Jansenism are those who will most readily accept casuistry.[81] Bernanos expressed his frustration with a Catholic ethics focused upon casuistry with the line that "the more a person feels the need to consult casuists in order to know the amount starting from which stealing money may be considered a mortal sin, we may say that his social value is nil, even if he abstains from stealing."[82] Schindler is therefore concerned to examine practices from the perspective of their form, which will be either one that is open to the work of grace and the cultivation of virtue or one that is foreclosed against the same; and he fur-

---

78. CSA, 20.

79. D. L. Schindler, "Luigi Giussani on the Religious Sense and the Cultural Situation of Our Time," *Communio: International Catholic Review* 25 (1998): 141-150; L. Giussani, "Religious Awareness in Modern Man," *Communio: International Catholic Review* 25 (1998): 104-140.

80. P. Henrici, "Modernity and Christianity," *Communio: International Catholic Review* 17 (1990): 140-151 at 150.

81. Balthasar, *Bernanos: An Ecclesial Existence*, 298.

82. G. Bernanos, *We the French*, cited by Balthasar in *Bernanos: An Ecclesial Existence*, 298.

ther argues that the most excellent expression of the form of love is to be found in the theology of the Eucharist and in liturgical practices.

VI. Contemporary Convergences

In a recent work, *After Aquinas: Versions of Thomism,* the Scottish Dominican Fergus Kerr concluded that few now doubt that de Lubac was right. Few contemporary theologians continue to hold the flag for the interpretation of nature and grace that flows from Cajetan to Garrigou-Lagrange, though his Italian-American confrere, Romanus Cessario, has recently counseled younger scholars not to assume that one eminent French Jesuit and 100,000 Communio scholars can't be wrong.[83] This issue of the best theological account of the relationship between nature and grace was one of the most bitter theological controversies of the twentieth century.[84] The question of how to re-evangelize Western culture is central to the Pontificate of Benedict XVI, and this question cannot be answered outside a framework for understanding the relationships among nature, grace, and culture. In the world of Anglophone theology, David L. Schindler has done more than anyone else to put a framework together, working on foundations set by a line-up of Continentals: Balthasar, de Lubac, Giussani, Bernanos, Gilson, Guardini, John Paul II, and Benedict XVI.

The alternative frameworks currently being promoted include: the neo-conservative or "Whig Thomist" framework, whose foundations were set by, inter alios, Suárez, Lord Acton, John Courtney Murray, Heinrich Rommen, and Jacques Maritain; the liberation theology project, which drives on a mixture of Marxist sociology and Rahnerian theology; the various "pluralist theologies," including those of Paul Knitter and Hans Küng; and, most recently, the postmodern "open narrative" project of Lieven Boeve from Leuven.[85]

83. R. Cessario, "Cardinal Cajetan and His Critics," *Nova et Vetera* (Winter 2005): 115.

84. For a good historical summary of the controversy, see A. Nichols, "Thomism and the *Nouvelle Theologie,*" in *Beyond the Blue Glass: Catholic Essays on Faith and Culture* (Farnborough: The Saint Austin Press, 2002), 33, 52.

85. For a selection of works from a "Whig Thomist" perspective, see the following: R. J. Neuhaus, *The Naked Public Square: Religion and Democracy in America* (Grand Rapids: Eerdmans, 1986); G. Weigel, *Soul of the World: Notes on the Future of Public Catholicism* (Grand Rapids: Eerdmans, 1994); *Catholicism and the Renewal of American Democracy*

Of these options Schindler's is the most highly developed and deeply theological of those likely to receive Magisterial approval. The Whig Thomist project needs to engage with criticisms of its extrinsicist foundations and its blindness to the ways in which the culture of America is, in part, the manifestation of Puritan theology, which operates as a barrier to the flourishing of Catholic creedal rationality and Marian relationality. No one denies that Catholics in the United States can worship whenever they like, build whatever institutions they can afford, and not be hampered in the exercise of their faith in the same mode and to the same degree as Catholics in France or China. Still, this does not mean that they are not for reasons of social mobility inclined to become "Catholics in theory, but Protestant in practice." Moreover, the Whig Thomist project is very much a child of the Cold War era. It appeals to patriotic pro-Americanist sympathies, to the obvious advantages of free markets over Communist and socialist experiments, and it tends to view issues from the perspective of questions of liberty and authority, which is also appealing to those deeply rooted in a liberal culture. But it does not dig into the theologically deeper territory of the *logos* inherent within practices and the ways in which such practices are rooted in Protestant, Catholic, or even completely atheistic ontologies. This, however, is precisely what David L. Schindler has attempted to do. Schindler wants liberty, too, but not a Pelagian liberty rooted in a Stoic cosmology. The price of the U.S. Catholic social ascendancy cannot be the acceptance of sixteenth-, eighteenth-, and twentieth-century dualisms.

The liberation theology project is also highly developed in its theological foundations, but whole sections have been condemned by the Congregation for the Doctrine of the Faith for the priority it gives to praxis over belief and for its eschatology and Christology. The projects of Knitter and Küng have also been expressly criticized by Joseph Ratzinger (now Benedict XVI) as Prefect for the Congregation for the Doctrine of the Faith. With reference to what he called the "pragmatic" approach of Küng to build a community on the pursuit of peace, justice, and the integrity of creation, Ratzinger warned against transforming religion into political moral-

---

(Mahwah, NJ: Paulist Press, 1989); and R. A. Sirico, *The Soul of Liberty* (Grand Rapids: Acton Institute, 2003). For an overview of the liberation theology project see the following: L. Boff and C. Boff, *Introducing Liberation Theology* (Maryknoll: Orbis, 1987). For works of Lieven Boeve see L. Boeve, *Interrupting Tradition: An Essay on Christian Faith in a Postmodern Context* (Louvain: Peeters Press, 2003); and "Method in Postmodern Theology: A Case Study," in *The Presence of Transcendence: Thinking 'Sacrament' in a Postmodern Age*, ed. L. Boeve and J. C. Ries (Louvain: Peeters, 2001), 19-39.

ism. The postmodern project, for different reasons, is problematic. Boeve's version appears to be based on a different understanding of the development of tradition from that of Ratzinger/Benedict XVI. Some of the post-modern theological projects also tend toward what Ratzinger calls the "rejection of the categories of being and the subsequent tendency to solve the problem of history's mediation in the realm of ontology by cancelling it (that is, cancelling ontology) and declaring history alone to be that which is and is essential."[86] Also implicit within many of the postmodern projects is a denial of a role for the Magisterium as "operation ground control." This is not, however, to suggest that Benedict XVI is indifferent to the types of questions that the postmodern projects raise.[87] The relationship between revelation and history was one of the central themes in his scholarship in his early academic years.[88] In his work *Principles of Catholic Theology,* he went so far as to argue that "the fundamental crisis of our age is understanding the mediation of history within the realm of ontology."[89]

Schindler's theology of culture could therefore perhaps be enriched by incorporating into his already existing framework some of the insights of the early Ratzinger and de Lubac in this territory of the relationship between revelation and history. In other words, a fully developed approach to the theology of culture requires the appropriation of de Lubac's critique of the neo-Thomist account of nature and grace (this has already been done by Schindler), the appropriation of critiques of Kantian rationality and Pelagian accounts of the will (this has already been covered to some degree by Schindler and even more so by Hanby), the appropriation of contemporary critiques of the notion of an autonomously secular realm (see below), and the appropriation of the work of de Lubac, Ratzinger, and John

86. J. Ratzinger, *Principles of Catholic Theology* (San Francisco: Ignatius, 1982), 161.

87. Boeve argues that postmodern theologians evaluate the neo-conservative (prototypically Ratzinger's) correction of the autonomy of the modern subject as a construction of a new but old master-story that is hegemonic and in the end repressive, because the Other, the Transcendent, is fully known, is mastered. See L. Boeve, "*Gaudium et spes* and the Crisis of Modernity: The End of the Dialogue with the World," in *Vatican II and Its Legacy,* ed. M. Lamberigts and L. Kenis (Leuven: Peeters, 2002), 94. However, one might respond that this is not exactly Ratzinger's position. While Ratzinger believes that there is a master-story and that the Church's responsibility is to be a mediator of that story, the Other (the Trinitarian God) is never mastered, but masters us, divinizes us, in the nuptial mystery of the union of the soul with God.

88. See, for example, J. Ratzinger, "Revelation and Tradition," in K. Rahner and J. Ratzinger, *Revelation and Tradition* (New York: Herder and Herder, 1966).

89. Ratzinger, *Principles of Catholic Theology,* 160.

Montag, S.J., on the inadequacies of both the propositional and modernist theories of revelation.[90]

Ironically, Schindler's account of the relationships among nature, grace, and culture is converging with the projects of numerous scholars outside of the Catholic academy — a phenomenon that might in part be explained by the fact that scholars from the various Reformist and Anglican traditions are not hampered by the accommodationist interpretation of *Gaudium et Spes*. For example, Schindler's thesis that the process of transcending the culture of America requires the recovery of the centrality of the liturgy and sacrament as form represents a point of convergence with the work of the Cambridge Anglo-Catholic Catherine Pickstock. Whereas John Paul II used the expression "the culture of death," Pickstock speaks of a "polity of death" to describe the culture of modernity, or what Schindler and Alasdair MacIntyre call the "culture of America." She connects the notion of a social order resting upon a "rhetoric of consensus" with the classical Sophist tradition, and she traces the modern version of sophistry, or what MacIntyre calls "ideological rhetoric," to the work of Duns Scotus. With the philosophy of Scotus, the will became a "self propelling power, detached from the lure of teleology." This detachment of the will from the lure of the good resounded outside the inner field of moral philosophy and effected deep and dramatic changes to social life. Once the will was asserted as a "self propelling power" it had to be curtailed by the rise of a new juridical authority — the nation-state — whose job is to prevent a dissolution of social order. Henceforth "both private actions within the conjugal and domestic realm and those performed over against the collective now consummated as the nation, are no longer situated within the eschatological dimension of time, but within an open-ended but empty and indifferent order of temporal successiveness."[91] In place of the common good there is now a theory of government based upon principles of contractual relations, just as the Scotist abandonment of the idea of participation in Being encouraged the establishment of contractual relations between creatures and God. The consequence of this Scotist-derived political philosophy is that the secular authorities erect a rival sacrality. The liberal

---

90. Ratzinger, in *Revelation and Tradition*; Henri de Lubac, *The Discovery of God* (Grand Rapids: Eerdmans, 1996). See also J. Montag, "The False Legacy of Suarez," in *Radical Orthodoxy: A New Theology*, ed. J. Milbank, C. Pickstock, and G. Ward (London: Routledge, 1999).

91. C. Pickstock, *After Writing: On the Liturgical Consummation of Philosophy* (Oxford: Blackwell, 1998), 136-137.

political order begins to parody the theological. Politics becomes a "pseudo-liturgical power whose absolutist colonization of every realm of life parodies the traditionally sacramental structure of all forms of social interaction."[92]

Fundamental to the erection of this rival sacrality is the promotion of a new understanding of the *saeculum.* A raft of contemporary scholars, including the Oxford evangelical Oliver O'Donovan, the more Anglo-Catholic John Milbank, and the Catholic William T. Cavanaugh have traced the mutation in the concept of the secular realm from simply pertaining to the things of this temporal world, to a sphere impervious to the sacred, outside the realm of the theological. They further argue that, within the traditional meaning of the term *saeculum,* society as a whole could never be secular. Rather, "the appearance of a social secularity could only be created by understanding society as a quasi-mechanical system, incapable of moral and spiritual acts," and thus, "the false consciousness of the would-be contemporary secular society lies in its determination to conceal the religious judgements that it has made."[93] Accordingly, Cavanaugh holds that the theory of the neutrality of the contemporary liberal state is itself a kind of *mythos* by which our participation in one another through our creation in the image of God is replaced by the recognition of the other as the bearer of individual rights, which may or may not be given by God, but which serve only to separate what is mine from what is thine.[94] Such alternative liberal myths involve relations of mutual support and come together as a single culturally embodied package. In the language of Schindler and John Paul II, the cultural package is a "structure of sin."[95]

Against the idea that the *saeculum* is, or can be, a theology-free zone, the Archbishop of Canterbury, Rowan Williams, suggests that those who read St. Augustine's *City of God* arrive at the paradox that the only reliable political leader who can be guaranteed to safeguard such authentically political values as order, equity, and the nurture of souls in these things is the man who is, at the end of the day, indifferent to their survival in the relative shapes of the existing order, because he knows them to be safeguarded

92. Pickstock, *After Writing,* 152.

93. O. O'Donovan, *The Desire of the Nations: Rediscovering the Roots of Political Theology* (Cambridge: Cambridge University Press, 1997), 247.

94. W. T. Cavanaugh, *Theopolitical Imagination* (Edinburgh: T&T Clark, 2002), 44.

95. John Paul II, *Sollicitudo rei socialis,* paragraph 36; *Reconciliatio et paenitentia,* paragraph 16; and *Dominum et vivificantem,* paragraph 56. See "Significance of World and Culture."

at the level of God's eternal and immutable providence, vindicated in the eternal *civitas Dei*.[96] Williams counsels that this is not to say that Augustine believed that only the saint should be allowed to govern, but he did recognize a link between the peace of the temporal order and the virtue of those who live within it and who are charged with its governance.[97] This is consistent with the judgment of the eminent Augustinian scholar Gerald Bonner, who concluded that everything in Augustine's career would suggest that he considered a state governed by Christians to be a better polity than a pagan state, and with the recent work of Robert Dodaro, who suggests that, by reading the responses Augustine gives to Christians holding high office, such as found in his *Letter to Macedonius,* one can construct an Augustinian account of political virtue that is linked to the theological virtues.[98] Thus to acknowledge that Christians and non-Christians have similar temporal needs, such as food, clothing, shelter, and peace, is not to argue that theological virtues are irrelevant to the achievement of such goods, or, conversely, that the site of this achievement is theologically neutral territory. As Balthasar wrote: "this space [of history] belongs to Christ, it is in no sense an empty space but one that is shaped and structured and completely conditioned by certain categories. The framework of its meaning is constructed of the situations (the interior situations) of Christ's earthly existence."[99]

Within the Catholic tradition, however, there are, of course, numerous

96. R. Williams, "Politics and the Soul: A Reading of the City of God," *Milltown Studies* 55 (1987): 67.

97. This is not to suggest a general equivalence between the theology of Schindler and that of Rowan Williams. Obviously there are important differences in ecclesiology and theological anthropology between them. Williams believes that it is possible to ordain women, for example. However, it is to observe that there is significant agreement in the territory of political theology, and further, that those who believe that there is no such thing as an autonomous secular order can be found in many circles that could not be classified as "conservative Catholic."

98. G. Bonner, *God's Decree and Man's Destiny: Studies on the Thought of Augustine of Hippo* (London: Variorum Reprints, 1987); R. Dodaro, "Between the Two Cities: Political Action in Augustine of Hippo," in *Augustine and Politics,* ed. J. Doody et al. (Oxford: Lexington, 2005), 99-117. Note: Dodaro is a Catholic priest of the Order of St. Augustine and is included here simply because his recent work backs up the judgments of Rowan Williams and other non-Catholics in the Radical Orthodoxy circles. He is not being cited in this paragraph as an example of a Protestant scholar whose work is converging with that of Schindler's.

99. Hans Urs von Balthasar, *A Theology of History* (New York: Sheed and Ward, 1963), 66.

convergences between the work of Schindler on theology and culture and the work of other scholars in the Communio circles. From the United Kingdom there are the contributions of Stratford Caldecott, Director of the Centre for Faith and Culture in Oxford and editor of *Second Spring,* and Aidan Nichols, O.P., from the Divinity School at Cambridge. Caldecott's interest in the distributist (economic) theories of G. K. Chesterton dovetails with Schindler's critiques of liberal economic theory, and Nichols shares Schindler's interest in the application of Balthasar's insights to the development of a theology of culture. To this end, in *Christendom Awake,* Nichols offered a Trinitarian paradigm for the assessment of cultures, according to which a culture's tacit "paterological" dimension is defined by its idea of transcendence; its Christological dimension is discerned by considering the integrity, clarity, and harmony (or otherwise) of its institutional structures; and its pneumatological dimension is judged by reference to the moral ethos of its institutional practices.[100] From the French-speaking world there is the contribution of the theological anthropology of Marc Cardinal Ouellet and his work on the theological significance of human experience; from Spain, the criticisms of secular rationality and the liberal tradition of Archbishop Xavier Martinez; from Italy, the contribution of Angelo Cardinal Scola on the nuptial mystery; from Canada, the contribution of Kenneth L. Schmitz on the problems of German idealism and the metaphysical insights contained in his work *The Gift: Creation;* and from the United States, the Dawsonian theology of history of Glenn Olsen and the endorsement of Schindler's criticisms of the culture of America by James Cardinal Stafford. From the Papacy, there is also the contribution of the theology of the body and philosophical anthropology of John Paul II and the neo-Augustinian and very Balthasarian emphasis on the relationships between love and beauty, and love and reason, of Benedict XVI, as well as the latter's attempt to mediate between modernist and Suárezian approaches to the question of the relationship between history and revelation.[101]

---

100. A. Nichols, *Christendom Awake* (London: Gracewing, 1999), 16-17.

101. S. Caldecott, "Cosmology, Eschatology, Ecology," *Communio: International Catholic Review* 15 (1988): 305-318; X. Martinez, "'Beyond Secular Reason': Some Contemporary Challenges for the Life and the Thought of the Church," *Communio: International Catholic Review* 31 (2004): 557-586; G. Olsen, "Cultural Dynamics: Secularization and Sacralization," in *Christianity and Western Civilization,* ed. Wethersfield Institute (San Francisco: Ignatius Press, 1995), 97-122; M. Ouellet, "Hans Urs von Balthasar: Witness to the Integration of Faith and Culture," *Communio: International Catholic Review* 18 (1991): 111-126; "Paradox and/or

Tracey Rowland

The combined efforts of all of these scholars could be summarized by the statement that they are working toward an account of nature, grace, and culture that overcomes the dualisms of faith and reason, nature and supernature, secular and sacred, historically situated virtue and ahistorical natural law, Scripture and tradition, revelation as theoretical propositions and revelation as personal experience of the Divine; and instead they are providing an understanding of these topics within what Nichols calls, and Schindler affirms, a "trinitarian taxis."

Supernatural Existential," *Communio: International Catholic Review* 18 (1991): 259-280; K. L. Schmitz, "Catholicism in America," *Communio: International Catholic Review* 19 (1992): 474-477; "Faith and Reason: Then and Now," *Communio: International Catholic Review* 26 (1999): 595-608; A. Scola, "Christian Experience and Theology," *Communio: International Catholic Review* 23 (1996): 203-206; "Freedom, Grace and Destiny," *Communio: International Catholic Review* 25 (1998): 439-461; "Human Freedom and Truth According to the Encyclical *Fides et Ratio*," *Communio: International Catholic Review* 26 (1999): 486-509; "The Nuptial Mystery: A Perspective for Systematic Theology," *Communio: International Catholic Review* 30 (2003): 209-233; "Nature and Grace in Hans Urs von Balthasar," *Communio: International Catholic Review* 18 (1991): 207-226; "On the Trinitarian Encyclicals of John Paul II," *Communio: International Catholic Review* 18 (1991): 322-331; J. Stafford, "Knights of Columbus State Address Dinner: Keynote Speech," Washington, D.C., August 3, 2004; "Reflections on *Veritatis Splendor*," *Communio: International Catholic Review* 21 (1994): 363-366.

II

Praeambula fidei: David L. Schindler and the Debate over "Christian Philosophy"

Nicholas J. Healy Jr.

> *We are seeking the principles and the causes of the things that are, and obviously of things qua being.*
>
> Aristotle, Metaphysics VI, 1

> *Now among those who went up to worship at the feast were some Greeks. So these came to Philip . . . and said to him, "Sir, we wish to see Jesus."*
>
> John 12:20-21

The 1930s in France saw many of the leading figures of twentieth-century Catholicism engaged in a heated debate over the possibility and meaning of a specifically "Christian philosophy." The debate was sparked when the French historian of philosophy Emile Bréhier delivered a series of lectures in Belgium in 1928 published under the title *Is there a Christian Philosophy?*[1] The substance of Bréhier's answer is that "there is no Christian philosophy, never has been and never will be, because the very idea is unthinkable."[2] For Bréhier, "Christianity is essentially the mysterious history of the relationship of God and man, a mysterious history which can only be revealed, while philosophy has rationalism for its life-blood, that is to say a clear and distinct consciousness of the reason that is in things and in

---

1. E. Bréhier, "Y a-t-il une philosophie chrétienne?" *Revue de métaphysique et de morale* 38 (1931): 133-162.
2. M. Nédoncelle, *Is There a Christian Philosophy?* (New York: Hawthorn Books, 1960), 100.

the universe."[3] Bréhier's position provoked a sharp response from Étienne Gilson both in writing and at a famous meeting of the Société française de philosophie held at the Sorbonne in the spring of 1931. Gilson argued that the history of Patristic and medieval thought establishes beyond doubt the indebtedness of philosophy to revelation for key notions such as creation, providence as paternal goodness, the concept of person, and so forth. Accordingly, Gilson proposed the following definition of Christian philosophy: "I call Christian, every philosophy which, although keeping the two orders formally distinct, nevertheless considers the Christian revelation as an indispensable auxiliary to reason."[4]

Gilson's thesis was severely criticized both by Bréhier and by several Catholic philosophers who were concerned to uphold the distinction between philosophy and theology and to safeguard the autonomy of reason. "As so often happens," observes Henri de Lubac, "Bréhier found himself nearly forgotten," and the Catholics were left arguing among themselves about the meaning of the notion of "Christian philosophy."[5] Maurice Blondel and Jacques Maritain both penned substantial essays on the theme in 1932.[6] And on September 11, 1933, the Société thomiste devoted its *Journées d'études* to the question of "Christian philosophy." The list of participants includes many of the leading figures of the Thomist revival initiated by Leo XIII's *Aeterni Patris*: M.-D. Chenu, Y. Congar, A. Forest, E. Gilson, P. Mandonnet, A.-G. Sertillanges, Y. Simon, B. de Solages, and F. Van Steenberghen (among others).

At this meeting Gilson continued to defend the idea of a specifically "Christian philosophy," basing his view on what he claimed was the manifest influence of revelation on the development of medieval philosophy. The opposing side was upheld by Pierre Mandonnet, the founder and honorary president of the Société thomiste, who claimed that "to think or argue from the faith is to engage in theology."[7] Mandonnet's position was

---

3. Bréhier, "Y a-t-il une philosophie chrétienne?"

4. E. Gilson, *The Spirit of Medieval Philosophy* (New York: Charles Scribner's Sons, 1940), 37.

5. H. de Lubac, "On Christian Philosophy," *Communio: International Catholic Review* 19 (1992): 480.

6. M. Blondel, *Le problème de la philosophie catholique* (Paris: Bloud et Guy, 1932); J. Maritain, "De la notion de philosophie chrétienne," *Revue néoscolastique* 34 (1932): 155-186 [ET = *An Essay on Christian Philosophy* (New York: Philosophical Library, 1955)].

7. R. McInerny, *Praeambula fidei: Thomism and the God of the Philosophers* (Washington, DC: Catholic University of America Press, 2006), 94; hereafter cited as PF.

strongly supported by Ferdinand Van Steenberghen, who published a summary account of the debate in the *Revue néoscolastique*.[8] In the eyes of both Mandonnet and Van Steenberghen, the notion of "Christian philosophy" inevitably leads to a confusion between philosophy and theology and thus should be avoided.

Looking back at the francophone debate, it is possible to identify certain hidden assumptions that contributed to the question's intractability. Joseph Owens observes how "[o]ften . . . a kind of blindness to the adversaries' conception of philosophy seemed to hinder communication."[9] Mark Jordan develops the same point more generally:

> Consider how differently the question about Christian philosophy sounds when one substitutes different definitions of philosophy. If philosophy is a search for a way of life leading to blessed tranquility, then the believer must certainly hold that Christianity is the only true philosophy. If philosophy is, however, the knowledge of the ultimate constituents of the physical cosmos, then perhaps it lies somewhat apart from Christianity, though even that project is not entirely unconnected to the doctrine of creation, say. . . . Or perhaps philosophy is the knowledge of those things that can be known with mathematical certainty. . . . It comes as no surprise, then, that Bréhier and Gilson or Van Steenberghen and Gilson cannot agree about Christian philosophy, when they do not agree about philosophy itself.[10]

A second and related ambiguity that often goes unnoticed in contemporary accounts of the debate concerns the meaning of the "autonomy" of philosophy. Ralph McInerny, for example, criticizes Gilson for "calling into question the autonomy of philosophy"[11] without seeming to notice that Gilson has in fact offered a different (and I would argue more adequate) account of autonomy than the one McInerny seems to assume. If, generally speaking, autonomy always requires the absence of any dependence whatsoever, it is of course true that any indebtedness of philosophy to Christian revelation would undermine the autonomous nature of a philosophical ar-

8. F. Van Steenberghen, "La IIe journée d'études de la Société thomiste et la notion de philosophie chrétienne," *Revue néoscolastique* 35 (1933): 539-554.

9. J. Owens, *Towards a Christian Philosophy* (Washington, DC: Catholic University of America Press, 1990), 8.

10. M. Jordan, "The Terms of the Debate over 'Christian Philosophy,'" *Communio: International Catholic Review* 12 (1985): 293-311, at 298-299.

11. PF, 36.

gument. On the other hand, if one conceives autonomy not simply as independence, but as the integrity proper to a created reality, then an intrinsic influence of faith on philosophy is not automatically at odds with the legitimate autonomy of philosophy.[12]

At a deeper level, the reason why the notion of "Christian philosophy" continues to generate interest and controversy is grounded in the mystery of Christian revelation itself. Christianity claims to be at once a gift of faith that is radically beyond human reason *and* a renewal from within of everything human, including reason. In the words of Henri de Lubac, "Christianity is universal not only in the sense that Jesus Christ is the Savior of all men but also in the sense that all of man finds salvation in Jesus Christ."[13] *All of man* emphatically includes the loving search for wisdom that is designated by the term "philosophy" and that reached a high point in Athens four centuries before Christ. The question of how the mystery of Christ relates to the comprehensive claims of Greek wisdom is "not merely ancient, it is also perennial."[14]

It should be noted that the question of "Christian philosophy" is not simply a matter of determining how philosophy relates to theology. The more difficult question is whether and in what sense the mystery of Christ makes a difference to philosophy qua philosophy. It is interesting and salutary to note that this question was not asked by the Church Fathers, for whom Christianity was simply "the true philosophy."[15] Nor was the question asked in this form during the high medieval period. Thomas Aquinas, of course, has much to say about the legitimate use of philosophy within theology. He often describes this use by analogy to the miracle at Cana, where water is turned into wine. That said, Aquinas never applies the term "philosopher" to any Christian thinker, since this was a term he reserved for pagans.

---

12. Of course, this is simply a claim that the notion of "Christian philosophy" is not immediately incoherent; it still remains to show how philosophy can be "Christian" and still be philosophy. The only point I wish to make at this juncture is that opponents of the idea of a "Christian philosophy" need to beware lest unconfessed assumptions about the integrity of the substantive "philosophy" lead them to dismiss prematurely, without the requisite philosophical argumentation, the possible fittingness (or even necessity) of the adjective "Christian."

13. H. de Lubac, "The Authority of the Church in Temporal Matters," in *Theological Fragments* (San Francisco: Ignatius Press, 1989), 211.

14. Jordan, "The Terms of the Debate," 294.

15. For Patristic texts on this theme, see H. U. von Balthasar, "Philosophy, Christianity, Monasticism," in *Explorations in Theology*, vol. 2, *Spouse of the Word* (San Francisco: Ignatius Press, 1991).

The question about what difference, if any, the mystery of Christ makes to philosophy as such is a relatively new one. Perhaps this is why Maritain describes the question of "Christian philosophy" as the "central point of the history of *our time* . . . and probably as the central point in the age to come."[16]

The terms of the question need to be framed in light of the declaration of the First Vatican Council that

> there exists a twofold order of knowledge, distinct not only as regards their source, but also as regards their object. With regard to the source, because we know in one by natural reason, in the other by divine faith. With regard to the object, because besides those things which natural reason can attain, there are proposed for our belief mysteries hidden in God which, unless they are divinely revealed, cannot be known.[17]

In light of this important teaching, the question of "Christian philosophy" can be reformulated as follows: Can there be a philosophy that is intrinsically influenced by the revealed mysteries of God and yet distinct from theology?

The debate over the possibility and meaning of "Christian philosophy" is worth revisiting for several reasons. There is a growing consensus that one of the most serious problems in Catholic theology since Vatican II is "the disappearance of serious engagement with philosophy."[18] Significantly, the last two Popes have devoted a great deal of attention to this problem. In his now famous address at the University of Regensburg, Pope Benedict XVI lamented the unfortunate consequences both for Christianity and for the dialogue among cultures that have resulted from repeated attempts to purify Christian faith of Greek philosophical reflection. Over and against this "de-Hellenization," Benedict argued that, because "the truly divine God is the God who has revealed himself as logos," there is a "profound harmony between what is Greek in the best sense of the word and the biblical understanding of faith in God."[19] In light of this harmony, Benedict called for a rediscovery of "the whole breadth of reason," a rediscovery that will succeed "only if reason and faith come together in a new way."[20]

16. J. Maritain, *Science and Wisdom* (London: Geoffrey Bliss, 1944), 129; my italics.

17. Vatican I, Dogmatic Constitution on the Catholic Faith *Dei Filius,* III: DS, 3008.

18. Fergus Kerr, "Foreword: Addressing This 'Giddy Synthesis,'" in Lucy Gardner et al., *Balthasar at the End of Modernity* (Edinburgh: T&T Clark, 1999), 13.

19. Benedict XVI, "Faith, Reason and the University: Memories and Reflections," Address to the University of Regensburg (September 12, 2006).

20. Benedict XVI, "Faith, Reason and the University."

Benedict's emphasis on the "convergence" of faith and reason should be read against the backdrop of the even more vigorous assertion of their unity that we find in his predecessor's *Fides et Ratio*. In this encyclical John Paul II issued "a strong and insistent appeal . . . that faith and philosophy recover their profound unity which allows them to stand in harmony with their nature without compromising their mutual autonomy" (48). Theologians are urged "to pay special attention to the philosophical implications of the word of God" (105), and philosophers are asked "to be open to the impelling questions which arise from the word of God" (106). It is incumbent on all "to look more deeply at the mystery of man, whom Christ has saved in the mystery of his love," and thereby to rediscover the "intimate bond between theological and philosophical wisdom" (107, 105).

For John Paul II and Benedict XVI, the current crisis of reason is intimately related to the "fateful separation" of faith and reason that, in their view, stems from the late medieval period. Accordingly, both Pontiffs call for a renewal of "philosophical speculation conceived in dynamic union with faith," whereby faith both "purifies reason" and sheds light on the proper objects of philosophical reflection. At the heart of this "strong and insistent appeal . . . that faith and philosophy recover their profound unity" there clearly lies a concept of "Christian philosophy." It is my contention that the two Pontiffs significantly advance our understanding of what this "Christian philosophy" is beyond the *status quaestionis* of the 1930s debate. Not only do they hold, with Gilson, that there can be a unity of faith and philosophy. They go a step further and address the difference that Christianity makes to philosophy per se. And on this score, they hold that the unity of faith and philosophy safeguards and deepens the autonomy of philosophy itself. "In the mystery of the Incarnate Word," John Paul II writes, "human nature and divine nature are safeguarded in all their autonomy, and at the same time the unique bond which sets them together in mutuality without confusion of any kind is revealed" (*Fides et Ratio*, 80). If one substituted the words "philosophy" and "revelation" for "human nature" and "divine nature," respectively, one would have formulated the central teaching about "Christian philosophy" that animates the thought of the last two pontificates on the subject of faith and reason.

More than any other contemporary Catholic philosopher, David Schindler has patiently explored how the mystery of God's incarnate love informs and renews philosophical reflection and thereby provides the deepest answer to the crisis of reason in modern liberal cultures. From his doctoral dissertation, "Knowing as Synthesis: A Metaphysical Prolegomenon to Critical Christian Philosophy," through his forthcoming two-volume work *Ordering Love,* Schindler's writings have embodied and embraced a twofold concern: first and foremost, that of a renewed understanding of being in terms of love; second, a critical engagement with contemporary culture in light of the mission of the Church to recapitulate all things in that love insofar as it is definitively revealed in Christ (Eph. 1:10). The question of "Christian philosophy" marks the intersection of these two concerns and, in this sense, represents the driving force behind Schindler's work.

Schindler's thinking is animated by the insight, which is catholic in the deepest sense of the word, that being receives its fundamental order and meaning from the love definitively revealed in Jesus Christ and that "all of nature and all of the anthropological (political, economic, cultural) orders that extend nature into culture" are "invited to share in the *communio* whose reality in history is the Church."[21] The mystery of Jesus Christ not only reveals that God is love, but also discloses that creation itself, in all of its different orders and despite its sinful condition, is made in the image of love and is destined for communion with God in the Church. In terms of "Christian philosophy," this means that the love revealed in and through Jesus Christ is not simply an "addition" that remains foreign to properly rational reflection. With respect both to the human subject and to the proper object of philosophy, love allows for a deeper understanding of the being of the world and the mystery of God, who can be known by reason as the "beginning and end of all things."[22]

I suggested earlier that the question of "Christian philosophy" can be reformulated as follows: Can there be a philosophy that is intrinsically influenced by the revealed mysteries of God and yet distinct from theology? My aim in what follows is to show how Schindler provides what amounts to the most comprehensive and subtle account — at once philosophical and theological — of this affirmation. I propose to do so by laying out Schindler's contribution to the question of "Christian philosophy" against the backdrop of the unresolved debate of the 1930s. Accordingly, part I of the present essay will outline the four basic options of the debate as represented by Étienne Gilson, Ferdinand Van Steenberghen, Jacques Maritain, and Maurice Blondel, respectively.[23] Part II will consider the contempo-

---

21. HW, xi.
22. Vatican I, Dogmatic Constitution on the Catholic Faith *Dei Filius,* II: DS, 3004.
23. Although Maritain and Gilson were in basic agreement with one another, their po-

rary state of the question in light of John Paul II's *Fides et Ratio* in conjunction with a recent book by Ralph McInerny, *Praeambula fidei: Thomism
and the God of the Philosophers*. Only then will we be in a position, in part
III, to evaluate Schindler's distinctive understanding of the nature and task
of Christian philosophy.

I. The Debate of the 1930s — Four Basic Options

As mentioned above, Bréhier's radical rejection of the possibility of Christian philosophy provoked divergent responses from Catholic authors.
Among the various solutions put forward, it is possible to identify four
representative answers, each of which continues to find adherents today. I
will briefly summarize the four positions before identifying some unresolved issues that, in my judgment, were not clarified in the context of the
original debate itself.

A. Etienne Gilson: Faith as an Indispensable Auxiliary to Reason

Responding to Bréhier's charge that the idea of "Christian philosophy" is
contradictory, Gilson turned to the realm of history:

> The question [is there a Christian philosophy?] can be answered in the
> affirmative if we treat the problem as a historical one. We have then to
> decide whether Christianity has in fact played a visible part in the for-
> mation of certain philosophies. If we find philosophical systems, purely
> rational in their principles and methods, which could not have come
> into existence without the Christian religion, then the philosophies thus
> defined deserve to be called Christian. This notion does not correspond
> to a pure essence, that of a philosopher or that of a Christian, but to the
> possibility of a complex historical reality, that of a revelation which is
> productive of human reasoning. The two orders remain distinct, al-
> though the relationship which unites them is an intrinsic one.[24]

---

sitions do not entirely coincide. Accordingly, their respective positions are presented as two
distinct options.

    24. *Bulletin de la Société Française de Philosophie* 31 (1931): 39; cited in Nédoncelle, *Is
There a Christian Philosophy?* 85-86.

Gilson returns to the historical evidence in his Gifford Lectures, published as *The Spirit of Mediaeval Philosophy:* "the content of Christian philosophy," he writes there, "is that body of rational truths discovered, explored or simply safeguarded, thanks to the help that reason receives from revelation. Whether this philosophy ever really existed or whether it is nothing but a myth, is a question of fact on which we shall have to turn to history for a decision."[25] As a privileged example of a properly "rational truth" that came to light through the impetus provided by revelation, Gilson cites the Thomistic understanding of God as *ipsum esse subsistens* and the attendant notion of being *(esse)* as unlimited perfection and the actuality of all acts. Other examples include the Christian idea of providence as paternal goodness and solicitude, and the unique dignity of personal being.

Gilson's argument, then, essentially appeals to the principle that holds that *ab esse ad posse valet consequentia.* The test of whether there can be such a thing as "Christian philosophy" is whether there has been such a thing as "Christian philosophy." For him, the central test is historical influence: Has there in fact been a philosophy, or philosophies, that could not have existed apart from the Christian religion? As we have just seen, Gilson's own answer to this question is a resounding "Yes."

It is important to stress, however, that Gilson still maintains a fairly strict formal distinction between philosophy and theology. The complex historical reality of Christian philosophy involves, he holds, an initial illumination from revelation, but this light then fructifies a form of thinking and arguing that is authentically rational. "It is of the essence of philosophy," he writes, "to pursue the knowledge of causes in the light of the natural reason."[26] As John Wippel observes, Gilson's position "implies that philosophy has discovered certain naturally knowable truths only at the positive suggestion of revelation. Once such truths have been pointed out by faith, of course, the Christian philosopher is invited to investigate their rational foundations."[27] It is just this strictly philosophical character of a

---

25. Gilson, *The Spirit of Mediaeval Philosophy,* 35. Armand Mauer provides a helpful overview of Gilson's various treatments of Christian philosophy in an introductory essay to Gilson, *Christian Philosophy: An Introduction* (Toronto: Pontifical Institute of Mediaeval Studies, 1993).

26. Gilson, *The Philosopher and Theology* (New York: Random House, 1962), 192.

27. John Wippel, "Thomas Aquinas and the Problem of Christian Philosophy," in his *Metaphysical Themes in Thomas Aquinas* (Washington, DC: Catholic University of America Press, 1984), 13.

Nicholas J. Healy Jr.

"Christian philosophy" that one of Gilson's chief opponents in the 1930s debate, Ferdinand Van Steenberghen, denies.

B. Ferdinand Van Steenberghen: Reason as Autonomous

From his summary account of the 1933 meeting of the Société thomiste until the end of his distinguished career, the Louvain Thomist Ferdinand Van Steenberghen objected to the notion of "Christian philosophy" on the grounds that it violated the autonomy of reason.[28] He acknowledged that Christian faith "might have an indirect and accidental effect on a Christian's philosophizing, by establishing the internal peace, serenity, and love of truth required for research. Like the cinema or a walk in the park, revelation might suggest ideas or angles for nuancing a concept."[29] But properly speaking "philosophy is a scientific effort which attempts a general explanation of reality insofar as it is an object of natural human knowledge."[30] That is to say that the object, principles, methods, arguments, and conclusions of philosophy are strictly or purely rational. To the extent that philosophy were to acknowledge an indebtedness to revelation, i.e. to become "Christian philosophy," it would no longer be philosophy but theology. For Van Steenberghen, then, the idea that faith can influence properly rational reflection on the latter's own immanent terms represents an unfortunate confusion of nature and grace, philosophy and theology. The autonomy of philosophical reason rules out any intrinsic influence on it from the side of revelation.

C. Jacques Maritain: The Distinction Between "Nature" and "State"

At first sight, Maritain's position looks little different from Gilson's confident assertion of the historical reality of "Christian philosophy." Nevertheless, Maritain introduces a new note, in that he attempts to affirm Gilson's ideas while at the same time doing justice to the concerns about the integ-

28. In addition to the reference in note 8 above, see Van Steenberghen, "Etienne Gilson, historien de la pensée médiévale," *Revue philosophique de Louvain* 77 (1979): 496-507.

29. I borrow this summary account of Van Steenberghen's position from Marilyn McCord Adams, "History of Philosophy as Tutor of Christian Philosophy," in *The Question of Christian Philosophy Today,* ed. Francis J. Ambrosio (New York: Fordham University Press, 1999), 39.

30. Van Steenberghen, "La IIe journée d'études," 546-547.

rity of philosophy raised by opponents of Gilson such as Van Steenberghen. Thus, though Maritain begins his 1932 "Essay on Christian Philosophy" by noting his "basic agreement" with Gilson, he goes on to qualify that "whereas [Gilson] has intentionally adopted the historical standpoint, I should like to attempt to bring together some elements of a solution on the doctrinal level."[31] The core of Maritain's solution is a distinction between what he, drawing on Thomas, calls the order of specification and the order of exercise, or between "nature" and "state." A consideration of the *nature* of philosophy focuses on the essence of philosophy in itself, in abstraction from its existential conditions. By contrast, the *state* of philosophy has to do with the concrete manner in which persons philosophize, with both "reason and heart" engaged.

For Maritain, then, the notion of "Christian philosophy" refers to the *state* and not to the *nature* of philosophy. To be sure, the state of philosophizing can and should benefit from Christian faith, both objectively in terms of aspects of revelation that pertain to the natural order and subjectively in terms of a "reinforcement and refinement" of intellect. Nevertheless, the nature of philosophy as such cannot be Christian. Maritain explains why in the following passages:

> Whoever fails to recognize that the philosophic domain is of its nature within the reach of the sole natural facilities of the human mind — whatever else his conception of philosophy may embrace — negates philosophy; he does not define it.[32]

> Viewed as formally constructed philosophy, Thomistic philosophy — I do not say Thomistic theology — is wholly rational: no reasoning issuing from faith finds its way into its inner fabric, it derives intrinsically from reason and rational criticism alone; and its soundness as a philosophy is based entirely on experimental or intellectual evidence and on logical proof.[33]

As these passages make clear, Maritain in effect sides with Van Steenberghen in denying that Christian faith can touch the nature of philosophy without robbing that nature of its integrity.

---

31. J. Maritain, *An Essay on Christian Philosophy* (New York: Philosophical Library, 1955), 4.

32. Maritain, *An Essay on Christian Philosophy*, 14.

33. Maritain, *An Essay on Christian Philosophy*, 15.

D. Maurice Blondel: Reason Acknowledging Its Inadequacy

A fourth position in the debate about "Christian philosophy" is represented by Maurice Blondel, who, like Van Steenberghen, objected to Gilson's use of the term "Christian philosophy," though he did so on quite different grounds. The best way into Blondel's position is an entry from his diary that includes a meditation on his vocation as a philosopher:

> Like every man, I have a role, a mission to fulfil, a vocation. And I feel more and more drawn to the project of showing, in thought as in my life, the natural necessity of the supernatural and the supernatural reality of the natural. . . . I must show the actual paths of reason towards God incarnate and crucified; I must conciliate the claims of modern thought; I must move science and philosophy by the methods which are dear to them and which they are right to love; I must remain natural as long as anyone and longer than anyone in order to show more singly, more peremptorily, more pacifically, more broadly, more impersonally, the inevitable need for the supernatural. How few men are disposed to follow along those laborious paths, to open up a scientific road among so many obstacles, to understand equally the legitimate exigencies of the modern mind and the redoubtable intransigencies of Christian truth, to fill in the intervening space, and to throw into the abyss between them, so as to fill it, one's life, one's heart, one's reason, one's faith, one's future in time and eternity, the whole of oneself? It is to that task that I must consecrate myself.[34]

The task Blondel sets himself in this passage is to move philosophy from within and by its own proper method ("remaining natural longer than anyone") toward a reality that is utterly beyond philosophy. In response to Bréhier's criticism that this project was an exercise in apologetics and not a work of philosophy, Blondel replied: "I nowhere give any evidence of entering into the least content of the Catholic religion. I stop at the threshold; and, as a philosopher, I finally refuse to pronounce the one little word that I would have to utter as a believer."[35] Blondel took himself

---

34. M. Blondel, *Carnets Intimes* (Paris: Éditions du Cerf, 1961), 496; cited in Alexander Dru, "Introduction," in M. Blondel, *The Letter on Apologetics & History and Dogma* (Grand Rapids: Eerdmans, 1994), 44-45.

35. Blondel, "Y a-t-il une philosophie chrétienne?" *Revue de métaphysique et de morale* 38 (1931): 604.

to be remaining within "the legitimate scope of philosophical conclusions," which by their own intrinsic nature lead to "the threshold of that real operation in which alone the human act and the divine act, nature and grace, can unite."[36]

In order to bring philosophy "towards God incarnate and crucified," then, Blondel deemed it necessary to reject all attempts to "Christianize" philosophy. In other words, Blondel is reluctant to use the term "Christian philosophy" precisely because he thinks that philosophy on its own terms tends naturally to the point where it is forced to acknowledge its radical insufficiency before the deepest questions of existence.[37] Blondel's jealous guarding and even promotion of philosophy's "scientific autonomy" is animated by his conviction that such autonomy is itself openness to the supernatural destiny of every human being. Consequently, Blondel does fuller justice *both* to Gilson's *and* to Van Steenberghen's real concerns than Maritain with his distinction between the state and the nature of philosophy. Nevertheless, even Blondel falls short, as we will see in a moment.

E. Concluding Postscript: Henri de Lubac's Review of the Debate

The most brilliant account of the respective positions outlined above as well as of the overall significance of the debate is found in a short essay that Henri de Lubac published in 1936 under the title "On Christian Philosophy." After summarizing the views of Maritain, Gilson, and Blondel, and showing how the three accounts of "Christian philosophy" presuppose and complement each other, de Lubac proceeds to identify the hidden weakness of each proposed solution:

> According to Maritain, Christian philosophy is *not* and does not want to be strictly Christian: if, among the elements it examines, some are contained in the deposit of revelation, the coincidence is fortuitous. . . . All one can say is that Maritain, being otherwise Christian, finds himself sometimes aided, "comforted," as from outside, in his work as a philosopher by the suggestions of his faith.
>
> Christian philosophy according to Gilson, is *no longer* Christian,

36. Blondel, *Letter on Apologetics,* 164.
37. After initially rejecting the term "Christian philosophy," Blondel settled on the notion of "Catholic philosophy"; his concern for philosophy's proper autonomy nonetheless characterized his position from beginning to end.

Nicholas J. Healy Jr.

whatever its empirical origins may be, since for him revelation is the generator of reason. As a "constant effort to lead the irrational in us to a state of rationality," philosophy purely and simply annexes for itself what Christian revelation has provided it.

As to Christian philosophy according to Blondel, it is *not yet* Christian. For him philosophy is in a last stage of pure rational reflection, but it is noticing of itself that it does not "tie neatly together." It is thus a philosophy which will itself be open to Christianity, but which by rights does not at all proceed from it.[38]

According to de Lubac, then, the difficulty with Maritain's proposed distinction between *nature* and *state* — which denies "reasoning from faith" entrance into the "inner fabric" of philosophy — is that it evacuates the idea of "Christian philosophy," leaving it with very little meaning in the end. Faith may offer extrinsic suggestions or subjective comfort, but it is irrelevant to philosophy as such. The difficulty that de Lubac sees in Gilson's thesis — revelation provides an initial impetus to reason, which then seeks rational grounds for truths discovered with the help of faith — is that this position offers no principled resistance to the error of rationalism, which seeks to find purely rational grounds for the revealed mysteries of the faith. Gilson's response to this objection is that the domain of "Christian philosophy" pertains only to those "natural truths" which are "capable of passing from the stage where they are believed to a stage where they become 'known.'"[39] But, as de Lubac notes, two difficulties remain. First, where can we find the criteria to make this distinction? Second, supposing the legitimacy of the distinction between natural truths and properly supernatural mysteries of the faith, the question of "Christian philosophy" would simply reemerge with respect to the relationship between philosophy and the revealed mysteries of the faith.

De Lubac's own position comes closest to that of Blondel, whose account of the orientation of nature toward the supernatural he finds necessary to justify the claim of Maritain and Gilson that "reason illumined by faith functions better than reason which does not benefit at all from this light."[40] "[P]hilosophy," de Lubac writes, "by its own movement and without exterior prompting, tends toward revelation. Philosophy [will be

38. De Lubac, "On Christian Philosophy," 495-496. De Lubac does not consider the position of Van Steenberghen, but his criticism of Maritain applies equally to the former.
39. De Lubac, "On Christian Philosophy," 493.
40. De Lubac, "On Christian Philosophy," 492.

Christian] by being aware of its radical insufficiency."[41] However, as indicated by the long passage cited above, de Lubac identifies an important weakness in Blondel's understanding of philosophy. The idea that philosophy's relation to Christian faith is exclusively a matter of reason acknowledging its insufficiency (philosophy as *not yet* Christian) would seem to preclude the essential Christian truth that faith can purify, heal, and renew reason from within. That is, it is not enough to conceive faith as arriving only at the end of philosophy's journey, at the point where reason reaches its limit; the burden of an incarnational "from within" is that faith can be present to reason from the very beginning and all along the way.

In light of the threefold difficulty sketched above, de Lubac asks: "Isn't there nevertheless some other way of defining Christian philosophy, some way which does not reflect the ways we have just described, but which would instead establish itself in their wake, thus coming closer to the unity we seek? . . . One can define it in a few words: the synthesis of all knowledge, operating in the light of faith."[42]

While de Lubac's definition of "Christian philosophy" has the advantage of being traditional, even he leaves a crucial question unresolved. If philosophy is "a synthesis of all knowledge operating in the light of faith," how is philosophy still distinct from theology? De Lubac seems to think that the important thing is not what we call his "synthesis of all knowledge in the light of faith," but whether it is in fact a fulfillment of philosophy per se: "Couldn't we say that this is not philosophy, but theology? Once the ideas have been clarified, the words are hardly important."[43] But this answer is not quite satisfactory. The question remains: Can we affirm a permanent, intrinsic, content-ful influence of faith on philosophy per se, while safeguarding, indeed, exalting, the legitimate autonomy of philosophy and thus an abiding distinction between philosophy and theology?

II. *Fides et Ratio* and the Current State of the Question

In the intervening years, the debate over "Christian philosophy" has continued to generate interest as well as numerous publications.[44] Hans Urs

41. De Lubac, "On Christian Philosophy," 487.
42. De Lubac, "On Christian Philosophy," 497.
43. De Lubac, "On Christian Philosophy," 499.
44. Mark Jordan lists most of the relevant literature up to 1985 in "Terms of the Debate" (see note 10 above).

von Balthasar engaged the question in his 1946 essay "On the Tasks of Catholic Philosophy in Our Time," and, one year later, in his introduction to his book *Truth of the World.*[45] Maurice Nédoncelle published a book on the theme in 1960, and symposia were organized around the question in Namur, France, in 1983 and in Washington, D.C., in 1993.[46] In 1990 Joseph Owens gathered his various essays on the question in a volume titled *Towards a Christian Philosophy.* Most recently, Ralph McInerny devoted a considerable part of his book *Praeambula fidei: Thomism and the God of the Philosophers* (2006) to a reconsideration of the issues discussed at the 1933 meeting of the Société thomiste. Of course, the most significant intervention came in the form of an encyclical letter, *Fides et Ratio, On the Relationship Between Faith and Reason* (1998), which deals explicitly with the meaning of the disputed term "Christian philosophy."

These bibliographical data suggest the following procedure. Before expounding David Schindler's contribution to the question at hand, I propose to set forth a brief consideration of McInerny's book, which brings out with admirable clarity the basic issues that need to be addressed by anyone who would argue for an intrinsic relation between philosophy and revelation. After having examined McInerny's position, I will then introduce the teaching of John Paul II's *Fides et Ratio,* highlighting how the encyclical deals with the issues raised by McInerny — and, in so doing, resolves, on one level at least, the debate about "Christian philosophy." Finally, against this backdrop, I will present the contribution of David Schindler, whose account of the issues raised by McInerny provides the most cogent theological and philosophical justification of the teaching of *Fides et Ratio.*

A. McInerny on the Impossibility of a "Christian Philosophy"

In his acclaimed book *Praeambula fidei: Thomism and the God of the Philosophers,* Ralph McInerny concurs with the judgment of John Paul II (and Benedict XVI) regarding the harmful effects of a "negative attitude towards philosophy and the *praeambula fidei.*"[47] At the same time, McInerny

45. H. U. von Balthasar, "On the Tasks of Catholic Philosophy in Our Time," *Communio: International Catholic Review* 20 (1993): 147-187; TL 1:7-33.

46. Cf. *Pour une Philosophie Chrétienne,* ed. Pierre-Philippe Druet (Paris: Éditions Lethieulleux, 1983); *The Question of Christian Philosophy Today,* ed. Francis J. Ambrosio (New York: Fordham University Press, 1999).

47. PF, 38.

presents a strikingly different account of the root causes of the current crisis of reason. According to McInerny, key developments within twentieth-century Thomism are partly to blame for the contemporary disparagement of philosophy. Alongside de Lubac's theology of nature and grace and Chenu's critique of rationalism, McInerny singles out for criticism Gilson's conception of "Christian philosophy." He describes how, in response to the challenge of a separated philosophy, "new thought was given to the way in which Christians engage in philosophy, to the notion of Christian philosophy. Ironically, in some cases, this led to the calling into question of the autonomy of philosophy, and therefore of the *praeambula fidei*."[48] After summarizing Gilson's interventions at the contentious 1933 meeting of the Société thomiste, McInerny concludes: "Clearly it is not easy to understand what is meant by the autonomy of philosophy in some versions of Christian philosophy. From the point of view of our interest, the *praeambula fidei*, it is easy to see how confidence in it was weakened by some versions of Christian philosophy."[49] The key mistake of Gilson was "to have made philosophy Christian in its essence."[50]

McInerny's solution to the problem of "Christian philosophy" is essentially the same as Van Steenberghen's and Maritain's. He writes:

> Maritain distinguished philosophy from its state. . . . Anyone who philosophizes is influenced by a host of existential factors, in most cases unnoticed. . . . For the believer, the faith that is at the core of his being, a virtue of the speculative intellect, animates, or should, his every activity, most emphatically including philosophizing. . . . For all that, and this was Mandonnet's point, a philosophical argument, whatever its existential provenance, cannot include as the condition of its acceptability revealed truth.[51]

Christianity may be existentially relevant to the one who philosophizes, but philosophy as such is independent of faith; it is "an autonomous discipline whose arguments do not depend on the acceptance of any revelation."[52]

Earlier in this essay I suggested that hidden assumptions about the nature of philosophy contributed to the intractability of the question of

48. PF, 37.
49. PF, 38.
50. PF, 37.
51. PF, 107.
52. PF, 35.

"Christian philosophy." In this respect, McInerny is admirably clear. He defines philosophy, for instance, as "the principles and procedures . . . taught by Aristotle";[53] or, "the sort of activity that is conveyed by the treatise of Aristotle."[54] In case there is any doubt that McInerny means to identify "philosophy" with the activity and principles of Aristotle, consider how he poses and answers a question about whether there is a philosophy specific to Thomas Aquinas:

> There are two possible explanations of this presence of Aristotelianism: either Thomas adopted the principles and procedures of philosophy as taught by Aristotle because he thought they were true, or he had a different conception of philosophy than Aristotle's into which he was able to assimilate Aristotelian tenets as well as others. In favor of the second alternative is the fact that Thomas also exhibited sympathy for Platonic teachings. Must there not, then, be a larger whole, a specifically Thomistic philosophy, into which both Platonic and Aristotelian elements fit to the degree that they are in accord with its principles? I will endeavor to show that the first alternative is the correct one. The second has plausibility because Thomas did indeed advance the Aristotelian program beyond Aristotle. . . . But this . . . was done in terms of philosophical outlook that is fundamentally Aristotelian. Moreover, there are no peculiarly Thomistic philosophical principles that could supplant the Aristotelian ones he adopts.[55]

Notice what happens to the question of "Christian philosophy" in light of McInerny's questionable identification of "philosophy" with "the principles and procedures . . . [of] Aristotle." For if philosophy is essentially the principles and procedures of Aristotle, then whatever novelty Christianity brings falls outside the range of philosophy considered as such. In the passage cited above, McInerny explicitly excludes the possibility of reconceiving the nature and task of philosophy, in continuity with Aristotle, but fundamentally beyond Aristotle in the sense that he is integrated into a greater whole. Here McInerny is at odds with the argument of *Fides et Ratio* both in terms of the meaning of "philosophy," which John Paul II describes as "asking the question of life's meaning and sketching an answer to it" (3), or as "a search for the ultimate and overarching meaning

53. PF, 160.
54. PF, 127.
55. PF, 160.

of life" (81), and in terms of the objective contribution of Christian faith to the principles and procedures of properly philosophical reflection. More on this below.

The second thing to notice about McInerny's solution to the problem of "Christian philosophy" is his assumption that the "autonomy of philosophy" requires its total independence from faith. As noted above, this is the core of his criticism of Gilson, and, more generally, it is the reason why he includes a critical discussion of the debate over "Christian philosophy" in a book that seeks to reinvigorate philosophical thinking within the Catholic tradition. "If there is any mark to the arguments and analyses that make up the *praeambula fidei*," he writes, "it is that they are independent of faith and Scripture, something of which human beings are naturally capable."[56]

Now, it is not my purpose here to mount a critique of McInerny, who essentially follows Maritain's account of "Christian philosophy." The important thing about McInerny's position for our purposes is simply that it brings out so clearly the nub of the problem around which the controversy over "Christian philosophy" revolves — What is the autonomy of philosophy? — a question that is in turn bound up with two others: What is philosophy? and what is autonomy? McInerny himself seems to conceive both philosophy and autonomy in such a way that a philosophical argument or philosophy taken as such must be neutral or indifferent to revealed truth. This position assumes without argument that the evidence available to natural reason in its encounter with its proper object cannot be influenced in any way whatsoever by faith. For John Paul II, on the other hand, the influence of faith can and should inform every aspect of philosophy, from the initial encounter with reality through reflection and argumentation.[57] It is to John Paul II's exposition of this claim in *Fides et Ratio* that we now turn, an exposition admirably summed up by Benedict XVI in *Deus Caritas Est*: "[f]aith enables reason to do its work more effectively and *to see its proper object more clearly*" (28).

56. PF, 107.

57. There is, of course, a kernel of truth in McInerny's assertion that philosophy is "an autonomous discipline whose arguments do not depend on the acceptance of any revelation" (PF, 35). The relevant question is whether the evidence available to reason (upon which any properly philosophical argument rests) is neutral or indifferent to faith.

B. *The Teaching of Fides et Ratio*

In the sixth chapter of *Fides et Ratio*, titled "The Interaction Between Philosophy and Theology," John Paul II writes that "the relationship between theology and philosophy, is best construed as a circle. Theology's source and starting point must always be the word of God revealed in history, while its final goal will be an understanding of that word which increases with each passing generation. Yet, since God's word is truth (cf. Jn. 17:17), the human search for truth — philosophy, pursued in keeping with its own rules — can only help to understand God's word better" (73). Earlier in the encyclical John Paul II had described the fruitful relationship of unity and the distinction between faith and philosophy whereby each contributes something essential to the other. Conversely, "each without the other is impoverished and enfeebled" (48). "Deprived of reason," John Paul II writes, "faith has stressed feeling and experience, and so run the risk of no longer being a universal proposition. It is an illusion to think that faith, tied to weak reasoning, might be more penetrating; on the contrary, faith then runs the grave risk of withering into myth or superstition" (48). On the other hand, "[d]eprived of what Revelation offers, reason has taken sidetracks which expose it to the danger of losing sight of its final goal. . . . [R]eason which is unrelated to an adult faith is not prompted to turn its gaze to the newness and radicality of being" (48). In contrast to the trajectory of modern thought, which has tended toward a "fateful separation" of faith and philosophy, the experience of the great Christian theologians of the tradition confirms the fruitfulness of a circular relationship between revelation and philosophical reflection. Likewise, the "courageous research of more recent thinkers," among whom Jacques Maritain and Étienne Gilson are mentioned, offers an example of "philosophical enquiry which was enriched by engaging the data of faith" (74).

John Paul II proceeds to distinguish three different "stances" of philosophy in relation to Christian faith. First, there is "the stance adopted by philosophy as it took shape in history before the birth of the Redeemer and later in regions as yet untouched by the Gospel" (75); the second stance, often designated as "Christian philosophy," is "philosophical speculation conceived in dynamic union with faith" (76); the third stance occurs when "theology itself calls upon [philosophy]" (77).

Regarding the first stance, John Paul II says that "[w]e see here philosophy's valid aspiration to be an autonomous enterprise, obeying its own rules and employing the powers of reason alone. Although seriously handicapped by the inherent weakness of human reason, this aspiration should be supported and strengthened" (75). There are two points to note relative to this affirmation of philosophy's "valid autonomy" *(rectae autonomiae).* First, John Paul II distinguishes between an authentic sense of autonomy, often qualified by adjectives such as *recta* (75), *aequa* (75), *legitima* (79), or *iusta* (80), and the "illusion of autonomy which would deny the essential dependence on God" (80). The latter is characteristic of the "separate philosophy" pursued by some modern philosophers who claim a wrong sort of self-sufficiency for philosophical thinking. Second, "autonomy" does not mean neutrality to God or to the revealed mysteries of faith. David Schindler explains why not:

> [Philosophy,] even when practiced in historical circumstances in which the Gospel has not yet been preached, is for all that still not *neutral* toward the Gospel. A so-called "pagan" — pre-Christian or non-Christian — exercise of reason, in other words, is not to be confused with a "purely natural" reason, as though a lack of an explicit positive (or negative) relation to the Gospel or the supernatural signified a simple indifference of reason toward the Gospel — or indeed a reason unaffected by the sin of Adam (cf. FR, 22). On the contrary, as stated, philosophy's independence of revelation in such circumstances always implies — "contains" the implication of — openness to this revelation. This is why any (eventual) refusal of revelation involves damage already to philosophy itself. The historical appearance of the fullness of truth — the historical event of God's self-revelation in Jesus Christ — cannot be a matter of indifference, even-already to philosophy as such.[58]

Against this backdrop, it becomes clear how the second stance of philosophical thought, "Christian philosophy," is in some sense paradigmatic for *philosophia* as such. To be sure, this term "in no way intends to suggest that there is an official philosophy of the church, since the faith as such is not a philosophy" (76). Nevertheless, the term does seek to indicate "a philosophical speculation conceived in dynamic union with faith" (76) — within the circulation of faith and philosophy mentioned above. The influence of faith is not merely "negative" in the sense that philosophers who are also believers know that their philosophical conclusions, if true, will never contradict the faith. Faith also contributes positively to philosophy. This is why there is such a thing as a "Christian philosophy" that "includes

---

58. "Knowledge as Relationship," 513.

those important developments of philosophical thinking which would not have happened without the direct or indirect contribution of Christian faith" (76).

For John Paul II, then, faith has a "positive" influence on philosophy. This positive influence has two aspects: "The first is subjective, in the sense that faith purifies reason," providing philosophers with the requisite humility to engage questions "which are difficult to resolve if the data of revelation are ignored." Examples here include the problem of evil and suffering, the personal nature of God, and, finally, "the radical metaphysical question, 'Why is there something rather than nothing?'" (76). This leads to the second point: the influence of faith on philosophy is "objective, in the sense that it concerns content. Revelation clearly proposes certain truths which might never have been discovered by reason on its own, even if in principle not inaccessible to reason" (76). With this claim, *Fides et Ratio* touches the neuralgic point of the debate of the 1930s. It is difficult to deny that both the words of John Paul II regarding objective content and his examples of truths brought to light with the help of revelation — a free and personal God who is the Creator of the world, the reality of sin, the notion of the person as a spiritual being, and the idea of human dignity — recall Gilson's argument in *The Spirit of Medieval Philosophy*.[59]

Anticipating an objection to his account of "Christian philosophy," John Paul II explains that the fact of revelation's positive contribution to rational reflection does not mean that "philosophers have . . . become theologians, since they have not sought to understand and expound the truths of faith on the basis of revelation" (76). The implication is that Christian faith can and should influence the "rational method" proper to philosophy. In other words, instead of distinguishing between the *nature* and *state* of philosophy, or, as John Wippel has suggested, between the "moment of discovery" and the "moment of proof,"[60] *Fides et Ratio* suggests that philosophy as such, precisely in its nature as a "rational method," can and should be influenced by a light that comes from revelation. The delicate point that needs to be clarified is that the influence of faith, which is both subjective and objective, is not a threat to reason's natural integrity or "autonomy." Nor does the influence of faith upon reason entail a col-

---

59. This does not mean, Schindler notes, "either that the pope accepts Gilson's thesis in all of its aspects, or even that Gilson's understanding is in every respect adequate" ("Knowing as Relationship," 514n.6).

60. Wippel, *Metaphysical Themes in Thomas Aquinas*, 23-24.

lapse of the distinction between philosophy and theology, which remain "distinct not only as regards their source, but also as regards their object."[61] The claim of *Fides et Ratio* is that faith allows reason to function better as reason in relation to its natural object. As noted above, Pope Benedict XVI articulates the same thesis in *Deus Caritas Est* when he writes that "faith liberates reason from its blind spots and therefore helps it to be ever more fully itself. Faith enables reason to do its work more effectively and to see its proper object more clearly" (DCE, 28). I will return to this claim when considering David Schindler's position below.

The third and final stance concerns philosophy when it is explicitly called upon by theology. "Theology in fact," John Paul II writes, "has always needed and still needs philosophy's contribution" (FR, 77). In the concise formula of Hans Urs von Balthasar, *ohne Philosophie keine Theologie,* without philosophy there can be no theology. The pertinent point here is that even when it is taken up in service to theology, philosophy must maintain its proper autonomy if it is truly to be of service. The unsurpassed achievement of Thomas Aquinas serves as a guide and model for the task of integrating authentic philosophy within theology.

Let us try to summarize the foregoing brief exposition of John Paul II's teaching on faith and philosophy. On one level, the Pope's account of philosophy's three "stances" retrieves Maritain's distinction between *nature* and *state.* Nevertheless, John Paul II envisages a much more intrinsic relation between *state* and *nature* than does Maritain; the stance of "Christian philosophy" is paradigmatic for philosophy *tout court.* On this point, John Paul II retrieves the essential insight of Gilson, though with an important difference. For the Pope, in fact, revelation does not simply add new content at the beginning of philosophy's way. Rather, Christian faith permanently influences philosophy as such. Indeed, John Paul II agrees with Blondel that philosophy itself is intrinsically open to what can be given only from beyond reason. Finally, *Fides et Ratio* takes up the concern enunciated by Van Steenberghen and teaches that the intrinsic influence of faith, which is both subjective and objective, is not a threat to philosophical reason's natural integrity; rather, faith allows philosophical reason to function better as such in relation to its natural object. Indeed, the intrinsic influence of revelation on philosophy does not turn philosophy into theology, but liberates it to be more fully itself than ever before. This essential claim of *Fides et Ratio* is grounded in the mystery of the Incarnate and

---

61. Vatican I, Dogmatic Constitution on the Catholic Faith *Dei Filius,* III: DS, 3008.

crucified Word wherein human nature and divine nature are simultaneously unified and "safeguarded in all their autonomy" (FR, 80). The
most comprehensive and subtle articulation of the Christological under-
pinnings of *Fides et Ratio* is found in David Schindler's contribution to the
"Christian philosophy" debate, to which we now turn.

III. The Contribution of David Schindler

Beginning with his doctoral dissertation, "Knowing as Synthesis: A Metaphysical Prolegomenon to Critical Christian Philosophy," David Schindler
has approached the question of Christian philosophy from a variety of per-
spectives. Early on, he considered the question in the context of a creative
retrieval of the metaphysics of Thomas Aquinas as the key to overcoming
the limitations of process philosophy while doing justice to its legitimate
concerns. In the early 1980s, an extended dialogue with the physicist David
Bohm provided the occasion for clarifying the meaning of Christian philosophy in relation to the mechanistic assumptions of modern science.
Underlying Schindler's long-running argument with American neoconservatism is a discernment that liberalism's claim to provide economic
and political institutions that are empty of anthropological and religious
content presupposes a false view of the relationship between philosophy
and Christian revelation. After the death of Hans Urs von Balthasar in
1988, Schindler increasingly focused on the themes of Christology and the
ontological significance of childhood as central to the nature and task of
Christian philosophy. In a seminal essay written in 1993, Schindler broad-
ened the question in terms of the relationship between sanctity and the
methods and contents of the modern academic curriculum.[62] The meaning of "Christian philosophy" explicitly emerges in the discussion with
W. Norris Clarke and Steven Long on the themes of person, relation, receptivity, and Thomism.[63] Finally, his article "God and the End of Intelli-

---

62. David L. Schindler, "Sanctity and the Intellectual Life," *Communio: International
Catholic Review* 20 (1993): 652.

63. In chronological order, David L. Schindler, "Norris Clarke on Person, Being, and St.
Thomas," *Communio: International Catholic Review* 20 (1993): 580-592; W. Norris Clarke,
"Response to David Schindler's Comments," *Communio: International Catholic Review* 20
(1993): 593-598; Stephen A. Long, "Divine and Creaturely 'Receptivity': The Search for a
Middle Term," *Communio: International Catholic Review* 21 (1994): 151-161; George A. Blair,
"On *Esse* and Relation," *Communio: International Catholic Review* 21 (1994): 162-164;

gence: Knowledge as Relation," includes a compelling interpretation of *Fides et Ratio*'s treatment of "Christian philosophy."[64]

Surveying this extensive body of writings, we can identify two seminal theses on the meaning of Christian philosophy: the first thesis concerns the creaturely and ultimately Christological meaning of "autonomy"; the second thesis is that "love tells us what it means to act in the highest and deepest sense — and thereby what it means most fully *to be*."[65] Taken together, these two claims provide a distinctive and fruitful approach to philosophy. In the remainder of this section, I propose to examine each of these claims in turn. Having done so, I will then summarize in the conclusion the burden of Schindler's contribution to the debate over "Christian philosophy."

A. Christology and the Autonomy of Philosophy

To a large extent, the 1930s debate about the possibility of a "Christian philosophy" was a controversy over the nature of the autonomy of philosophy. As we noted above, all of the parties to the discussion wished to affirm this autonomy. Nevertheless, there was too little explicit consideration of the nature of autonomy itself. What is it for something — in this case philosophy — to be autonomous in the first place? Now, one of Schindler's fundamental insights is precisely that the autonomy of created things — philosophy included — is first and foremost a theological reality, whose deepest source and explanation lies in God's Trinitarian being. Schindler insists, especially in his later writings, that the autonomy of creatures is itself a requirement of the (free) economic revelation of God's Trinitarian being in creation and redemption (which form a distinction-in-unity). Consequently, any closure to revealed theology, implicit or explicit, will eventually deprive those so closed of the capacity to understand, affirm, and safeguard precisely autonomy of created things, philosophy included. Or, to put it positively, it is only through God's own self-gift to the world — in creation and redemption — that we can fully affirm the world (and all that is in it) as it ought to be affirmed. "All

W. Norris Clarke, "Response to Long's Comments," and "Response to Blair's Comments," *Communio: International Catholic Review* 21 (1994): 165-171; David L. Schindler, "The Person: Philosophy, Theology, and Receptivity," *Communio: International Catholic Review* 21 (1994): 172-190.

64. "Knowledge as Relationship," 511-519.
65. "Person and Receptivity," 174.

that is in it" emphatically includes human nature and the philosophical act in which human nature comes into its own in a central way.

Following Hans Urs von Balthasar, Schindler describes Jesus Christ himself as the *analogatum princeps* of every distinction between God and creation, between nature and grace, and between faith and philosophy. The mystery of Christ reveals the deepest and most perfect meaning of the "autonomy" of creation, philosophy included. It is helpful to contrast this idea with conventional approaches to the question of nature and grace or reason and faith, approaches that assume that Jesus Christ is relevant to only one side of the relation (i.e., Jesus Christ as the origin and archetype of grace). The teaching of the New Testament as received by the Church makes a much more comprehensive claim: Christ not only reveals the meaning of God and the mystery of his gratuitous communication of himself to creatures; Christ simultaneously reveals what it means to be fully human, indeed, to be fully creaturely. "The Incarnation of God the Son," writes John Paul II, "signifies the taking up into unity with God not only of human nature, but in this human nature, in a sense, of everything that is 'flesh': the whole of humanity, the entire visible and material world" (*Dominum et Vivificantem*, 50). The Incarnate Christ fully reveals the original purpose and structure of creation itself in its abiding distinction from God. For Schindler, the affirmation in paragraph 22 of *Gaudium et Spes* that Christ fully reveals man in fully revealing the Father both presupposes and interprets the teaching of Chalcedon that "the distinction between [Christ's] natures was never abolished by their union, but rather the character proper to each of the two natures was preserved as they came together in one Person."[66]

"Christ's person," Schindler writes, "establishes the real unity which is the context within which the distinction occurs . . . the integrity of Jesus' human nature, which is ever to be maintained (in the words of Chalcedon: *'in duabus naturis inconfuse'*; *'nusquam sublata differentia naturarum propter unitionem'*), is realized not outside but within his divine procession from and to the Father."[67] It is an inner requirement of the divine mission of the Son that he bring to light the true meaning and integrity of human nature in its distinction from the divine nature (*gratia non destruit, elevat, perficit naturam*).[68] This point bears emphasis, since Schindler is some-

---

66. DS, 302.

67. HW, 207.

68. N. Healy, *The Eschatology of Hans Urs von Balthasar: Being as Communion* (Oxford: Oxford University Press, 2005), 116.

times misunderstood to be affirming the opposite. God cannot reveal his being-as-love in the Son's "divine mission" of Incarnation unless he does so within the "integrity of Jesus' human nature, which is ever to be maintained." This statement, let it be noted, is far removed from any "pan-christism" that would misread the hypostatic union as replacing or absorbing into itself the communication of being to created natures at the level of *creatio.* True, the hypostatic union is the paradigm of this *communicatio entis,* but in a paradoxical way, for the Archetype simultaneously depends on what he is the Archetype of. Put more technically: the Son, in becoming Incarnate, not only communicates the divine *esse* to his humanity; at that very instant, and within that very act, he "recapitulates" the human creature's reception of the *actus essendi* within the limits of its creaturely nature. So much so that the Son lets himself depend on the very human nature he creates in the act of assuming it — a dependence expressed in his owing his Incarnation to the Yes of Mary. Mary's actively receptive Yes is creaturely autonomy — enfolded in, yet never simply reduced to, Christ. It is no accident that Schindler's thinking about the *iusta autonomia* of the creature circles continually around the fiat of the Mother of God.

For Schindler, then, the very fact that the integrity of Christ's humanity is an inner requirement of the Son's divine mission implies that this integrity receives its most comprehensive measure in that mission:

> the crux of the matter . . . is that the Son does not actualize the integrity of his human nature outside of, or apart from, the act of receiving his entire being and existence from the Father. To the contrary, the integrity of his human nature is perfected to the extent that it is assumed and taken into his one divine mission and person.[69]

The Son's "dependence" on the Father is the deepest ground of his autonomous being and acting as man. Autonomy includes receptivity. Freedom coincides with (free and loving) obedience. This is true not only for Christ, not only for Mary, but, in and through them, for all humans, indeed, for all creatures. To be sure, the free and loving human obedience of Jesus is the unique act of a divine person that, as such, has its origin from beyond the cosmos. Yet precisely as such it becomes — freely — immanent in the cosmos, indeed, is born from the cosmos (in Mary), and so discloses the deepest nature of the cosmos, whose nature is thereby shown to involve an autonomy-in-relation.

---

69. Healy, *The Eschatology of Hans Urs von Balthasar,* 116.

What we have just said about created being applies, *mutatis mutandis,* to rational reflection on being as such — philosophy. For Schindler, in fact, the autonomy of philosophy is embedded within the circulation of faith and reason — a circulation having a Christological (but not panchristic!) form:

> This paradoxical affirmation of (chalcedonian) Christology thus provides the *analogatum princeps* for understanding properly the relation between faith and reason. It is in the anterior unity between faith and reason in the God of Jesus Christ, as the origin and end of both, that the rightful distinctness between faith and reason occurs. The rightful distinctness of faith and reason, and of their respective formal objects, in other words, cannot be conceived first in terms of juxtaposition, as though in the first instance they lay side by side each other — and, *a fortiori,* not first in terms of opposition. On the contrary, as the encyclical states, "each is found in the other" — differently — , and each one's rightful scope for action occurs precisely within this mutual if asymmetrical penetration. Faith "contains" reason, and reason, in the one historical order of existence, is always-already — albeit implicitly — open from within to the order of faith. In a word, the relation between faith and reason is mutual and asymmetrical, analogous to the way in which the relation between divine and human in Jesus is mutual and asymmetrical. In neither case is the relation first extrinsic and "additive," much less inverse.[70]

It is significant that in the sequel to this passage Schindler goes on to present the coinherence of philosophy and faith through the lens of the connubium between the divine and human in Christ. What has been called the "nuptial mystery," always in the background of Schindler's later writings, is the paradigm of the non-mechanical distinction-in-unity that, for him, embodies the fecundity of being. In this nuptial paradigm, the oneness of being includes, even presupposes in a sense, distinction; the unity of being does not compete with distinction, but lets it be to the extent of depending on the very thing it lets be in this way:

> In a mechanical relation — as illustrated in Descartes, for example — , x and y each retain their integrity only from outside each other, in a state of what we have called juxtaposition. X remains truly distinct from y only by virtue of something like abstract-spatialized lines drawn be-

70. "Knowledge as Relationship," 516-517.

tween them, establishing as it were the boundaries of perfectly separate spheres. On the one hand, any unity between entities so distinguished can be established only "additively," insofar as the elements remain extrinsic (after the manner of a collection or sum). On the other hand, any attempt to make the unity between such entities internal now necessarily takes the form of reduction or confusion (a mixing together that violates the integrity of one or the other, or both). In a relation of love, things are quite different. Here we find a relation wherein the unity of the partners and the rightful distinctness of partners grow directly-intrinsically and not inversely-extrinsically in relation to each other. Each finds his or her integrity from inside and not outside their relationship. Married partners (in a genuine relationship), for example, do not grow less but more free and autonomous as they deepen their unity — even as each one's freedom is now different by virtue of that deepened unity. (The mechanical view of relation seems to imply, on the contrary, that the more you are unrelated, the more you are yourself.)[71]

Elsewhere Schindler describes the unity and autonomy proper to spousal love as follows:

> Consider an authentic love between a husband and a wife: each genuinely shares in the joys and sufferings of the other. "Sharing in" entails "affectivity" being affected by the other. Clearly this "sharing in," with its note of affectivity, is in some sense a perfection: we would hardly consider one who remained indifferent to his or her spouse's joys and sufferings a good love. Nor do we in fact intuitively think of their mutual capacity for being affected as a matter exhaustively of dependence: a kind of emptiness awaiting actualization. Were this the case, it would follow that the more actualized each partner became, the more unaffected by and indifferent to one another each would become; the more perfect the relationship, the less mutual would it become; in a word, the more perfect the person, the more unrelated would he or she become. But we sense instinctively and immediately that this is a perversion of love rather than its perfection.[72]

These two passages mark an important transition from a theological reflection on the (Christological) meaning of autonomy to a properly philo-

---

71. "Knowledge as Relationship," 517.
72. "Person and Receptivity," 172.

sophical reflection on creaturely autonomy. Schindler's claim is precisely that the primacy of the theological approach to autonomy itself requires a relative, but real, primacy of philosophy. For its part, philosophy's own original impulse was never to claim absoluteness, but to participate in the absolute through a transparent relativity (consider the Socratic "I know only what I don't know"). The ancient vocation of philosophy to lovingly seek the whole of truth[73] is both safeguarded and deepened within the astonishing revelation that God is love and the world was created in the image of love.

B. Love as the Meaning of Being

In order to complete the argument sketched above regarding the Christological meaning of autonomy, we need to stress that there is an obvious sense in which Christ comes to philosophy from the outside and must so come to it. The speculative Christologies we find in German Idealism notwithstanding, the appearance of Christ in this world is the supreme grace. Christ's coming is therefore from beginning to end a surprising gift of God above and beyond the bestowal of being in creation, a gift that cannot have its first origin within the world. By the same token, Christ's coming cannot be anticipated or deduced or constructed by any philosophical reflection on the world. Nevertheless, if, as *Fides et Ratio* teaches, Christ is relevant to philosophy as such, then this relevance must also emerge from within the purview of philosophy itself. Christ is, and always remains, *superior summo* to philosophy; yet he must also become — freely and by grace — *interior intimo* with respect to it. Schindler's suggestion is that the best way to do justice to this simultaneous transcendence of, and immanence in, philosophy is to ponder the novelty that, in his view, Christianity brings to philosophy: the insight, namely, that love is the deepest meaning of being, and that "love tells us what it means to act in the highest and deepest sense — and thereby what it means most fully to be."[74]

In order to grasp the import of this claim, we need to understand that Schindler wishes to overcome the identification of love with affectivity —

73. "Do you need to be reminded or do you remember that, if it's rightly said that someone loves something, then he mustn't love one part and not another, but he must love all of it . . . the philosopher doesn't desire one part of wisdom rather than another, but desires the whole thing." Plato, *Republic* V, 474c, 475b.

74. "Person and Receptivity," 174.

without, of course, denying the importance of the emotions. Indeed, Schindler even calls into question the identification of loving with willing, understood as one faculty or activity of the human soul among many. For Schindler, in fact, love is, or is constitutive of, the very *logos* of being, the *ratio entis* as such. As he never tires of repeating, love is an "order," an order seen, for instance, in the fact that the paradigmatic form of distinction is not primitive mutual indifference — as if cold unconcern, and not love, were the heart of things — but a mutual letting be within the being-let-be proper to all things that partake of the *communitas entis* in the light of the non-subsistent act of being.

Schindler's thinking on this point is in some sense a reprise of the Platonic teaching that the relation to the Good is what makes being to be being in the first place; being qua being is *"agathoeides," boniform,* which is why being qua being is beautiful. Nevertheless, Schindler rejects the notion that love is beyond being; there is indeed a "beyond" to love, but it lies within being itself. For Schindler, excess, indeed, fruitfulness is intrinsic to being. It is for this reason that he regards the paradigmatic instance of being, not simply as substance, but as substance constitutively related to the Source of being and, through this Source, to all fellow participants in being. For the same reason, Schindler insists that unity, which for St. Thomas is being-as-undivided, is the letting-be of its own distinctions, and the distinct elements are internally related through a mutual letting be of their own. For the same reason, these distinctions (in their paradigmatic case) are precisely *not* "divisions,"[75] but just that: *distinctions,* the fruit, and just so far also a ground, of the inner excess of being in its indivision. *Indivisio* is not absence of distinction, but communion in love.

Schindler undertakes a creative retrieval of the Thomistic "real dis-

---

75. It is true that St. Thomas says in *De Veritate* I, 1, that the transcendental *aliquid* expresses being insofar as it is "undivided in itself and divided from all others." Nevertheless, one could argue that Thomas is using the notion of division in this passage in two different, though perhaps related senses. For the division from all others that comes to light in the *aliquid* is precisely not a breaking up of the (analogical) community of being, but an inner requirement of it. In this sense, "division" is a synonym for what Schindler means by "distinction." That St. Thomas means something similar becomes clearer when we compare the formulation in *De Veritate* I, 1, to parallel statements, for example, to that of *Summa Theologiae,* I, q. 29, a. 10, where he says that to be a subsisting unit is to be "indistinct with respect to oneself and distinct from all others." Note that "indistinct with respect to oneself" does not mean lacking internal distinction or exempt from what the Germans call *Vermittlung.* It simply means that all these internal distinctions are the distinctions proper to an *unum* — and do not break up that *unum* into two separate beings.

tinction" in order to elaborate this account of being-as-love. In his earlier writings on this topic, Schindler sounds a more (though not exclusively) Gilsonian note: created *esse,* God's proper effect that is distinct from, and endowed with primacy over, essence, is the deepest and most comprehensive actuality of all acts and form of all forms. As such, *esse creatum* is God's creative self-gift at the very heart of created *ens,* which is thus constitutively related to God (and in God to all others) and shaped from within by the logic of the divine self-gift at the level of creation. In his more recent writings, Schindler has developed the (Ulrichian-Balthasarian) implication latent in his more Gilsonian reflection on being-as-gift. That is, since *esse creatum* is non-subsistent, it cannot sovereignly produce or unfold created essences out of itself, but is radically transparent to God's sovereign production of them. One implication of this transparency is that, at the very moment when *esse creatum* (super-formally) causes the "to be" of creaturely essences *ex nihilo,* it "needs" those essences to receive it, thus "presupposing" the very thing it causes in the act of causing them and as an inner dimension of the perfection of that act! The wealth of *esse creatum* includes a poverty — a poverty that not only distinguishes it radically from *ipsum esse subsistens,* but also reveals the latter's own primary unity of poverty and wealth, making God present at the heart of his creature as the paradigmatic fullness of being-as-love. Indeed, this consideration shifts the focus away from *esse* alone to the mutual letting be of *esse* and essence, which alone does justice to the order or logos of being as love.

Schindler's account of being-as-love culminates, then, in a retrieval of *esse creatum* as a kind of creaturely "language" into which God can speak his self-emptying Word of love through the Incarnation. Needless to say, Schindler denies that the economy of the Son's Incarnation is simply contained within *esse creatum* as this *esse* is communicated at the level of creation. The Incarnation has its first origin from (infinitely) beyond — or "before" — the reach of created *esse.* Nevertheless, as we have already seen, the Word, in becoming Incarnate, does not simply communicate the *esse divinum* to his assumed humanity; within that act, he also virtually contains, or recapitulates from within, the "experience" of receiving *esse creatum* from the Creator inside the limits of human nature. In this sense, the love revealed in Jesus does emerge, albeit always by a free grace, from within the reach of created *esse.* Indeed, it emerges from within the poverty built into created *esse's* wealth as the actuality of all acts; it emerges within created *esse's* "dependence" on the very essence it super-formally makes be. Again, the love revealed in Jesus does not have its primary origin from within created *esse*'s self-emptying into essence, or from the interplay between *esse creatum* and *essentia creata*. The point is simply that it has — by God's free and gracious choice — a secondary and subordinate origin there. Precisely in its radical transcendence of created being, the *caritas Dei in Christo* touches it from within its innermost core, recapitulating its deepest meaning as love. Indeed, if we remember that Christ owes his Incarnation in a secondary sense to the fiat of Mary, the archetypal creature, then we can say that the appearing of the *caritas Dei in Christo* owes itself in a secondary sense to the depths of the creature, whose depths it fully reveals for the first time in that owing.

IV. Conclusion

The notion of "Christian philosophy" implies that faith makes a difference to philosophy without thereby collapsing philosophy into theology. Schindler would be the first to acknowledge that the love of God revealed in the Incarnation "adds" something radically new to philosophy from outside its properly rational consideration of reality, whose deepest center is the pondering of the real distinction. In this respect, Schindler agrees with Gilson that Christian revelation has contributed, not just new inspiration, but also new content, to the philosophical enterprise. At the same time, Schindler would deny the charge of Van Steenberghen, McInerny, and Maritain that such a contribution necessarily violates the autonomy of philosophy. Why does it not? Because the content that revelation contributes to philosophy is in the end nothing other than the theme of themes proper to philosophy itself: being qua being, now seen in its own deepest meaning as love. To be sure, this "nothing other than," like the *Non aliud* of Nicholas of Cusa it echoes, is paradoxical: it is the wholly other — and only the wholly other — that is truly non-other. But that is just the point: it is precisely insofar as the *caritas Dei in Christo* appears from beyond the purview of created *ens* that it can emerge, indeed, receive itself from — and so disclose for the first time — the latter's deepest depth. It is the novel that is the key to what always already was. Surprise, even dramatic surprise, is the heart of rationality.

For Schindler, the autonomy of philosophy is Marian. It remains true, of course, that we could not even talk about the Marian character of philosophy had it not been for Mary's actual fiat. Nevertheless, to think about that autonomy enfolded within her fiat is not simply to do theology. It is also to do philosophy. Indeed, it is in some sense to do philosophy first, just as Mary's fiat was (by free grace) the prior condition of the Incarnation itself. Indeed, the Marian fiat is an endlessly fruitful recapitulation of the permanent source of philosophy itself: wonderment. Indeed, this wonderment was never simply an experience of autonomy; it was always the reception of an autonomy pervaded by relativity, the gift of a self-sufficiency that is such only by participation in the Good through humility before its mysterious *excessus* at the core of all intelligibility. Knowing God's love revealed in Christ does not provide the philosopher with any "answers" that would bypass this genuine philosophical task. On the contrary, it "urges" the philosopher to be faithful *usque ad finem* to philosophy's autonomy on its own terms, to patiently remain with the evidence that is available to reason. The Christian will remain longer with philosophy because of his or her faith. Faith helps reason to see that there is a secret at the heart of reality that never ceases to provoke wonder and gratitude. David Schindler's work bears witness to the essential truth that philosophical wonder depends on a childlike heart that receives all of reality as a gift.

"Constitutive Relations":
Toward a Spiritual Reading of *Physis*

Adrian J. Walker

I. Introduction

The title the editors have chosen for this volume of essays — *Being Holy in the World* — nicely captures one of the deepest sources of David L. Schindler's genius: his passion to get to the core of things, and, once there, to give over his entire existence to rendering it the greatest possible justice in the most comprehensive and most subtle possible speech. By entitling this book *Being Holy in the World,* in other words, its editors remind us that Schindler is a philosopher in the tradition of Plato and Aristotle, a man whose great theme is nothing less than the question of the "really real" and its Principle — of being and its relation to God.

Heideggerian-inclined readers will therefore be tempted to write Schindler off as a hopeless onto-theologian. They will be wrong, however. Schindler does indeed unapologetically preach and practice metaphysics.[1] Nevertheless, he knows that, as Thomas Prufer puts it, "God and creatures together are not the last whole."[2] He also holds that part of the metaphysical enterprise is precisely the effort to clear room for the advent of the "godly God,"[3] who defies any attempt to imprison him within some supposedly all-encompassing Ultimate Whole of our own making. And yet, Schindler, unlike most so-called "Continental Philosophy of Religion," avoids what I consider to be Heidegger's great mistake of propounding a

---

1. Cf. HW, 275-311.
2. Thomas Prufer, *Recapitulations: Essays in Philosophy* (Washington, DC: Catholic University of America Press, 1993), 40.
3. Martin Heidegger, *Identität und Differenz* (Pfullingen: Günther Neske, 1957), 165.

Adrian J. Walker

pseudo-negative theology that plays this godly God off against intelligible, determinate form.[4] Putting the same point positively, we can say that Schindler's metaphysics is *Catholic:* it thinks from the Incarnation, in which the "godly God" (here no longer just a cypher for *Seyn*) reveals his "godliness" as *Fatherhood* — in the womb of the Virgin Mary, who brings forth the paternal fruitfulness, the Son, without violating its transcendent godliness. Schindler shares Benedict XVI's conviction that "God does not become godlier by our removing him into a pure and inscrutable voluntarism. Rather, the truly godly God is the God who has shown himself as Logos and as Logos has lovingly acted for us and continues to do so."[5]

Schindler's readers are familiar with his hallmark claim that relation to God is constitutive of things full stop, and that relation to other things, enfolded within the primordial relation to God, is co-constitutive of them.[6] This "Constitutive Relation Thesis" (= CRT) is a record of Schindler's passionate effort to give adequate expression to the appearing of the More-Than-World from within the world in the circumincession of the transcendentals and at the intersection of nature and grace, philosophy and revelation. I do not wish to claim that CRT is the exclusive key to Schindler's rich and fecund thought, but only that it is one of many possible golden threads through it. I will venture to say, though, that CRT recommends itself because, as we will see in what follows, it contains, in germ at least, a precise, technical account of how the appearing of the More-Than-World in the world unites, without confusion or separation, things that conventional thinking tends to hold apart: divine immanence and transcendence, dependence on God and creaturely integrity, the primacy of revelation and the "subordinate priority" of philosophy.[7] CRT, then, brings to the fore Schindler's genius for overcoming dualism without leaving behind duality, an aspect of his thought from which I have personally benefited very much. My task in what follows, then, will be to present CRT

4. For a superb critique of Heidegger on this point, see D. C. Schindler, "'Wie kommt der Mensch in die Theologie?': Heidegger, Hegel, and the Stakes of Onto-Theo-Logy," *Communio: International Catholic Review* 32 (2005): 637-668.

5. Here is the same quotation but in a different translation: "God does not become more divine when we push him away from us in a sheer, impenetrable voluntarism; rather, the truly divine God is the God who has revealed himself as logos and, as logos, has acted and continues to act lovingly on our behalf." Benedict XVI, "Faith, Reason, and the University" (lecture at the University of Regensburg on September 12, 2006).

6. Cf. WPHD.

7. I borrow the phrase "subordinate priority" from David Crawford.

primarily from the angle of the "first, all-pervasive (transcendental) property of being"[8] that is the *unum,* relating the beautiful-good-true appearing of the More-Than-World in the world back to what I will call below the "fruitful" — which is to say: triune — unity of the Father revealed from the womb of Mary.[9] It is no accident that Schindler's thought gravitates toward the *Theotokos,* who is the *concretissimum* of mystery of being as the appearing of the More-Than-World in the world.[10]

The following essay seeks to show the plausibility of CRT against the backdrop of Schindler's intellectual concerns, first mainly, though not exclusively, by way of straightforward commentary (section II), then mainly, though not exclusively, by way of a free variation on Schindlerian themes that I hope he will recognize as a creatively faithful, which is to say grateful, retrieval of his thought — proof of its abiding power to generate thought in others (sections III-VI). Concretely, I want to show how CRT is an entryway into what I see as Schindler's project of reconciling Christian novelty with classical metaphysics in what Balthasar calls a "third way" of love that integrates what is best both in the ancients and in the moderns.[11] This project requires in turn what I will call a "spiritual reading" of Aristotelian *physis* (i.e., "nature" in an inner sense) which both transforms and preserves what the Stagirite understood nature to be. The result of this spiritual exegesis is the

---

8. Hans Urs von Balthasar, *Epilogue* (San Francisco: Ignatius Press, 2004), 55.

9. The wonder-provoking appearing of the More-Than-World from within the heart or womb of the world itself is the *arche* of Schindler's thought, as it is of all great philosophy and theology. It is thus no surprise that Schindler speaks again and again of the "primacy of beauty." At the same time, Schindler holds that the appearing of the More-Than-World from within the world is not just the outshining of beauty, but also drama. Schindler sees at the heart of things meaning — meaning, however, that contains event and fruitfulness, novelty and surprise, not as random unraveling, but as the inner richness of *logos* itself. Drama, in Schindler's sense, is not open-ended explosiveness, but the gratuitous, non-arbitrary convergence of eternity and time, necessity and freedom, form and event. By the same token, the appearing of the More-Than-World from within the world is not only dramatic, for Schindler, but logical: an intelligible, reliable confirmation of the reality of the appearing of the More-Than-World from within the world, which puts love at the heart of meaning, mystery at the core of rationality. The three Balthasarian transcendentals *(pulchrum, bonum, verum)* are, for Schindler as for Balthasar himself, circumincessive dimensions of one and the same appearing of the More-Than-World from within the world; they fill out the concreteness of the "analogy of being," which in turn makes possible what Schindler likes to call an "intrinsic" relation between nature and grace, philosophy and revelation.

10. Cf. HW; "Creation and Nuptiality."

11. See Hans Urs von Balthasar, *Love Alone Is Credible* (San Francisco: Ignatius Press, 2004), 51ff.

securing of the non-neutrality of nature vis-à-vis specifically Christian revelation[12] — but without dissolving nature into history in the name of that "dehellenization" which is alive and well in much of postmodern philosophy and theology, although under assumed names. Here Mary is the archetype, in that her virginal motherhood shows how nature can be open to the communication of the Trinitarian fruitfulness of the Father in Christ — and precisely so be most fully itself as nature. In developing these themes, I will be highlighting again and again the importance of Schindler's dialogue with Henri de Lubac and Hans Urs von Balthasar. My purpose in so doing is not to attempt to trace Schindler's "influences," but to illustrate the appositeness of the old saying that the quality of a man can be judged by the company he keeps. De Lubac and Balthasar, for their part, complement each other as helps to understanding what Schindler is about, the former shedding light particularly on the non-neutrality of nature, the latter shedding light particularly on how this non-neutrality allows the fruitfulness of the Father to appear in the world, centrally in the *Gestalt* of Christ.

I begin, then, by relating CRT to Schindler's concern to overcome dualism by opening up the non-neutrality of nature with respect to specifically Christian revelation. At the end of this opening discussion, I will suggest the hypothesis that CRT, as a claim about the non-neutrality of nature vis-à-vis Christ, is best understood in light of de Lubac's theology of nature and grace (section II). This hypothesis sets up the transition to the next section, where I will consider the non-neutrality of nature as a flashpoint in the encounter between Aristotle and Christian revelation, an encounter that calls for what I will call a "spiritual reading" of the former's understanding of nature in the light of the latter (section III). As we will see, this reading involves for Schindler the discovery of a certain motion from and to God in nature qua principle, and this motion best corresponds to what Schindler means by "constitutive relation to God." Since this affirmation of motion in the principle might seem like a flat contradiction to the strict Aristotelian, I propose to continue by resolving the apparent contradiction by drawing on what I take to be Schindler's creative reconstruction of the Thomistic doctrine of creation (itself a spiritual reading of sorts — section IV), as well as

12. By "specifically Christian revelation," I mean three interrelated things. First, I mean the revealed items that the Thomistic tradition distinguishes from those deemed in principle accessible to natural reason, such as the Trinity, the Incarnation, and the Eucharist. Second, I mean these items insofar as they make Christianity *religions-* and *geistesgeschichtlich* unique. Third, I mean this unique reality seen in one of its (for Schindler) central implications: love is somehow constitutive of the *logos* of being.

showing how Schindler goes beyond Thomas Aquinas himself in interpreting relationality as intrinsic to the perfection of act as such (section V). Here the Balthasarian complement to de Lubac will begin to play an important role, inasmuch as the motion-relation Schindler discovers at nature's heart is what I will call a "fruitfulness" that reflects, through the distance of analogy, the ur-fruitfulness of the Father, the revelation of whom is for the same reason the source of the spiritual reading of the Aristotelian account of nature. Having done this, I will conclude by suggesting how the virginal *Theotokos* is the living quintessence of the heart of the world from which the More-Than-World appears. She is the non-neutrality of nature, and so, literally, the matrix of a new ontology (section VI). Through her womb, the risen Christ, with the pervasive, but non-invasive subtlety of the Spirit, penetrates nature, not to destroy it, but to be born from it in this world and the next as the inexhaustible fruitfulness of the Father.

II. Constitutive Relations and Non-neutrality

The task before me in this section is, as just noted, to set forth CRT as an expression of Schindler's oft-repeated claim that nature, as such, is non-neutral with respect to specifically Christian revelation.[13] This claim raises three questions whose discussion will lay the groundwork for the rest of the essay: (1) Why is it important that nature should be non-neutral with respect to specifically Christian revelation? (2) What is so important about nature? (3) What does this non-neutrality have to do with CRT? I would like now to address each of these three questions in turn.

(1) Schindler is one of the (often unacknowledged) pioneers of the movement to "re-theologize theology" that has been steadily gaining ground in the English-speaking world in the last twenty years or so.[14] Schindler's offer also anticipates this movement's critique of the schizophrenia that characterizes modern Christianity and that often goes under the name of "dualism." In Schindler's account, this schizophrenia consists in a compartmentalization of the Christian soul into two unconnected

---

13. Cf. Schindler, "Grace and the Form of Nature and Culture," in *Catholicism and Secularization in America,* ed. David L. Schindler (Huntington, IN: Our Sunday Visitor, 1990); "Religion and Secularity."

14. For both the term and an account of the movement it stands for, see William L. Portier, "Here Come the Evangelical Catholics," *Communio: International Catholic Review* 31 (2004): 35-66.

halves. One half of this divided Christian soul is a mind that has capitu-
lated to modernity's secular reason. This leaves the other half of the Christian soul for an unworldly piety that for this very reason no longer has any
purchase on reality.[15] For Schindler, the first step toward overcoming
modern Christian schizophrenia is to realize that modernity, shaped outside of the obedience of the *Catholica,* yet in reaction to it, is not neutral
with respect to the claims of specifically Christian revelation. By the same
token, he seeks to break down the notion that the world itself is neutral
with respect to that revelation — a notion born, says Schindler, of nature-
grace dualism in Catholic theology and taken over, in altered form, as one
of the chief features of the modern account of the "really real."[16]

Schindler's critique of the modern claim of the world's neutrality takes
its best-known form in a powerful critique of liberalism. Schindler does not
make things easy for himself by focusing, say, on the rabid anti-clericalism
of Jacobin French liberalism; rather, he concentrates on the apparently tol-
erant liberalism of the English-speaking world. For, at first sight, this
English-speaking liberalism appears to be perfectly harmless toward religion, indeed, even friendly to it. After all, it claims to do no more than offer
citizens the freedom to choose their own solutions to the ultimate questions
uncoerced. Some have even argued — most notably the "Catholic Neo-
conservatives," such as Michael Novak, Richard John Neuhaus, and George
Weigel[17] — that this immunity from coercion is actually a positive, albeit
indirect, encouragement to seek and embrace religion. In response,
Schindler points out that the *privileging* of immunity from coercion vis-à-
vis religion entails that — as far as the public order is concerned — relation
to God is effectively a matter of choice.[18] In this respect, Anglo-American

15. Cf. "Trinity, Creation, and the Academy."

16. For Schindler's account of the theological roots of modernity, see his "Introduction
to the 1998 Edition," in *The Mystery of the Supernatural* by Henri de Lubac (New York:
Crossroad Publishing, 1998), xi-xxxi.

17. For Schindler's debate with the Catholic neo-conservatives, see chapters 1-5 of HW;
see also his "Christological Aesthetics and *Evangelium Vitae:* Toward a Definition of Liberalism," *Communio: International Catholic Review* 22 (1995): 193-224; see also, more recently,
WPHD, 347-413; "Truth, Freedom, and Relativism."

18. It should be borne in mind that Schindler does not reject immunity from coercion,
but seeks to subordinate it to a larger context of meaning. For Schindler, freedom is for
truth, even as freedom is intrinsic to the truth. For an excellent discussion of the truth-
freedom relation and the problem of immunity from coercion, see David L. Schindler, "Reorienting the Church on the Eve of the Millennium: John Paul II's 'New Evangelization,'"
Communio: International Catholic Review 24 (1997): 728-779.

liberalism's supposedly benign "neutrality[1]" is not at all the fair evenhand-edness it is alleged to be, but the tacit enshrinement of "neutrality[2]," the substantive, though often hidden, claim that nature — especially human nature — is constitutionally empty of any relation to God.[19] Anglo-American liberalism actually amounts to the creation of a public orthodoxy that drifts inevitably in the direction of human self-construction, and so to-ward atheism. Schindler has brilliantly shown how this subtle atheism, sit-ting unnoticed at the heart of American religiosity, blinds many to the col-lusion — at the level of logical entailment, and not of intention — between the founding principles of the liberal order and the denial of the good givenness of (physical) nature that links apparently disparate phenomena like bio-engineering and the push for gay marriage.[20]

This last point reminds us of the connection between Schindler's cri-tique of liberalism and his critique of mechanistic science, which reaches far back into his intellectual biography. This connection is unsurprising, for the new mechanistic science — essentially technological in character — and the new politics of modernity arose in tandem as mutually condi-tioning dimensions of a single "project," whose unifying theme is that na-ture is empty of any discernible teleology.[21] Schindler, not contenting him-

---

19. The neo-conservatives themselves recognize that the empty freedom of choice guaranteed on their view by the democratic state and the free market is, taken by itself in the abstract, an incomplete, even untrue representation of what a "thick" anthropology would construe freedom to be. Their goal is to seek to overcome this emptiness — without a restorationist overturning of immunity from coercion, a goal with which, stated broadly, Schindler himself agrees. The neo-conservatives attempt to negotiate this task by maintain-ing liberalism's clean theoretical separation of state, market, and society or culture, while in-terpreting this separation as the opportunity for freedom to fill up its own emptiness by drawing on sources from the cultural sphere. In this way they seek to unite in praxis the thick freedom of culture with the thin and empty juridical freedom of the market and the state as such. Schindler's first criticism is that this method of reconciling the primacy of the Good with juridical freedom repeats the old pure nature hypothesis in the garb of a theoreti-cally purely empty, purely unmoved choice. His second criticism, like unto the first, is that the ideology-institutions distinction is untenable, that state and the market are already cul-ture. Thus, to construe them as theoretically empty is already to define that culture as liberal. Moreover, once the principle of empty freedom is enshrined in the two domains where the real world does its real business in the liberal regime — the state and the market — it is only a matter of time before that principle eats up whatever Christian substance might be left on the cultural margins of those all-important areas.

20. Cf. "Significance of World and Culture."

21. See, for example, George Grant, *English-speaking Justice* (Notre Dame: University of Notre Dame Press, 1985).

self merely with a recovery of the distinctiveness of Christian discourse vis-à-vis secular reason, has attempted to expose, critique, and provide an alternative to mechanism.[22] Put positively, he has tried to show, in great and careful detail, how specifically Christian revelation is, through a series of analogical mediations, "intrinsically" relevant to the method and content even of the physical sciences.[23] Schindler's aim has not been to absorb the secular sciences into theology, but rather to help them into their true worldliness by freeing them from the false theologies of secularity that tacitly shape them under the guise of methodological "neutrality[1]."[24] For Schindler, specifically Christian revelation is either the key, not only to the depths of God, but also to the "heart of the world" — or else it is simply false, boring, and ugly.[25]

(2) Schindler's most recent work on bioethics reveals his conviction that the Aristotelian account of *physis,* reread in light of creation out of nothing, is the best alternative to mechanistic science.[26] Schindler lays particular stress on Aristotle's fundamental distinction between nature and artifice,[27] which sets a permanent limit to technology: not only is nature unmanufactur*ed* as a matter of fact, but it is essentially unmanufactur*able* in principle.[28] This is especially the case of living nature, whose offspring are "begotten, not made."[29]

At the same time, although the distinction between nature and artifice "goes all the way down,"[30] and nature is a bottomless depth, this depth is

22. See, for example, BM.

23. See, for example, David L. Schindler, "The Catholic Academy and the Order of Intelligence: The Dying of the Light?" *Communio: International Catholic Review* 26 (1999): 722; "Trinity, Creation, and the Academy," 406-428.

24. In this respect, Schindler differs from, say, John Milbank, who dismisses secularity as a myth. For Schindler, Christocentrism means precisely that the directly, not inversely, proportionate strength with which the divine and the human are affirmed in Christ is the "formula" for interpreting the formal structure of the God-world relation itself.

25. See, for example, "Toward a Culture of Life"; "Significance of World and Culture."

26. See, above all, "Reply to Austriaco."

27. See, for example, Aristotle, *Physics,* II, 1: 192b8-193a1.

28. Nature can, of course, be created, but creation is not a manufacture. It is precisely the impartation of a non-manufacturable being. God does not create an "artificial world" made of plastic like a fake flower, but precisely a natural world that, like a living flower, looks and feels real because it *is.*

29. See "The Meaning of the Human."

30. The nature-artifice distinction goes "all the way down." This means that it is constitutive of the world, both because the world articulates itself first into the makeable and the unmakeable and because the divine nature, which is the source of the world's being, is

not irrational, but manifests itself in characteristic operations, which have a meaningful relationship to the world around them. As Goethe would say centuries later, *"nichts ist drinnen, nichts ist draußen/Denn was innen ist, das ist außen."*[31] For the same reason, nature remains mystery beyond, but manifested in, the moving interplay between inside and outside — an image fit for the Incarnation of the Infinite: *heilig-öffentliches Geheimnis,* to cite Goethe again.[32] By the same token, Aristotle's *physis* recommends itself as a key component of Schindler's effort to break down the modern dualism between the world and specifically Christian revelation.[33] For Schindler, nature — especially in what he calls the "nuptial body" — is apt for the expression of being-as-love, and so is open from its core to specifically Christian revelation (which begins, after all, with the Son's assumption of human nature from the womb of a woman). This is not a plea for irrationality, but for the restoration of mystery to the heart of reason.[34]

(3) In order to grasp what CRT has to do with the non-neutrality of nature vis-à-vis Christian revelation, we need to recall Schindler's well-known commitment to a robust Christocentrism. This Christocentrism is

---

unmakeable par excellence — although it is communicable: in identity within itself and *per participationem* to us.

31. "Nothing is inside, nothing is outside/What is inside, that is outside." Johann Wolfgang von Goethe, "Epirrhema," cited after *Goethe: Natur* (Munich-Zurich: Droemer-Knaur, 1962), 74.

32. "Sacred[ly]-public mystery." Johann Wolfgang von Goethe, "Epirrhema."

33. Isn't this — an objector might ask — a relapse into an objectivist mode of thinking, which tries to reconstruct the world apart from its givenness to consciousness? Schindler does not deny the contribution of subjectivity to constituting the world. In fact, he explicitly affirms it. Nevertheless, Schindler remains convinced that the meaningfulness of the world for consciousness is not simply an achievement of consciousness, individual or transcendental. Like Balthasar in *Theo-Logic,* vol. 1, Schindler holds that the very setting of the conditions of the possibility of things meaningfully appearing is itself co-given by those things themselves. The physical is precisely not brute "thereness," but is a co-condition of consciousness in a non-psychologistic sense because already saturated with *logos* out of an inner depth of its own, and that depth is nature. By the same token, Schindler argues that the structure of consciousness — which he exposits using Balthasar's discussion of the "mother's smile" — reflects something like Henri de Lubac's "paradox of man": man's highest determinacy is to be a hyper-determinate readiness for the revelation of another that he cannot anticipate, and this already on the "natural level." The truth, as Balthasar argues in *Theo-Logic,* vol. 1, is neither inside nor outside, in the "subject" nor in the "object," nor even simply in their interplay, but in a subtle, hard-to-pin-down richness that enables that interplay, appears in it, yet is not a member of it: for Schindler, the non-subsistent *actus essendi.*

34. That mystery is an inner dimension of intelligibility is one of Schindler's most basic theses.

not new to Schindler, but is implied in the basic Christian claim that Jesus is Lord, which says that a *man,* Jesus of Nazareth, has *become* the *Pantokrator.*[35] Now, in becoming *Pantokrator,* Jesus simultaneously reveals the Father (and so the Trinity)[36] and shows himself to be the one in whom "all things hold together" (Col. 1:17). His exaltation to cosmic lordship is thus an event that affects the whole of reality, "in heaven, on earth, and under the earth" (Phil. 2:10). By the same token, to "realize," in Newman's sense, the claim that Jesus is Lord is to be obliged to see everything anew. If Jesus is indeed Lord, then everything in the universe must somehow reflect this overwhelmingly decisive fact, and there must be in some real sense a corresponding "Christian view of everything from soup to nuts," as the neo-Calvinist philosopher Roy Clouser humorously puts it[37] — everything, *including Aristotle's account of nature.* For Schindler, in fact, it is not enough simply to recover Aristotle against modernity; it is also necessary to rethink Aristotle's account of nature in order to open it to the novelty of grace — a task whose failure leads to modernity.[38]

Schindler often argues that the Achilles' heel of Western metaphysics is what he calls the "principle of identity" (A = A). More specifically with respect to Aristotle, he agrees (in part) with Hegel's critique of the Aristotelian understanding of substance/nature, which, according to Hegel, expresses a kind of ontological "siege mentality," in which self-identity re-

35. Of course, Jesus was always the Incarnate Son of God. Nevertheless, during the time of his earthly mission — so from his conception until his Resurrection — this Incarnate Son of God agreed to withhold from his humanity the glory that belonged to it by right. It was only on being raised from the dead that Jesus, as man, recovered the glory that he had with the Father before the foundation of the world (cf. John 17:5).

36. In being exalted to the status of *Pantokrator* at the right hand of the Father, Jesus is manifested as always having been the Son of God whose glory was temporarily veiled in the "form of a slave" (Phil. 2:7) during the time of his earthly mission. By the same token, he reveals God as always having been a Father. The Holy Spirit, who gets poured out by and through the risen Lord as the eschatological gift (cf. Acts 2:32-33), also pertains to this eternal intimacy between the Father and the Son that is now fully manifested and communicated *ad extra.*

37. Roy Clouser, "Is There a Christian View of Everything from Soup to Nuts?" *Pro Rege* 31 (June 2003): 1-10. I would like to note that Schindler would disagree heartily with Clouser's rejection of traditional metaphysics (which he inherits from his intellectual master, Herman Dooyeweerd). I would also stress that Schindler does not regard this Christian view of everything as a deductive system drawn from revelation. More on this below.

38. One of the main themes of Prufer's *Recapitulations* is that modernity is made possible by the divorce of the world-transcendent freedom revealed in Christianity from nature and the consequent secularization of that divorce.

quires an "ultimate indifference to others."[39] We could put the problem like this: Aristotle's account of *physis* is "ambiguous," insofar as it is commanded by an ideal of God as a "mover" that is "unmoved" in every significant sense. If, however, Christ, dead and risen, now holds sway over all of reality, including the reality of nature, then, Schindler argues, nature's ideal pattern can no longer be simply an "unmoved mover." If Christ's *kenosis* penetrates to the core of nature, then that core, almost by definition, cannot be an immovable invulnerability. Rather, nature must somehow include a being-affected-by-another in its very identity as nature. Relation (in the sense of being-affected-by-another) must be constitutive of nature. In this sense, CRT is a sort of synecdoche of Schindler's general conviction that the "event" of specifically Christian revelation — the Incarnation, life, Passion, and Resurrection of Jesus — "affects" both human and cosmic nature "intrinsically," that is, in a more-than-accidental fashion. For the same reason, it is the "acid test" of whether nature is non-neutral with respect to that specifically Christian revelation.

Clearly, Schindler is trying to walk a very fine line here. On the one hand, he argues that, if Christianity does not somehow "affect" nature from within, it cannot sustain its claim to unveil the meaning of reality as a whole, and we must surrender to modern dualism. On the other hand, Schindler knows that, if we mishandle this "affection," we will pay for the non-neutrality of nature by sacrificing it altogether to historicism, and so deprive Christ of the very foothold in the structure of worldly reality that we are trying to secure him. In order to negotiate the Scylla of neutral nature and the Charybdis of historicism, Schindler draws on Henri de Lubac's thesis that created spiritual natures, as such, desire an end that, paradoxically, they have no natural capacity to attain on their own (a thesis Schindler develops in the perspective of the robust Christocentrism of the affirmation of *Gaudium et Spes,* 22, that "Christ reveals man to himself"). This thesis is helpful for the tricky navigation Schindler must undertake because it reconciles nature's determinate immanent perfection with a "hyper-determinate" (Kenneth Schmitz) inexhaustibility within nature's own limits as an establisher of membership in the human species — an inexhaustibility

39. These phrases come from Kenneth Schmitz. For an informative account of Hegel's critique of the classical understanding of substance — and for the context from which the above cited phrases come — see Kenneth L. Schmitz, "Substance Is Not Enough: Hegel's Slogan: From Substance to Subject," in *The Metaphysics of Substance: Proceedings of the American Catholic Philosophical Association,* ed. Daniel O. Dahlstrom (Washington, DC: CUA Press, 1987), 52-68; in particular, 56.

that then, when grace is given, can be seen to have been an intrinsic openness to it.[40] This brings us to the claim that is the burden of CRT: the Christian event reveals, *in actus exercitu,* that nature is so constituted, already on the creation side of the God-creation relation, that its very being-in-itself, taken as a whole, *itself* has its being in Another (which is also "Non-Other"). Let us now begin our exploration of that claim by setting it in the context of what I will be calling a "spiritual reading" or "exegesis" of Aristotelian *physis* (section III). This will then set the stage for a discussion of how CRT concretely transforms while preserving Aristotle's concerns regarding nature (sections IV-V) and, in light of that, for a brief concluding account of what the non-neutrality of that nature vis-à-vis Christ means concretely for our approach to it, especially in the sciences (section VI).

III. CRT as a Spiritual Exegesis of Aristotle

CRT places Schindler right at the heart of the central debate in twentieth-century Catholic theology: the *querelle* between neo-scholasticism, with its emphasis on immutable natures, and various attempts to integrate "historicity" in one form or another into the theological enterprise. These at-

---

40. What I have called, borrowing from Kenneth Schmitz, "hyper-determinacy" is not at all indeterminate; indeed, it is a determinacy so determinate that it cannot be fully captured simply within the determinate limits of essence or form. Hyper-determinacy does not erase those limits, of course. Rather, it expresses itself within the limits of form and establishes them solidly — while simultaneously transcending them. By the same token, hyper-determinacy does not cancel definitely graspable form, but builds into it an inexhaustibility, a "more-than-can-be-definitely-grasped." The point, then, is this: the "more" just mentioned is not the enemy of essential form's definite graspability, but rather the inner condition of it, in the sense that the whatness of essential form is a one-many (as Plotinus would say) that as such does not owe its unity simply to itself, but to itself in dependence on a higher principle of oneness. When, therefore, I say above that human nature is inexhaustible in its own limits as an establisher of membership in the human species, I do not mean that we cannot definitely know, say, that Tom is an individual human being from conception on. The point is rather that this definite knowledge contains at every stage an implicit awareness of a "more" such that, as we see looking back from the platform of grace given, Tom has to become God (by grace) in order fully to justify even the definite knowledge we had of him as an individual human being from the beginning. Grace will surprise us by showing us Tom in a new, unexpected light — which shines from the resurrection that follows Tom's death — and yet precisely by doing that it will also confirm what we always already knew about him. Here we already discern the rhythm of the spiritual reading of *physis* that will occupy us in the next section of this essay.

tempts fall into two main schools. The one school essentially follows liberal Protestantism in taking modern historical consciousness as the standard against which Christian revelation must be measured.[41] The other school, which the papacies of John Paul II and Benedict XVI have proved to be more than a school, follows Henri de Lubac in using modern historicity as an occasion for rediscovering the authentically Christian sense of history as a corrective to neo-scholastic dualism — but without dissolving nature in favor of a raw historicism. Such, I take it, is the goal that lies behind CRT: not to dissolve nature in favor of history as ceaseless self-creation in the modern sense, but to bring Christian novelty to birth out of nature, in order to lay both the ancients and the moderns at Christ's feet. It seems to me that this project is still quite timely, in that, as I said in the introduction, most postmodern and post-liberal theology is still pursuing old-fashioned "dehellenization" in up-to-date French *haute couture*.

As we have already suggested, Schindler tries to steer his project of reconciling Aristotelian nature and Christian history between two dangerous extremes. On the one hand, he wants to avoid a dualistic juxtaposition between Aristotelian nature and Christian history, as if the latter were — to use a metaphor current in the critique of the neo-scholastic theology of nature and grace — a second storey built upon the former in an extrinsic fashion. On the other hand, Schindler's project has to avoid undermining the abiding truth in Aristotle's insistence on a certain static immutability of nature, lest we dissolve this nature into the unstable flux where becoming one-sidedly gains the upper hand over being, and it becomes impossible to say anything intelligibly about anything at all. This double desideratum demands, on Schindler's view, that we approach nature both "from above," that is, in terms of Christian novelty communi-

---

41. The debate between neo-scholasticism and historicity is, in turn, a modern echo of the ancient tension between Athens and Jerusalem, which Leo Strauss identifies as constitutive for Western thought. If we take Aristotle as standing for Athens (admittedly a somewhat reductive move), the question at issue is this: Is the First Principle immobile in every respect — or does the Principle also have a history in some sense? Much of Patristic and medieval theology can be read as an attempt to answer this question without sacrificing either philosophy or revelation, God's status as Principle or his status as Person. This attempt was arguably only partially successful, and its incompleteness was at least a *praeparatio remota* for modernity. At this point, the Athens and Jerusalem debate takes on a new form: the moderns use history to dissolve Aristotelian nature, while secularizing history into a ceaseless self-creation through technology. For a complementary account, see Benedict XVI, "Faith, Reason, and the University" (cited in note 5 above). Benedict emphasizes the turn to history in Protestantism.

cated in graced history, and "from below," in terms of a philosophy of nature that opens *physis* to, but that does not dissolve it in, that graced history — thus revealing to the retrospective view *post revelationem datam* that the inherent structure of nature was all along an availability for something like Christian novelty without recourse to anything like a Rahnerian "supernatural existential."

I would like to stress the retrospective nature of the view from grace to the non-neutrality of nature. Schindler knows perfectly well, in fact, that we cannot deduce Christianity from what we take to be the exigencies of nature, partly because we do not know fully what those exigencies are until Christ comes to claim nature for himself. At the same time, Schindler would insist that it is precisely this incommensurability between expectation and fulfillment that, in hindsight, appears as the index of the correspondence or fit between grace and nature. For the whole burden of CRT is precisely that nature, already as nature, possesses a constitutive yearning to be fulfilled, not simply on its terms, but on the terms of the Creator, even as his fulfilling intervention (which, given the nature of the case, must be historical) will in some respects reverse that yearning precisely because it is not in nature's power to program. Consequently, just as the lover discovers after falling in love that his happiness always really did depend essentially on this particular woman whose appearance in his life was a surprising gift, so, too, the retrospective believing gaze will discover in nature itself all sorts of unexpected anticipations and openings to Christ — even though no one could have known them to be such before Christ actually came. By the same token, even though Aristotle could not explicitly recognize foreshadowings of Christ in the structure of nature under their proper name, he could certainly have known them so to say anonymously under an alias. If, then, Aristotle could have been implicitly engaged, depending on the intrinsic quality of his wonderment, with either opening or closing the possibility of something like Christian revelation, a Christian reader of Aristotle ought to be like the scribe learned in the kingdom of God who brings forth from the Aristotelian text treasures old and new.

This suggests another way of formulating the project of reconciling Aristotelian nature and graced history that CRT represents: what Schindler is proposing is a spiritual reading of the former in the light of the latter that is analogous to the spiritual reading of the Old Testament in light of the New Testament.[42] For, once the holiness of God appears es-

---

42. To read the old spiritually is to read it in communion with Christ's Passover. The

chatologically from within the heart of nature — and this is what happens in the Virgin Birth — it becomes possible to reread Aristotle's own affirmation of nature as an abyssal depth, for him a reflection in matter of God's uncaused being (more on this below), as an anticipation, beside Aristotle's own explicit intention, of the manifestation of the holiness of the Biblical God from within the world. Such a rereading clearly gives Aristotle's account of nature a meaning that it did not have in Aristotle's own mind. Rather, it generates new meaning out of that account by placing it within a new Christological context in which all sorts of surprising foreshadowings become visible. And yet, however much this new meaning may reverse Aristotle's teaching about nature, it also both brings to light and preserves its deepest truth. This is because his feeling for the unfabricated and unfabricable depths of the natural is itself a response to the inexhaustibility-within-determinacy that Schindler thinks is characteristic of nature as principle, and it prepares a door for God to enter into the world.[43] Our task now is to test the viability of the spiritual reading of Aristotle that Schindler proposes by examining how CRT, in light of the doctrine of creation out of nothing, both challenges and preserves the Aristotelian understanding of nature as an immobile source of motion. For it is just here that the dramatic encounter between graced history and nature plays itself out most intensely in the West from the rediscovery of Aristotle in the twelfth century on.

Passover is a passage from death to resurrection. To read the old text in communion with this passage is thus to alienate it from itself, indeed, to subject it to a kind of death, but then to restore it to itself through this alienation — not, however, by some sort of dialectical mechanism, but through the living, free intervention of the Spirit in whom the Father raises Jesus from the dead. Do we hear echoes here of Hegel's *Aufhebung*? Rather, Hegel's *Aufhebung* is a secularized echo of the rhythm of spiritual reading. For an excellent account of the structure of promise-death-fulfillment as a surprising characteristic of spiritual reading, see Prufer's essay on Waugh's *Brideshead Revisited* in Prufer, *Recapitulations*, 91-102.

43. It is important to see that Schindler is not proposing an anachronistic criticism of Aristotle as a nature-grace dualist *ante litteram*, but reminding Christian readers of Aristotle that the novelty of Christianity has to affect how they appropriate Aristotle. Schindler would be the first to point out that the word "affect" is inadequate, insofar as it fails to capture the pervasive but non-invasive subtlety that makes this appropriation all the more far-reaching for giving it the almost anonymous quietness of the still small voice that cast Elijah on his face when he heard it in the cave on Mount Carmel. The resonance back and forth between Christianity and Aristotle is a subtle thing that we can rightly interpret only if we know what we are listening for, which we fully do only when the revelation of the biblical God's holiness from within the world gives us a motivation to do so.

IV. Aristotelian Objections

Speaking of motion, Aristotle says that it is "hard to know, but possible to be."[44] Motion is hard to "pin down,"[45] and it is so because, by its very nature as motion, it is continually slipping through our fingers; it is a flowing continuum that is only potentially divisible into instants.[46] It has the undivided wholeness proper to act, and yet this wholeness is not static, but exists only "underway." It is, if you will, a real "in-betweenness." This, I take it, is the true meaning of Aristotle's definition of motion as the "actuality [*entelecheia*] of a potency as a potency."[47]

Now, what I want to suggest here is that this definition is a compressed description of how potency exists as such, which is to say, precisely as a flowing transition. By the same token, it can also be read as a condensed reflection on how potency co-constitutes the world in its distinctive characteristic as world: as a perpetual flowing within the bounds of an equally perpetual static order (that being the contribution of *energeia*). If this is right, then Aristotle's definition of motion is at the core of his construal of world as *physis*: a coming to light of radiant form (*morphē*) out of a hidden depth (matter); the display always achieved, yet always, in its bloom, beginning to pass away.[48] Nature is the deepest truth about the world, because the world is matter, potency, erotic aspiration to eternal being[49] that is fulfilled within the embrace of Pure Act yet never brought to a complete halt. World is nature, nature is *erōs* for God, and *erōs* is the in-betweenness (*metaxu*) Plato describes in the *Symposium* as an attainment in failing to retain (or in letting go).[50]

Unlike mechanistic physics, then, which concerns itself with so-called laws of motion, but leaves the phenomenon of motion itself unexplained, Aristotle attempts to account for there being such a thing as motion in the first place.[51] He does this, as we just saw, by deriving motion from God —

---

44. Aristotle, *Physics*, III, 2: 202a2.

45. "*Chalepon autēn labein.*" Aristotle, *Physics*, III, 2: 201ba33.

46. Aristotle, *Physics*, VI, 9: 239b8-9.

47. Aristotle, *Physics*, III, 1: 201a10-11.

48. Except, of course, for the incorruptible heavenly bodies. Yet even they are in perpetual locomotion, or, better, are the reconciliation of static rest and motion that defines the structure of the cosmos as a whole. Perhaps this is why Aristotle refers to the universe at times as *ho ouranos*.

49. Aristotle, *Physics*, I, 8: 192a20-26.

50. Plato, *Symposium*, 203b1-204b6.

51. The great mistake of mechanistic science is its reliance on what might be called the

whose *ousia* is to be immobile actuality.[52] This explanatory move is no accident. For motion cannot even give rise to the quest for its origin unless it has just enough of what I will be calling the "perseity" of act/form to appear on the radar as a single phenomenon (as an "as such") but not enough to be self-explanatory. The very possibility of the project of accounting for motion as such thus depends on regarding motion as *"imperfect* act,"[53] which in turn points to an essentially immobile act/form guaranteeing the full perseity required to explain motion. As we know, Aristotle will then find what he is looking for in nature as a principle of motion[54] that depends in turn on God as the principle of nature.[55] Now, it is just here that the problem arises. For if

"billiard ball model of causality" (= BBMC) to explain motion. BBMC holds that causing motion means imparting locomotion to a thing through pushing it. But this is simply question-begging: Why should pushing impart locomotion? Indeed, is not pushing itself an instance of locomotion? At best, then, mechanical accounts in terms of BBMC are simply partial analytical descriptions of abstracted phases of motions, rather than explanations of motion as flowing stasis itself. Such explanation requires *sources* of motion, not just an enumeration of occasions, or more microscopic re-descriptions, of it; it requires what Aristotle called "natures." Of course, the idea that motion is something that has an essential source implies a different understanding of motion from the mechanistic one, namely, precisely as tied up with being in its transcendence of the push-and-pull of action and passion. On this difference, see Joe Sachs, "Introduction," in his *Aristotle's Physics: A Guided Study* (New Brunswick: Rutgers University Press, 1995), 1-31; and Simon Oliver, "Motion According to Aquinas and Newton," *Modern Theology* 17 (2001): 163-199.

52. Aristotle, *Metaphysics,* XII, 6: 1071b20.

53. "Movement seems to be an *energeia,* but an imperfect one [*atelēs*]." Aristotle, *Physics,* III, 1: 201b31-32.

54. Aristotle, *Physics,* II, 1: 192b21.

55. See, for example, Aristotle, *Metaphysics,* XII, 7: 1072b13-14: "so from such a principle the universe and nature is suspended." The point I am making here becomes evident if we connect *Metaphysics,* XII, with the analysis of the priority of act over potency in *Metaphysics,* IX. When we do, we get the following picture. Nature, for Aristotle, is not just the principle of motion, but also its end — it is also a principle of rest in its own achieved being (see Aristotle, *Physics,* II, 1: 192b21 et passim). There is, then, an *ideal identity* between principle and end, which establishes a kind of pattern for the movement that happens between them. This ideal pattern is, for Aristotle, itself immutable and is therefore what guarantees our ability to have stable concepts about the material mobile — to have a science of nature. Now, in order for the ideal pattern to be immobile, the end has to have been already realized from the very beginning. The problem is that the mobile, insofar as it is in movement, has never fully realized the ideal pattern of its movement at any given point in that movement. It has done so only imperfectly (motion as "imperfect act"). This problem can be solved — ultimately — only if there is something whose "ideal pattern" and its "realization" are always already perfectly one, without any intervening movement or time. Mobile things depend for their immutable ideal patterns of movement on something that is immobile because its ideal pattern

nature, qua principle of motion, must be the bearer of a certain immobile perseity of act-form to be a source of motion as such, then to want to put motion into the principle as such, in the way Schindler does, is apparently to remove the very thing whose positing was required to account for motion in the first place. Seemingly, we must choose: either immobile act/form as the ideal — or the unintelligibility of motion, hence, of the world; either immobile act/form as the ideal — or violation of the principle of non-contradiction.

I think that it would be a mistake to try to respond to this objection by dismissing the principle of non-contradiction (PNC) as the assertion of an a-relational identity after the manner of the statement that A = A. Consider PNC under the following formulation: X cannot be A and not be A at the same time and in the same respect. So stated, PNC does no more than exclude the absolute negation of X's *being* A, providing, of course, that X *is* A after all. PNC, then, is the expression of a "conditional absoluteness" that, on reflection, leads philosophy to see that things have their being relatively to God.[56] Far from suggesting an a-relational universe, in other words, PNC can only hold sway over one that is "constitutively related" to God. And with respect to God himself, PNC does not rule out real distinction, but simply places it beyond the interplay of alternative possibilities existing within the world. God grounds PNC as Trinity, even as the relative absoluteness of worldly being PNC establishes is an analogical trace of the Trinity within the interplay of same and other.[57] But if PNC is not to be set

---

is always already actual. But this absolutely immobile is not merely something having an ideal pattern. It is itself its ideal pattern, indeed, it is "ideal patternness" *as such*, always already perfectly realized. By the same token, the absolutely immobile is the perfect identity of intelligibility and actuality, being and concept — and precisely as such the immobile guarantee of the immobile intelligibility of moving natural things.

56. PNC reflexively elaborates, in other words, the paradoxical structure that generates wonder as the principle of philosophy — the appearing of an absoluteness of being in the non-absolute — and so stands as a kind of promissory placeholder for God as the ultimate guarantor of that paradoxical structure who also appears within it (which is why, formulated context-less by itself, PNC is abstract and easily dismissed as trivial or question-begging).

57. In excluding the absolute negation of X's being A *hic et nunc*, PNC therefore also excludes the simultaneous position of X's being B *hic et nunc*. This is not the establishment of an empty A = A, however. For PNC only rules out X's being B *now*, while leaving open the possibility of its being B *later* — and so establishes A and B as alternative possibilities standing in the mutual referentiality characteristic of the interplay of same and other (as in Aristotle's doctrine that change is between contraries). In this interplay, being A has a certain absoluteness — but only relatively to the possibility of being B.

aside as an assertion of abstract identity, but retained as the formulation of the question to which CRT is the exact answer, how does Schindler deal with the objection that motion in nature as principle is contradictory?

(a) Schindler meets this objection with a reconstruction of the Thomistic teaching about creation out of nothing, which itself both challenges and preserves the Aristotelian understanding of nature within a kind of spiritual exegesis of its own. According to Aristotle, as we have seen, nature is an immobile source of motion. In other words, nature is a source and measure of becoming, but it does not itself become, on pain of forfeiting its status as a source and measure of becoming. "Natural forms are unmoved movers, neither coming to be, nor ceasing to be, and natural motion *(entelecheia atelēs)* is the recapitulation of indwelling form."[58] For similar reasons, Aristotle does not think that the world, which, after all, is really just nature displayed against its proper background, could have become, in a sense of having had a first moment of existence.[59] On Aquinas's reading, Aristotle is partly right, insofar as nature, as such, does not come into being by means of the same sort of genesis of which it itself is the principle.[60] Thus, if that sort of coming into being were the only sort there were, then the world could indeed have had no beginning. And yet, nature *does* come into being for Aquinas, namely, by way of creation out of nothing, which is not a natural motion within an already existing matter, but God's act of liberally giving being, *esse,* to matter and form at once, while presupposing absolutely nothing external to him.[61] But notice what happens: precisely because God's creative act does not just give *esse,* it does not suppress, but brings about, nature as a subordinate, receptive principle of *esse* in its own right. This is why Thomas Aquinas can say in *Summa Contra Gentiles,* II, 54, 5, that "[F]orm is a principle of being, because it is the complement of the substance, whose act is being itself: as the transparent is the principle of the air's shining because it makes it the proper subject of

58. Prufer, *Recapitulations,* 8.

59. Aristotle, *Physics,* VIII, 1: 250b10-28. See also this passage from Prufer: "The fully developed offspring is prior to the seed from which it develops and prior to both is the generator whose form is the end of the generated. The making of nature is the cycle: reconciliation in eidetic identity of the priority of eternally anterior actuality with the priority of the eternally to be actual end; that which is to be or anticipated completeness is the anterior activity of the complete form from which the seed proceeds." Prufer, *Recapitulations,* 8.

60. Creation is not a *mutatio* or *motus.* See, for example, Thomas Aquinas, *De Potentia,* 3.2.

61. See, for example, Thomas Aquinas, *De Potentia,* 3.1.

light" — thus retrieving Aristotle's sense of nature as unmanufacturable depth that explains, without being explained by, the interplay of worldly causes, within Christian creationism.[62] In a sense, the Thomistic doctrine of the participation of secondary causes in the all-embracing causality of the first cause[63] is an attempt to account for the primordial sourcehood of Aristotelian nature in the context of a robust Christian doctrine of creation with the help of the Neoplatonic notion of participation.[64]

62. Only the Christian doctrine of *creatio ex nihilo,* understood as both free and necessary, as both principial and personal, accounts for the immutable intelligibility of natures without attributing any quasi-divine status to them. St. Thomas achieves this balancing act by reducing the intelligibility of created essences to the divine intellect, which in the same act in which it knows the divine essence also knows them as possible, but not necessarily existing, participations in that essence. See, for example, his discussion of the divine ideas in *Summa Theologiae,* I, q. 15, a. 1.

63. See, for example, Thomas Aquinas, *Summa Theologiae,* I, q. 104, a. 2.

64. Schindler has referred in his most recent work to the non-subsistence of *esse creatum,* a Thomistic topos that Gustav Siewerth and Ferdinand Ulrich recovered for contemporary philosophy. Schindler, following these two thinkers, makes much of Aquinas's statement in *De Potentia,* 1.1, that *esse* "signifies something complete and simple, but non-subsistent." This sentence presents *esse* as a Neoplatonic fullness in which all things participate ("complete and simple"), while distinguishing this fullness from God ("non-subsistent"). This disentanglement of the divine source and its created image, which Plotinus runs together under the rubric of the One, implies that *esse* must cause by sourcing the causality of all four causes, even as its sourcing depends on the finite substance exercising *esse* as the unitary supposit of its fourfold causality. The result is a seeming paradox: on the one hand, since *esse* is the actuality of acts, essence is nothing in itself apart from it, so that there is nothing to receive *esse* prior to God's gift of it; on the other hand, *esse* depends on the very essence that it makes be as quasi-formal cause. Thus, while holding to a certain primacy of *esse,* without which creaturely essence, indeed, the whole creature, is nothing in itself, Schindler insists that the primacy of *esse* includes a kind of dependence on creaturely essence and so on the creature of which it is the essence. Of course, this dependence is not so to say inflicted on *esse* from the outside, as if it were a quasi-physical entity that could be physically worked on by essence. Rather, *esse*'s dependence on essence is the result of a hypothetical necessity built into the very non-subsistence of *esse,* which, being non-subsistent, cannot be realized as cause without a subsistent something to be the cause of. But that is just the point: *esse* causes, not by doing something to the creature, but precisely by letting the creature be a subordinate but real co-source out of its essence of the concrete realization of *esse* as the act of existing of a subsistent substantial being. The real distinction is not a halving of the creature into two independent things, but the qualification of its unity as a participated, dependent, receptively structured quasi-source of itself displaying in a kind of reverse mirror-image the generosity of the Creator in a constitutive *exitus-reditus* structure. See Gustav Siewerth, "Das Sein als Gleichnis Gottes," in idem; Ferdinand Ulrich, *Homo Abyssus. Das Wagnis der Seinsfrage,* 2nd ed. (Freiburg: Johannes Verlag, 1998).

The Thomistic retrieval of the Aristotelian notion of nature as an immobile source of becoming implies that, however much nature is a source, there is never a time when it does not owe its sourcehood, or even its existence, to God.[65] Conserved in *esse* by God, nature as principle is never finished depending on God for and in every phase and exercise of its principality. By the same token, no matter how much nature gives substance a platform for its self-constitution in being, this self-constitution is not absolute, but relative to the divine source that is incessantly indwelling it and communicating to it both being and the act of self-constitution in being. The very act of subsistence, of substantial self-constitution in being on the basis of nature, therefore structurally contains an *exitus* and *reditus* from and to God that can be called motion in an analogous sense. Since this movement is an "ontological" motion consisting in referentiality to God, and not a physical change, it can constitute nature as principle in Aristotle's sense without contradiction, as long as we bear in mind that it does not constitute after the manner of an immanent component or principle of essence, but operates in a trans-essential order connected with *esse* as *"magis intimum cuilibet"* precisely because it is not in the order of essence.[66] Physical change, for its part, is the "temporal underside" of ontological motion, and Schindler stresses that to see physical motion is to glimpse this ontological motion, through the mediating lens of analogy, as a supra-temporal ur-drama between God and the creature. Physical change is indeed itself dramatic because it involves a real novelty that is not simply the mechanical unfolding of what always already was on the level of ontological motion. Nature and history, in other words, are for Schindler two sides of one thing in the same fact of being created, and so each can be interior to the other without history's being mere automatic unfolding of nature or nature's being dissolved into mere temporal flux.

(b) Insofar as the *exitus* and *reditus* internal to creaturely subsistence represents a "fromness" and "towardness," Schindler denominates it a "relation," indeed, a "constitutive relation to God" — as, for example, in his discussion of *esse ab, in,* and *ad* in his debate with Norris Clarke over when receptivity begins in the creature. This identification of ontological motion with constitutive relation to God immediately raises another objection. For Aristotle himself arguably already understood nature as a being-moved-by-God, and yet he did not feel compelled to identify this being-moved as a

---

65. See, for example, Thomas Aquinas, *Summa Theologiae*, I, q. 104, a. 1 ad 1.
66. "Most intimate to each thing." Thomas Aquinas, *Summa Theologiae*, I, q. 8, a. 1.

Adrian J. Walker

"relation," as Schindler does. It would be unfair to attribute this silence to an alleged lack of appreciation for the relational side of the world on Aristotle's part, though. Aristotle's God, free from the interplay of action and passion that characterizes the world, communicates to the world something of that freedom: nature.[67] Moreover, precisely because nature enjoys this freedom, constituting the interplay of intra-worldly antitheses, rather than being constituted by it, it assures that this interplay — and so the basic character of the world — is not a system of mechanical interactions, but a web of giving and receiving of actuality. So much so, in fact, that Aristotle can say in book XII of the *Metaphysics* that things cohere in a single cosmos insofar as they have a share in one another on account of their common ordination to God.[68] Clearly, then, the disagreement between Schindler and Aristotle does not lie in the fact that the former affirms a relational cosmos as the first effect of the non-technological divine generosity whereas the latter is simply closed to the idea of such a cosmos. I would like to suggest in what follows that the real point of disagreement between the two thinkers lies rather in their differing accounts of the nature of the receptive principle that both agree must be present as an intra-worldly correlative of God's non-technological causation of the world.

There are, in fact, two different ways of using the receptive principle for ruling out the idea that God causes by a technological acting-on. The first way, which is Aristotle's, is to say that, just as God's causal influence is timeless, every new natural entity that arises already exists in the potency of matter, from which it is drawn forth by an already actualized member of its species — and so on back *ad infinitum*: egg-chicken-egg-chicken forever.[69] The natural entity therefore does not need to wait for God's action to bring it into existence, but is always already shining forth from the darkness of matter in response to that action. By the same token, there is no special act of dependence on God that the natural entity would need to perform separately from its own act of constituting itself in existence within the world on the platform of matter. At the same time, matter is ambivalent, both a help and a hindrance, and the natural entity must not only constitute itself as a *subjectum* on the platform of matter, but must also master the platform's tendency to undermine what builds itself up on it —

67. This, I take it, is an upshot of Aristotle's affirmation that God moves as loved: Aristotle, *Metaphysics*, XII, 7: 1072b3.
68. Aristotle, *Metaphysics*, XII, 10: 1075a16-25.
69. The following discussion applies to sub-lunar matter, not to the ethereal matter of the heavenly bodies.

a tendency that will nonetheless eventually overcome the individual, although not the eternal species. This mastery requires in turn that the natural entity establish for itself a core of freedom from the push-and-pull of action and passion. Since, for Aristotle, relation can exist only within this push-and-pull, it must lie outside of the substantial being's core of liberty, as an accidental entity inherent in the substance. For a strict Aristotelian, "constitutive relation" is almost a contradiction in terms.

Aristotle's position is thus as follows. According to the *Categories*, relation is the subject's definability-in-reference-to. . . .[70] But definability-in-reference-to occurs only where things act on one another. God and nature, however, are precisely not two things in interaction. Rather, what nature receives from God is not his action upon it, but a share in his superiority to the interplay of action and passion altogether. God's causing frees nature from exhaustive determination by the interplay of action and passion, inside and outside, substance and relation that is imposed by matter, and so lets nature be an immanent co-source of the world, rather than the mere product of it. For the same reason, because being moved by God *is* nature as freedom from the interplay of intra-worldly antitheses, to call it a "relation," when in reality relation is a trace of that interplay, is a kind of category mistake on Aristotelian terms. Just as I can't be my being-moved-by-God, because my being-moved-by-God makes there be an I to be moved in the first place, so, too, my being-moved cannot be a relation, because it is the establishing of me as a supposit of relations in the first place.

It would be a mistake to interpret CRT as simply accepting Aristotle's framework for thinking about substance and relation without qualification, but then insisting on making relation as Aristotle understood it within that framework somehow less accidental. Schindler's point, I think, is that we need to challenge the framework itself, in order to work out a new account of relation that would do justice to Aristotle's concerns, while also absorbing the full impact of the manifestation of divine liberality[71] in

---

70. See the discussion in Aristotle, *Categories*, 7.

71. This is not to say, of course, that Aristotle had no inkling of the divine liberality that would be confirmed by the Christian account of creation out of nothing. If he hadn't, then St. Thomas's account of creation out of nothing as I have described it would be un-Christian to the extent that it tried to do justice to Aristotle. It seems to me that Aristotle's definition of nature as an intrinsic principle of motion and rest represents just the sort of inkling I mean. The intrinsicality of nature, in fact, is an oblique expression of creation as a liberal communication of being that, as such, liberates the creature into its own — giving it a ground within

creation out of nothing as an alternative way of explaining the role of the receptive principle in preserving divine causality from technology.[72] The problem with the Aristotelian framework, in fact, is that it dialectically smuggles into our construal of nature's freedom from worldly push-and-pull a new version of that very push-and-pull itself, insofar as the assumption of the eternity of the world places God and matter in a certain antithesis of mutual conditioning that carries over into the relation between substance and matter.[73] Creation out of nothing, by contrast, in freeing divine causality from this dialectic, also brings to light a new form of genesis for substances, which in turn liberates their self-constitution to include being-

---

itself under which is no further ground of the same order. Aristotle could discover nature as an inner principle of motion and rest because creation out of nothing gives creatures a "relative absoluteness." That having been said, the ability to valorize the Aristotelian account of nature with a view to making explicit these implications depends on reading it spiritually in light of Christian revelation. By the same token, the failure to read Aristotle in the light of Christ at the very least makes it easier to resolve the ambiguities in his thought in the direction of a one-sided conceptualism.

72. Aristotle believed that God causes, indeed, is the causation of the world. Does God's causation extend to matter, according to Aristotle? It is difficult to say, although one might read him as saying that, insofar as God causes limited actuality, he must also cause potency, hence matter, by a kind of concomitancy. In this sense, Aristotle's understanding of divine causation can be interpreted as overlapping partially with the Christian doctrine of creation out of nothing. What seems to be missing from this account, however, is the idea that God freely decides to perform an act of efficient causation whose result is the world (coming into being out of nothing). Indeed, Aristotle would probably say that God's being his causation of the world rules out just such a free act, which would involve the divinity in a change unworthy of its changeless perfection. Of course, we could agree with this, too, insofar as the divine causal act is not an accidental addition to the divine being. Nevertheless, Aristotle does not make even a rational distinction between the divine causative act and the constitutive identity of God, whereas Christianity does — except, of course, when it comes to the supracausation of the Son and the Spirit: the Father is his generative act, and so forth. Perhaps we could say that the "problem" with Aristotle is that he does not have available a distinction between the generation of the Son and the production of the world that would enable him to introduce a non-complexifying distinction between the divine causative act and the divine being — that is, to make creation free and deliberate without involving God in the wrong kind of compromise with the world.

73. Aristotelian matter is ambivalent. On the one side, it is purely passive; on the other side, it somehow imposes itself with a certain necessity upon divine causality. Of course, Aristotle might concede that the necessity of matter is a conditional one. That having been said, it is at least an open question whether Aristotle does not identify the condition with God's very being, full stop. If this is the case, then God remains, arguably contrary to Aristotle's own intentions, eternally yoked with, and so conditioned by, matter (insofar as God, and not, say, God's will, *is* the conditional necessity of matter).

affected-by-another[74] — even while transposing this being-affected to a different ontological register beyond the wear-and-tear of action and reaction within the physical world.[75] Creation out of nothing thus opens up a new receptive principle, which, no longer conditioning God's creativity from without, also needs no longer be reduced to pure passivity to minimize its impact. What emerges is what Schindler has called an "active receptivity," a good heteronomy constituting the very core of the autonomy of substance beyond the opposition between *heteros* and *autos*. This active receptivity is not identical with matter, of course, but it does reveal itself in the material in a way that affects how we see the interplay of worldly antitheses, too. Extending Aristotle's own insight that nature's freedom from this interplay preserves its non-mechanical character, we can say that physical change, as the temporal underside of ontological motion, is an index of a good vulnerability built into the principle itself thanks to which it manifests the fruitfulness of the Creator.

74. We can agree that substances must have a certain freedom from the push-and-pull of action and passion in order to be the bearers of a non-mechanical world. But, having registered our agreement, we need to go on to ask why Aristotle needs to locate relation solely in this push-and-pull in the first place. The answer, I think, lies in his doctrine of the eternity of the world/matter. As one would expect from a teaching that aims to reduce temporal novelty to eternal order, this doctrine limits the possible ways in which substances can come into being to one: the one by which we observe them to come into being within the world, namely, out of preexisting matter. By the same token, Aristotle cannot consistently admit any kind of being-affected-by-another that is not simply an example of the matter-based push-and-pull he is trying to free substances from in the first place. The being of relation therefore exhausts itself in the intra-worldly push-and-pull of action and passion, and so can never be more than an accident to be excluded as such from the substantial core of natural entities.

75. Schindler does not deny, of course, that the creature is also the subject of its own dependence on the Creator — that follows from the fact that creation is not a technological doing-to — and that there is even a sense in which relation to God is the property of a substantial *suppositum* consequent upon its having been created. Nevertheless, this aspect of the creature's relation to God now presupposes another: relation to God is first something God himself brings about in the creature, and only secondarily something the creature recuperates (in a dramatic way, to be sure) as its subject. The creature is the subject of its relation to God — but this subject-hood originates from the very relation it is the subject of. It is as if creatures, because coming into being out of nothing, were a pure relativity to God, impossible to pin down in itself, that was then, by virtue of divine generosity, given to itself as its own substantial *suppositum* of itself, while never simply catching up with itself. The point is not that nature loses its autonomy, but that this autonomy is itself, and as a whole, relative to God, albeit in a non-alienating way. The very integrity of nature is itself a moving reference to a Wholly Other that is Not-Other.

Whereas Aristotle understands relation in terms of matter's ambivalence as the world's capacity for divine causality coupled with its propensity to drag that causality into self-alienation, Schindler, rereading the receptivity of matter in light of Christian faith, discovers at the heart of finite being a heteronomous autonomy reflecting the liberal self-giving of the Creator — a heteronomous autonomy that he dubs "constitutive relation to God." I would like to stress that Schindler is not faulting Aristotle for failing to see something that he himself sees only because of the gift of the Christian faith that was not yet available to the Greeks. Indeed, Schindler would surely acknowledge that matter remains ambivalent — it is both the root of our individual existence in the world and at the same time the seed of that existence's inevitable end — and would want to stress that it is not within man's power to overcome this ambivalence. But that is just Schindler's point: in order for Aristotle's own intuition about the non-technological character of divine causality to come to fruition, he is saying, our experience of the ambivalence of matter has to be changed — by the revelation of creation out of nothing and of the Resurrection. What changes, of course, is not the fact of this ambivalence, but the otherwise almost inevitable association of physical death with cessation of participation in the divine. This is not to say that Christian revelation makes light of the horror of death. Rather, contemplation of the Passion of Christ makes it possible to do full justice to this horror — we reject any cheap "kenoticism" that identifies being and death — while discerning in that horror something deeper: the pledge of a new fruitfulness in the Resurrection. Here a new ontological register emerges to enable a distinction between the push-and-pull of self and other, inside and outside leading to death — and the fruitful polarity of finite being that this push-and-pull rides on without exhausting its meaning. This brings us to the theme of the next section: motion as fruitfulness, a fruitfulness that distantly, but really, echoes the primordial fruitfulness of the Father. This will be the context for us both to identify the source and to carry through the spiritual rereading of the understanding of perseity behind Aristotle's account of motion, which, as we will see, reverses and achieves it by uniting perseity with mutuality, power with vulnerability.

V. Motion as Fruitfulness

So far, I have been explaining CRT in connection with Schindler's creative reconstruction of St. Thomas's own spiritual exegesis of Aristotle in light of the doctrine of creation out of nothing. The novelty of CRT emerges most clearly from its Thomistic background insofar as Schindler asserts, not just that there is a movement-relation within nature as principle, but that this movement-relation is nature's constitutive impossibility of being exhaustively determined within its boundaries as an establisher of membership in a species — and that this impossibility pertains to nature's perfection in actuality. The real novelty of CRT, in other words, is its affirmation that nature's status as a principle of species-specific motion within the world is the expression of an inexhaustibility that is most basically a positive "fruitfulness" or ability to bring forth what one is not the first origin of: to bear the More-Than-World from the heart of the world itself. At the very moment when the creature depends most radically on, and so is distinguished most completely from, God, it most fully participates in, and so to say "magnifies," the fontal goodness of the Origin — as itself bearing an analogous constitutive relationality, indeed, the *analogatum princeps* of it, as we will see below. It is at this point that Schindler's reconstruction of the Thomistic account of the constitution of finite substance in the perspective of creation as gift converges with Balthasar's account of *Gestalt* — at the point where this *Gestalt* becomes Mary mirroring back the humble sovereignty of the Father, participating in his begetting of the Son by the power of the Spirit.

CRT, then, amounts to a claim that the creature's constitutive relation-movement to God is not merely an "imperfect act," much less a merely potential indeterminacy, but a hyper-determinate active readiness to bring forth novelty from itself upon being fecundated by the free intervention of a/Another: an inexhaustible fruitfulness. The movement-relation within nature, however much it is concretely bound up with a potency that limits the fullness of act, is for Schindler the revelation of a "new" sense of the perfection of act as always containing something like fruitful relation, which is thereby elevated to a kind of ontological ultimacy. What Schindler is calling for is nothing less than a rethinking of Aristotle's identification of what I above called "immutable perseity" as the ontological ideal. This is ultimately a theological problem, since, as Aristotle himself already saw, the immutable perseity of nature as principle and the immutable perseity of God go hand in hand and stand or fall together.[76] By the

---

76. This is because, as noted above, the explanation of motion per se hangs for him on its being a deficient perseity that depends on the existence of an immobile perseity: secondarily nature insofar as, being in act, it is principle; but primarily God as *Actus Purus*.

same token, rethinking the status of perseity as the ontological first best must not lead us in the direction of a process theology that denies the received doctrine of the immutability of the divine nature. We must not only rethink perseity but also preserve the abiding truth of Aristotle's account of it against the pure processuality of historicism. This, as we will presently see, is precisely the achievement of Trinitarian doctrine, which indeed offers the paradigmatic form of the spiritual reading of Aristotelian perseity in light of the central Christian experience that one must die to rise to new life through participation in the divine communion of love.

What, then, does the immutable perseity of God look like on Aristotle's account, so far as we can make it out? The most striking thing about this account for a Christian reader is that Aristotle's God is without action (in the sense of *praxis*) or friendship.[77] If we want to understand God's immutable perseity, Aristotle seems to be telling us, we cannot draw on our experience of ourselves as part of the world in the rough-and-tumble, give-and-take with other parts of the world, but, at best, on the experience we have of ourselves when we contemplate, for then we seem to be more-than-human,[78] even to merge with the divine.[79] On this reading, it would be pointless to seek for action and friendship in God, not because God is selfish, but precisely because he is not a self at all — because action and friendship belong to selves, and selves are composites[80] belonging in the physical world of which God is the cause, but not in any sense a part. The perseity of Aristotle's God, then, is not the perseity that an individual composite self would have if, by some impossible catastrophe, the universe in which it is at home were to disappear around it, leaving it absolutely solitary in the void. Divine perseity on Aristotle's reading is rather the simple immateriality that reigns prior to any of the mutual exteriority of self and world, inside and outside, being and knowing, which goes with being a composite self in the first place.

77. Prufer, *Recapitulations*, xii.

78. Aristotle, *Ethics*, X, 7: 1177b26-29. Even for human beings, action and friendship characterize the perfection of the human soul as the life-principle of a body interacting with other things and people in a natural world and in a city, but not necessarily the *nous*. Of course, whether in pure nous we are still accessible to ourselves as anything we would recognize as selves in the first place is just the question that Aristotle's account of the immutable perseity forces us to ask.

79. Aristotle, *Ethics*, X, 7: 1177b30 ("the intellect is something divine with respect to the man").

80. Aristotle speaks of sub-contemplative man as *"to syntheton,"* the composite, in *Ethics*, X, 7: 1177b28-29.

Now, Trinitarians can benevolently read Aristotle as thinking prior to the appearance of any meaningful distinction between the mutuality bound up with exteriority and complexifying duality, which Trinitarians would be the first to exclude from the divine nature, and a new sense of mutuality that does not require exteriority or complexity for its instantiation. It is, in fact, only the Resurrection that fully opens up this distinction: confirming Christ as one person who is true God and true man, the Resurrection displays him as the revelation both of the fact of Trinitarian personhood and of the way in which the unity of the human composite can manifest it through the distance of analogy. Just as the condition of this analogy is the "spiritualization" of the body Paul talks about in 1 Corinthians 15,[81] its structure is that of a spiritual reading. Indeed, in some sense it is *the* primal spiritual reading: dying to self and rising with Christ dead and risen, we bring our ideal of perseity with us through the fire — and the result is a spiritual *relecture* of divine simplicity that, while still negatively removing all complexity from God as it did before, does so in the service of underscoring the unique sort of reality characterizing the "real distinction" among the divine persons.[82] Divine simplicity on a Trinitarian reading, in fact, does not mean that the distinction among the hypostases in God is less real than the distinction between earthly individuals, but that it is real in a different, and therefore infinitely richer, way: not as an individualization of the divine nature within the horizon of universal and particular, but as personhood in fruitful mutuality beyond the opposition between universal and particular altogether.

In some sense, the very distinction between person and nature in God, which is the bedrock of Trinitarian doctrine, is the outcome of the early Church's struggle to reconcile Christian teaching about Father, Son, and Holy Spirit with the theolegoumenon of divine simplicity through a spiritual reading of the latter in light of the former. In this sense, the nature-person distinction is a way of saying that God is what we would now call "person*al*," meaning that he exists as the subject of acts of knowledge and will, as he does in the Old Testament — but without therefore ceasing to be the all-encompassing First Principle. In this context, Trinitarian doctrine does not invoke simplicity for the sake of a "damage control" that would

---

81. For further details, see Adrian J. Walker, "'Sown Psychic, Raised Spiritual': The Lived Body as the Organ of Theology," *Communio: International Catholic Review* 33 (2006): 203-215.

82. See Thomas Aquinas, *Summa Theologiae*, I, q. 28, a. 1 *et passim*.

minimize the personal distinctions, but in order to affirm that the divine being subsists as one person*al* entity — neither in the finitude of the individual nor in an a-personal infinity, but in a *communio personarum* where mutuality of person*al* knowing and loving is not the finitizing reciprocal limitation of individuals, but unlimited, albeit not form- or structureless, sharing. In this carefully qualified sense, the revelation of the Trinity is the revelation of a new ontology of perseity that incorporates, while transforming non-destructively, the Aristotelian account of that perseity according to the law of spiritual reading, which is, in fact, inscribed in God's way of being person-in-relation beyond the opposition and interplay of self and other, inside and outside, and the like.

Of course, everything begins with the fontal plenitude whom with Jesus we dare to call Father, and so with the ur-miracle of the mysterious distinction between the Father and his divine nature. For it is with this distinction that the person*al* character of the Covenant God of the Old Testament, יהוה, clearly becomes the new sense of person mentioned above (which, as Ferdinand Ulrich reminds us, implies in turn the emergence of a new, trans-essential ontological register beyond the interplay of all worldly antitheses that we could call "spiritual").[83] Admittedly, we must insist with St. Thomas that the distinction between the Father and his divine nature is not a "real" one, lest we introduce complexity into God.[84] At the same time, the very teaching that there is only a "rational" distinction between the Father and his divine nature[85] implies that the Father, as Father, is *conceptually* irreducible to that nature, even for himself.[86] It implies, then, that for the Father to be the one, subsistent, intelligent, willing Reality we call "divine nature" is for him to stand, in a mysterious way, over against that nature — as a person*al* supposit of that nature whose subsistence coincides with relation to another such personal supposit: "subsistent relation."[87] This doubling without diremption or loss of sim-

---

83. Ferdinand Ulrich, *Homo Abyssus,* 2nd ed. (Freiburg: Johannes Verlag, 1998), 168.

84. See, for example, Thomas Aquinas, *Summa Theologiae,* I, q. 28, a. 2.

85. See, for example, Thomas Aquinas, *Summa Theologiae,* I, q. 39, a. 1.

86. Note that, even for Thomas, the conceptual irreducibility of the Father to his divine nature exists in some sense even for the Father, insofar as he cannot know himself as God without generating, and so being in relation to, the Word in whom that self-knowledge is fruitful.

87. True, Thomas maintains a conceptual distinction between substance and relation, which he uses in order to affirm that relation does not constitute the divine person, looked at as a distinct subsistent, in virtue of being a relation, but insofar as it is really identical

plicity does not alienate the divine nature from itself, but fulfills it as a
hyper-determinate selfhood beyond self that transcends the self/other interplay altogether.[88]

The Father is the *plenitudo fontalis,* the infinitely fruitful, hyper-
determinate (not indeterminate) source who not only can generate novelty in an *ad extra* history of creation and redemption without losing his
absoluteness, but also can make that history the extension into time of
his act — that he is — of timelessly placing novelty at the very heart of
the immobile perseity of the First Principle itself, even as this extension
is a new kind of newness beyond all intra-worldly antitheses.[89] Notice,
moreover, that this novelty is the miracle (which the Father *is*) of both
bringing forth another and, at the same time, of taking that other seri-

---

with the divine substance or essence (see, for example, *Summa Theologiae,* I, q. 29, a. 4). On
the one side, then, Thomas maintains the superiority of substance over relation all the way
into the Trinity, at least on the conceptual plane. On the other side, though, Thomas holds
substance and relation apart in the way I have suggested to the end of explicating how the
one, person*al* divine being contains *communio* beyond what we experience as the interplay
of inside and outside. In this sense, we can legitimately invoke Thomas in support of the
claim that the doctrine of the Trinity implies that, when the distinction between self and
world drops away, what is left is not simply an identity of being and consciousness without
mutuality, but precisely a real, but non-complexifying mutuality of love in the mutual love
who is the Spirit (see, for example, *Summa Theologiae,* I, q. 37, a. 1 ad 1). The real difference
here is that Thomas, in part in order to do justice to Aristotle, makes the self-world distinction fade first into a non-complexifying mutuality at the level of knowing. Following
Balthasar, Schindler would want to emphasize that the nature-person distinction in the Father is a perpetual ur-miracle — which the Father *is* — of being oneself in the sharing of
oneself. This primal miracle is neither simply the natural overflow of the contemplative
unity of what, here below, would be the self and world, being and consciousness, nor an act
of the will, much less a blind upsurge of volition. The primal miracle is neither knowing
nor willing, not because it is blind or unfree, but because it is — to speak anthropomorphi-
cally — the eternal, always already accomplished, self-liberation of subsistent knowing and
willing from mere individuality, which is the same as the self-constitution of subsistent
knowing and willing as properly personal. It is the ur-glory that contains the good and the
true reconciled within the Trinity as the non-complex super-*Gestalt* in which God appears
as love.

88. In *Summa Theologiae,* I, q. 39, a. 1, Thomas explains that the real distinction among
the divine persons on account of mutual opposition and the rational distinction between
each person and the divine nature are two sides of the coin of the one simple divine being.

89. This is the significance of Thomas's doctrine that the visible mission of the Son is
his procession viewed with the non-complexifying, non-accidental, yet free adjunct of the
temporal effect of subsistence in a human nature. See, for example, *Summa Theologiae,* I,
q. 43, a. 2.

ously as a novelty for oneself. There was never a time when the Son was not, so much so that we can agree with Adrienne von Speyr when she says that the Son is always already present to the generative act, letting himself be generated,[90] indeed stirring up the Father's *erōs* to generate him — simultaneously with, and as a result of, his unoriginate origination of the Son.[91] The Son is no "copy" *(Abklatsch)* of the Father,[92] and just so is he con-substantial with the paternal Origin, a subordinate but real source of the Spirit, who is the confirmation that fruitful novelty and stable eternity are one in the Principle — as himself the personal embodiment of the unity of novelty and identity, of mutuality and simplicity, of person and nature, of self and other, and so forth. This is why Augustine insists on the role of the Holy Spirit as *communio:* by *uniting* Father and Son *as persons,* he reconciles the simplicity of the divine nature with the interpersonal dimension of the Godhead, and just so seals

90. See Adrienne von Speyr, *Die Welt des Gebetes* (Einsiedeln: Johannes Verlag, 1992), 41.

91. This is not to deny for an instant the asymmetry in the Father-Son relation, such that the Father produces the Son, but never *vice-versa.* However much we insist on the asymmetry in the Father-Son relation, though, we cannot interpret it as implying that whatever "happens" between them goes only in one direction, from the Father to the Son, and never in the other direction, from the Son to the Father. As Thomas himself asserts, the Father is as really related to the Son as the Son is really related to the Father; the asymmetry between Father and Son is clearly not such that the Father could be without the Son, in the way, say, that God could be without the creature, or the column without my standing to the right of it. Indeed, although the Son does not generate the Father, the Father *in some sense* owes his Fatherhood to the Son. In what sense? Clearly, the Father does not owe the generative act by which he is a Father to the Son, but has it *a se.* Nevertheless, unless the Son exists, the Father cannot be said to have generated. This is all the truer the truer it is that "there was never a time when the Son was not." Unless the Son exists as consubstantial God from all eternity, then, the Father cannot really be a Father. Thus, at the very "eternal moment" when the Father generates the Son, he receives from the Son, not Godhead or Fatherhood, to be sure, but the Son himself, as the inner completion of his generative act. This completion is double-sided. On the one hand, it is interior to the paternal generative act; from this point of view, it adds nothing to it, but results entirely from it. On the other hand, since this completion consists in another *hypostasis,* this latter has to perform an act of its own in order to count as the desired completion. This act is, of course, the act of receiving itself entirely from the Father — but that is just the point. The act of self-reception that the Son subsistently is remains internal to the Godhead of the Father to such an extent that the Son, while resulting from the generative act, is not posterior to it, but accompanies it, articulating, expressing, and embodying *for* the Father the "motive" of the generative act — paternal love fully given and, in the moment of the gift, fully reciprocated. Indeed, overflowingly so: the Holy Spirit.

92. Adrienne von Speyr, *Die Welt des Gebetes,* 65.

God's infinity as intensive[93] (as opposed, say, to simply negative-remotive) and precisely thus as properly personal.[94]

With that we return to Schindler's claim that the revelation of the Trinity is also a revolutionary rethinking of Aristotelian perseity, which overcomes any lingering traces of a "monopolar" conception of act. God's self-revelation "from above" corrects Aristotle's association of mutuality with material individuality, and so reveals a new sense of the spiritual that, like the Holy Spirit, is not conditioned, even negatively, by the interplay of intra-worldly antitheses. The properly spiritual is not the material; yet it is not simply immateriality as the remotion of matter. Rather, it is an immateriality that is so free from matter that it does not have to define itself in opposition to it, but can pre-contain the passivity of matter in a non-material, non-passive way — as a fruitfulness that combines apathic fontal power with a real being-moved-by the other, albeit in a transcendent sense of motion and otherness that does not involve the First Principle in any patripassian muta-bility.[95] God's self-revelation, precisely when it most gloriously distinguishes him from the world, opens up a new experience of the world as world, and so of the intra-worldly interplays themselves, a new experience that does not overturn philosophical negative theology, but preserves it from the temptation to imagine God as still somehow conditioned dialectically by the worldly dualities of which he is supposedly the negation. If fallen reason hardens the moved interplay of intra-worldly antitheses or polarities into a dualistic push-and-pull under the sign of the either-or, the Spirit recalls to our always wandering attention that this interplay is not the last word even

---

93. On the connection between the Spirit and this intensive infinity, here as a super-abundance of joy, see especially Augustine, *De Trinitate,* VI, 10.

94. On the connection between the properly spiritual and the properly personal in God, see Antonio López, "*Donum Doni:* An Approach to a Theology of Gift," in this volume. The following paragraph is especially indebted to the reading of López's article.

95. It is important to stress that the Father's ability to be "touched" by "otherness" is an intrinsic implication of his own fontal power, which, putting him beyond the push-and-pull of other and same, frees him to be "touched," yet without suffering any of the alteration from the outside that occurs when *we* are touched by otherness. Moreover, the Father's fontal gen-erosity is never seen directly, but only in the mirror of the self-reception of the Son, as this is seen in the mirror of the self-reception of Mary, as this is seen in turn in the mirror of the self-reception of created essence. The point is that, at each stage, the fontal power of the origin is seen, so to speak, indirectly in the dignity of the receiver that this fontal power enables vis-à-vis itself by the intrinsic implication mentioned above. For this dignity therefore displays a transcendent foundation of the receptivity of the receiver in the origin, yet without ever mak-ing it directly available in an objectifying way that would evacuate the origin of its mystery.

about the world, that the movement between the poles of worldly being is not simply an imperfect determinacy, but a hyper-determinacy, a positive inexhaustibility or fruitfulness. The Spirit reminds us that nature is what Balthasar calls a *Gestalt:* a form whose immanent perfection is not a premature closure for self-protection against accident, decay, and death, but an "in-betweenness" that, in active readiness, leaves open a space for something like the grace of God that saves from death by taking death upon itself, as Homer and the Tragedians seemed to have intuited from afar.

VI. The Virgin of the Sign

Let us briefly recall the trajectory of the argument so far. I started off by presenting CRT as a claim about the non-neutrality of nature vis-à-vis specifically Christian revelation that Schindler develops against the background of a de Lubacian theology of nature and grace (section II). Having noted that this claim would require a spiritual rereading of Aristotelian *physis* (section III), I went on to answer likely objections to such a *relecture* in light of Christian teaching about creation out of nothing (section IV). In the course of obviating these objections, I tried to make plausible the idea that a certain motion of *exitus-reditus* — what Schindler means by "constitutive relation to God" — is inherent in nature as act/principle. This led me to the notion of "fruitfulness," the inability to be exhaustively determined within the confines of one's own nature — which, I claim with Schindler, not only is the perfection of nature, but is a key to the spiritual rereading of the perseity of act in light of the fruitfulness of the Father in the Trinity (section V). De Lubac's thesis about nature and grace, interpreted in light of Balthasarian *Gestalt,* places the individual exemplar of the human species at the heart of an *analogia fecunditatis:* the individual human being remains recognizably such for all eternity precisely because he is by nature a *Gestalt* that, through the Resurrection, finds its fulfillment in manifesting, indeed, giving birth to, God precisely from within the contours of his (spiritualized) human nature.[96] Insofar as this *Gestalt*

---

96. The connection between Balthasar and de Lubac becomes clear when we consider that the latter's theology of nature and grace is in some ways an elaboration of Julien Green's statement that *"tout est ailleurs":* all is elsewhere. On the one hand, it affirms that *"tout est":* there is such a thing as a whole, and it triumphantly resists every mechanistic attempt to reduce it to its components. On the other hand, this *tout* is *ailleurs,* elsewhere than just within the confines of its parts, as if it were itself just one more part among many. Indeed, precisely

involves the individual in a death to self (which nature wants but cannot give itself) and a rising to new life, it brings to light a "new" ontology that transforms, yet preserves everything that we knew from classical philosophy about motion, nature, and the perseity of act.

CRT, then, construes the non-neutrality of nature toward specifically Christian revelation in terms of the enacted analogy between natural fruitfulness, also and precisely bodily fruitfulness, and the paternal fruitfulness.[97] The point I would like to stress here is that this enactment is completed only where the link between death and fruitfulness, which so struck Aristotle,[98] is transvalued by the Redemption. This transvaluation begins when the virginal motherhood of Mary opens a distinction between a good death[1], built into the structure of nature itself qua paradox, and the sin-tainted death[2] with which it is entangled concretely — thus making death[1] fully available to manifest the paternal fruitfulness and so to guide a rethinking of perseity, relation, motion, and the like. For Schindler, then, the virgin *Theotokos,* who anticipates the apathic incorruptibility of the Resurrection, even while distinguishing it from invulnerable self-enclosure, is the living key to the spiritual rereading of Aristotle's account of nature, indeed, of nature itself, and so, literally, is the matrix of a new

---

because the whole is elsewhere, precisely because it is not exhaustively determinable within the bounds of its own parts, indeed, within the bounds of the world, the whole is a whole in the first place: a unity that is, as Aristotle saw, more than the sum of its parts (even as this "more" frees the parts from what would otherwise be a technological-mechanical control from above, allowing them to participate in the giving of unity). Insofar as such a unity re-enacts the mystery of the God-world relation within its own confines, and so serves as an expressive medium for God to appear in the world as God, it is what Balthasar means by *Gestalt.* The passage from Green is cited in Alexander Schmemann, *The Journals of Father Alexander Schmemann 1973-1983* (New York: St. Vladimir's Seminary Press, 2000), 1 *et passim.*

97. De Lubacian paradox is never better on display on the nature side of the nature-grace distinction than in human begetting. For the doubling of the principle of generation into male and female is the thickest revelation in this world that the intrinsic perfection of nature is an impossibility of fulfilling itself within its own bounds: fruitfulness.

98. This becomes especially clear in Aristotle's account of the finality of sexual differentiation generation — to give the species the chance to receive something of the divine eternality that is denied to the individual on account of its matter-bound mortality. See above all Aristotle, *On the Generation of Animals,* II, 1: 731b24-732a10. Note here the connection between Aristotle's account of *erōs* and *thanatos* and his alignment of the female with matter; only when creation out of nothing makes both form and matter equally dependent on God and the Resurrection untangles the sex-death connection does it become possible for the active receptivity of woman in the *Theotokos* to stand for the perfection of nature vis-à-vis the divine.

ontology.[99] It is she who shows how the creature's constitutive relation to God is a principle of fruitfulness that reflects, or rather refracts through the gap of radical non-identity, what might be called the "vulnerable omnipotence" of the fontal plenitude of the Father. What, then, does the non-neutrality of nature mean concretely for our attitude toward the world?

There is an icon motif called, if I am not mistaken, the "Virgin of the Sign." The motif depicts Mary, in the *orans* position, with a circle open in her stomach. Inside this circle is Jesus, with the legend *"ho on,"* "he who is." The incarnating Word, the iconographical tradition is telling us, enters into Mary, not by forcing her open from the outside, but by *coming from* inside of her, from a depth deeper than her own. The Virgin of the Sign sums up, it seems to me, the burden of CRT: just as Mary bears the Incarnate Word without loss of her virginal integrity, so, too, Christ enters into natures in a way that really "affects" them without destroying their integrity. Christ really "adds" something to nature and concepts, not by mutating their inner *logos,* or by mixing foreign elements into it, but by allowing them to bring him forth from out of themselves — from out of a depth that is both a new creation of his presence in them *and* the deepest truth they in some sense always already had. This suggests a threefold process: (1) we can distinguish between change[1] and change[2] vis-à-vis nature; (2) we can rule out change[1] as a way of affecting nature; (3) we can nonetheless hold to the reality of a change[2] of natures worked by Christ — and so preserve the immutability of natures Aristotle affirmed, though at the "cost" of giving it a new meaning that changes it (in the sense of change[2]) from top to bottom. This threefold process is nothing other than the spiritual reading of *physis* with which I have been concerned in this essay.

The Incarnate Logos, then, "affects" (change[2]) all beings, and so also the knowledge of all beings, from the inside, albeit not as a component of beings. Of course, even more so than in the case of metaphysics with respect to mathematics,[100] relation to Christ will never appear as a thematic

---

99. This means that the virginal fruitfulness of Mary, as an anticipation of the Resurrection, is the full warrant and measure for construing the fruitful embrace of man and woman as a distant echo of the Father's fruitfulness — not just in spite of, but also in, death. Mary's virginal fruitfulness is the key to the sacramentalization of human begetting in Christian marriage, and is therefore the deepest source of a spiritual rereading of the relation between death, person, and natural fruitfulness that preserves the perseity Aristotle found in nature while opening it from within to the Paschal Mystery.

100. The formal object of metaphysics is immanent in the formal object of mathematics in such a way that, without appearing per se as a principle of, or step in, mathematical ar-

principle of, or step, in the arguments of the secular sciences, but will come to light only when we reflect on that relation on the level of the highest science — *revealed* theology. And yet, just as in the former case, here, too, the jump up to a higher science is not simply an arbitrary option of the religiously minded, but is actually necessary *fully* to unfold the excess of intelligibility whose implicit presence within the secular sciences is the key to their fruitfulness, precisely within their own limited spheres.[101] Christ has

---

gumentation, it is nonetheless pervasively relevant to that argumentation at every point. While not converting mathematics into metaphysics, or confusing the formal object of the former with that of the latter, this pervasiveness guarantees the fruitfulness of mathematical concepts — first *from within the specific horizon of mathematics itself.* For the doing of mathematics, that may be enough; the reflexive explanation of how mathematical concepts are fruitful in terms of being occurs within the "higher science" of metaphysics. But that is just the point: the immanent fruitfulness of mathematics is itself so rich that *it can't be fully unfolded within the limited horizon of mathematics per se.* It is this fact, and this fact alone, that explains how mathematics can raise questions that mathematicians, as such, can't deal with, but have to become metaphysicians in order to resolve, even as they are pertinent to understanding what mathematicians are doing when they do mathematics.

101. Aristotle himself already knew that things' natural striving goes, not just to themselves, but to themselves as imitating God. God is immanent to nature, not as one of its constitutive principles, but as, so to say, the "principle of its principles," or, if you will, the cause of its immanent causes. God does not appear among these principles or causes, not because he is not relevant to them, but because his relevance is so deep and so comprehensive that it cannot be accounted for in terms of those principles *alone,* but only in terms of those principles as seen in the light of the principles of a higher science. In the end, that higher science is *theologia,* not just as it exists in our minds, but as it exists in God's mind, indeed, as God. The contemplation of God as he is in himself, then, would seem to be necessary to understand even the world on its own terms. Aquinas, for his part, transposes Aristotle's insight about God's nature-grounding immanence in nature into the register of creation, when he says that, at the heart of every created nature, is something that is no longer yet another created nature, nor yet another principle of such nature, but the *actus essendi,* which pervades the whole of that nature, yet without being "mixed up" with it in any way. By the same token, the real distinction enables Thomas to maintain that the natural movement of created intellect, to understand all things in their Principle, can be fulfilled intrinsically only by a gracious elevation conforming that intellect to that Principle beyond the innate power of nature. Compare this text from Maximus the Confessor: "So since none of the beings knows at all either what it itself or anything else is by essence, it follows that none of the beings by nature has foreknowledge of any of the things that will come to be, either, except the God above the beings, who knows both what he is by essence and has foreknown the existence of all the things made by him even before they came into being, and who will by grace liberally bestow upon beings the knowledge of what he and one another are by essence and manifest to them the *logoi* of their own coming into being, which pre-exist uniformly in him." Maximus the Confessor, *Quaestiones ad Thalassium,* 60: PG 90, 623d-625a.

an intrinsic relevance to the sciences in a way that changes our usual understanding of "intrinsic": precisely because he is not an immanent principle of, or step in, the specific arguments of the sciences, he can pervasively
touch every such principle and step from an inner depth lying even deeper
in them than they are in themselves.

Of course, though Christ's Incarnation already touches all of being
from within, the full manifestation of his presence in things is still to come.
In the meantime, Jesus enters into the natures of things hiddenly, thanks to
the Holy Spirit, who, without dissolving his individual humanity, gives it a
"subtlety" that allows it to pervade and penetrate all natures and their *logoi*
without invasion and destruction. Nevertheless, he really does enter into
them — or rather, since, as Logos, he was already in them, he enters into
them in a new mode that now includes his pneumatic humanity. This new
mode does "change" natures (change²) — but only in the way that Christ
"changes" the Virgin of the Sign (change²). The risen Christ, in other
words, truly takes possession of all things *from within* as *Pantokrator,* thus
making all things re-live, singly and collectively, what the Virgin of the
Sign lived as the archetype of the creature: a fruitfulness without loss of integrity corresponding to, and revealing the meaning of, the vulnerable
power of the Father that he makes present in his Incarnation. Christ is the
connection between the fruitfulness of the Paternal Principle, which he reveals in the Incarnation, and the insight that all natures reflect precisely
this fruitfulness of his through the virginal fruitfulness of Mary.

CRT, it should by now be clear, is not simply a novel hypothesis, but a
way of talking about what has to be true about the world if specifically
Christian revelation is going to have a real influence on how we understand it even on its own terms. CRT does not mean, however, that revelation brings to the world a theological or philosophical system deduced
from the mysteries of the faith. Schindler knows that specifically Christian
revelation is not even primarily about the world in the first place, but
about the More-Than-World: God. But he also knows that precisely because it is given "from above," and so does not compete with other
worldviews on the same level, specifically Christian revelation brings with
it a new sense of the worldliness of the world. The wholeness of the world,
we now see, is an intactness beyond, but not opposed to, the mere totality
of integral parts — the intactness of *Gestalt* in the unity of form and light,
the intactness of a virginal womb ready to reveal the More-Than-World
from the heart of the world in the splendor of the transcendentals. CRT,
then, is not first the proposal of some new theological or philosophical

cure-all, but an invitation to relearn how to see nature, in its infabricable originality, with eyes of wonderment trained in the light of the dawning of God's glory from within it. Here the apathic contemplation of Aristotle's wise man and his own naturalist's passion for the physical world converge in what Ignatius of Loyola called "indifference": not lack of interest in differences, but intense interest in them within the catholic equilibrium of the whole — which lies not only in this or only in that part, but in all together in their common reference to God, who reveals himself in the intraworldly antitheses as the one who infinitely transcends them.

Beyond Mechanism: The Cosmological Significance of David L. Schindler's *Communio* Ontology

Michael Hanby

I. Introduction: Schindler's Comprehensive Vision

Entailed in a proper understanding of God *as* God is an understanding of the world as creation: something at once distinct from God and thus possessing integrity of its own and yet intrinsically dependent in its very distinction from God upon its participation in God's own life for its being and meaning. Something like this is the only coherent sense of that audacious — and to the modern mind, quaintly anachronistic — claim of the Second Vatican Council, which insists that Jesus Christ reveals man's true nature and destiny "in the very revelation of the mystery of the Father and of his love."[1] It follows that if we are thinking coherently of God and if the world is indeed creation, then even under the distortions imposed by sin there can be no aspect of the world that falls outside of this relation of utter dependence, no aspect of it that can fail to reflect and participate in the divine life, and thus no aspect of it whose inner meaning is not objectively revealed in analogous ways through the incarnation of Jesus Christ. It follows further that failure to apprehend this relation with sufficient rigor or to regard the whole of reality as constituted by it from within will issue in a double defect. Not only will the doctrine of God assumed in this notion be flawed, but the corresponding understanding of nature and of the world will be defective precisely in their worldliness and naturality.

Perhaps no theologian who came of age in the post-Conciliar Church, and certainly none writing in English, has understood the implications of this more deeply, extended them more broadly, understood the defects of

1. *Gaudium et Spes*, 22.

alternative understandings more thoroughly, and thus grasped the real import of the Council's call to *aggiornamento* more correctly, than David L. Schindler. He succinctly sums up this insight in the theological principles, offered as interpretations of the Council's teachings, undergirding his remarkable essay "Trinity, Creation, and the Order of Intelligence in the Modern Academy": "God-centeredness and world-centeredness properly understood are not opposed; on the contrary, they mutually imply one another."[2] This mutuality is a function of the Incarnation of the Son, who assumes rather than absorbs human nature, uniting it through love to his own relationship with the Father, thereby empowering "the integral distinctness of [Christ's] human nature *as human*."[3] "Thus, the mutuality of God-centeredness and world-centeredness means that the world's (destined) ever-greater union with God coincides with, even as it provides the anterior condition for, the world's ever-deeper integrity as world."[4] The source of this paradoxical differentiation in unity is of course the inter-Trinitarian life itself. "Within God himself (infinite) union generates (infinite) difference," precisely because the processions within the divine being are processions of love.[5] Hence Schindler will insist that "being receives its basic order and meaning from love."[6]

The implications of all this are enormous, for, if they are true, they necessarily impinge upon the most basic features of the natural order and should thus impinge upon how we are to understand that order if we would grasp it aright.

> In sum, the movement toward God in Christ (through the Church, by the Holy Spirit) is not something tacked on, as it were, to a space and time and matter originally constituted on their own and in abstraction from this movement. On the contrary, the movement toward God in Christ lies at the core of space, time, and matter in their original constitution, and hence in their original meaning precisely *as* space and *as* time and *as* matter.[7]

It should go without saying that the entire modern — i.e., post-Christian — world is to a great extent historically, theoretically, and politi-

2. "Trinity, Creation, and the Academy," 407.
3. "Trinity, Creation, and the Academy," 408.
4. "Trinity, Creation, and the Academy," 408.
5. "Trinity, Creation, and the Academy," 408.
6. HW, xi.
7. "Trinity, Creation, and the Academy," 410.

cally predicated upon what is at best a deep distortion and at worst the out-right rejection of this understanding, except that the now normative character of this rejection, on the one hand, and the persistent attempts by neo-conservatives to reconcile Anglo-American liberalism with Catholic orthodoxy, on the other, tend to obscure this and deaden us to its implications. Yet if our claims heretofore are correct, it means that the physical and metaphysical first principles of the modern world and their social, political, economic, and intellectual embodiment are predicated on a distorted conception of God and a correlative failure to understand nature in its naturality. At first glance this appears to be an odd claim, given the ostensible success of modern science in understanding nature, but I am hardly the first to note what seems to be an inverse relationship between our increased technological command of nature and the intelligibility of human life *qua* human. It has been a persistent if slightly muted theme in literature and certain strains of philosophy (e.g., Kierkegaard) since the nineteenth century, and we see it reiterated by Vatican II and Pope John Paul II.[8] One may wish to stress the legitimate distinction between the natural and the artificial to object that it is just those peculiarly human facets of our existence that are not "natural," but it is the burden of Schindler's work — and I am sympathetic to this burden and appreciative of his success in meeting it — to show just how deep are the stakes in this point and to dispute it.

The pervasiveness of these first principles and the tenacity of their grip upon the modern imagination have had a profound influence on how the Council's call to embrace the world has been received both inside and outside the Church, arguably making it difficult for claims such as *Gaudium et Spes,* 22, to have their full effect.[9] Consequently, to articulate

---

8. See, e.g., *Evangelium Vitae,* 21: "Consequently, when the sense of God is lost, the sense of man is also threatened and poisoned, as the Second Vatican Council concisely states: 'Without the Creator the creature would disappear. . . . But when God is forgotten the creature itself grows unintelligible.' Man is no longer able to see himself as 'mysteriously different' from other creatures, he regards himself merely as one more living being, as an organism which, at most, has reached a very high stage of perfection. Enclosed in the narrow horizon of his physical nature, he is somehow reduced to being 'a thing,' and no longer grasps the 'transcendent' character of his 'existence as man'" (citing *Gaudium et Spes,* 36).

9. For Schindler's criticisms of the rival ecclesiologies still determining the Anglo-American reception of Vatican II, see HW, 1-40. Inasmuch as both the "left-wing autonomy" of liberationist integralism and the "right-wing autonomy" of neo-conservative liberalism misunderstand the genuine nature of worldly autonomy, there is between these alternatives, as between so many others, less of a real disagreement than immediately meets the eye.

the full ontological implications of *communio* ecclesiology one must simultaneously criticize the first principles of modern social, political, economic, and intellectual life, not primarily for the sake of *communio* ontology per se, and certainly not in order that the world might be extrinsically and juridically subordinated to the Church, but rather so that the Church might liberate the world for the genuine "legitimate autonomy" proclaimed for it by the Council.[10]

All of the various distortions imposed upon the God-world relationship by the first principles of liberal society across the various spheres of human life are analogically related by a feature common to them all: a mechanistic understanding of *physis* that evacuates nature of intrinsic meaning, institutes a new regime of knowledge appropriate to nature thus construed, and subsequently dictates that "God" is only accidentally and extrinsically related to a world capable in principle of exhaustively explaining itself (typically through the ministrations of science).[11] This mechanistic ontology is presupposed, analogously manifest, and juridically enforced throughout the various spheres of liberal society, which occludes its own deep metaphysical commitments by promoting its own principled and methodological neutrality in matters metaphysical and theological. Yet this allegedly neutral viewpoint recapitulates the metaphysical commitments of modern mechanistic philosophy, with the consequence that vast areas of human life, certainly those typically identified with religion, mirror the extrinsicism that the mechanistic viewpoint imposes upon the God-world relationship. Faith and love, for instance, are regarded as essentially extrinsic and thus arbitrarily related to reason and knowledge.[12]

The Church, far from being seen as an ontological reality integral to the very form and destiny of the cosmos in its original constitution, is likewise regarded sociologically as an "arbitrary addition" to a culture whose essential secularity and a nature whose essential godlessness are assumed. Thus its role is confined to that of a counselor providing moralistic guidance to the world in its pursuit of secular justice.[13] Betraying a deep and abiding dualism of quantitative matter and qualitative mind, questions of

---

10. *Gaudium et Spes*, 36.

11. BM, 7-11.

12. Schindler, "The Religious Sense and American Culture," in *A Generative Thought: An Introduction to the Works of Luigi Giussani*, ed. Elisa Buzzi (Montreal: McGill-Queens, 2003), 84-102.

13. HW, 6-11.

gender, marriage, and family are treated in similar terms, as *merely* moral
questions, matters of value that reveal nothing of nature in its original and
teleological constitution, and therefore represent a voluntaristic imposition upon the qualitatively neutral facts of nature. Incursion by the Church
more generally into matters thought to be the special province of science is
regarded in similar terms. The scientific enterprise is (falsely) conceived
from the outset in a relation of indifference to metaphysical and theological considerations. The Church's role, if it is to have one, is once again to
step in with moral casuistry when scientific applications threaten to cross
a moral boundary. To accept this role is of course to accept defeat *a priori*,
since the operative conceptions of nature, knowledge, and truth in modernity make these boundaries appear arbitrary. And it is not only secular opponents of the Church who fall into these habits of thought, but also well-
intentioned proponents of the Church's teachings. Consider the remarks of
Robert George, a highly respected Catholic scholar and member of President Bush's Commission on Bioethics, regarding a "test case" we will explore at the conclusion of this essay, the case of ANT-OAR as a method for
extracting embryonic stem-cells.

> There is no mystery about when the life of a new human individual be-
> gins. It is not a matter of subjective opinion or private religious belief.
> One finds the answer not by consulting one's viscera or searching
> through the Bible or the Koran; one finds it, rather, in the basic texts of
> the relevant scientific disciplines. Those texts are clear. . . . Of course,
> science cannot by itself settle questions of value, dignity, or morality.[14]

Though George is attempting to defend the Church's teaching that life begins at conception, he does so on the basis of presuppositions that are fundamentally mechanistic and dualistic and so cannot but undermine that
teaching in the end. In so doing, he is merely repeating the animating assumptions of modern, Western culture. As we shall see more clearly below,
these are thus hardly metaphysically and theologically neutral. Implicitly
denied in all cases where these assumptions are operative, even where they
are sincerely affirmed, is the claim made above: that all aspects of the
world are *intrinsically* though analogically constituted precisely as world in
relation to the circumincession of Trinitarian love manifest in Jesus Christ

---

14. Robert George, interviewed by Kathryn Lopez, "Scientific Breakthroughs," *National Review Online*, 29 June 2005, available at http://www.nationalreview.com/interrogatory/george200506290814.asp; quoted in "Response to Joint Statement," 374.

and extended into the world through the Church.[15] Yet to deny this is to fall into profound theological confusion that ultimately casts the intelligibility of nature itself into doubt.

Thus far we have merely noted the effects of modern mechanistic ontology, largely assuming its constitutive features. We will consider Schindler's more precise explication of these features in more detail below. What is important to notice at present is the unity and character of Schindler's work and the relation of his analysis of mechanism to those areas of his thought dealing more explicitly with ecclesiology, liberal politics, economics, gender, and contemporary intellectual life. Positively speaking, his entire body of work can be seen as the attempt to bring the implications of the Incarnation to bear *intrinsically* upon the whole of reality, especially those areas regarded by liberal society as beyond the purview of theological reflection. The reality of the Incarnation carries within it the need to regard love — a unity whose infinite depth coincides with infinite difference — as the meaning of being in all its analogical manifestations. This variation on the ontological priority of goodness, whose ultimate meaning is disclosed in the Yes of Christ's resurrection, means that ontological generosity trumps human malice, and consequently that the distortions of the liberal order, like the distortions of sin more generally, could never succeed in eradicating the beauty of creation or extinguishing the *imago dei*. There is thus much that remains beautiful and good in modernity, often in spite of itself, many genuine achievements that are acknowledged and praised by the Council; and, consistent with his own ontological commitments, Schindler himself is quite generous in upholding that in modernity which is worthy of affirmation even as he criticizes its organizing logic.[16]

15. With regard to the effect of these presuppositions upon the constitution of academic disciplines, Schindler raises a dilemma. "The question, then, is two-fold: whether the purely formal methodological procedures of the academy already, in their very form, import a content; and whether that content is neutral toward or weighted against the content of an authentic Catholicism." He then contends that the priority of method within liberalism entails the correlative notions of mechanism and subjectivism and poses yet a further question. "Granted, then, that acceptance of liberalism's priority of method commits us to a worldview whose content is mechanism and subjectivism, in what sense is this content opposed to an authentic Catholic worldview?" The answer is much like what I've sketched here: these correlative notions entail a rejection of the ontological primacy of love manifest in the Son's mission from the Father, and the analogy of being that flows from it. See HW, 161-169.

16. See especially HW, 177-188, though Schindler is magnanimous toward modernity's social and intellectual achievements more generally in this book.

Nevertheless, we have suggested that in its organizing logic modernity is constituted as such by the tragic denial of this ontological generosity and by the concomitant defacement of this image, even as it has sometimes attempted to assert it. Modernity is thus an alternative account of the meaning — or rather, tragically, the meaninglessness — of being, and this alternative is contained in the fundamental priority modernity accords to mechanism. This account is just as comprehensive, but its breadth is secured by tyrannically reducing the being of the world to what can be known (and controlled) by its methods. Consequently, Schindler's analysis of mechanism should not be regarded as an isolated feature of his thought pertaining only to the so-called "religion and science" debate, but rather as a critique of the ontological violence at the heart of the liberal order, though not to be equated with a simplistic *rejection* of that order. As a consequence of its inherent reductionism, this order tends to treat all real differences as so many indifferent and interchangeable variables, thus tragically and ironically suppressing those differences in the name of celebrating them. As this order expresses its avowed indifference by locating the economic activities of economic production and consumption at the heart of social life, the dangerous result, Schindler argues (following Balthasar), is a world without women or children. Which is to say that it is a world dangerously at risk of being inhospitable to persons as such.[17]

II. The Problem of Mechanism

Apropos of its importance within David Schindler's global vision, the critique of mechanism and its implications occurs at various places throughout his corpus. Perhaps nowhere is it stated at once more thoroughly and more succinctly, however, than in one of his lesser known essays from the proceedings of a conference on the topic hosted by *Communio* at Notre Dame and published in 1986.

In this essay, the real metaphysical significance of the new mechanistic treatment of nature emerges in Schindler's contrast between the mechanistic philosophy set forth paradigmatically by Descartes and the earlier tradition advanced by Aristotle and transformed by Aquinas.[18] The essential point of contrast concerns the nature of matter.

17. HW, 269-274.
18. This is not to say that Schindler does not appreciate "the enormous refinement in

On the Aristotelian side, the issue turns on the relationship between matter and nature *(physis)* more generally. In one sense, nature is matter. "Nature means the primary material — *ex hou prōtou* — of which any natural object consists or out of which it is made."[19] As Schindler explains:

> Nonetheless, in a second and indeed more proper sense, nature for Aristotle is *not* matter: for nature in the full and proper sense for Aristotle is something actual and matter in its basic meaning is not actual — it is what has the capacity for becoming actual. It follows that nature in its full and proper sense must be — not matter — but that — the act or activity — in virtue of which nature, and hence matter, are said to be actual. What I wish to suggest here, then, is this: that the meaning of *physis* (nature), is for Aristotle disclosed in the first instance by the meaning of act (that in virtue of which something is said to be actual). I thereby wish to suggest that the meaning of matter, in the sense of matter *as it is a part of nature in its proper — actual — sense,* is likewise disclosed in the first instance by the meaning of act.[20]

The primacy that Aristotle accords to act, and the concomitant notions of form, wholeness, finality, and immanence, serve to locate the question of nature within an understanding of being as such that is ontologically primary. Departing momentarily from Schindler's analysis, we should note that it is just this location of beings within the question of being that makes Aristotle's conception of nature amenable to the transformations

---

the mechanistic understanding of nature (matter) as extension or quantity: Descartes's matter as inert substance undergoing change of place has become an enormous variety of microsubstances, as it were (elementary particles), undergoing change of place. More importantly, whereas Descartes's mechanism made the explicitly metaphysical claim that material entities really were (in themselves) simply mechanical in their activity, a more methodological mechanism would abstract from the question about what material entities really are (in themselves), and restrict itself rather to treating those entities as if they were mechanical in their activity — treating them, that is, just so far as they manifest in mechanical ways." However, in a culture still operating under concepts of knowledge established by the earlier forms of mechanism, in which "natural" knowledge is largely restricted to what can be quantitatively represented, there is little formal difference in practice between the two approaches. It has become quite fashionable for scientists and philosophers alike to renounce the reductionism that says that we are "nothing but" the sum of our component parts or antecedent causes, but modern, scientific habits of mind provide no means for accounting for the "what more" in a way that can be publicly regarded as true. BM, 6.

19. Aristotle, *Metaphysics,* 5.4. 1014[b] 27-28; cf. also *Physics,* 2.1; BM, 2.
20. BM, 2.

wrought in it by Aquinas, who encompassed it within his famous distinction between the *esse ipsum* of God himself and the *esse creatum non subsistens* of creatures.[21] The latter notion is of fundamental importance for Aquinas, for the non-subsistence of created being apart from those things which participate in it means that the very "being of being" consists fundamentally in an act that is simultaneously dependent and receptive, on the one hand, and self-giving or kenotic, on the other.[22] The perfection of being consists precisely in its being given away, but nothing can be given that hasn't "first" been received.[23] Thus, expanding upon Aquinas, or at least upon the standard interpretation of Aquinas by many subsequent "Thomists," Schindler stresses that created being both participates in and has the structure of love — of being itself precisely in being from and for another. Schindler makes this point all the more pervasive and explicit by enfolding the implicitly Thomistic understanding of created being in *Beyond Mechanism* within a Balthasarian understanding of the nuptial relation between the Trinitarian God, which is eternally for and from another in the relation between Father and Son, and the Marian Church, which is at once receptive and kenotic both with respect to the Bridegroom and in her orientation to the world. To locate this relationship fundamentally in the hypostatic union of Christ is simply to say once again that "the Son of God's incarnate union with the world, in a word, itself makes possible and deepens the continuing difference of the world as world."[24] We note all of this here in order to indicate the integral relationship between Schindler's appropriation of a Thomist-Aristotelian conception of nature in *Beyond Mechanism* (and elsewhere) and his conception, drawn from Balthasar, of the ontological primacy of the nuptial bond between Christ and the Marian Church. Each is an aspect of a seamless garment, a fact that is easily overlooked if one pits St. Thomas *against* Balthasar, or if one is intent on viewing Schindler more as a commentator on Balthasar than as an original thinker in his own right. Yet "God-centeredness and world-centeredness properly understood are not op-

---

21. On the importance of *esse non subsistens* as developed by Ferdinand Ulrich, see the extraordinary essay by Schindler's son, D. C. Schindler, "What's the Difference? On the Metaphysics of Participation in a Christian Context," *The Saint Anselm Journal* 3.1 (2005): 15.

22. For a more technical explanation of the priority of receptivity as a primordial perfection of *esse* and not merely of *agere*, and for Schindler's amendments to Aquinas (following and altering Norris Clarke), see HW, 275-311.

23. "First" here indicates an ontological rather than a temporal priority.

24. "Trinity, Creation, and the Academy," 408.

posed"; if they do indeed "mutually imply one another," then a seamless garment is exactly what we should expect.[25]

If it is true that the God-world relationship is intrinsic, then it will be logically and ontologically impossible for the mechanical ontology to remain neutral with respect to this relationship. Rather, it will simply reconfigure that relationship in accordance with its own presuppositions and ends. One may object that while this is certainly the case in the mechanical philosophy of the seventeenth century, which invoked God variously as first efficient cause and metaphysical guarantor of rationality, the intellectual trajectory opened up by this philosophy made it possible for later science to join with Laplace in denying the need for a God hypothesis, thus establishing at last its pragmatic independence from metaphysical and theological speculation and its autonomy within its own self-enclosed sphere. Indeed, early mechanical philosophy did so transform the concept of God as to make it ostensibly irrelevant to later iterations of that philosophy, but to take the disappearance of God as an axiom of mechanistic ontology to mean that science is not always and already laden with constitutive assumptions of a metaphysical and theological nature is to completely misunderstand the nature of science's legitimate autonomy, the relationship between science and metaphysics, and the contemporary situation with regard to these questions. Judgments as to the meaning of matter, causality, and nature, the nature and limits of reason, the goods of scientific inquiry in relation to broader human goods, and the validity and necessity of metaphysical questions are the presuppositions of science, not its conclusions.

From the very outset these judgments exert profound internal pressure on the shape of the scientific enterprise, the understanding of nature within which science does its work, and the nature of the "God" whom this conception of nature will permit us to imagine. The commonplace contrast between naturalistic and supernatural explanations, a distinction presupposing a world of theological speculation, exemplifies *both* the magisterial authority ascribed to science by modern culture *and* the way in which metaphysical assumptions are intrinsically constitutive of the modern scientific enterprise. And in a culture that does not recognize metaphysics and theology as legitimate forms of knowledge, much less as the organizing principle and final cause of *all* knowledge, it is inevitable that science will *become* metaphysics and theology, patrolling the boundaries

---

25. "Trinity, Creation, and the Academy," 407.

of acceptable theological speech. This is true of modern science generally, but it is especially true of modern evolutionary biology, which is often positively evangelical in insisting that its claims somehow invalidate the doctrine of creation, even while it imposes its own extrinsicist picture of the God-world relationship upon the question.

The Cartesian conception of matter that Schindler juxtaposes to that of Aristotle functions in precisely this fashion. For Aristotle (and certainly for Thomas), "the meaning of nature (matter) is only understood by considering the meaning of activity in the first instance, not in terms of specifically *human* being, but rather, more basically in terms of being (ousia)."[26] Descartes's system, by contrast, rests upon his fundamental method of hyperbolic doubt, which effectively redefines the very meaning of metaphysics and thus precludes anything like an Aristotelian conception of nature (or Thomistic conception of God) at the outset.[27] Emptying being of its transcendental attributes, collapsing it into extended or un-extended substance, and subjecting these to hyperbolic doubt, Descartes transforms the very meaning of metaphysics. No longer is metaphysics to be regarded as the science of being *qua* being, for this is no longer an intelligible question. In Descartes's hands, "metaphysics" now treats "the principles of all *knowledge*." Thus "metaphysics" was to be the root of "the tree of philosophy," whose "trunk" was physics and whose branches would become the so-called applied sciences.[28]

It is this same method of hyperbolic doubt, by which Descartes famously destroys the dubious world of the senses in order to reconstruct it as a clear and distinct idea for the mind, that allows him to dispense with the so-called occult qualities of the scholastics and make straight the path for mechanical philosophy. Yet these drastic measures are warranted only on the assumption of a radically voluntaristic God, a God whose power is unconditioned by the transcendental attributes of being, whose will is severed from intellect, from goodness, and from the processions of Trinitarian love. Indeed, Descartes *needs* the *deus malignus* of the *Meditations* to justify his extreme doubt. Schindler is correct to juxtapose the Aristotelian and Cartesian understandings of matter, but we should stress perhaps even

26. BM, 8.

27. The controverted question of whether the *Meditations* reflects a real skeptical crisis on Descartes's part is methodologically irrelevant.

28. Descartes, *Principles*, in *The Philosophical Writings of Descartes*, trans. John Cottingham, Robert Stoothoff, and Dugald Murdoch, vol. 1 (Cambridge: Cambridge University Press, 1985), 186.

more than he does that all mechanical ontologies depend, first, upon the rejection of the question of being whereby God's difference from, transcendence to, and immanence within the world can be elucidated; second, upon God being emptied of traditional predicates ascribed to the divine essence and employed to articulate the Trinitarian processions; and, finally, upon the Trinity being relegated to an arbitrary realm of faith and piety essentially extrinsic to reason and, correspondingly, to so-called revealed religion, whose God is quite distinct from the God who may be of use to philosophy.[29] The God correlative to mechanistic ontology is not the *actus essendi* or *esse ipsum,* in whom all creatures somehow live, move, and have their being, and it is certainly not the Trinity of love manifest in the drama of the Incarnation. It is rather a unitary causal object, one finite thing confronting the other finite thing that is the world. This is the only thought of "God" that can be accommodated from within a mechanistic ontology; indeed, this is the thought of God continually conjured up by modern society and modern science in order that it might be denied.

What is the essential difference between Cartesian, mechanistic nature and its Aristotelian antecedent? In Aristotle's view, matter is a relative concept, dependent for its actuality on the intrinsic acts of formality and finality by which it is instantiated in any of its actual instances as this or that sort of being. In short, its actuality depends upon *nature* in its more fundamental sense. There is no *actual* matter that is not a tree, or a dog, or a house, or a person, no matter that is not already intrinsically actualized by form. For Descartes, by contrast, matter "becomes precisely identical to a nature from which mind (anything like forming and finalizing activity) has — always and already — been removed."[30] Matter, in other words, is clearly distinguishable from mind, which for purposes of the mechanical philosophy Descartes reduces to extension. And for Descartes, whatever can be clearly distinguished can be clearly set apart from everything else, as things on either side of a line. Matter and mind — "that is, anything like the immanent activity of forming and finalizing" — are simply different, separate, and apart from one another.[31]

Descartes reduces the meaning of *physis* to matter now regarded as actual in its own right, and he empties matter of all inherent formal and final

<hr>

29. See Michael J. Buckley, S.J., *At the Origins of Modern Atheism* (New Haven: Yale University Press, 1987), 68-144.

30. BM, 3.

31. BM, 4.

activity and all qualitative properties save extension. Thus nature (that is, matter) becomes essentially inert and inherently meaningless. All formal and final activity in "nature," i.e., the work of "mind," must therefore be essentially *extrinsic* and thus accidental to nature in its new, most primary sense. This new understanding of nature is the source of the modern "mind-body problem." For all its intractable flaws, Descartes's dualistic attempts to locate mind "in" matter, which gave philosophical expression to the prevailing sense that there must be more to the human being after all than could be accounted for by Cartesian and Newtonian nature, helped for a while to postpone the complete erasure of nature in the human sphere.[32] That would not arrive until the latter half of the nineteenth century with the arrival of Darwinian biology.[33] Nevertheless, it is important to see that the dualistic and materialistic attempts to resolve issues like the "mind-body problem" both presuppose this same basic conception of nature,[34] which means that the primary problem with the so-called material-

32. "Of course, it is still possible to conceive the mind, as Descartes in fact does, in some sense inside matter. But note how . . . the meaning of 'inside' (inner, internal) now gets transformed. The mind's immaterial agency is (can be) inside matter (the body) only after the manner of what is disjoined or separate (somewhat after the manner in which we might picture something like a gremlin lurking at the center of a machine: not in, immanent within — the machine; but rather remaining external to the machine albeit now from somewhere imagined to be its center). It is not hard to see how, subsequently, the activity of the mind (and indeed that of any agent taken to be immaterial: e.g., God) comes to be understood as something private: that is, as something hidden by rather than disclosed in the matter (bodies) taken to be public." BM, 9.

33. Depew and Weber contend that the real scandal of Darwinism in the nineteenth century lay in its success in at last making biology a legitimate Newtonian science. See David J. Depew and Bruce H. Weber, *Darwinism Evolving: Systems Dynamics and the Genealogy of Natural Selection* (Cambridge, MA: MIT Press, 1997), 57-84. For a theological criticism of the effects of Darwinian reductionism, see my article "Creation without Creationism: Toward a Theological Critique of Darwinism," *Communio: International Catholic Review* 30 (2003): 654-694. This criticism should not be taken to mean, however, that the Church has a stake in denying evolution as such or even in denouncing Darwinian explanations of it as *simply* false. The problem is that it isn't simply true either. Lacking a proper metaphysical foundation and relation to theology, Darwinian evolution inherently takes refuge in the flawed metaphysics whose legitimacy it must deny.

34. When Richard Lewontin, who is more philosophically astute than many of his colleagues in evolutionary biology, dismisses the latent epiphenomenalism of many of his contemporaries and expresses his hope that the so-called "mind-body problem" will be resolved according to the only "coherent materialist position . . . that the mental and neural are simply two aspects of the same material physical state," he begs the crucial question of what constitutes a physical state, and arguably recapitulates the very dualism he is rejecting. See

ism or naturalism of modernity is not its denial of spirit, but its denial of *matter and nature,* or, rather, the actuality of the natural forms according to which material things actually exist. The problem with materialism, one might say, is that it isn't materialistic *enough.* The same should be said of empiricism.

To say that nature is actually missing from modern naturalism is to call attention to the new way in which the mechanistic viewpoint regards the "wholeness" of nature, indeed the only way wholeness could be regarded. For Aristotle, the manifestations of nature in this or that respect are always the expression of the internally active unity of form and internally ordered to a *telos* beyond itself. Because of the priority of this immanent act and the inherent orientation of each thing to a good beyond itself, the wholeness of each thing "is always, in principle, more than the sum of its parts."[35] Because Descartes empties nature of itself, it "can be a whole only in the manner in which what is exhaustively extension is whole, that is, precisely as quantity — a quantified bit or the sum of quantified bits."[36]

> The heart of that understanding consists in a two-fold claim: (a) that matter is an absolute concept, something apart from, not-relative to, anything "more" like internal — formal and final — activity; (b) that nature, now absorbed into matter in this way, is whole (in any of its instances) only in the sense of being a collection which is exactly the sum of its externally interactive parts.[37]

When the wholeness of a thing is reduced to "the sum of its externally interactive parts," nature itself, as that principle of unity which precedes and transcends this organization, is eliminated, and with it, the real ontological identity of things in their distinction and difference from other things.

This redefinition of *physis* makes possible the remaining critical elements of a mechanistic worldview, succinctly described by the physicist David Bohm in the proceedings of *Beyond Mechanism:*

> (i.) The world is reduced, as far as possible, to a set of basic elements.[38]

Lewontin, *It Ain't Necessarily So: The Dream of the Human Genome and Other Illusions* (New York: New York Review of Books, 2001), 95.

35. BM, 4.

36. BM, 4.

37. BM, 5.

38. Bohm is speaking in terms of developments in modern physics that follow upon

(ii.) These elements are essentially basically *external* to each other, not only in being separate in space, but more important, in that the fundamental nature of each is independent of that of the other. Thus, the elements do not grow organically as parts of a whole, but rather, they may be compared to parts of a machine, whose forms are determined externally to the structure of the machine in which they are working.

(iii.) [T]he elements interact mechanically, and thus are related only by influencing each other externally, e.g., by forces of interaction that do not deeply affect their inner natures.

In addition, it is admitted that such a goal is yet to be fully achieved, as there is much that is still unknown. But it is essential for the *mechanistic reductionistic program* to assume that there is *nothing* that cannot eventually be treated in this way.[39]

Thus we can begin to see how this mechanistic conception of nature lies at the root of all those interrelated forms of *extrinsicism* governing modern thought and culture that were introduced in the opening section of this essay, from the relationship of God to the world, to the relationship of reason to faith and love, to the anthropology and notion of freedom at the heart of the liberal social and political orders. Let us briefly consider a few instances of this extrinsicism, beginning with the relationship between God and the world.

The *ordo rationis* of this relationship is complicated. As we saw in the case of Descartes, the new conception of matter was actually *predicated* upon a voluntaristic concept of God that warranted his redefinition of metaphysics, even as the redefinition of both metaphysics and matter ensured that God could henceforth be conceived only in *extrinsicist* terms. To precisely the extent that the Cartesian God must be extrinsic to creation, divine transcendence and thus the genuine difference between God and world are compromised, thus making Descartes's notion of God as incoherent as it is heretical. The same is true of Newton, who was even more explicitly heretical than Descartes and who, distrusting metaphysics, did even more than Descartes to elevate physics to the status of first philosophy. (For

---

Descartes and Newton. But, formally, his remarks apply to these earlier philosophies. He continues, "Typically, these have been taken as particles, such as atoms, electrons, protons, quarks, etc., but to these may be added various kinds of fields that extend continuously through space, e.g., electromagnetic, gravitational, etc." BM, 14.

39. BM, 14-15; emphasis original.

our purposes it matters little that Newton added mass to his essential definition of matter.)[40] Dispensing with the question of being as distinct from the question of discrete substances and failing to see that true transcendence entails immanence, Descartes and Newton found it impossible (and undesirable) to regard God's inward presence in creatures after the fashion of Aquinas, as *constitutive* of creaturehood in its very difference from God and as that toward which all things intrinsically aim.[41] Thus the final causes that Newton ascribes to God in the *General Scholium* that concludes his *Principia Mathematica* are not intrinsic to a thing's nature as with Aquinas, not "part of creation's ontology," whereby it is given to itself to develop in freedom, "but merely imposed from without by a God whose rule is supreme."[42] The difference is as profound as that between a child and a lawnmower.[43] Despite the tendency on the part of Newton to divinize absolute space — or perhaps because of it, since this, too, compromises the difference between God and the world — the Cartesian-Newtonian image of God's relationship to the world is that of two finite things, externally related to each other, confronting one another from across a chasm through the external relationship of force. To the extent that the world's relationship to God is extrinsic, it is accidental, disclosing nothing of the world as world, and, to just this degree, arbitrary.[44] God's career as a factor in the explanations of natural philosophy was destined to be a short one.

40. See Simon Oliver, *Philosophy, God, and Motion* (London: Routledge, 2005), 156-190; Stephen D. Snobelen, "'God of gods, and Lord of lords': The Theology of Isaac Newton's General Scholium to the *Principia*," *Orisis* 16 (2001): 169-208.

41. "Now since God is very being *(ipsum esse)* by His own essence, created being *(esse creatum)* must be His proper effect; as to ignite is the proper effect of fire. Now God causes this effect in things not only when they first begin to be, but as long as they are preserved in being. . . . Therefore as long as a thing has being, God must be present to it, according to its mode of being. But *being is innermost in each thing and most fundamentally inherent in all things since it is formal in respect of everything found in a thing. . . . Hence it must be that God is in all things, and innermostly.*" Aquinas, *Summa Theologiae*, I, q. 8, a. 1; emphasis mine.

42. Each comes perilously close to depicting the action of God upon creatures in terms of force. Oliver, *Philosophy, God, and Motion*, 160. See also Margeret J. Osler, "Whose Ends? Teleology in Early Modern Natural Philosophy," *Orisis* 16 (2001): 152-153.

43. The example is Adrian Walker's. We will see it again below. See Walker, "Altered Nuclear Transfer: A Philosophical Critique," *Communio: International Catholic Review* 31 (2004): 677-679.

44. "[I]t follows that, in so far as one does continue to affirm anything like a distinct activity on the part of any immaterial agent (mind, God) on nature (matter), that activity can just so far be conceived only in terms of what comes from outside: hence in terms of the sort of activity from without which we commonly call forceful." BM, 9.

Michael Hanby

This also goes a long way in explaining the fate of metaphysics and theology as forms of knowledge in the modern world, though to understand this better we must consider the perhaps familiar story of how the new understanding of nature affects the meaning of knowledge more generally. "The mechanistic understanding of nature, which entails a disjunction between nature (matter) and what is not nature, entails in turn a disjunction between the sort of knowledge proper to the study of nature (e.g., physics) and the sort of knowledge proper to what it would take to be non-nature (e.g., metaphysics and theology)."[45] What is now "non-nature" as a consequence of this new conception of matter is, strictly speaking, all the formal and qualitative distinctions through which the natural world necessarily manifests itself to us as meaningful.[46] This accounts for modern philosophy's preoccupation with epistemology as first philosophy. Once the "real world" is reduced to quantifiable bits of indifferent matter, the world of our perception, that is, the world that we actually inhabit, becomes *merely* our perception, destined for the heterogeneous and untrustworthy realm of opinions and "values." The only knowledge that can then be trusted is that which corresponds to the world reduced to fit this conception of knowledge: knowledge that can be represented as quantifiable data. Theology and philosophy cease to be regarded as knowledge at all; for acts of love and faith, rather than being integral to the very form of knowledge and the acts that properly complete knowledge in its very rationality, are regarded as extrinsic to the act of knowing. They are, once again, accidental, arbitrary, and suspicious. But all of this is due in no small measure to the fact that the objects of faith and love have been made extrinsic to the object of knowledge at the ontological level.

Mechanism and extrinsicism mutually entail one another, and together they further entail both atomism and nominalism. That is to say, by severing being and knowledge from love and goodness, mechanism makes not just the world's relation to God extrinsic and accidental, but relation-

---

45. BM, 10. For a more detailed critique of the modern academic disciplines on this same basis, see HW, 143-176.

46. Hence the last century has witnessed what one might call a "war on essentialism" that is equally fierce in philosophy and biology. In the latter field, this essentialism is referred to as "typological thinking," to be eschewed in terms of "population thinking," which defines species, including the human species, simply as historically interbreeding populations. Biologist Ernst Mayr provides the now-classic definition: "Species are groups of actually interbreeding populations, which are reproductively isolated from other such groups." Mayr, *Animal Species and Evolution* (Cambridge, MA: Harvard University Press, 1963), 19.

ality as such. As Bohm's earlier remarks indicate, each thing is most fundamentally itself in an inertial state of indifference to every other thing, and insofar as it is indifferent, each thing is inherently meaningless, identical to, and interchangeable with every other thing, except insofar as their difference can be quantitatively expressed.

The anthropological correlate to this ontology finds its expression in the liberal conception of freedom, and its social embodiment in the liberal order dominated by the mutually legitimating activities of commercial exchange and scientific research.[47] The evacuation of being, and the expulsion of all form, finality, and meaning from nature, necessarily entail the abandonment of any coherent, substantive, and teleological sense of *human* being and nature. That is to say, the liberal order presupposes that persons have already been emptied of personhood. It presupposes an atomistic world of so many indifferent and interchangeable variables, amenable to the reductive tyranny of an economic and technological order that regards them as little more than the sum of their economic functions of production and consumption, on the one hand, and the sum of their DNA, on the other: as Schindler puts it, a world without women and children in which real difference is obliterated for the indifferent and where the gift character of our existence, and the receptivity appropriate to that gift, are denied. Moreover, where being and human being are emptied of all inherent substantive and teleological content, human freedom can be understood only negatively, as immunity from coercion for an agency untethered from any goal inherent in it by virtue of its humanity. Not only, then, does the political order preoccupy itself with the task of regulating and "protecting" the violence of such heteronymous exercises of this agency (requiring ever more absolute power to do so), but human *doing* becomes a surrogate definition for human *being,* and requires for its exercise a space free of "extrinsic" impediments. In consequence, because nature is inherently empty and meaningless, the givenness of nature itself in its manifestly biological dimension is at best taken as an end in itself (hence the dominance of medicine and the role of the "heroic physician" in modern society). At worst, it is regarded as a coercive restriction upon human freedom and autonomy, to be seized upon, manipulated, and overcome according to our preferences (hence the advent and resurgence of eugenics). Since human nature and hu-

---

47. On the isomorphism between the liberal political order and the assumptions of modern (Darwinian) biology, see Richard C. Lewontin, *Biology as Ideology: The Doctrine of DNA* (San Francisco: Harper, 1992).

man persons appear to be no more than the aggregate of their component parts or their social function, there is no inherent limit upon our manipulation of these parts in order to maximize our utility and minimize inefficiencies with respect to these functions.

Within the confines of modern and liberal ontological judgments, it is simply impossible to offer principled philosophical grounds for recognizing inherent limits upon these manipulations. Any attempts to do so will appear moralistic and arbitrary and thus tend to be subordinated to the "objective" claims of an all-powerful science, which is burdened with the task of providing poor answers to intractably philosophical questions while eschewing philosophy. All of the principal debates of the present moment — whether the issue is stem-cell research, abortion, euthanasia, same-sex marriage, biotechnical manipulation of the human genome, or genetically modified agricultural products — conform by and large to this pattern, which obscures the logic of the underlying ontology that makes them thinkable in the first place and binds them into a unity.

What unifies these debates is a common conception of nature that undermines nature's very intelligibility. What is ultimately at stake in the question, and in the advance of an ontology of *communio,* is much more than is ordinarily implied by "morality," and nothing less than whether the world we and our progeny will inhabit is in any sense human and humane. Perhaps as much as any theologian of the post–Vatican II generation, David Schindler has drawn our attention to the depths of the Church's answer to this question.

III. Case in Point: ANT-OAR

I conclude this essay with a recent "test case" that I hope will display these depths by developing Schindler's ontology of love in a bit more detail and showing its relevance to our understanding of biology as both a natural "fact" and an intellectual discipline. I choose the context of a controversy in order to illustrate both the advance of the mechanistic view in the realm of human nature and the subtlety and the power of its sway over otherwise earnest and faithful Christian minds. This example will also show us something of the unity and coherence of Schindler's thought across time.

When *Beyond Mechanism* was published in 1986, Schindler could not have envisioned that the depths of human unintelligibility warned against by *Gaudium et Spes* would be equaled by a corresponding increase in the capacities of biotechnology to dissect and manipulate the human genome, such that, nearly twenty years later, a very public controversy would rage over the harvesting of stem cell lines for medical research, either from the "surplus" embryos frozen away in fertility clinics — itself an odd fact that in twenty years' time has come to be regarded as normal — or, perhaps even more ominously, from embryos "manufactured" through SCNT (cloning) for that purpose.

To circumvent the moral difficulties of these procedures and to satisfy both the desire of the scientific community to exploit the promise of stem cell research and the desire of the pro-life community to avoid feticide, a technical solution endorsed in a joint statement by some thirty-five prominent pro-life scholars was proposed that claims "to produce pluripotent stem cells without creating and destroying embryos and without producing an entity that undergoes or mimics embryonic development."[48] The method, a form of altered nuclear transfer (ANT) called oocyte assisted reprogramming (OAR) operates as in conventional cloning (SCNT) by inserting a donor cell with a reasonably complete human genome into a human oocyte (egg cell), with the twist that one or both cells have been genetically manipulated in advance to determine which genes are expressed and which remain silent, thus preventing the enucleated egg from reprogramming the human genome into an epigenetic state consistent with embryonic development. Given what Fr. Nicanor Austriaco, a supporter of ANT-OAR, calls "the primacy of epigenetics over genetics" in determining cellular identity, that is, the event by which the reasonably complete human genome present in all human cells subsequently expresses itself in "the epigenetic state associated with embryos," the *a priori* manipulation of which genes are switched on in the enucleated egg is said to prevent the essential event constituting a new human organism from ever taking place.[49] The end result of the subsequent cell division is not a "true human blastocyst," so the argument goes, but rather a cell mass akin to a teratoma (tumor). "From these pluripotent cells endowed with the nuclear genome of the nucleus donor, human embryonic stem lines could be obtained and cultured as from blastocysts."[50]

48. "Response to Joint Statement," 369.

49. This is in spite of the fact that the procedure mimics human conception. See three articles from *Communio: International Catholic Review* 32 (2005): Fr. Nicanor Pier Giorgio Austriaco, O.P., "Altered Nuclear Transfer: A Critique of a Critique," 174-175; Adrian Walker, "The Primacy of the Organism: A Response to Nicanor Austriaco," 177-187; and Schindler, "Reply to Austriaco," 795-824.

50. Roberto Colombo, "Altered Nuclear Transfer as an Alternative Way to Human Em-

Schindler and others contended that ANT-OAR provided no reason for certainty that the process was not technically and morally tantamount to the cloning of defective human embryos for the purpose of harvesting stem cells.[51] They challenged the philosophy of biology underlying the joint statement, contending that the signatories were able to maintain the compatibility of their endorsement of ANT-OAR and their avowed pro-life position only by assuming the reductionist and mechanistic definition of an organism that they ostensibly rejected and by begging more fundamental, metaphysical questions about the ontological status of organic unity and the necessity for philosophical and theological mediation of empirical, biological claims at the origin of life. In begging these questions and ceding the responsibility for adjudicating them to positivist science, they thereby compromised their "ability to mount a truly consistent, reasonable, and persuasive defense of human life."[52]

There can be no question of my recapitulating in what's left of this essay that intricate and complex debate, which was conducted among several thinkers on either side of the issue across several issues of *Communio* and other journals. I wish only to exploit Schindler's assessment of the principal issues of that debate, the definition of an organism and the criteria by which to make that determination, in order to demonstrate, first, the recalcitrance of mechanistic ontology, but second and more fundamentally, the relevance of the theological claims made at the outset of this essay for our understanding of biology as an order of being and knowledge.

Implicit in the priority accorded to epigenetics over genetics by Austriaco and other proponents of ANT-OAR are two interrelated problems for a position hoping to remain consistent, not simply with a pro-life position, but with the deepest logic of a Christian understanding of creation and God. The first problem is a version of reductionism we encountered above. Mediated by the perspective of contemporary systems biology, this form of reductionism is more subtle than earlier versions inasmuch as it recognizes the unity of a "dynamic network of interrelated parts."[53] Still, to the extent that this unity results from and is exhausted by

---

bryonic Stem Cells: Biological and Moral Notes," *Communio: International Catholic Review* 31 (2004): 646.

51. See Walker, "Altered Nuclear Transfer: A Philosophical Critique," 649-684.

52. "Response to Joint Statement," 370. See the remarks of Robert George, cited above.

53. Jose Granados, "ANT-OAR: Is Its Underlying Philosophy of Biology Sound?" *Communio: International Catholic Review* 32 (2005): 726, quoting Austriaco, "On Static Eggs

this interrelation, it is doubly reducible — to the sum of its component parts and to its antecedent causes. It therefore remains classically mechanical. Austriaco, like many contemporary scientists, would of course deny that organisms are *nothing but* the sums of their parts. But the systems biology perspective can afford of its own resources no integral sense of what the "something more" might consist in. Consequently, his argument reasserts this mechanistic understanding, despite his claims to the contrary. He insists that embryonic cells and teratoma cells "are different ontologically *because* they are *organized* and *behave* differently." "Form," in other words, follows upon organization, which means that failure to manifest the epigenetic state characteristic of embryos can be taken to indicate that what was present in the first instance was not an embryo. Schindler dubs this "ontological consequentialism," recognizing that it actually dispenses with a substantive notion of nature altogether.[54]

Austriaco's deference to empirical science's capacity to determine the ontological identity of an organism indicates the second problem, inherent in mechanistic ontology from Descartes onwards: a positivism that fails to recognize that empirical observation will always necessarily be "essentially mediated — not replaced — by a philosophical criterion which, as such, is trans-empirical."[55] This positivism masks the inherently mechanical and philosophical character of the ANT-OAR criterion, embodied in the decision to accept the criteria offered by systems biology. Coupled with the consequentialist implication that "substantial identity can be known simply on the basis of and is *nothing more than* the epigenetic state,"[56] this empiricism is reducible to one of two varieties: either a "reductionist empiricism," which holds that "being is exhaustively expressed in its empirical effects or manifestations," or a "dualist (Kantian) empiricism," which requires "only that the knowledge of being is realized in terms of being's empirical effects."[57]

Schindler contends that this empiricism confuses the orders of being

---

and Dynamic Embryos: A Systems Perspective," *National Catholic Biological Quarterly* 2 (2002): 661.

54. "Reply to Austriaco," 800, citing Austriaco, "Are Teratomas Embryos or Non-Embryos?" *National Catholic Biological Quarterly* 5 (2005): 706; emphasis Schindler's. The term "ontological consequentialism" first appears on 804 of "Reply to Austriaco."

55. "Reply to Austriaco," 798.

56. Whether this is the case is the "decisive question" that the original "Response" claimed ANT-OAR supporters failed to acknowledge or answer.

57. "Reply to Austriaco," 805.

and knowledge and betrays Austriaco's claim to ground his elision of epigenetic state and ontological identity in the Thomistic axiom *agere sequitur esse* (acting follows being) rather than in a flawed mechanical philosophy. This confusion leads him to define being by its first effect, the coordinated interaction of its parts, which warrants in turn the claim that the ANT-OAR product is a tumor rather than an embryo. The controversy then turns on whether Austriaco's understanding of an organism's unity can legitimately claim the authority of Aquinas and Aristotle. Articulating an alternative sense of the axiom affords Schindler the opportunity to develop a positive notion of organic unity that accords with the ontological commitments discussed in previous sections. These terms are dictated by Austriaco's claim to ground his argument in a Thomistic axiom; and Schindler's decision to contest it on these grounds is interesting in its own right, given what some would claim is a tension between Schindler's Balthasarian and Thomistic commitments.[58] While the question of what constitutes legitimate Aristotelian-Thomism is crucially important, and important for Schindler, the more important issue in the use of these terms is their utility in expressing something about the nature of organisms that is available in principle apart from the Aristotelian understanding.[59]

The plain ontological sense of the axiom *agere sequitur esse* — that acting follows, is consequent upon, is causally derivative of, being — implies a distinction between the two terms that precludes the reducibility of one to the other. Thus, as we might have gathered from our earlier discussion, in Aristotelian terms "an organism is defined first by its substantial form, not by its manifest organization, which, on the contrary, is the first (ontological, not temporal) consequence of form. Form is causally anterior to organization, which is the effect of form"; ontologically, it supplies to the organism an all-at-once character out of which it temporally unfolds and develops.[60] It follows, then, that form establishes the unity of an organism that is irreducible to, and even in some sense *precedes*, its manifest organization or temporal development.[61] This is not to say, as some of Schindler's

---

58. HW, 275-311.

59. While we have now seen several instances in which Schindler exploits Aristotelian terms to advance his claims about nature, he does not always employ this terminology, and he is not claiming that those in various fields who would allow *communio* ontology to transfigure their work from the inside must necessarily become strict Aristotelians. See, e.g., HW, 143-176.

60. "Reply to Austriaco," 806.

61. "Thus a systems biology perspective as conventionally conceived, which views an or-

critics alleged, that empirical observation of manifest organization is un-necessary. To the contrary, Schindler maintains that "to insist on a cogni-tional act that goes beyond the empirical to the metaphysical is not at all to suggest that one can or should stop looking at the physical. . . . [I]t is to look at the physical more comprehensively."[62] Nor is it to suggest that the formal unity of the organism precedes its development in time, or that this unity is somehow "separate" from or independent of that manifest organi-zation and coordination of parts. However, it is to insist that the unity of the organism as such exceeds and transcends the coordination of its parts — part of what is meant by the all-at-once givenness of the organism — even though Schindler insists upon a mutual but "asymmetrical" relation-ship of interdependence between the organism in its formal wholeness and its development and organization of parts (a point whose importance will become apparent).

Inherent in this claim is a distinction between ontological and chrono-logical dependence (which ultimately redounds to a more complex and variegated conception of causality than is entertained within the mecha-nistic framework of modern science).[63] The parts can be *ontologically* de-

---

ganism as an interacting system, cannot as such be claimed as an expression of authentic Aristotelianism. On the contrary, the unity indicated by the (total) system of an organism's in-teractive parts always presupposes for the Aristotelian the presence of the substantial form; and this (total) system of parts thus signifies the immediate and simultaneous but always on-tologically subordinate effect of the unifying presence of form. To confuse these two different senses of unity is to conflate an Aristotelian-Thomistic hylomorphic organism with what re-mains, for all its subtlety, a Cartesian mechanistic body." "Reply to Austriaco," 807-808. Trans-posing his argument into the Aristotelian terms of active potency, Austriaco claims that the failure of the ANT-OAR product to evince the manifest organization of an embryo means that it never was an embryo rather than that it was a radically defective embryo.

62. "Response to Joint Statement," 375.

63. In his reply to Austriaco, Schindler casts this asymmetrical dependence and the mutuality of form and matter in Aristotelian terms: "In accord with a rightly understood Aristotelianism, this priority of form in establishing the organization of the whole does not at all deny, but on the contrary simultaneously presupposes, a material platform, as it were, upon which form itself depends. The all-at-once unity provided by form necessarily presup-poses the progressive development and integration of material parts. The crucial point for Aristotle, however, is that this . . . occurs only-always from within, and simultaneously by virtue of, the (absolutely) prior all-at-once unity and agency of form. There is, in other words, a mutuality of form and matter (materia apta) in accounting causally for the unity of the organism as a-whole-in-parts and parts-in-a-whole, but this mutuality is asymmetrical. What may be termed the relative priority of matter/material parts ('potency') in accounting for that unity always presupposes what may be termed the absolute priority of substantial

pendent upon the whole for the determination of their meaning as parts, even if the development of the whole is *chronologically* dependent upon the unfolding and development of the parts, as in the case of an embryo maturing into a child and a child maturing into an adult. This distinction is at the root of the difference between organisms and machines, between the artificial and the natural.[64] In the example noted above from Adrian Walker, a lawnmower as a designed artifact may indeed empirically manifest the blueprint in the mind of its designer, but its unity comes about only as a consequence of its piece-by-piece assembly from an extrinsic agent. An embryonic organism, by contrast, is given to itself — given to be — in a radically different way. Precisely because an embryo is already an organic unity, it contains its blueprint, so to speak, within itself, and it normally unfolds out of itself the parts it needs to exist as a unity consisting of but transcending the irreducibly complex interaction among its irreducibly complex systems.

What is the upshot of this understanding of organic unity, beyond its immediate usefulness in denying the Thomistic credentials of the ANT-OAR advocates? Without denying that organisms can manifest themselves in mechanical ways or that mechanical manipulation through medicine can serve genuine goods, Schindler has rejected the reductive and dangerous conception of unity characteristic of mechanistic ontology, encompassing the legitimate applications of mechanical diagnosis within a more comprehensive understanding of being, in which wholes are always and intrinsically *more* than the sum of their parts or their antecedent causes. In other words, the priority of form to matter and whole to parts invokes the constitutive role of mystery, not "as an unknown lying somehow simply behind or beyond the organism in its proper structure," but rather as the essentially

---

form ('act')" (809). On the distinction between ontological and chronological dependence and unity, see Walker, "Altered Nuclear Transfer: A Philosophical Critique," 677-680.

One note on the "mechanistic framework" of modern science. The shift away from Newtonian determinism toward statistical mechanics does not fundamentally alter the mechanistic character of the framework. As Bohm notes, "It has to be emphasized, however, that this question of determinism or indeterminism has little or no relationship to that of mechanism vs. non-mechanism. For the essential point of mechanism is to have a set of fundamental elements that are external to each other and externally related. . . . Whether these elements obey deterministic or statistical laws does not affect the question of the mechanical nature of the basic constituents (e.g., a pin-ball machine or roulette wheel that would operate according to 'laws of chance' is no less mechanical than a machine whose behavior is completely knowable and predictable)." BM, 21.

64. See Walker, "Altered Nuclear Transfer: A Philosophical Critique," 677-679.

gifted and excessive character of things to themselves that is "woven into the fabric of organic reality, into the very nature of an organism."[65]

The inherently excessive and mysterious character of human being — not as something "spiritual" dualistically opposed to, but contained within, the material and biological dimension, but rather precisely *as* material and biological — places (or ought to place) inherent and principled limits on our pretensions exhaustively to understand and control nature, limits that cannot be supplied from within the concept of nature (and knowledge) operative in the ANT-OAR proposal or mechanistic ontology more generally.[66] The limits imposed by mystery, once again, do not occur at the "boundaries" of our knowledge as something that might in principle be overcome, but are inherent in and constitutive of both natural objects and our knowledge of them, and increase in proportion to knowledge's advance. Moreover, to speak once more in Aristotelian terms, precisely because each of the "composite aspects" of the organic whole — form and matter — are mutually, though asymmetrically, dependent on each other, this implies that the organism in the fullness of its substantial being is also dependent, unable fully to account either for its existence or its essence: "it must somehow be given to itself, not self-generated but received."[67] Nature is fundamentally receptive (feminine/contemplative) before it is active, or rather receptive in its activity. Thus the mystery inherently constitutive of creatures as such opens of its own inner logic into the mystery of the "givenness — and indeed giftedness of organic being." In the previous section we discussed briefly how love provided the fundamental structure of created being that was at once receptive and kenotic. Schindler's account of organismic unity, developed through the ANT-OAR controversy, now opens toward that understanding from the other side, as it were, from within the inner logic of organismic wholeness. That is, the mystery intrinsically establishing nature in its naturality opens of its own accord into the mystery of being, difference, and love.[68] Inasmuch as self-reception is

<hr />

65. "*Veritatis Splendor* and Bioethics," 197.

66. "The difficulty, then, is that ANT, failing to take account of the ontological mystery proper to organic life, is just so far incapable of providing any principled or reasonable means of checking the tendency of the dominant scientific culture as these bear on (human) organic life at these most subtle and fragile moments." "*Veritatis Splendor* and Bioethics," 198.

67. "Reply to Austriaco," 821-822. In replying to Fr. Austriaco, Schindler locates ontological dependence within the context of Thomas's real distinction.

68. Hence the ontological significance of the Marian Church as both the antecedent condition for and the crown of this relation.

integral to created beings as such, the mystery and movement of love is thus not something accidentally "tacked on, as it were, to a space and time and matter originally constituted on their own and in abstraction from this movement,"[69] but is rather constitutive of this originality.

Acknowledgment of the constitutively mysterious character of creatures requires a fundamental rethinking of the relationship between faith, knowledge, and desire, and a correlative recovery of the distinctness-within-unity of truth, goodness, and beauty. It requires us to admit that the health of biology as an intellectual discipline depends upon its acknowledging that there are principles of biology (as natural "fact") inaccessible *to* biology the discipline as it is currently conceived, inasmuch as it is incapable in principle of admitting on its own terms how creatures might be more than their component parts and antecedent causes. To do this, which is to admit once again the reality of "natures," biology must be intrinsically open to the mediation of other "higher" forms of knowledge and to the inherently beautiful and mysterious aspects of being with which they are concerned. The same is true of other branches of knowledge.[70] As Schindler puts it,

> In the end, we can form proper ethical judgments with respect to bio-technological science's production and manipulation of embryonic stem cells for health-serving ends only insofar as we can recover adequate notions of nature and human-organic life (as gift). And this recovery comes about only as we ponder biology, anthropology, and theology in all their ontological breadth and depth.[71]

We have thus come full circle to the theological claims put forth at the outset of this essay. To recover an adequate notion of nature by pondering

---

69. "Trinity, Creation, and the Academy," 410.

70. These principles are accessible through concepts other than those supplied by Aristotle. Indeed, variations of it flourished in Christian Neoplatonism long before the Christian appropriation of Aristotle afforded it more precise philosophical expression. Advocates of Intelligent Design have potentially stumbled onto it in their notion of "irreducible complexity," though the philosophical and theological limitations of this program prevent them from recognizing this. My recourse to this notion should not be taken as an endorsement of Intelligent Design in any of its current articulations. I am publicly on record arguing that the ostensive conflict between Intelligent Design and neo-Darwinian biology is largely an illusion, since each assumes the same mechanistic ontology and, consequently, similar understandings of nature and of the relationship between science and other forms of knowledge.

71. "*Veritatis Splendor* and Bioethics," 201.

the forms of natural things is to recover a conception of nature at once more comprehensive and less reductive than those dominant in modernity: more comprehensive because it includes *both* the mechanical manifestations of nature *and* those formal and qualitative features which mechanistic ontology regards as epiphenomenal; less reductive because it refuses to make the world less than the mystery it is by insisting that its reality conform to a defective concept of knowledge, allowing the forms of natural things to show forth of their own inner logic that the mystery of love constitutes them in their naturality. In other words, entry into the mystery of love manifest in the nuptial union between Christ and his Church and determinative of nature in its naturality liberates the sciences to *be* the sciences, not least by relieving them of the burden of being *scientia divina*. Just so does it also liberate the world to be the world, to be the fullness of mystery and gift that it actually is and that so much of modern life is intent on denying. Thus do we demonstrate more thoroughly that "ever-greater union with God coincides with . . . the world's ever-deeper integrity as world."[72]

72. "Trinity, Creation, and the Academy," 408.

III

David L. Schindler and the Order of Modernity: Toward a Working Definition of Liberalism

Larry S. Chapp and Rodney A. Howsare

I. Toward a Definition of Liberalism:
Contemplative Receptivity vs. Creative Agency
as the Most Primitive and Anterior Truth about Man

Fergus Kerr, in his recent book outlining the history of twentieth-century Catholic theology, is somewhat critical of the "nuptial" reading of the Adam and Eve narrative given by Pope John Paul II in his theology of the body.[1] Kerr points out that the standard reading of this narrative in the tradition has always been to emphasize man's role as God's "steward" or "viceroy" on earth, rather than, as John Paul asserts, as anteriorly and more primitively "nuptial" in the sense of an inner orientation toward love of the other. In other words, Kerr wants to say that the primary image of God presented in Genesis is that of a divine King whose power over the created realm is, at least partially, now handed over to human beings who, bearing in themselves the imprint of this divine "kingly" image, now have as their primary responsibility the exercising of authority and "dominion" over creation. Certainly, there is a great deal in Kerr's reading of Genesis that is consonant with elements of the Church's exegetical tradition. However, Kerr's critique of the application of nuptial categories in this regard seems, at the same time, to be an exercise in question begging, since the issue at stake in the exegesis of this narrative within a properly Christian order is not whether human beings are to exercise authority and dominion over creation, but rather precisely what form the human dominion over cre-

---

1. Fergus Kerr, *Twentieth Century Catholic Theologians* (Oxford: Blackwell, 2007), 75-179.

ation is to take. In other words, if Kerr is correct, then the deepest reality of human nature is creative *action* — that is, human nature is to be viewed most primitively as an active agency, and the primary responsibility of this agency is to act as the chief architect of the form of the world. On the other hand, if John Paul II is correct, then the polar opposite would prove true, i.e., that our fundamental humanness is defined most primitively as a contemplative openness to the giftedness of creation as typified in the nuptial relation of Adam and Eve. Thus, in John Paul II's reading, our "dominion" over nature as God's steward is a dominion first rooted in the order of contemplative love that roots our freedom constitutively as a fundamental orientation to the gift of the "other," as opposed to the rather empty notion of a raw autonomous freedom that is only later "specified" through its moral obligations.

David Schindler's approach to the definition of modern liberalism mirrors this debate closely. This is made clear in an important programmatic essay where he develops a basic definition of liberalism through a meticulous metaphysical reduction of its public claims.[2] In what follows, we will follow the structure and logic of this essay closely in order to get to the essence of Schindler's definition of liberalism as well as his critique of its shortcomings. It shall be the burden of this essay to show that, for Schindler, liberalism is inherently flawed as an "idea," regardless of whatever good may be gleaned from the various political arrangements organized under its banner, and that this basic flaw resides in a twofold dualism between the world and God on the one hand and between man and the world on the other. It will then be clear why it is that Schindler's definition of liberalism is so pertinent to the debate concerning John Paul II's nuptial reading of human nature. Finally, in the light of this definition and critique of liberalism, we will conclude with a more specific analysis of Schindler's response to his liberal (of the largely conservative variety) critics in order to draw some conclusions concerning the state of our contemporary situation.

Schindler begins his analysis by first making clear his agreement with the assessment of the crisis of modern culture offered by Pope John Paul II in his encyclical *Evangelium Vitae*.[3] It was in this encyclical that John Paul II made his now well-known distinction between a "culture of life" and a "culture of death" as representative titles for two radically different

---

2. "Christological Aesthetics."
3. "Christological Aesthetics," 193-196.

ways of structuring human society. The Pope's point is not to paint the Church as the sole locus for the culture of life and "modernity" as the sole locus for the culture of death. Rather, it is to point out that there is an on-going clash or tension between two competing forces within the very heart of modern liberal culture. Thus, despite the many legitimate achievements of the modern world, we seem, at the same time, to be dogged by systemic evils that threaten to eclipse, many times over, the good that has been achieved. The oddness of our contemporary situation is, in fact, often quite stunning: modernity is characterized by a deep commitment to a vast array of fundamental human goods while at the same time denying those goods to whole segments of the population through the adept defining away of their humanity through legal fiction. John Paul II refers to this strange situation as the "light and shadows" of modern culture, by which he means that there is an inherent clash between good and evil that is built right into the fabric of the modern project that renders any so-called "progress" in the modern world deeply ambiguous. Schindler quotes John Paul II here with approval: "This situation, with its lights and shadows, ought to make us all fully aware that we are facing an enormous and dra-matic clash between good and evil, death and life, the 'culture of death' and the 'culture of life.' We find ourselves not only 'faced with' but necessarily 'in the midst of' this conflict" (*Evangelium Vitae*, 28).

Schindler points out that this strangely conflicted situation poses to us a simple question with regard to the role played by liberalism in its con-struction: Is liberalism sound in its fundamental principles, and therefore are the evils we see today mere distortions and corruptions of these origi-nating liberal ideals or the inevitable by-product of liberalism's flawed metaphysical understanding of reality?[4] And perhaps more importantly, is liberalism capable of developing from within its own resources a princi-

---

4. Neoconservative Catholic thinkers such as George Weigel, Michael Novak, and the late Richard Neuhaus have opted for the notion that liberalism is sound and even "Catholic" in its basic principles, even as it has undergone "corruption" in modern culture through the work of a few cultural elites. America in particular, founded as it was by the more religiously neutral and irenic "anglo" version of liberalism rather than the more anti-clerical Continen-tal Enlightenment, is particularly Catholic in its originating ethos. Thus, the task of the Catholic in modern America is to affirm the basic principles of anglo-liberalism and to seek the restoration of their original meaning in our public life. David Schindler, has, as is known, rejected this thesis of American exceptionalism and argued strenuously against it. For a fuller treatment of this debate, see Schindler, "Church's 'Worldly' Mission"; see also the discussion entitled "Catholicism and American Culture" between Mark Lowery, George Weigel, and David Schindler in *Communio: International Catholic Review* 18 (1991): 425-472.

pled response to the evils inherent in the culture of death, or are those very principles inherently responsible for these evils, thus requiring a complete rethinking of the foundations of the liberal project?[5] Schindler's answer to that question is unequivocal: "Thus, first of all, the current spiritual crisis cannot be adequately understood 'merely' as a kind of moral aberration — or simple corruption of the will; on the contrary, the crisis involves also the order of intelligence and thereby that which gives institutions their inner 'logic' or 'shape' . . . the assumptions which most fundamentally constitute the culture of death as a 'structure of sin' are those concerning the primitive — and ultimate — ordering of human being and consciousness."[6]

In other words, we must first begin with a fundamental definition of liberalism that goes beyond the vague political sentiments and slogans of the moment and inquires instead after the metaphysical root of liberalism as an "idea." To that end, in what follows we will begin with a generic definition of liberalism followed by a threefold distinction among different kinds of liberalism. We will then conclude with Schindler's analysis of what is at the root of liberalism's "ordering of human being and consciousness."

Schindler defines liberalism in its metaphysical core as a "dualism . . . between truth and freedom and between nature (reason) and grace (God of revelation)."[7] Along these same lines, he quotes Balthasar's description of the soul of modern man as an *anima technica vacua.*[8] What he means by this is that embedded in the heart of liberalism is a notion of nature's autonomy from God in a negative sense, i.e., that God's transcendence is viewed, to borrow a phrase from Robert Barron, as "competitive" with the integrity of the world such that in order for the world to be truly "worldly" it must assert its independence and distance from God. Obviously, this view of the nature-grace dynamic has historical causes and roots far too complex to dissect here.[9] However, the salient point is that nature in mo-

---

5. "Christological Aesthetics," 195-196.
6. "Christological Aesthetics," 197.
7. "Christological Aesthetics," 207.
8. "Christological Aesthetics," 198.
9. Indeed, Schindler identifies the ultimate source of these various dualisms as being theological in nature. In a related essay, Schindler comments on the theology of Alexander Schmemann and makes the point that one of the fateful moments in the history of theology came when Western theologians began to make oppositional distinctions between the realm of the mystical/symbolic and the realm of the "real" in debates over the exact meaning of the "real presence" of Christ in Eucharistic theology. When the "realness" of Christ's presence in the Eucharist is emphasized over and against the "mystical" nature of this presence, then a false objectivist and mechanical understanding of nature has already raised its head. The ul-

dernity is conceived of as independent from God in the sense of a "separation" that renders the divine ever more alien to the worldly structures of the world. All elements of the sacral realm are thus bleached from the natural world, reducing nature to the mere manifestation of various configurations of matter, with matter itself thought of in a monadic fashion as self-contained and all relations between material entities viewed as inherently extrinsic and mechanical. Thus, nature has no inherent theophanic and/or anthropological meaning that thereby situates nature completely outside the realm of metaphysical value. This, in turn, signifies the loss of any sense of nature as a "gift" to be contemplated or adored and opens the door to a raw activism on the part of man vis-à-vis the "matter" that is now at his disposal to do with as he sees fit. We also might mention here liberalism's tendency to privilege or presuppose non-sacramental forms of religion (individualist, voluntarist, congregational, etc.).

This radical dualism between God and nature thus also applies to man, who now views the autonomy of his own freedom increasingly as the assertion of his will over and against that of a God who now appears, at best, as a mere spectator to our own Promethean assertion of will, and at worst as an alien, heteronomous threat to the full integrity of our freedom. The world, now devoid of an inner orientation to God, becomes merely a mechanical and plastic reality to be molded by a human freedom equally devoid of metaphysical grounding in God. It becomes the job of the spiritual subject to give meaning to a world now devoid of inherent meaning.[10] Once this final step is realized, the emptiness or vacuity of our souls becomes apparent; nature, no longer inherently meaningful, becomes a mere set of "facts" to be technically manipulated. All that remains is for the en-

---

timate context of Schindler's comments here is his discussion of Schmemann's thesis that nature is always already precisely as nature oriented toward the worship of God and exists precisely as nature as a sacrament of the divine presence. If we do not view nature as inherently oriented toward worshiping the glory of God, then a more extrinsic relationship between God and the world emerges with all of the dualistic and mechanistic tendencies noted above. Cf. "Creation and Nuptiality."

10. We have noticed a paradox in our students that bears out Schindler's point in this regard: on the one hand, they generally have little sympathy with Idealist views that allege that the world has only the meaning we give it, or that all we can know of the external world is that world as it is represented to us through the categories of the subject. They tend, in this regard, to be closer to naïve realists. And yet when it comes to the notion of freedom and moral truth, they become absolute Idealists: sex acts, for instance, have only the moral meaning that the subject wants to give them; they have no intrinsic moral meaning, just as the human body, in their view, has no intrinsic meaning.

tire realm of the human to fall under the sway of our own "technique" as human relations become governed by the same extrinsicist ethos now translated into the modality of social "control." The consequence of this in anthropological terms is that a new image of man emerges wherein our deepest reality is characterized as a raw "activism," in which absolutely nothing about our existence is treated as a "gift" to be contemplated, adored, and protected; rather, everything about us is seen as simple "material" to be used in our own constructive project as we see fit. *Homo sapiens* (man viewed as oriented to wisdom) is now replaced with *homo faber* (man, the creative constructor of reality). Schindler concludes this line of thinking as follows: "it is because the Western soul is so empty (*vacua*, light) that its relations to others are so preponderantly in terms of 'doing' and 'having,' hence so manipulative (*technica*, unbearable) — and conversely. It is because the Western soul is so empty that its patterns of thought and action are so mechanistic — and conversely. In a word, *there is a direct link between a subjectivity (or will) become arbitrary and an objectivity (or reason) become 'techne.'*"[11]

What we are then left with is an unlimited, yet hollow freedom — hollow because it is cast adrift without any inward orientation to the realm of the true, the good, or the beautiful — and a natural world that is viewed at best as a gigantic Tinker Toy for our amusement and at worst as an alien force that needs to be subdued to the aimless whims of our hollow will. But underneath this dialectic of arbitrary will and technical reason lies the most salient aspect of liberalism's definition of what it means to be human: *we are first and foremost the creative and active agents of how both the world and human culture are to be formed.* As Schindler states: "a conception of the self as primitively constructive or creative is at the source of the autonomy that must be challenged if we are to have principled ontological protection against relativism and atheism."[12]

To be sure, if you were to examine history and seek for explicit statements from liberal thinkers that would justify this definition, you would be hard-pressed to find them. The overt motivation behind liberal political regimes has always been some form of "liberation," e.g., liberation from ecclesiastical control, from political tyranny, from poverty, from ignorance, from disease, from social unrest, and so on. Indeed, Schindler would go so far as to stipulate that the founders of the American Republic were just

11. "Christological Aesthetics," 199; emphasis in original.
12. "Christological Aesthetics," 217.

such fair-minded men who merely sought a more "rational" form of life and were even well-disposed to the role of the Christian faith in the life of the new country.[13] However, the point is not what their overt motivations and sentiments may have been or whether they were "pro-Christian" or "anti-Christian." The point, rather, is the metaphysical logic of their ideas and the fact that, no matter what form liberalism takes, it always has inherent in the logic of its metaphysical assumptions the trajectory sketched above.[14] To make this clear, Schindler engages in a threefold distinction among different types of liberalism precisely to show that no matter what its form might be — putatively benign toward religion or overtly hostile — liberalism always contains the logic of dualism and an anthropology that emphasizes a creative activism toward the construction of the form of the world that is at the very core of how liberalism orders human consciousness. We will now examine each of these types of liberalism in turn.

Schindler borrows the nomenclature of Alasdair MacIntyre, who characterizes the three forms of liberalism as radical liberalism, liberal liberalism, and conservative liberalism.[15] The first type, radical liberalism, views the relation between God and world, as well as that between freedom and truth, as one of direct opposition. Thus, as Schindler states, in this type of liberalism "legitimate autonomy . . . is seen to imply atheism."[16] This is the type of liberalism that has now morphed into what commonly goes by the name of postliberalism, owing to the radicality of its claims. However, as Schindler notes, there is nothing really postliberal about it at all, since it is, in truth, the mere radicalizing of all the latent metaphysical claims of liberalism as such. And in light of the widespread acceptance of abortion and euthanasia in modern American culture (which Schindler takes to be profound evidence of a thoroughly mechanized view of human

---

13. "Christological Aesthetics," 212-218.

14. Notice, in this regard, the important reference to Michael Buckley in Schindler's "Church's 'Worldly' Mission." In n. 22, on p. 383, Schindler quotes Buckley accordingly: "Much more may be involved in . . . a progress of ideas than their own internal necessity, but internal necessity remains and governs inherently. Given enough time, intrinsic contradiction and ineluctable implications will out. The origin and choice of particular ideas may be free; their exploration may be voluntary; but their consequences are necessary. . . . The falsity of consequences exposes the fallacies of an initial idea, the equivocations of its language, or the paralogisms inherent in the form by which its content is explored and its conclusions reached." Schindler is citing Buckley's *At the Origins of Modern Atheism* (New Haven: Yale University Press, 1987), 334-335.

15. "Christological Aesthetics," 209.

16. "Christological Aesthetics," 207.

life itself and an out-of-control assertion of the autonomy of the self), Schindler identifies this type of liberalism as the dominant form in America today, at least with regard to those elements of contemporary culture which John Paul II has identified as the form of structural sin known as the "culture of death."[17] And certainly, in this view, man is characterized as raw creative freedom, whose sole stance before the natural world is one of master to slave.

The second form of liberalism, liberal liberalism, is what Schindler would call "liberalism as such." The form of dualism that characterizes this type of liberalism can be called a dualism of "hard dichotomy."[18] In this type of dualism, a sharp distinction is drawn between the subjective and objective orders, wherein the "objective" order is viewed as the realm of the mechanistic and strictly quantifiable (facts) and the "subjective" order as the realm of arbitrary will (value). Certainly, some of the more famous purveyors of this view (e.g., Descartes) did not directly view such a dichotomy as implying atheism. Nevertheless, as Schindler states, "thinking about nature nonetheless entails for him a primitive methodological abstraction from the concrete God of revelation."[19] Thus, the inner logic of this view, even if it does not overtly assert atheism, tends nevertheless in the direction of a de facto methodological atheism that easily lends itself to the overt metaphysical atheism of radical liberalism. Finally, liberal liberalism shares radical liberalism's view of man as most primitively a creative agent who gives shape to the world through a manipulation of its mechanics in the form of an ever-increasing mastery of "technique."

The third type of liberalism, conservative liberalism, is characterized by a "soft" dualism that seems at first glance to be more consonant with Catholic theology. In this form of dualism nature is granted a certain legitimate autonomy from God in order to create the space necessary for the world's development precisely as "world." This was the preferred path of neo-scholastic theology. However, the mistake neo-scholastic theology made in this regard was to view nature as not inwardly and intrinsically oriented toward God and thus, in some sense, as "complete in itself" even without divine grace. Grace can elevate nature into the divine sphere but does so "extrinsically," so to speak, by lifting nature into the divine life through an act of pure gratuity that bears no intrinsic relation to the inner

17. "Christological Aesthetics," 208-209.
18. "Christological Aesthetics," 207.
19. "Christological Aesthetics," 207.

orientation of nature as such. Thus, the grace of divine life comes to be viewed as an "add on" to a structure that is already complete in itself. The problem with this view in the context of our current discussion is obvious. If nature is complete in itself, there is a tendency to downplay the status of its very being as a "gift" from God and the theophanic sacramental quality of its "worldly" teleology. The primary vocation, therefore, of all creaturely being to offer worship to the glory of God is eclipsed in favor of a world whose *sole* natural purpose *qua* nature is now viewed as the attainment of more mundane ends. And this goes for man as well, who now ceases to be the high priest of creation (cf. Schmemann's *homo adorans*), offering praise to God on behalf of nature out of a spirit of contemplative adoration, and who now becomes, most primitively, a creative agent whose primary purpose is the working out of the worldly ends of his nature. The best that scholastic theology could say in this regard was that one could discern in the natural law a completely natural moral obligation to honor and give worship to the Creator. But stating that our nature has, as one of its moral obligations, the requirement to honor God is very different from acknowledging that nature, *qua* nature, is inwardly oriented to God, i.e., *to God as that which is its most proper fulfillment.*

The scholastic emphasis on nature as "complete in itself" accounts as well for its overstating of what could be strictly known about God through reason. Owing to this dualistic understanding, scholasticism felt justified in abstracting its analysis of the world from the concrete revelation of God in Christ. In other words, since revelation is viewed as an extrinsic "add-on" to nature, one ought to be able to see in nature all that one needs rationally in order to fulfill one's moral duty to honor the Creator. Since "honoring the Creator" is one of the moral duties of our nature, it is necessary that reason provide us with sufficient light to see all that this means on a natural level. But this approach has the strange effect of forcing revelation to fit into the form of the natural law as worked out in advance. Schindler quotes Balthasar here: "Teachers behaved as though man knew from the outset, before he had been given revelation, knew with some sort of finality what truth, goodness, being, light, love, and faith were. It was as though divine revelation had to accommodate itself to these fixed philosophical conceptual containers that admitted of no expansion."[20]

And it is precisely here, in the most putatively "benign" of the three

20. Hans Urs von Balthasar, "Theology and Sanctity," in *Explorations in Theology,* vol. 1: *The Word Made Flesh* (San Francisco: Ignatius Press, 1989), 186.

versions of liberalism, that we actually see most clearly the nub of the problem with liberalism as such. The problem with abstracting the concept of nature from any overt reference to Christian revelation is that it robs nature of the only thing that can possibly unite its conflicting polarities. Specifically, the only thing that can bridge the divide between truth (reason, the form of the "objective" world) and freedom (will, love, the realm of subjective "value") is beauty (glory). When truth and freedom are viewed dualistically, there is no sense in which they mutually interpenetrate or participate in the other. The relation between them becomes purely extrinsic and accidental.

In order to shed some light on the way out of such extrinsicism, Schindler turns to Balthasar, whose entire theological project begins with a focus on beauty or divine glory as the focal point for a renewed theology. Balthasar had found his studies as a young Jesuit scholastic to be "dreary" owing to the fact that even Catholic theology had bought into liberalism's dualism of form and love and had, therefore, divided theology into tracts on dogma (truth, rationalistically conceived) and spirituality/moral theology (the realm of the "good"). But what this did to theology was to take that which should be united in the reality of the Trinitarian God and to separate them by precisely abstracting them from their proper grounding in the unity of revelation. This has the effect of robbing both the true and the good of their inner *ratio* — an inner orientation toward a final integration in Trinitarian love — and thus rendering each in its own way strangely attenuated and hollow. Only beauty (or its analog, divine glory) can act as this point of integration. Schindler summarizes this point in a lengthy quote worthy of full citation:

> If, then, in the light of the classical-Christian philosophical tradition, we accept with Balthasar that the *ratio* of beauty lies in its simultaneous participation in, and hence integration of, truth and goodness, we arrive immediately at what most shapes his theological undertaking: the claim, namely, that the dreariness of theology can be overcome only by granting primacy to the beauty which precisely unifies the *verum* and the *bonum*. . . . it is the absence of the primacy of beauty which gives this separation its first and most proper meaning: beauty is the technical name for this missing *unity* — or *intrinsic relation* — between form and love.[21]

21. "Christological Aesthetics," 201-202.

What Balthasar is saying, in other words, is that the various dualisms inherent in the modern liberal project had their origin in the dualism of modern theology. We see this theological dualism already in the medieval era's dividing of the tracts on God into *de Deo uno* (which came first and dealt with the God we can know through nature or reason) and *de Deo trino* (which came afterward and dealt with the God of revelation). And it is precisely the rootedness of all modern forms of liberalism in what is ultimately a theological reality and debate that renders even the two forms of liberalism thought to be more congenial to religion (liberal and conservative liberalism) problematic. Indeed, conservative liberalism might be the most problematic of all, since it seems to give theological warrant and "cover" to the kind of dualism that is at the very heart of the liberal project.

In contrast to this theological dualism, Schindler points out that only in the revelation of the Trinitarian God do we see where love and form are truly coincident: "the Trinitarian God incarnate in Jesus Christ [is] the one place where the ultimate, and therefore most fundamental, unity of form and love is found. Only in Jesus Christ do we find the *Logos* who is *Love*, the *Logos* of *Love*. . . . [T]he primary name of this God who is the unity of Logos and Love is beauty, or better, Glory."[22] And locating beauty in the divine unity of truth and freedom (Glory) points to a deepening of how we understand truth and freedom in an earthly context as well. For in God there is a *circumincession* of truth and freedom wherein they both retain their unique distinctiveness, but it is now a distinctiveness that is precisely constituted by an anterior orientation to the unity of the *bonum* to the *verum* and vice versa. Schindler concludes with an insight that is critical to his definition of liberalism: "Beauty thus enables us to see that the love affirmed as the basic meaning of God and, in an analogous sense, also of the entire world, is a matter *simultaneously* of truth *and* goodness — and in turn of intelligence *and* will, of objectivity *and* subjectivity. Again, all of this is summed up in the recognition that, in Jesus Christ, God is revealed as Beauty: Form is revealed as Love, even as Love is revealed as Form."[23]

We now come full circle to the debate mentioned at the beginning concerning John Paul's nuptial reading of Genesis. What Christ reveals to us is precisely that the universe should be viewed as governed by an order of love, since it is the creation of a Trinitarian God who is the complete unity of love and truth. The realization that creation so conceived is also

22. "Christological Aesthetics," 202-203.
23. "Christological Aesthetics," 204.

the fruit of a double gratuity of love on God's part (the gratuity of both our creation and redemption in Christ) gives rise to our awareness that all of reality has the character of *gift*. God is the Creator, the Giver, while man is the receiver. What this means is that the most primitive stance of man vis-à-vis reality should be one of contemplative wonder, i.e., we are first and foremost receivers of the gift of existence — an existence we did not make and cannot unmake — and not, as Fergus Kerr and others imply, creative agents whose primary and most anterior task is the creation of the form of our existence. Our paradigm here is the fiat of the Virgin. That is not to say that man's role is in no way that of creative agent, for indeed we are called, as Genesis indicates, to act as God's stewards on earth. However, the point is rather that our creative agency, if it is not to fall prey to liberalism's opposition of form and love, must always be grounded in an anterior stance of contemplative receptivity. Schindler states:

> Man is — should be — first contemplative: or better, as seen in the light of Mary, the "archetypal" creature, man is first receptive (cf. the *Fiat*), as the condition for becoming authentically creative — that is by magnifying the always anterior creativity of the Father (cf. the *Magnificat*). This primarily contemplative disposition of man extends not only to God the giver, but to all of God's gifts. Man's disposition toward every other creature, in other words, is first contemplative; and only such an anterior contemplative disposition permits man then to be properly "creative" toward the others.[24]

Furthermore, in the light of the foregoing reflections on the anterior unity of truth and freedom in God we can see that this order of love is thus not a question of mere piety but involves both the intelligence and the will, both truth and freedom, both objectivity and subjectivity. This is an absolutely critical point. Schindler is not claiming that if we could just be more "pious" all would be fine. His claim is that imbedded within the metaphysical claims of liberalism is an orientation toward an anthropology of raw existential activism that pits truth against freedom and, in the end, destroys both. This happens because even in the more theologically inclined versions of liberalism there is already, in our view, an abstracting of the proper ends of nature from the revelation of God in Christ — a revelation that alone can show us what the true ends of our nature are. This abstracting from revelation causes us to miss the unity of truth and freedom in

24. "Christological Aesthetics," 204.

God and thus to miss that even worldly truth and freedom can find their fulfillment only in their anterior unity in the order of beauty and love. But this can be seen only from a posture of contemplative receptivity that first begins with an acknowledgment of the "givenness" and "giftedness" of all things. Schindler concludes this line of thinking as follows:

> Here I wish to highlight how the notion of beauty reveals "the contemplative outlook" to be a matter (also) of order and intelligence. The creaturely love that expresses itself in terms of a primacy of contemplation, wonder, and awe is not a matter "merely" of piety but (also) of the fundamental *order* of civilization. The claim is thus comprehensive in its implications: what it means is that creaturely *love,* with its primarily contemplative outlook, is to provide the most basic *form* of all the orders — economic, political, cultural, academic — that make up civilization.[25]

II. Toward a Definition of Liberalism:
Schindler and His Neo-conservative Critics

The American who reads the foregoing analysis cannot seem to resist the following question: Even if Schindler is right, what is to be done? In other words, at least the various forms of liberalism as delineated above in terms of MacIntyre's famous quote issue forth in some concrete set of objectives, objectives that can be, theoretically at least, realized within the concrete situation of liberal democracies. The liberal liberal, for instance, in seeing various forms of liberal liberation as already graced can actually identify the advancement of the kingdom with the various strategies of liberating the oppressed (women, minorities, the poor, etc.). Here the Church's mission *is* the world's mission; perhaps, put more strongly, the Church's mission *is* the mission of the Democratic Party, even if this entails a willingness to turn a blind eye to the murder of over a million unborn children every year. Meanwhile, the conservative liberal can do two things: first, protect a traditional theology *within* the church — against all forms of liberal liberal reductionism; and, second, campaign against the more morally repugnant aspects of liberalism in the "public square" on the basis of natural law arguments recognizable by all. Again, at least both of these positions can find a platform within the current political arrangement. But what, to repeat the question, can be done if Schindler is right?

25. "Christological Aesthetics," 205.

Larry S. Chapp and Rodney A. Howsare

Part of Schindler's answer to this question can be found in his various clashes with Catholic neo-conservatives, especially Michael Novak, Richard John Neuhaus, and George Weigel. In the remainder of this essay, then, we will take a brief look at this debate in order better to understand the full implications of the fundamental issues outlined above. But before we look at some of the specific issues that arise in this context, we think it important, in advance, to raise two particularly nettling tendencies in the liberal approach that have to be kept in mind with regard to Schindler's critique of neo-conservatism.

First, there is the tendency of liberalism always to make room for the very criticism that is being waged against it, to grant it, as it were, a place at the liberal table. We are reminded here of an article that appeared in *Theological Studies*, which attempted a reconciliation of Balthasar and Lonergan along lines in which Lonergan could provide the methodology and terms to engage the larger culture, while Balthasar was given charge over the intra-ecclesial contents of the faith.[26] One is tempted to respond with the old "with friends like these . . ." line. For would this not be simply to jettison everything that makes Balthasar, well, Balthasar? Has not Lonergan always made room for doctrinal content? Is not the Balthasarian point precisely that the *method* must be appropriate to its object, must be, that is, precisely *Christocentric?* Is it not, finally, the starting point that is exactly what is at stake?

But let us now turn to some similar comments regarding Schindler's approach from conservative liberal Michael Novak:

> For those deep in Catholic understanding, the more theological works of de Lubac and Balthasar quicken mind and heart. However, in writing for Jewish, Protestant, and secular readers, I find the theological language of de Lubac and Balthasar too rich for common understanding. It seems better to go as far as I can with a more "worldly" language, while pointing beyond it, as both Balthasar . . . and de Lubac . . . sometimes did. . . . Taking Balthasar's vision as his own, Schindler asks a number of important and useful questions of NNW [Neuhaus, Novak, Weigel]. Indeed, one wonders why he simply does not consider himself a colleague, entering as it were into *communio* with us, while accomplishing this part of our common project himself.[27]

26. Robert M. Doran, "Lonergan and Balthasar: Methodological Considerations," *Theological Studies* 58 (1997): 569-607.

27. Michael Novak, "Schindler's Conversion: The Catholic Right Accepts Pluralism," *Communio: International Catholic Review* 19 (1992): 148.

In other words, "Let Schindler do all the intra-ecclesial work of trinitarian metaphysics, we (NNW, that is) have always appreciated this sort of christocentrism; it's just that we have a different role, namely, to engage the larger culture." Schindler's task in such a view is "intra-ecclesial," while Novak's, et al., is "extra-ecclesial." Of course our point here is that this begs the very question that Schindler is raising: Can the best way of dealing with the world be worked out while prescinding from questions of a more theological or metaphysical nature? Or, more to the point, is not entering into the culture under the terms set by that culture precisely what Schindler is questioning? This brings to mind another quip from Alasdair MacIntyre, "Liberalism is the only meta-narrative that has convinced the world that it is not a meta-narrative."[28]

The second tendency is more specifically related to the conservative — or what Schindler will sometimes call the neo-scholastic — version of liberalism. This is addressed in the first part of the essay in terms of the dualism between nature and grace, but we wish now to specify it. With regard to Schindler's debate with the neo-conservatives, a double move is made that is really a necessary implication of the first tendency, just mentioned. First, conservative liberals, unlike their liberal counterparts, make a very clean line between the kingdom of God and the kingdoms of this world. This enables them to avoid liberal liberalism's tendency to see this-worldly reforms as being already salvific, or, conversely, of defining salvation purely in terms of this-worldly liberation. As Novak puts it:

> A democratic regime is not the kingdom. It is not a church, or even a philosophy. . . . It is designed to create *space,* within which the soul may make its own choices, and within which spiritual leaders and spiritual associations may do their own necessary and creative work.[29]

So, first, according to this view, Schindler has gotten himself overly worked up over a system that is interested only in this-worldly sorts of arrangements and goods. To offer a theological or even *philosophical* critique of it is to mistake it for being more than it is, *space.* But, then, second, there is this paradoxical tendency on the part of conservative liberals to start singing the praises of this or that aspect of liberalism as if it really is something

28. MacIntyre made this comment during a talk on Edith Stein given at the *Lumen Christi* Institute in 1998.

29. Michael Novak, "Boredom, Virtue and Democratic Capitalism," *Commentary* 88 (September 1989): 34, cited in Schindler, "Church's 'Worldly' Mission," 390.

more than just space, as if it really does begin to advance new (and better) forms of thinking and new (and better) virtues. Indeed, in the article just cited Schindler goes on to quote Novak in several contexts boasting about this or that new thing that can be credited to democratic capitalism.[30]

The fact that this second move is neo-scholastic in nature should not be overlooked, for it is very much akin to the move made by neo-scholastics vis-à-vis the *ressourcement* school regarding the natural knowledge of God and the Trinity. It is not as easy as simply saying that de Lubac, Balthasar, et al. wish to grant a greater dynamism to nature than the neo-scholastics. This is true. De Lubac fought a long battle in order to restore the Patristic/scholastic notion that human beings have a *natural* desire for the beatific vision. But what is often missed is the paradoxical outgrowth of the older, neo-scholastic position. By radically reducing reason and nature's role on one end, neo-scholasticism has to grant it an ever greater role, even over theology, at the other. We are speaking here, in particular, of the territory granted to purely natural reason with regard to God's existence and nature, so that once God does speak for himself in Jesus Christ, certain things have already been worked out that now cannot (will not?) be given up. This is not the place to go into all of the differences between the neo-scholastics and, say, Balthasar regarding the immutability of God or the question of God's relationship to the world, but it is hard to overstress this final point. For all of its talk of a purely secular politics with purely this-worldly ends in mind, conservative liberalism ends up granting much more to the political than is warranted in a properly Christian view, just as the purely natural theology of the neo-scholastics ends up granting much more to natural theology than any Christian theology should grant it. "Liberalism is the only meta-narrative that has convinced the world that it is not a meta-narrative," indeed!

Having laid out these two "tricky" moves of liberalism, we are in a better position to look at Schindler's response to the question stated above, What is to be done? In the light of the foregoing, it may seem that Schindler's only option — in the light of his rejection of the two forms of liberalism just noted — is some form of monism, some form, that is, of *theocracy*. In an interesting article assessing Schindler's debate with George Weigel, Mark Lowery raises this very issue:

One gets a sneaking suspicion, looking at the debate from this angle, that the real issue lurking behind the scenes is that of religious freedom.

---

30. "Church's 'Worldly' Mission," 391.

There is no question of Weigel's view on the matter: Catholic monism has been "decisively rejected by the Magisterium." . . . What does Schindler think? Might he have second thoughts about the prudence of *Dignitatis Humanae,* or see it in tension with (rather than a clear development beyond) the earlier Catholic position?[31]

It is precisely this question, raised in the context of the Schindler/neoconservative debate, that will allow us to unpack some of the implications of the first part of this essay.

Schindler's first response may seem obvious, but it is crucial in the light of the two liberal tendencies just mentioned: liberalism is itself already monistic, precisely in the terms laid out by MacIntyre in part I above. In a variety of articles over the years Schindler has pointed out the nature of this monism in terms of liberalism's view of the human person (as being first creative in imaging God and as being a substance standing in itself, prior to being relational); its view of freedom (as being first and foremost freedom of choice, rather than being conditioned by the prior reception of a gift); its view of God (as being extrinsically/mechanistically related to the cosmos, in largely Deistic fashion, rather than as being "more interior to things than they are to themselves"); its view of the Church (as being first voluntarist in nature, rather than sacramental/hierarchical); its view of the relationship between God and humanity (as being one of over-and-against-ness, rather than one of an analogy best seen in the hypostatic union); etc. The point that Schindler is making here, and the specific concerns just raised make his case a convincing one, is that these are precisely the kinds of issues that have to be addressed in order to work out the proper role of the Church in a liberal society, and, furthermore, that these issues cannot be properly worked out while prescinding from questions of a theological and philosophical nature.

His second response is to say, in no uncertain terms, that he affirms *Dignitatis Humanae* and the proper separation of Church and state, but with a crucial caveat: that Catholicism and not liberalism be allowed to define the nature of that freedom or that separation.

[First,] Love demands respect for the other as other — and thereby for the freedom of the other. Force or compulsion or imposition have no place, when and insofar as the unity or integration that is sought is one

---

31. Mark Lowery, "The Schindler/Weigel Debate: An Appraisal," *Communio: International Catholic Review* 18 (1991): 430.

of love. Secondly, then, the priority of love seems to me to entail both a rejection of any notion of the state which would permit coercive means to bring about religious unity, and a relative openness with respect to any notion of state which would protect religious freedom. . . . In this sense, the Church's evangelizing mission, as one of love, carries in principle some form of the distinction between state and society.[32]

Of course, this can get complicated, but it is precisely here that the Schindlerian/*Communio* position comes out in all its distinctiveness, just as it is here that Schindler's position comes closest to Benedict XVI's insistence that Europe cannot afford to forget its Christian roots. This is not just a matter of special pleading, nor is it a quest for power. The point, for both thinkers, is that the very notion of the person that modernity wants to preserve, and the very notion of freedom that comes with it, and the very notion of religious freedom that comes with that, was born in and so is in need of Christian soil.

A final point about Schindler's response to the question of religious freedom must now be made in reference to the role of John Courtney Murray. While we have no intention of entering into Schindler's substantive analysis and criticism of Murray's thought, the following points are crucial. In Schindler's view, Murray's position involves two important strategies. First, he puts as positive a spin as possible on the American founding, distinguishing it as strongly as possible from the anti-clericalism of the French Revolution. Schindler is willing to grant this. Second, Murray reads the articles of the American founding as "articles of peace," that is, as articles empty of any specific notion of the nature of human freedom or the nature of religion. It is this second strategy that Schindler refuses to grant. This requires brief attention.

The first thing to be said with regard to the difference between Schindler and Murray concerns the latter's tendency to understand religious freedom primarily in the negative terms described above, namely, as an absence of coercion. While Schindler does not deny this aspect, he thinks that a properly Christian notion of religious freedom requires that *priority* be given to freedom's natural orientation *toward* truth and goodness. "The issue is whether a positive relation (to God) or a negative relation (absence of compulsion) is to establish the primary context for the meaning and exercise of freedom."[33] The second point concerns the state-

32. Schindler, "Response to Mark Lowery," *Communio: International Catholic Review* 18 (1991): 462.

33. "Response to Mark Lowery," 465.

ment in *Dignitatis Humanae* that it is the responsibility of the government to "help to create conditions favorable to the fostering of religious life" (par. 6).[34] Again, a significant difference between Murray and Schindler arises in response to this suggestion. Murray, in keeping with the notion of religious freedom just mentioned, understands this in largely *negative* terms: i.e., that the state should not interfere with the free exercise of religion. In order to defend this reading, Murray makes a distinction between the role of the state and that of the society. Any positive promotion of religion, then, would reside, not with the state, but with the private institutions of "society." Schindler, on the other hand, while accepting a distinction between these two orders, raises an important qualifier, and this qualifier has to do with reading the founding documents as "articles of peace." The crucial point here is that these documents both were written in and will necessarily be read in the light of "definite theological-philosophical presuppositions," and that even if we grant the most positive reading of our founding possible (e.g., the Scottish Enlightenment as opposed to the more anti-clerical Continental one), we are still a far cry from a properly Catholic notion of freedom.[35] In short, the freedom is still a freedom of indifference as opposed to a freedom situated within a prior restlessness *for* God.

One more time, then, to the question, What is to be done? The very question seems to imply that Schindler's position is untenable insofar as it does not allow for a real impact on the world given our current political atmosphere. In response to this question, which Schindler seems to get asked an awful lot, he is often given to resorting to two favorite quotes: first, "Success is not a Gospel category"; and second, "Liberals give the impression that if Jesus had just been lucky enough to be born into a liberal society he could have avoided a rather ignominious end." We would like to unpack the meaning of these two lines in order to round out our discussion of Schindler's definition of liberalism.

First, the Christian's mission to the world can only ever be a mission within Christ's mission. Christ's mission, furthermore, consists in reconciling the world to the Father through his death and Resurrection, made present in subsequent world history by an act of the Holy Spirit in the Eucharist. This goes back to the importance of anthropology or to the definition of the person. Schindler insists that all persons are created for nothing

---

34. Cited in "Response to Mark Lowery," 466.
35. "Response to Mark Lowery," 467. For a fuller treatment of Murray's position, see "Religious Freedom and Liberalism."

less than the unity with the Father made possible through Jesus Christ and the Holy Spirit. This is what the person *naturally* desires. The danger in liberal regimes has to do with the limit that is placed on the Christian's mission *in* the world. By privatizing everything that makes Christianity Christianity, liberalism allows the Christian to enter into the so-called public square only in terms of a purely natural morality. If we can talk about things like Christ and the Trinity only when we are among other Christians, what precisely does the Christian have to offer the world? Just as Christ leaves behind nothing of his divinity when he enters into the heart of the world, so the Christian can leave precisely nothing of Christ behind when he enters into the world today. This, of course, does not entail an endless clamoring about Jesus at all times. But it does suggest that the transformation of the world that the Christian seeks must begin from the ground up. The problem with liberal regimes, in Schindler's view, is not primarily *moral*; it is primarily *ontological*. It involves, in short, a forgetfulness of God. The moral problems that tend to flourish in the context of such forgetfulness are not merely aberrations but betray a fundamental logic. The Church's mission to the world, then, must attend to the problem at its root if it is not to amount to something like rearranging furniture on the *Titanic.*

Second, Christ's mission did not win him many votes and appears to have made very little impact on the politics of the Roman Empire (at least directly, at least immediately). Furthermore, Christ does not seem to have lost much sleep over this apparent lack of success. Indeed, far from winning votes or changing laws, Christ's mission landed him on the Cross. He offers little assurance to his immediate disciples that their end will be any different. "The world hated me; it will hate you." This means two further things. First, the success of Jesus' mission — and it was, after all, not a failure — must be measured in categories very different from those of modern politics and culture wars. Second, there will be a cross. Jesus did not come to bring peace but a sword. Because he addresses man at his very center, his message gives rise to fierce responses, positive or negative. "The kingdom of God is violently advancing and the violent shall take it by force." "He who is not for me is against me." In short, Jesus does not seem to have a high regard for neutrality. Nor does he relegate such a situation to the future. The kingdom is precisely at hand. Schindler's point in this regard is that the Church's transformation of the world will occur, not at the political, but at the pre-political level — to the heart of the world, from the center of the Church — and that its success will look a lot like its Master's.

A Balthasarian Theological Economics:
Making Sense of David L. Schindler's Happy Baker

D. Stephen Long

David Schindler makes it difficult for a Protestant theologian such as myself. That is to say, he makes it difficult to be a Protestant. One of the most important justifications for any ongoing protest is that Catholicism subordinates Christology to some overarching framework of "nature" or "being," which would be a kind of neo-paganism. Nature or being becomes a category separated from grace or Jesus, and to understand Jesus we must first place him within a "larger" philosophical framework that is autonomous from theology. Then politics, ethics, economics, and all other "secular estates" proceed on the basis of reason or nature alone. This would mean that an economic ethic could be developed without reference to Jesus, which would be a clear violation of Holy Scripture. Such an economic ethic would be a version of that *analogia entis* Karl Barth rightly warned us against. It is, he so boldly pronounced, nothing less than an "invention of the Antichrist."[1] I still find that kind of Catholic theology present in some eco-feminist and neo-conservative theology. Oddly enough, they share a common feature. A putatively theologically neutral social science offers us an account of nature — whether it be political, economic, or moral — upon which theology then works. Theology becomes removed from political, economic, and moral concerns, and it must be related to them "after the fact" through a socio-analytic mediation.

If Catholic theology is predicated on a subordination of theology to

---

1. Barth wrote, "I regard the *analogia entis* as the invention of Antichrist, and I believe that because of it it is impossible ever to become a Roman Catholic, all other reasons for not doing so being to my mind short-sighted and trivial." Karl Barth, *Church Dogmatics*, I/1: *The Doctrine of the Word of God: The Word of God as the Criterion of Dogmatics* (Edinburgh: T&T Clark, 2004), xiii.

philosophy (especially through the social sciences), if it subordinates our being made righteous in Christ to some larger category called nature, which is known without him and actually lets us know him simply by affirming it as nature *qua* nature, then Protestants have reason for an ongoing protest. But Schindler, working in the tradition of de Lubac and Balthasar, recognizes the threat Barth identified and offers a compelling alternative. Barth's *analogia entis,* they all argue, misconstrues Catholic moral theology, a misconstrual shared by those who use it to protest against Catholicism as well as by those Catholics who affirm it to distance Catholicism from Protestant Christocentrism. Because Schindler follows Hans Urs von Balthasar in order to distance his economic ethics from this faulty *analogia entis,* to understand the importance of his work on economics we must first understand what Balthasar accomplished. Schindler's important contribution to Balthasar is that he developed what Balthasar only alluded to, namely, a theological economics.

I. The Balthasarian Context for Schindler's Moral Theology

One of the most important engagements with Karl Barth's theology remains Balthasar's *The Theology of Karl Barth,* published with ecclesiastical approval in 1951. Balthasar took up the challenge Barth posed to Catholicism. He begins that work with a chapter called "A House Divided," in which he states:

> If we are aware of the true nature of the Church, we must feel this [Catholic-Protestant] split not only as a daily wound but even more as a constantly burning shame. The essence, and not merely the name, of the Church is agape: unity in love. So every lapse from this unity calls the very substance of the Church into question. It is impossible not to ask each day with renewed concern — even if this has to go on for centuries — about the reason and necessity for this shame, which for us who have remained within the ancient precincts of the Church is no less burning than it must be for those who felt, certainly with a heavy heart, that they had to leave.[2]

Balthasar's engagement with Barth remains one of the most important ecumenical engagements in contemporary theology. It was animated by this

2. KB, 3.

sense of a "constantly burning shame," which, far from producing a liberal tolerance, required an honest, if not brutal, airing of differences. Barth challenged the Roman Catholic Church to "think through her own doctrine on nature and grace and the dogmas on justification developed by Trent." Balthasar responded, "Let Reformed theology really think through to the end its doctrine of the visible Church, of obedience and Law, and also its dialectic of man *simul justus et peccator!*"[3] If we think through these doctrines, if we think through what is true in them and what is not, if we "reform" them, then, Balthasar hoped, "new life will at least begin to flow again through the Church's limbs, grown so sclerotic over the centuries."[4]

Balthasar's engagement with Barth's theology, and especially his correction to Barth's understanding of the *analogia entis,* is a thinking through of these doctrines for the sake of the Church's unity. This includes bluntly telling Barth where he is wrong and listening to him say the same thing in return. The most unlikely of conversation partners, Barth and Balthasar, each of whom were unapologetic defenders of their ecclesial traditions, provide the richest ecumenical engagement in theology precisely because they never intended compromise nor assumed some third neutral position outside of their respective ecclesial homes. The issue between them is whether the *analogia entis* as a formal principle prevented Catholicism from acknowledging adequately that Christ alone is the Lord of the Church.

As Balthasar rightly notes, Barth found the *analogia entis* to be the invention of the Antichrist because it provides Catholicism with "an overarching systematic principle that is merely an abstract statement about the analogy of being and not a frank assertion that Christ is Lord."[5] For Barth, the *analogia entis* is not a material doctrine but a formal principle that defines the entirety of Catholicism. It is the "naturalization of grace"; such a naturalization allows the Church to seek and overpower God with human institutions, with works and laws.[6] It unwittingly defends a secular politics, economics, and ethics, for it assumes "nature" alone can teach us how to understand and live within them. In so doing, it attempts to trap God within this nature.

If Barth found this understanding of the *analogia entis* to be the prob-

3. KB, 7.
4. KB, 7.
5. KB, 37.
6. KB, 52.

lem with Catholic theology, Balthasar turned Barth's critique against his Reformed theology and found a similar problem with it, especially as Reformed theology drew on an understanding of the redeemed creature in terms of *simul justus et peccator*. Grace was only a divine and never a creaturely activity. It was always transcendent and never immanent. Thus Balthasar found Protestant doctrine confining human activity to nature alone; it assumed the very doctrine of pure nature it identified as the problem with Catholicism: "We now learn that the proper place for the true activity and cooperation of the creature is the realm of nature or creation, while the realm of grace is reserved for God's activity alone. While there is a real 'mediation' in the order of nature, this is ruled out in the order of grace."[7] For Balthasar this will not do. Moreover, he finds it inconsistent within Barth's own theology because Barth adopts an account of secondary causality that "unfolds along the lines of Thomism" even though Barth and Thomas Aquinas approach theology from very different points of departure.

Balthasar finds in Barth a contradiction that, when thought through, requires human activity to be more than confined to the realm of nature. This contradiction is based on two of Barth's admissions. First, the "creature in its creatureliness and autonomy is a secondary cause." Second, "true freedom must be interpreted in terms of the economy of grace." If both of these are true, then, Balthasar states, "only one conclusion is possible." This one conclusion, "contrary to Protestant doctrine," is that "the causality of the creature achieves its true character and its fullest maturity in the order of grace."[8] Thus Catholics hold forth the "possibility of reigning with God in grace, faith, obedience, prayer and, above all, in petitionary prayer," which is a possibility Balthasar thinks Barth tacitly acknowledges but refuses to honor in his doctrine of the Church. This allows Balthasar to refuse to dismiss Barth as a fideist. For Barth, "faith awakens man to an action that is proper to him. This action not only lies within the scope of his created nature, it actually corresponds to the highest natural determination of his creatureliness."[9] The model for this is the Incarnation, which for Balthasar is also the basis for the *analogia entis*. A proper reading of the Catholic *analogia entis*, in which "nature is the presupposition for grace," would make the best sense of Barth's own theology.[10] When Barth thinks

7. KB, 132.
8. KB, 135.
9. KB, 140.
10. KB, 165.

through his Reformed account of nature and grace, he will recognize that an emphasis on human activity in the order of grace is not laying hands on God, but allows grace to do its proper work. This, in turn, will allow a more properly "secular" politics, economics, and ethics that neither eschew the Lordship of Christ nor render nature atheological.

David Schindler's theology makes it difficult for Protestants because he develops what Balthasar pointed toward in his critique of Barth, and what is often missing in Balthasar's work itself: the political and economic significance of his theology. Schindler develops the properly secular role for politics, economics, and ethics.[11] His development of this properly secular role first challenges a mechanistic ontology that came to define the secular in the modern era. But in rejecting this account of the secular, Schindler does not reject the secular altogether. Instead, he shows how a Christian ordering of grace and nature leads to a better account of the secular than occurred within that mechanistic ontology. This ordering of grace and nature reflects a Trinitarian ontology of love. Only such an ontology helps us understand why a happy baker, who first bakes intrinsically good bread because she loves such goodness, matters theologically.

II. The Properly Secular

The role of the "secular" in contemporary theology is well-contested territory. From (to my mind faulty) interpretations of Bonhoeffer that thought the task of the Church was to embrace the secular to John Milbank's alternative situating of the secular as a form of social-scientific policing of theology, the place of the "secular" in Christian theology has been a central issue. Schindler engaged this debate with an interesting twist both in his 2002 essay "Religion and Secularity in a Culture of Abstraction" and in his 1996 publication *Heart of the World, Center of the Church*.

In the 2002 essay, Schindler takes a surprising position, one he can take only because of the relationship between grace and nature both Balthasar and de Lubac provided. Schindler writes, "I believe with the 'left'

---

11. In an important and yet unpublished essay, "Trinitarian Doctrine and Moral Theology: Reflections after Balthasar," Frederick C. Bauerschmidt makes the point that Balthasar rightly avoided reducing theology to ethics but that this concern also prevented him from adequately developing a political and economic theological ethic. Schindler's work develops the direction toward which Balthasar pointed.

that American religiosity typically harbors an inadequate sense of and appreciation for the secular; and I believe with the 'right' that American secularity has wrongly emancipated itself from religion — has emancipated itself in ways that presuppose, however unconsciously, an inadequate sense of religion."[12] Schindler, like Milbank, finds that the secular is an invented space in which God is viewed as a threat from whom we must be liberated. This secular space becomes a political order that forces speech of God into a private or "non-public" space (as John Rawls identifies this secular space). But Schindler also finds that the left is correct to criticize the "Christian right" for failing adequately to appreciate the secular. In fact, recovering a proper sense of the secular drives much of his work, especially his work on economics.

But here is where Schindler's work is interesting and provides an alternative to the well-defined political options in the United States. The recovery of a proper sense of the secular is not to be done by challenging a few godless persons on the political left as much as it is to challenge those whose very belief in God unwittingly underwrites the secular. Schindler writes, "To put it in its most radical and indeed what seem to me also most precise terms, the disappearance and indeed the death of God is a phenomenon occurring not only in the 5 percent of Americans who do not profess belief in God, but also and more pertinently in the 95 percent who do."[13] This is due to an "extrinsicism," which leads to an aggressive secularizing. The emphasis on grace as extrinsic to creation, and on God's transcendence, leads to a false understanding of nature as devoid of grace. Thus it lacks any intrinsic, immanent form ordered to God. The result is that, in attempting to protect God's transcendence and the otherness of grace as a gift, we fail to recognize how grace integrates with nature, and so we concede too much of the latter to an improper secular.

Schindler finds evidence of such an improper secular in John Courtney Murray's defense of political liberalism, especially as Murray underwrites a "rationalism" that produces a "false sense of human-rational autonomy."[14] Murray sets forth a double finality for the human creature that divides the end of creation from that of redemption and interprets this as a secular-sacred distinction, which he also correlates to a state-church distinction.[15]

---

12. "Religion and Secularity," 33.
13. "Religion and Secularity," 34.
14. HW, 77.
15. These distinctions are found in Leon Hooper's interpretation of Murray.

Theology and politics are given distinct domains. The result is an inability to recognize the *political* work of sanctification. Schindler contrasts Murray's division of the ends of redemption and creation with that of de Lubac. Schindler never goes so far as Milbank, who suggests there is no gratuity in addition to that of creation.[16] Creation and redemption are distinct, but they do not have distinct or separate ends. The end of creation is "placed *within,* internally subordinated to, the supernatural end."[17] This still allows for principles of political liberalism such as "religious freedom," but it refuses to valorize them on the basis of a liberal ideology, which is difficult (if not impossible) to disentangle from political liberalism. For this reason, Schindler, unlike Murray, does not need to endorse what political liberalism offers as "articles of peace," distinct from "articles of faith." Instead, he finds reasons for a properly secular that are strictly theological and thus never autonomous in relation to the Church, even though they allow certain creaturely activities such as politics to have an independence from the Church's "juridical order."[18]

A properly secular would not be a space free from God. It is instead the infusion of creaturely existence with a call for sanctification that must be worked out not only in the Church but also within the secular. Schindler identifies the difference between Murray and de Lubac in terms of "two different conceptions of the civilization toward which Christians should be working." De Lubac's is a "civilization wherein citizenship is to be suffused with sanctity." Murray's is "a civilization wherein sanctity is always something to be (privately/hiddenly) added to citizenship."[19] The difference between these two can be found in an economics that assumes exchanges are to be grounded in an ontology of love understood as gift or in a market conceived as a neutral, fair mechanism based on the will's choices as political liberalism sets forth. The properly theological-secular will require the recognition of an immanence that is not a neutral or naturally pure realm to which grace must be added. Instead, all things, even in their immanence, desire holiness. Once creaturely existence is shorn of this desire, then we will seek to turn it into an abstract, mechanized order. Schindler follows Balthasar in finding that this mechanistic order produces "a displacement of the cen-

16. At least Milbank suggests this is "closer" to his own position than it is to de Lubac's: *Theology and Social Theory* (Oxford: Basil Blackwell, 1990), 221.

17. HW, 79.

18. HW, 84.

19. HW, 80.

trality of glory in our understanding of God and of beauty in our understanding of the secular order of things."[20]

A properly secular order will challenge both a nature that knows no desire for holiness and thus becomes nothing but a mechanism and a nature that is turned into grace and thus is ruled by the Church's juridical order. What does this properly secular look like? Schindler writes,

> Those who would, in light of faith, have an adequate notion of secularity must just so far overcome the disjunction between the intelligent order or the truth of things and beauty — a disjunction summed up sharply in Nietzsche's dictum that "truth is ugly." . . . Consider, for example, how even the material elements of the food prepared by the mother for her children take on the character of gift: that is, they are not only neutral instruments of her loving will. . . . What I am proposing is that this holds true, by way of analogy, for the entire cosmic order in its relation to God: every last bit of cosmic-cultural space, time, matter, and motion reveals — is destined to reveal — the face, the form, of God: the order of the event of God's great act of creative love. . . . Beauty, in short, is cosmic *order* understood as *gift*.[21]

Schindler repeatedly returns to this baker who bakes out of love in order to explain how the properly secular is a condition for the possibility of a politics of sanctification. It becomes the basis for an analogy to a properly secular economic order. But as the above discussion shows, the properly secular must challenge modernity's mechanistic understanding of the universe as well as late scholasticism's sharp nature-grace distinction. Both of these must first be discussed before we can see why happy bakers matter.

III. Beyond Mechanism

The properly secular is that time between the times when all of life, including politics and economics, yearns for God but still needs guidance to have those desires properly ordered. Such desires can never be destroyed; we can never be purely modern. In this properly secular time, the secular is not to be identified with religion. Schindler knows nothing of an embrace of the secular as the truest form of some kenotic movement of the Triune

20. "Religion and Secularity," 43.
21. "Religion and Secularity," 52-53.

God. But the secular is where our everyday lives, how we earn our living, how we work, how we relate to others, becomes the material that expresses the immaterial. This is because such activities can never truly be just "material." Too much must be forgotten, too much repressed, to compel us to see only "materiality." But modernity tempts us to see only the material. This temptation emerges not only on the political left but also on the political right, where the secular is viewed as a "neutral" materiality that must be activated by an extrinsic grace before it becomes the condition for the possibility of holiness.

Since his earliest work, Schindler has contrasted an Aristotelian with a Cartesian understanding of nature. For Aristotle, nature has an "immanence," which finds in the material an immaterial (spirit) that is characterized by the relationship among matter, nature, and a unifying activity. Matter is a "relative concept; it is something which can properly be understood in its actuality, only and always in relation — to nature." Matter is not a discrete, atomistic thing. It makes sense only via a holistic account of nature. Nature "is characterized by act or activity which is immanent, formal, final, unifying, and complete or whole."[22] This means that any organism — biological, social, political — is something more than the sum of its parts. It has a "form" that gives it a "wholeness" that cannot be viewed simply by breaking down and analyzing component features. Yet this form does not simply supervene on the otherwise brute material elements; it is immanent within them.

Schindler finds that this understanding of nature radically shifted with Descartes. Now nature becomes mere material; it is neutral and completely accessible to us such that we can know it by breaking it down into its component parts. It loses any sense of a form that gives it a wholeness within which it is rendered intelligible. The shift in Descartes leads to a mechanism in which anything "immaterial" (mind or spirit) is cordoned off and denied an immanent role in nature. It becomes a mere instrument. Matter can then be reconfigured, rearranged by an immaterial reality (spirit, will) that now always stands outside of it and encounters it as other on the basis of a struggle. The immaterial subdues the material; they are locked in conflict. The immaterial is now construed as "non-natural." This has three consequences. The first is that our understanding of "immateriality" is adversely changed; it becomes "force," which has negative consequences for how we think both of the mind acting on the body and of God

22. BM, 3.

acting on the world.[23] Immaterial forces effect change in matter solely by coming to them from the outside and imposing upon them. The result is a technological reality in which manipulation of a putatively neutral material becomes the means for "human" advancement. Such a mechanistic understanding of nature not only influences our understanding of the universe, but it also affects how we think about politics and economics. The second consequence is a stark fact/value distinction. Facts identify the "neutral" realm of matter. Values are those non-natural acts of will that seek to manipulate a recalcitrant nature, always coming to it from the outside. The third consequence is that metaphysics and theology become cordoned off from science. This can be seen not only with the social sciences, but with physics as well.[24] Eventually science proclaims an independence from both metaphysics and theology, which means that it claims complete intelligibility without any attention to what is good, true, or beautiful as well as to hope, faith, and charity. The world loses any enchantment; enchantment is to be found only in the production of cultural fantasies.

Schindler's efforts to move "beyond mechanism" in ontology are not limited to his forays into science. Because he also finds that this instrumental account of matter and nature has an undue influence in theology and economics, he seeks to identify its role in both of them and move beyond it by simply pointing out its unsustainability. Mechanism produces a moralism that is self-defeating. "A cosmos originally understood as 'neutral' or 'dead' stuff, hence as essentially blind and dumb until appropriated as an instrument of moral or pious choices, indicates a cosmos that is originally indifferent to God. And such a cosmos itself already and as a matter of principle maneuvers piety — the pious use of the cosmos — into what now becomes mostly a moralistic — because primarily arbitrary — imposition on the cosmos."[25] Mechanism does not produce a more permissive society, but a more legalistic one. If we thus refuse to recognize the good's immanent role in nature, it returns as a distorted and legalistic moralism that denies the freedom upon which mechanism turns it into a value.

Schindler differentiates this Cartesian mechanism from a Marian rela-

23. BM, 9.
24. "The mechanistic understanding of nature, which entails a disjunction between nature (matter) and what is not nature, entails in turn a disjunction between the sort of knowledge proper to the study of nature (e.g., physics) and the sort of knowledge proper to the study of what it would take to be non-nature (e.g., what one might call metaphysics and theology)." BM, 10.
25. "Religion and Secularity," 38.

tionship with nature. Descartes and Mary represent two different "methods" or "logics." Descartes's is that of the machine; Mary's is that of love. Descartes's is thoroughly modern in that nature is based on a simple identity between being and presence. What something is can be identified exhaustively in terms of its empirical reality. Here is the basis for empiricism and that flawed and failed philosophy known as logical positivism. Contemplating Mary and her relationship to nature makes no such simple identity, but always assumes a relationality according to which we can know something well only because of multiple relationships between it and us and the "form" within which it is received. We see Mary as Theotokos at the same time that we see her naturally give birth to Jesus. Both are made possible because of the love by which she receives this most miraculous gift. Schindler writes, "In short, what we learn from the Marian *fiat* is not only that the meaning of being is love, but that, in order fully to see this, *we must ourselves be in love*."[26] Only this ontology of love, rather than a mechanistic ontology, can account for the properly secular.

IV. A Graced Nature

Given the hold a mechanistic universe has upon modernity, it comes as no surprise that a theological rendering of nature gets supplanted by a modern notion of nature as a realm of brute facticity. This has dire consequences for the relationship between theology and economics. Nature becomes the realm of pure presence; it is no more than what it appears to be. We do not see economic exchanges as anything other than what they are. For example, a Chinese sweatshop in which fourteen- and fifteen-year-old girls labor for thirteen to fifteen hours a day, unable to converse during that entire time, making beads and trinkets, is not assessed in terms of its larger relation to the New Orleans Mardi Gras festival and how those beads are used. In his film *Mardi Gras: Made in New Orleans,* producer David Redmon shows us the conditions within which Mardi Gras beads are made in China and the reasons why they are distributed in New Orleans. He then shows those conditions to both sets of agents who make them possible. The Chinese girls who watch the beads being exchanged look in disbelief and wonder about what kind of people the Americans are. The New Orleans partygoers are generally appalled by the conditions in the factory, but see little to no rela-

26. HW, 200-201.

tionship between their own activity and what occurs in that Chinese factory. Each component of the process can be viewed as a mere instrument, a detachable component that could always be other. The justification for such practices is always, "If we don't do it, somebody else will," or "At least we give those Chinese girls alternative possibilities for their lives." There is a link here between promiscuous Western sexuality and a very different Chinese sexuality, but those in the film fail to recognize that each now requires the other for its own cultural reality.

Some New Orleans partygoers express concern that when the Chinese factory girls realize what we do with the beads, they will be disappointed. Their "artwork" goes unappreciated only to be swept up and destroyed by city sanitation officials after an evening of orgiastic excess. But the Chinese factory girls do not care; they always thought the beads were ugly and wondered why anyone would want them in the first place. Love, gift, and beauty have no bearing on their work. The fact that both the Westerners and the Chinese find the beads produced worthless and a waste of time bears no relation to the "natural" production of goods to which both contribute. Nature has become a brute thing, something to be endured and manipulated without any significance other than what we place into it by our own will. The idea that something might be produced because it has an inherent beauty and is loved becomes laughable, naïve, and at best extrinsic to the actual conditions of production. This is an example of why the relationship between grace and nature matters theologically. If grace and nature can be divided, and each given its own proper end without an inherent relationship between them, then we will be trained to examine the means of production in China as nothing but a brute fact to which at best "value" can be added.

Schindler recognized the connections between de Lubac's and Balthasar's theology and contemporary political economy. He states, "it is Balthasar's position, following the patristic and High Scholastic tradition, that grace orders nature from the beginning of nature's existence. Firmly maintaining the distinction between nature and grace, Balthasar's affirmation is nonetheless meant to exclude dualism of both a 'hard' and a 'soft' sort."[27] The "hard" distinction imagines a "pure nature" that is "conceived first in terms of its own finality, to which was then 'superadded' a second, now 'supernatural' finality."[28] The "soft" distinction between nature and

27. "Christology and Public Theology," 248.
28. "Christology and Public Theology," 248.

grace fails to recognize grace as an ordering from "within" that gives "form to nature."[29] For Schindler, Balthasar's "transcendentally" integrated grace and nature differs significantly from Rahner's "a priori" account: "These different tendencies are of momentous consequences: what is at stake is nothing less than whether (in what sense) nature (man; reason; world) will be the measure for grace (God; revelation; Church), or grace for nature."[30] Another way of putting this is to ask whether Christology measures nature and the Church measures politics and economics, or whether the "neutral" and putatively more universal modern accounts of nature, politics, and economics measure Christology and ecclesiology. For Schindler, following Balthasar, it must be the former:

> Balthasar's sense of the way unity (of divine person in Jesus Christ) establishes the context within which alone distinctness (of divine and human natures in Jesus Christ) can be properly understood, provides the archetype (analogy) for his understanding of the unity of grace and nature.[31]

No category called "nature" can be construed as larger than Christology. But this does not mean that "nature" gets lost by being completely absorbed into Christology.

The significance of this distinction can be seen in how Schindler qualifies Plantinga's Reformed understanding of "Christian scholarship." Plantinga calls for the pursuit of academic disciplines "from a specifically Christian perspective." Although Schindler finds much in this to affirm, it could easily lose the role of the properly secular. Therefore he replaces Plantinga's "specifically Christian" with "analogously Christian (or Catholic)" in order "to insure that the integrity of the discipline, insofar as they involve reason and nature, not be lost."[32] This illustrates well Schindler's development of the *analogia entis*. He would agree with the Reformed that no purely secular exists; there is no "neutral" academic discipline that is not always already related in some fashion to theology. But nor is there a "specifically" Christian physics, economics, political science, etc., in a direct, univocal sense. Christians need not reject the wisdom accrued through a secular nature or reason by countering it with specific Christian claims. We do not expect an airline pilot to fly by different principles be-

29. "Christology and Public Theology," 249.
30. "Christology and Public Theology," 249.
31. "Christology and Public Theology," 251.
32. HW, 152.

cause he confesses the Nicene Creed, nor an economist to develop some private Christian language for understanding exchanges because she has been baptized. We expect them both first to understand the natural integrity of their disciplines. But this does not imply some pure nature distinct from theology upon which theology works after the "autonomous" science presents the "facts." Immanent to these disciplines is a natural desire for God that gives them a form. Theology makes that form manifest, and, in so doing, grace corrects, fulfills, and perfects nature.[33]

V. A Trinitarian Ontology of Love: *Communio* Ecclesiology and the Happy Baker

Schindler's "analogously Christian" approach to scholarship takes the form of a Trinitarian ontology of love, which has its social and political analogue in a *communio* ecclesiology. He sets this forth in *Heart of the World, Center of the Church,* which takes as its "thesis" that "all of created being finds its integrity finally only in the divine communion of love revealed by the trinitarian God in Jesus Christ, in and through his sacramental Church."[34] Christ's two natures (divine/human) find an analogy in the relationship between the Church and the world.[35] Once again we see the influence of Balthasar and de Lubac: "In a word then, the key for Balthasar–de Lubac is that nature from the beginning is embedded (de facto) in only *one concrete historical order,* namely, that of person and love, as these are ultimately revealed in the life and death of Jesus Christ."[36] Nature and Christology, natural virtues such as justice and supernatural virtues such as love, can be distinguished but never separated.

We are now in a position to understand the important alternative

33. In an essay entitled "Moral Theology," in the *Oxford Handbook of Systematic Theology* (Oxford: Oxford University Press, 2006), I try to explain this more fully using Wittgenstein's helpful distinction between surface and depth grammar.

34. HW, xii-xiii.

35. HW, xiii. We see here also how the influence of Barth on Balthasar provides a corrective to Murray in Schindler's work. Schindler writes, "both Balthasar–de Lubac and Murray affirm an analogy of being — and thereby are able to identify structures of reality that are 'common,' indeed universal. The difference between them lies in the way they see it as possible or appropriate to detach the analogy of being from the analogy of faith." "Christology and Public Theology," 259.

36. "Christology and Public Theology," 258.

Schindler's work provides in theological economics. When it comes to ethical method, he does not adopt only a "narrative" or a "natural law" ethics, but rather adopts both in such a way that they are also "transcended."[37] For this reason he cannot embrace the natural law approach of neo-conservatism, for it concedes too much autonomy to nature without subjecting that term to the narrative history that his critique of mechanization and of the doctrine of pure nature requires. Nor can he simply adopt a thoroughgoing historicism that has no place for an immanent form producing a natural desire for God in all things. This would be to lose the doctrine of creation.

His Christology requires an economic alternative, and one that takes the Church as the "center" of the natural order. Love, not interest and power, gives being its proper form. His *communio* ecclesiology finds liberation theology neglecting this ontology of love by allowing the world to integrate the Church.[38] This inevitably evacuates the Church of substantive content and empties it into a secular realm of power politics. But *communio* ecclesiology does not then advocate for a reduction of the Church to a strongly juridical institution that stands outside the secular order as a demarcated space. The contest between these two gives an unpalatable either-or; both liberationists and neo-conservatives wrongly draw on the Church's social teaching about the secular: "In a word, the legitimate autonomy of the secular order affirmed at Vatican II (*Gaudium et Spes,* nn. 36, 59) comes to signify either a world with which the Church has already, implicitly, been identified, or a world to which the Church remains an 'arbitrary' addition."[39] To see nature well, even in its properly secular role, we must see it through the Church, for it mediates to us the Body of Christ.[40] It is on this basis that Schindler develops

37. Here Schindler also follows what he sees to be Balthasar's approach to ethics: "Balthasar's position includes even as it transcends both these approaches [narrative and natural law] to ethics." "Christology and Public Theology," 260.

38. The similarity between Schindler's critique of liberation theology and Milbank's in his "Founding the Supernatural," in *Theology and Social Theory,* both of which were written without awareness of the other's argument, is quite interesting. The common link, of course, was de Lubac and Balthasar.

39. HW, 5.

40. This is the heart of the argument in HW: "what this book proposes is that all of created being, in its integrity even as 'natural,' in a truly analogous sense 'subsists' in the Church!" (xii). This is a Christological claim because it assumes that "all things have their predestined integrity in and through Jesus Christ (cf. Heb. 1:2), hence in and through Christ's body and bride, the Church" (xii).

his theological economics. If his theology is not true, his work in economics would not make sense. But if his theology is true, his economics would resonate not only with people of faith but also with reason grounded in an ontology of love. This, as we will see, is why happy bakers matter: they are reasonable.

Adam Smith begins his *Wealth of Nations* with his famous statement about the butcher, brewer, and baker. Each looks only to his own interest and never appeals to a common humanity. Smith asserts that in this way common humanity is better served than when we intentionally seek to serve it. Schindler argues that this misses something significant. Does the baker love what she does? Smith's "proposal," he states, "makes no significant difference whether the baker bakes for love or for profit."[41] This statement could easily be misconstrued in two directions. First, it could be misinterpreted as suggesting that what an economic system needs is happy bakers in a trivial sense, like those greeters at the entrance to Walmart who tell us to "have a nice day." Schindler's counter-Smithian proposal could be wrongly viewed as reflecting this kind of modern, ideological sentimentality. But this would require a second willful misconstrual, which so presses against the heart of Schindler's work that it misunderstands it completely. To interpret Schindler's happy baker as a species of modern ideological sentimentality would require the assumption that our will gives an otherwise inert nature its meaning. This is the basis for that modern ideological sentimentality which robs persons of their true nature by forcing them to be "homeless" in the very work they do. The happy baker cannot be happy and do her work with love simply because she wills to do so despite her external circumstances; she must bear witness to, and bring to completion, something already immanent in any form of exchange — an ontology of love.

What would this mean for economics? It means at least three things. First, profit must be considered in terms of intrinsic goods and not simply as an index of human wills. Second, creativity must be considered as also a matter of receptivity. Third, the Catholic "third way" beyond the either-or of capitalism/socialism, which is represented in Catholic social teaching, cannot be rightly understood without the proper role for the Church in economics.

41. WPHD, 361.

A. Profit and Intrinsic Goods

Schindler developed this first theme in his *Heart of the World, Center of the Church:*

> A baker trying to live out his Christianity in his life as a businessperson, to imbue the reality of his economic life with the Gospel — in a word, to live in the spirit of the "new" liberation theory and praxis indicated in *Centesimus Annus* — would thus attempt to order profit differently from the way suggested by Smith. He would seek first to make a loaf of bread that was intrinsically good — in terms of its taste and health-producing qualities and the like — and he would seek to do this from the beginning for the sake of being of service to others in society, of enhancing their health and well-being.[42]

Bringing out the form of goodness in all things must be the first requirement for the Christian vocation as a businessperson. It cannot first and foremost be a desire for profit, for this would be to reduce production to the mechanized reality of inert matter that bears no theological significance.

This does not imply any naïveté about profit. Schindler continues, "To be sure, he would recognize profit as a necessary condition of his continuing ability to provide this service to others. He would recognize that he was realizing his own good in this service to others. But that is just the point: his legitimate concern for profit, and his own 'self-interest,' would be integrated from the beginning and all along the way into the intention of service." In contrast to Buddhism (and I would add Kantianism), Schindler's understanding of exchange does not assume an "elimination of the self and its interests," but a "mutual enhancement." It assumes that "a self that first (ontologically, not temporally) serves the other, and thereby finds itself, is not identical with a self that first seeks itself, and thereby serves the other. A selfishness become mutual is not yet mutual generosity."[43] Schindler's theological economics bears a striking resemblance to Oliver O'Donovan's. He encourages us to abandon the term "exchange" altogether and to think of a theological economics through the language of "communication." O'Donovan develops an analogy of faith that begins with the Church as "the 'communication of the Holy Spirit' (2 Cor. 13:14)" and moves to an understanding of the market as also a

42. HW, 123.
43. HW, 123-124.

"communication."[44] Schindler's understanding of intrinsic goods fits well O'Donovan's development of koinonia as a necessary basis for economic exchange.

B. Creativity and Receptivity

Michael Novak is well known for emphasizing the importance of human creativity as a defense for modern liberal economics. He refers to human participation in the market as co-creation. Schindler finds this problematic. It is why he states that "creativity is a transitive act."[45] Creativity is not only what issues outward from the agent but is just as much what the agent is willing to receive, especially a disposition to receive the intrinsic goodness found in the immanent form present in the created order. Schindler follows the teaching of John Paul II, recognizing that "man images the *creativity* of God the Father and Creator only in and through the *receptivity* of Jesus Christ and his mother Mary."[46] He critiques Novak for relying on the Scottish Enlightenment for an understanding of human agency. Such an understanding misses true freedom by failing to take into account Mary's fiat, which is a form of receptivity that defines all faithfully formed human agency.[47] Related to this is an understanding of participation. Schindler states, "a dimension of receptivity is already inscribed in any notion of participation adequately conceived."[48] The kind of liberalism neo-conservatives draw upon cannot allow for an adequate notion of participation, because the created order is fundamentally inert until the human will infuses it with value. For this reason, neo-conservatives are "unable to grasp the pope's critique of *consumerism as a 'structure of sin.'*"[49] The accommodation of neo-conservatives to the cur-

---

44. O'Donovan, *Ways of Judgment* (Grand Rapids: Eerdmans, 2005), 243. He goes on to say: "The abstract character of exchange appears as soon as we recognize that market-transactions, too, are also communications. The market itself, the community of transaction, belongs to neither party alone but to the two parties together; it is not exchanged between them, but held in common. In order to exchange our exclusive property, we must participate in what is not anyone's exclusive property" (247).

45. HW, 124.

46. HW, 118.

47. HW, 95.

48. HW, 103.

49. HW, 130.

rent configuration of global capitalism fails to embody the spirit of Catholic social teaching. It fails for at least two reasons. First, it has an inadequate understanding of human agency that takes the Father as the paradigm of human action, when the paradigm should be the Son and therefore also Mary's receptivity. Second, it assumes the neutrality of the "political, economic, and academic institutions" that constitute "Anglo-American liberalism."[50] That Catholic social teaching cannot privilege these institutions for the Church is the "third way."

C. The "Third Way" as Ecclesiology

Much has been made of the inadequacy of the so-called Catholic "third way." Beginning with Leo XIII's *Rerum Novarum* in 1891, Catholic social teaching sought a way beyond the conflict between capitalism and socialism. However, in the twentieth century theologians on the left who wanted to incorporate Marxism into the heart of Catholic social teaching, and theologians on the right who sought to incorporate the liberalism of the Scottish Enlightenment, either proclaimed that no "third way" existed or that their position represented the true "third way." Schindler's work does not look for a "third way" by adopting or reforming some perspective on the social sciences. This route is theologically naïve, because "an economic system itself already embodies, indeed is also, a theology and an anthropology and a culture."[51] Only an explicit recognition that we must begin with the third way, which the Church represents, and radiate outward to the world from that center analogically can allow for a theological economics that does not simply baptize some counter-Christian theology via putatively neutral economic institutions. At the heart of the third way is ecclesiology, because Jesus Christ is the heart of the world and the center of the Church.[52]

---

50. HW, xiv. Schindler states: "a *communio* ecclesiology entails a challenge to these central features of Anglo-American liberalism: to its claim of neutrality on the part of its political, economic, and academic institutions; and to its (often unconscious) conception of the (being and acting of the) self in its relations to God and others."

51. WPHD, 349.

52. HW, 9.

Freedom, Biologism, and the Body as Visible Order

David S. Crawford

In a pivotal passage from *Veritatis Splendor,* John Paul II points out two seemingly contradictory directions modernity takes in its understanding of freedom. First, it tends to absolutize freedom as the irreducible core or foundation of human dignity. As such, freedom is treated as self-generating, as a kind of pure spontaneity. To the extent that it is subject to anything beyond itself, autonomous self-determination is limited and undermined. Indeed, the encyclical suggests, such a view posits that freedom must ultimately generate its own truths in order to remain free (VS, 32). From this perspective, any limit on freedom appears to be a limit on human dignity.[1] Second, it simultaneously tends toward various types of determinisms, such as those often implied by the biological, behavioral, and social sciences (VS, 33). According to this second alternative, whatever we experience as freedom is in fact already determined and shaped by necessary internal and external forces and is therefore anything but free. While seemingly at odds, these two accounts share a common starting

---

1. As Ratzinger observes: "In the consciousness of mankind today, freedom is largely regarded as the greatest good there is, after which all other good things have to take their place. In legislation, artistic freedom and freedom of speech take precedence over every other moral value. Values that conflict with freedom, that could lead to its being restricted, appear as shackles, as 'taboos,' that is to say, as relics of archaic prohibitions and anxieties. Political action has to demonstrate that it furthers freedom. Even religion can make an impression only by depicting itself as a force for freedom for man and for mankind. In the scale of values with which man is concerned, to live a life worthy of humanity, freedom seems to be the truly fundamental value and to be the really basic human right of them all. The concept of truth, on the other hand, we greet rather with some suspicion." Joseph Cardinal Ratzinger, *Truth and Tolerance: Christian Belief and World Religions,* trans. Henry Taylor (San Francisco: Ignatius Press, 2003), 231.

point. If the former understanding sees freedom as an act of indifferent choice prior to any given order, the latter tacitly agrees with this core meaning but then observes that in fact it can exist nowhere.[2] Here, it seems to me, we have a simple statement of the dilemma raised by dominant notions of freedom today. Freedom is both exalted as the basis of absolute self-invention and dignity and simultaneously haunted by the dread of absolute, if tacit, domination.

The threats to freedom so conceived are of course infinite. However, the human body itself is perhaps the most important of these, as is evidenced in many developments in Western society today, such as the crisis in the meaning of "gender." While the body's inherent order and meaning are necessarily seen "outside" freedom, the body clearly also "shapes" freedom. But insofar as the body is "outside" freedom, this "shaping" cannot be considered a part of freedom. The body, therefore, not only enables but also radically limits freedom in ways that the agent has not chosen. Hence, the body constantly threatens to submerge freedom in the domain of the "pre-rational" and the "sub-personal."

As has already been hinted, extrinsic or dualistic views hardly guarantee a genuine human freedom. Indeed, part of my argument in this essay is that it is impossible to arrive at an adequate sense of either freedom or the body without seeing them as integrally related. One of the most interesting efforts to clarify the integral character of this relationship can be found in the work of David L. Schindler. As he puts it:

> Freedom derives its proper meaning in and through the person's substantial body-soul unity, his creation by God, and his nuptiality. The act of choice characteristic of freedom thus bears from the inside out a form and purpose shaped by the relation to the body, to God, and to other persons. Freedom discovers its primitive and proper meaning as a free and spiritual act from within these relations.[3]

Of course, talk of "shaping" freedom will heighten rather than assuage the "dread" mentioned a moment ago. The shaping caused by relation to God

2. Cf. also Robert Spaemann, "Genetic Manipulation of Human Nature in the Context of Human Personality," in *Human Genome, Human Person and the Society of the Future: Proceedings of the Fourth Assembly of the Pontifical Academy for Life*, Vatican City, February 23-25, 1998, ed. Juan de Dios Vial Correa and Elio Sgreccia (Vatican City: Libreria Editrice Vaticana, 1999), 340-350, at 340.
3. "Significance of World and Culture," 129.

and other persons raises the specter of heteronomy, while the shaping of the body suggests biologism. Key here is seeing the body (as well as the relation to God, other persons, and the world as a whole) as radically inside of, and indeed helping to co-constitute, freedom. It is this last point that Schindler seems to me to have developed so richly. In what follows, I will argue that the body "co-constitutes" freedom precisely as a visible order expressing not only the soul as form but also the order and destiny of the cosmos. In doing so, the body also discloses the meaning of inclinations and desire.

I

To make sense of this co-constitutive role of the body, however, we might begin with a brief discussion of what Hans Jonas calls an "ontology of death" characteristic of modern cosmological-biological thought.[4] If ancients interpreted the cosmos as most fundamentally alive (panvitalism), Jonas tells us, moderns understand it as fundamentally composed of "dead" matter. If for ancients the problem was to explain death as the overriding anomaly, for moderns the problem is to explain the emergence of life, and therefore freedom, from the interaction of material forces. These explanations, Jonas points out, typically take one of two general forms for modernity: materialism or idealism.

According to the former, life is an epiphenomenon of the interaction of material elements and forces. But from here freedom hardly seems possible. Hence we are left with materialist determinisms of various types. What we experience as freedom ultimately would be traceable back to non-free determination. Any gap between this determinism and actual events would have to be laid at the feet of the indeterminacy of chance rather than freedom.[5]

While the second alternative, idealism, would seem to be the salvation of freedom, it can be so only by severing (or rescuing) it from the body. Here freedom as rational autonomy takes on particular importance. The problem, however, has always been how to reconnect transcendental free-

4. Hans Jonas, *The Phenomenon of Life: Toward a Philosophical Biology* (Evanston, IL: Northwestern University Press, 1966), 15.
5. Indeed, Richard Swinburne uses the indeterminacy built into quantum physics to disprove physical determinism (*The Evolution of the Soul*, rev. ed. [New York: Oxford University Press, 1997], 231ff.). Cf. Robert Kane, *Free Will* (Malden, MA: Blackwell, 2002), 6-7.

dom to the real world, to the body and the world of sensation and causality.[6] "[P]ure consciousness is as little alive as the pure matter standing over against it," Jonas tells us. "It lives as departed spirits live and cannot understand the world anymore."[7] The problem with the idealist alternative, then, is its implicit removal of freedom from time and space. Hence the body and its manifestations, such as appetite, will always remain at least suspicious interlopers. The question then arises as to how such a freedom can ever begin to act. To speak of freedom as pure spontaneity is to speak of something inexplicable and arbitrary — something without order or ratio. But if we allow that desire and reason move freedom, we end with the paradox mentioned above: namely, that freedom is given actuality by what we have already conceived as non-freedom or necessity. Such a result tends to land us back in our materialist starting point. The implication is a freedom oscillating between rebellion and surrender, a freedom that needs to set itself apart from the body and human nature to be free but which finally needs the body to be real.

The answer to our conundrum, Jonas suggests, is to view the organism in terms of form and finality. Indeed, he argues that freedom begins analogously even at the most primitive level of organic life, say that of the amoeba, because even here there are the form and *telos* implied in simultaneous participation-in and standing-over-and-against the rest of the cosmos. He describes this level of freedom as a "manner of executing existence, distinctive of the organic *per se*."[8] As he grants, "freedom," here, is "an ontologically descriptive term which can apply to mere physical evidence at first." "Yet," he continues, "even as such it must not be unrelated to the meaning it has in the human sphere whence it is borrowed, else its extended use would be frivolous. . . . Thus the first appearance of the principle in its bare, elementary object-form signifies the break-through of being to the indefinite range of possibilities which hence stretches to the farthest reaches of subjective life, and as a whole stands under the sign of 'freedom.'"[9] In a word, while he sees freedom as proper to the mind, at the

---

6. Jonas, *The Phenomenon of Life*, 26-33. Cf. also Jaegwon Kim, "Lonely Souls: Causality and Substance Dualism," in *Soul, Body, and Survival: Essays on the Metaphysics of Human Persons*, ed. Kevin Corcoran (Ithaca, NY: Cornell University Press, 2001), 36.

7. Jonas, *The Phenomenon of Life*, 22. Or, as Robert Spaemann puts it, "[h]uman persons are neither things nor mere subjects but living beings: their being consists not in thinking but in living" ("Genetic Manipulation," 341).

8. Jonas, *The Phenomenon of Life*, 3.

9. Jonas, *The Phenomenon of Life*, 3.

same time he argues for an anticipation even at the level of the body or at the level of organism as such. This approach does not amount to falling back into a false materialism, because it takes the body — even of the amoeba — as necessarily more than simply material. In contrast to modernity's mechanistic presuppositions, life and the primitive "freedom" it implies stand both within and over-and-against their environment, metabolizing what is needed and rejecting what is not. Materialism cannot finally explain mind and freedom because it paradoxically cannot explain the specifically material aspect of the body. This is clear, Jonas points out, when we consider that the body is constantly reconstituting itself through metabolism. It is never simply materially self-identical over time; rather, it is precisely the characteristic of organisms to struggle to maintain their existence. Thus, its identity must be verified in terms of formal and final cause and not only in terms of its material content. In other words, a purely materialistic/mechanistic explanation not only runs into trouble explaining spiritual or conscious life. *It also runs into trouble explaining the body itself.*

Now of course these alternatives are not exhaustive of the resources of modern thought. As Schindler grants, for example, "contemporary physics has long since abandoned in any direct or simple form a Cartesian or, better, a Newtonian, model of nature."[10] The ambiguity outlined above nevertheless remains a real one. One might point out that contemporary physics hardly escapes Jonas's "ontology of death." One might also point out that science as it is actually practiced in a multitude of pertinent areas (e.g., biology) continues to presuppose an essentially mechanist approach.[11] One might finally consider the way the "body-soul problem" is treated in dominant philosophical discussions.[12]

10. "Significance of World and Culture," 139.

11. An example of the way in which biology remains fundamentally mechanistic in its outlook can be found in the recent proposals known as "Altered Nuclear Transfer" and "Oocyte Assisted Reprogramming" (ANT-OAR), aimed at generating pluripotent stem cells while avoiding the ethical issues entailed in the destruction of human embryos. Cf. Schindler, "Response to Joint Statement."

12. The debate among "substance dualists" and their detractors, for example, in various ways presupposes and continues the basic dilemma just outlined above. Among the former, Richard Swinburne argues that "those persons which are human beings (or men) living on Earth, have two parts linked together, body and soul" (*The Evolution of the Soul*, rev. ed. [New York: Oxford University Press, 1997], 145). The body and soul are "two parts linked together": "pure mental properties" belong to the soul, "physical properties" belong to the body, and "mixed properties" belong to both (145ff.). Bodies are "vehicles of knowledge and

Finally — and following Schindler's lead — one might point to the ambiguity implied for freedom and the body at the level of experience as it is mediated by liberal society and culture.[13] Here, the person is almost inevitably identified as the conscious actor, one who can claim and exercise rights. This mediated experience profoundly shapes our understanding of freedom and the body and brings with it a view of human destiny and the cosmos. Crucial in this regard is the liberal mission to insulate individual choice from prior, "comprehensive" visions of the meaning of life or the good. According to this view, freedom must therefore be understood in abstraction from nature in general and especially bodily nature, since these could only threaten autonomous choice. In other words, liberalism continues "to presuppose just the external relation between (bodily) nature and freedom lying at the root of the mechanistic conception of nature or the biological-physical world."[14] Here again, we find the oscillation between the body and freedom, but now expressed culturally (politically, juridically, economically, and so forth) by a rejection of the fully personal character of the body in favor of freedom. Indeed, liberal society increasingly rejects the body in its structures and meaning as *above all else* threatening to individual autonomy, as can be seen in the feminist and gay polemic against "anatomy" or "biology as destiny." Accordingly, freedom must conceptually precede the body. Increasingly, in fact, it is simply becoming the object of freedom, to be manipulated and shaped according to freedom's prior establishment of the self. Freedom itself is thereby reduced

---

operation" (146). Stewart Goetz tells us: "Just as I find myself having the basic belief that I am a soul, so also I find myself having the basic belief that I have freedom of the will in the libertarian sense that I am free to make undetermined choices for purposes" ("Substance Dualism," in *In Search of the Soul: Four Views of the Mind-Body Problem*, ed. Joel B. Green and Stuart L. Palmer [Downers Grove, IL: InterVarsity Press, 2005], 33-74, at 56-57). Goetz then goes on to argue that dualism is effectively necessary for "libertarian freedom" (58). Cf. also J. P. Moreland and Scott B. Rae, *Body and Soul: Human Nature and the Crisis in Ethics* (Downers Grove, IL: InterVarsity Press, 2000). Eric T. Olson, on the other hand, takes a materialist approach (e.g., *The Human Animal: Personal Identity without Psychology* [New York: Oxford University Press, 1997]; *What Are We? A Study of Personal Ontology* [New York: Oxford University Press, 2007]). Here the person is the organism itself, while personhood, and all that it entails, is not a substance, as substance dualism supposes, but a "phase sort," like being a philosopher, an athlete, an infant, or an adult (*The Human Animal*, 25, 30).

13. Needless to say, it is quite common in other fields to define the person solely in terms of consciousness — for example, in the jurisprudential debate over abortion and euthanasia (e.g., Ronald Dworkin, "The Concept of Unenumerated Rights: Whether and How *Roe* Should Be Overturned," *University of Chicago Law Review* 59 [1992]: 403n.36).

14. "Significance of World and Culture," 139.

to being, in its essential starting point, disembodied and indeed androgynous.[15] This is why the recent phenomenon of "gender bending" is intended as a politics and a metaphysics.

II

1. Freedom so constituted imagines the person without an ordering vocation, or better, perhaps, it imagines the person as giving himself a vocation. Thus, John Rawls tells us that "[h]uman good is heterogeneous because the aims of the self are heterogeneous. Although to subordinate all our aims to one end does not strictly speaking violate the principles of rational choice . . . it still strikes us as irrational or more likely as mad. The self is disfigured."[16] However deeply we may feel a desire for this or that "end" or "good," none of them can finally be truly considered an end or a good because none of them can be conceived as making a claim on us entirely. To give oneself entirely would be to give oneself irrevocably. But to do this would be to eliminate the power to make further choices. Thus, movement toward commitment to an end must be seen as movement away from freedom (and, by implication, human dignity). The response must be to attenuate the holding power of ends. Each therefore risks abandonment in

15. Hence, the current drift in society toward a sexless or androgynous anthropology, or what the late Italian philosopher Augusto Del Noce called a "gay nihilism" (cf. Angelo Scola, *The Nuptial Mystery*, trans. Michelle Borras [Grand Rapids: Eerdmans, 2005], 148-49; Livio Melina, "Homosexual Inclination as an 'Objective Disorder': Reflections of Theological Anthropology," *Communio: International Catholic Review* 25 [1998]: 57-68, at 65). There are also a large and influential number of thinkers within the ambit of Catholic thought who suggest a version of freedom along these lines. Here I have in mind writers for whom the body itself would lack normative implications in its structures but who simultaneously see it as possessing important implications at an affective level. An example of this would be the work in sexuality of Michael Lawler and Todd Salzman. See their *The Sexual Person: Toward a Renewed Catholic Anthropology* (Washington, DC: Georgetown University Press, 2008); "*Quaestio Disputata*, Catholic Sexual Ethics: Complementarity and the Truly Human," *Theological Studies* 67 (2006): 625-652. On the question of liberalism's implicitly androgynous anthropology, see my "Recognizing the Roots of Society in the Family, Foundation of Justice," *Communio: International Catholic Review* 34 (2007): 379-412, and "Liberal Androgyny: 'Gay Marriage' and the Meaning of Sexuality in Our Time," *Communio: International Catholic Review* 33 (2006): 237-265.

16. John Rawls, *A Theory of Justice* (Cambridge, MA: Harvard University Press, 1971), 554, cited in Alasdair MacIntyre, *Whose Justice? Which Rationality?* (Notre Dame: University of Notre Dame Press, 1988), 337.

shifting aims. The result is not so much a rejection of restlessness (this would be impossible), but a replacement of the classical idea with a version of "restlessness" as aimlessness.[17]

The Christian tradition, on the other hand, sees freedom as real because it is embedded within human origins and destiny. Thus, Schindler argues that human freedom is never its own source; it is never simply or purely spontaneous or self-originating. Rather, its "originality" and genuine novelty are always first embedded within its origin in God and, in a real sense, all others. Hence,

> [i]n the words of philosopher Robert Spaemann, the fundamental act of freedom is "letting be": the letting be of the being-given of myself to myself by God and others — the letting be of the effectiveness of God and others in me that originally constitutes my being as a gift that itself gives. My freedom at its core and thus in each of its acts actively-receptively recollects my being-given as gift and thus as apt for giving. . . . [I]t recuperates the relation to God and others in which I find myself always already a participant and of which, consequently, I am *never first or simply the origin.*[18]

As such, then, freedom has an original and internal structure or shape; it is most radically constituted as a response.[19] Not only is this view at odds with notions of freedom as primary and self-generating, but it also points to the crucial role of the body in human freedom. As John Paul II taught, the "being-given" that stands behind freedom is expressed in the body, which possesses an inherently nuptial or familial form. The body, he tells

17. Cf. David C. Schindler, "Freedom Beyond Our Choosing: Augustine on the Will and Its Objects," *Communio: International Catholic Review* 29 (2002): 618-653, at 626ff.

18. David L. Schindler, "The Embodied Person as Gift and the Cultural Task in America: *Status Quaestionis*," *Communio: International Catholic Review* 35 (2008): 397-431, at 418-419.

19. Cf. John Paul II, *Veritatis Splendor*, 10: "The moral life presents itself as the response due to the many gratuitous initiatives taken by God out of love for man. It is a response of love." John Paul II also emphasizes the "relational dimension" of freedom in *Evangelium Vitae*, 19. See also Hans Urs von Balthasar, "Nine Propositions on Christian Ethics," in *Principles of Christian Morality*, by Heinz Schürmann, Joseph Ratzinger, and Hans Urs von Balthasar, trans. Graham Harrison (San Francisco: Ignatius, 1986), 77-104, esp. 79-86, in which it is argued that the moral life is fulfilled only in the person of Christ, in whom the Christian becomes son or daughter, *heteros* rather than *heteron*. Hence, the "fragments" and beginnings of extra-biblical ethics find their radical fulfillment in Christ. Cf. also Schindler, "Freedom Beyond Our Choosing," which argues that freedom is most fundamentally "consent."

us, should not be considered a mere preamble to freedom. Rather, "it is in the unity of body and soul that the person is the subject of his own actions" (*Veritatis Splendor,* 48). Hence, Schindler concludes along with John Paul, "[t]he body, in its physiology as such, is not 'premoral' but 'moral': it bears an order characterized by 'the anticipatory signs, the expression and promise of the gift of self, in conformity with the wise plan of the Creator.'"[20] Because the body must be characterized as inherently "familial" (that is to say, as bearing the form or shape of filiality, nuptiality, paternity, and fraternity), so too must freedom.

The "moral life in its largest sense therefore originates in a religious and indeed ontological quest: a quest for the meaning of life that is prompted by and has its fulfillment in a movement initiated by God himself."[21] This search for meaning points to a relationship that encompasses the whole of life. Here freedom presupposes the *motus rationalis creaturae in Deum.*[22] Moral reasoning and freedom are "set in motion" as "an echo of, or indeed a response to, a call from God who is the origin and goal of our being."[23] Placing the question of the moral life in this context not only locates the purpose and meaning of human freedom and activity in relation to man's created origin and end; it also "involves . . . the *whole of his being,* recapitulated to be sure through the will."[24] Indeed, the order of freedom and action is also an order of human nature in its fullness and specifically in its embodiedness. "Jesus' gift of love, in other words, penetrates and thus comprehends the whole of his bodily existence, fulfilling the latter in its *natural integrity as bodily.*"[25] For Schindler, therefore, to properly understand the body and freedom requires seeing the former as participating in the latter's constitution.

2. Now, in part, Schindler's concern to reintegrate the body into freedom can be addressed from within the traditional treatment of freedom as rational appetite. Here freedom arises in an attraction to the good, and ultimately to the perfect or complete good or beatitude. Thus, freedom and all

20. "Significance of World and Culture," 112-113; citing *Veritatis Splendor,* 48.

21. "Significance of World and Culture," 115.

22. St. Thomas Aquinas, *Summa Theologiae,* I, q. 2, prologue; cf. Livio Melina, *Sharing in Christ's Virtues: For a Renewal of Moral Theology in Light of* Veritatis Splendor, trans. William May (Washington, DC: Catholic University of America Press, 2001), 48ff.

23. "Significance of World and Culture," 116; cf. *Veritatis Splendor,* 10.

24. "Significance of World and Culture," 115; emphasis added.

25. "Significance of World and Culture," 115.

human action turn on the conversion and movement of the creature toward union with God. As such, they are fundamentally teleological, drawing on man's desire for the beatific vision. "Final and perfect happiness," St. Thomas tells us, "can consist in nothing else than the vision of the Divine Essence."[26] This desire for complete happiness ultimately represents the desire of the human creature himself, at his deepest level, for a fulfillment that can in the end only be given "supernaturally" in the beatific vision. Hence, Henri de Lubac tells us that *desiderium naturale* "constitutes" us because it represents the movement of our nature itself.[27]

While it is clear that this desire for God is fundamentally rooted in man's spiritual faculties of intellect and will *(voluntas)*, it is also true that this desire drives all subordinate and penultimate movement. "Man must, of necessity, desire all, whatsoever he desires, for the last end."[28] This means that the particular inclinations[29] are themselves an expression of the basic desire for the final end. Indeed, in his criticism of indifferent freedom, Servais Pinckaers tells us that the "most decisive point . . . was the breach between freedom and the natural inclinations, which were rejected from the essential core of freedom."[30] The order given within these inclinations and brought to its fullness by practical reason, virtue, and law is not fundamentally a suppression or an imposition that limits worldly free-

---

26. *Summa Theologiae*, I-II, q. 3, a. 8.

27. Henri de Lubac, *The Mystery of the Supernatural* (New York: Crossroads, 1998), 167; or again, "God's call is constitutive. My finality, which is expressed by this desire, is inscribed upon my very being as it has been put into this universe by God. And by God's will, I now have no other genuine end, no end really assigned to my nature or presented for my free acceptance under any guise, except that of 'seeing God'" (55).

28. *Summa Theologiae*, I-II, q. 1, a. 6. St. Thomas goes on to say that this is evident because: first, whatever is desired must be desired either as a perfect good or as tending to a perfect good (i.e., for the sake of some other good); second, the perfect good is the first cause of action and therefore the first cause of movement toward secondary objects. This starting point has of course been challenged by writers such as Germain Grisez who question the validity of the traditional notion of "restlessness" and argue that actors act for diverse basic goods that are not ordered under some one perfect good. Cf., e.g., Grisez, "The True Ultimate End of Human Beings: The Kingdom, Not God Alone," *Theological Studies* 69 (2008): 38-61; "The Restless-Heart Blunder," Aquinas Lecture, University of St. Thomas (2005), at http://videoarchive.stthom.edu. Cf. also Peter Ryan, S.J., "Must the Acting Person Have a Single Ultimate End?" *Gregorianum* 82 (2001): 327-55; and "How Can the Beatific Vision Both Fulfill Human Nature and Be Utterly Gratuitous?" *Gregorianum* 83.4 (2002): 717-754.

29. Cf. *Summa Theologiae*, I-II, q. 10, a. 1; also I-II, q. 94, a. 2.

30. Servais Pinckaers, *The Sources of Christian Ethics* (Washington, DC: Catholic University Press, 1995), 332.

dom for the sake of a higher end; rather, it is the necessary implication of and interior presupposition of freedom as such in all of its realizations. It is man's "conformation" (*Veritatis Splendor,* 21) or connaturality, always drawing on what is already in him, to the order of love. That man desires *at all* is a sign or manifestation of his desire for God. Here then we have a version of freedom that succeeds in reconciling itself with nature in such a way that the latter is necessary and integral to freedom's very structure or form, operation, and meaning. As Pinckaers puts it:

> The root of freedom develops in us principally through a sense of the true and the good, of uprightness and love, and through a desire for knowledge and happiness. Or again, by what the ancients called *semina virtutum,* the seeds of virtue, which give rise to these natural dispositions — the sense of justice, of courage, truth, friendship, and generosity — which cause us to give spontaneous praise to acts so conformed and to condemn their absence, at least in a general way. Such dispositions project a certain ideal of life, which gives direction to our desires and forms and influences our moral judgments.

Far from lessening our freedom, such dispositions are its foundation. We are free, not in spite of them, but because of them. The more we develop them, the more we grow in freedom. In this we discover the true, specifically moral meaning of the famous principle of ancient philosophy, *sequi naturam,* "follow nature," so frankly adopted and Christianized by the Fathers of the Church.[31]

In concert with this tradition, Schindler emphasizes that freedom is set in motion, that it has an élan. He tells us that "[h]uman freedom . . . is an ordered desire," that the "movement proper to freedom from its beginning comes filled with 'in-*form*-ation' given through the call of God, through the attractiveness of God as good. This always-in*form*ed desire is what may be termed love: human freedom is by nature love — a natural love, if you will."[32] The desire of the human person is that of a complex whole, taking up all of the penultimate ends that together constitute human good, including, for example, self-preservation and procreation, which are very clearly rooted in bodily life. Thus, human desire and freedom, partly expressed in natural inclinations, are themselves an expression of the person, who is a composite of body and soul.

31. Pinckaers, *The Sources of Christian Ethics,* 357-358.
32. "Significance of World and Culture," 116.

3. As significant as this starting point is, however, Schindler offers a different emphasis, and one that seems to me to be important for a full response to the problematic versions of freedom outlined above, including their implied androgyny. While the inclinations are in part an expression of the person's embodiedness, they are not yet the body and its intrinsic order as such.[33] Schindler's important development, then, is his emphasis on the question of "order" or "form" as correlative to the order already indicated in desire. Indeed, he tells us, freedom "presupposes an *anterior order and goodness* already given . . . in the body's original human-created constitution."[34] His emphasis is on the body qua body. Hence, he reminds us of

> "premodern" (e.g., Aristotelian) biology according to which "the soul is the cause [*aition*] or source [*archē*] of the living body," in the threefold sense of being the body's end and form and source of its movement. That is, the soul gives the body its first order of meaning, even as the body then simultaneously, in its very nature *as* a body, enters into and is partially constitutive of the original order of freedom itself.[35]

Or again, "[t]he soul gives the body its first meaning *as a body,* although, given the unity of soul and body, the causal relationship is always mutually internal, albeit asymmetrical."[36] Or:

> Given the unity coincident with distinctness between soul and body, each contributes to the meaning of the other, in their respective differences *as* soul and *as* body: the soul contributes to the meaning of the body qua body, even as the body, in a subordinate sense, contributes to the meaning of the soul qua soul.[37]

A couple of points, it seems to me, can be drawn from the foregoing passages. The first can be arrived at by asking whether the "body qua body" or the body's "anterior order and goodness" can be understood exclusively in terms of the body as a source of inclinations when it comes to understanding the constitution of freedom. Clearly for Schindler some-

---

33. Cf. my "Natural Law and the Body: Between Deductivism and Parallelism," *Communio: International Catholic Review* 35 (2008): 327-353.

34. "Significance of World and Culture," 120; emphasis added.

35. "Significance of World and Culture," 119.

36. Schindler, "The Embodied Person as Gift," 400.

37. Schindler, "The Embodied Person as Gift," 400n.4.

thing more is involved. This is why he prizes so highly the teaching of John Paul II that the body "reveals man" and therefore that

> a primordial *sacrament* is constituted, understood as a *sign that effica-ciously transmits in the visible world the invisible mystery hidden in God from eternity.* And this is the mystery of Truth and Love, the mystery of divine life, in which man really participates. . . . The sacrament, as a visible sign, is constituted with man, inasmuch as he is a "body," through his "visible" masculinity and femininity. The body, in fact, and only the body, is capable of making visible what is invisible: the spiritual and the divine. It has been created to transfer into the visible reality of the world the mystery hidden from eternity in God, and thus to be a sign of it.[38]

This "anterior order and goodness" is manifest in the body understood as a "sign" or "sacrament." *It seems the body, then, is partly constitutive of freedom, not only in its being a source of inclination, but also in its very visible structure and meaning as a body or, in the words of John Paul II, in its visibility as sign.* The body itself in its visible *ratio* as a whole must help constitute human freedom from the very beginning, and not only in secondary ways: e.g., qua instrument, context, opportunity, or limit, or even qua foundation of appetite.

The second point can be arrived at by asking what it means to speak of the body as contributing an order. Of course, form and matter are distinct, and Schindler is not saying that the body possesses a kind of form outside of the soul's causality.[39] Indeed, he argues that "[t]he body . . . is never, after the manner of Descartes, simply physicalist 'stuff' that somehow has its own 'organization' prior to and independent of the order provided by the soul."[40] No, the soul is the formal "cause" of the body, while we have to say that the body in its subordinate way also "completes" the soul as the human person's material cause. The intellectual soul is, as it were, made to inform a body. Hence, hylomorphic unity indicates a kind of "mutual" or mutually "internal" causality. We might think that this mutuality of soul and the body qua body is simply a way of talking about the body as the material expression of the soul as form. However, Schindler is insistent that the body's contribution is more than its expression, that the mutuality he is

---

38. John Paul II, *Man and Woman He Created Them: A Theology of the Body*, 203; emphasis original.

39. Cf. Aquinas, *Summa Theologiae*, I, q. 76, a. 4.

40. Schindler, "Embodied Person as Gift," at 401.

speaking of is indeed circumincessive, albeit also radically asymmetrical (with form having an absolute priority).[41] Matter in a real way "completes" form. Indeed, the idea of *materia debita* or *materia apta* suggests that behind this completion is a necessary order.[42]

Now embodiedness entails created, cosmic order. The body must be of a kind that is apt for its concrete existence as part of a cosmos — or better, both as part of a cosmos and simultaneously as standing over-and-against the rest of the cosmos in maintaining its own continuance as a living organism. The nature of the human person is to be a substantial unity of body and soul living in creation; *in this sense then, the physical nature of embodied human being also orders the kind of soul the human soul is.* This is true even eschatologically, however radically spiritualized the resurrected body will be.[43] The soul is what it is because the nature of the human per-

---

41. For example, Schindler both praises and qualifies Edith Stein's statement that "'[t]he insistence that sexual differences are "stipulated by the body alone" is questionable from various points of view. (1) If *anima = forma corporis*, then bodily differentiation constitutes an index of differentiation in the spirit. (2) Matter serves form, not the reverse. This strongly suggests that the difference in the psyche is the primary one." In response, Schindler tells us that "[a]n important truth is affirmed here which nevertheless demands further clarification. Given the unity coincident with distinctness between soul and body, each contributes to the other, in their respective differences *as* soul and *as* body" ("The Embodied Person as Gift," 400n.4, quoting Edith Stein, *Self Portrait in Letters, 1916-1942* [Washington, DC: ICS Publications, 1994], 98-99).

42. Schindler tells us: "[t]here is, in other words, a *mutuality* of form and matter (*materia apta*) in accounting causally for the unity of the organism as a-whole-in-parts and parts-in-a-whole, but this mutuality is *asymmetrical*. What may be termed the *relative priority* of matter/material parts ('potency') in accounting for that unity always presupposes what may be termed the *absolute priority* of substantial form ('act'). . . . Substantial form and material parts are at the same time mutual causes and mutual effects of each other, but they are so in different ways — with radically asymmetrical kinds of priority. . . . [T]he mutual (but asymmetrical) relationship between substantial form and materia apta in the constitution of an organism entails that the hierarchy presupposed in this relationship is for all that not tyrannical. That relationship, in other words, is not deterministic. Though there is a necessary relation between substantial form and materia apta in the constitution of an organism, this necessary relation presupposes the enduring distinction between these two, such that the agency of neither can ever be reduced to, or thus ever exhaustively determined by, the agency of the other. To be sure, the substantial form of an organism makes the organism as a whole and in each of its parts be the kind of being that it is, and the substantial form thus formally determines the organism. . . . But the point is that substantial form, for all of its formal determination of the organism, always itself presupposes the distinct and simultaneous contribution of the materia apta in the determination" ("Reply to Austriaco," 808).

43. See, for example, John Paul II's *Dominum et vivificantem*, 50, where it is stated that

245

son is to be *corpore et anima unus*. And this nature receives its order in part from the "nature" or character of the rest of created and indeed material reality, which is apt (in an integral and non-mechanistic way) to be taken up in the spiritual and free realm of human being. Hence, the body brings its own order to freedom, not in the sense that the body possesses form or exists already outside of its hylomorphic constitution as caused by the soul, but insofar as human freedom is the freedom of the substantial unity of body and soul that is the person in the created order with all of its material, cosmic dimension.[44]

It is important to recall, at this point, that we are not speaking here only of the requirements of biological life in a reductive sense. Hence, to speak of the order implied by a body is not to fall back into the materialistic determinisms discussed earlier (i.e., it is not "biologism" in this sense). Rather, we are speaking of a cosmological-biological order that is an expression of creatureliness. As Schindler tells us, "physical nature bears an *interior order* (e.g., form and finality) rendering nature, precisely from within what are its essential, hence, abiding mechanical properties, apt for (eventual) integration into the organic-human and in turn sacramental-holy."[45] Thus, insofar as freedom arises out of the body, it is simultaneously an expression of the meaning and destiny inscribed in physical nature. Indeed, for God, "the Creator Spiritus, thinking and making are one and the same thing. His thinking is a creative process. Things are, because they are thought. . . . [A]ll being is therefore what has been thought, the thought of the absolute spirit. Conversely, this means that since all being is thought, all being is meaningful, 'logos', truth."[46] The "logos" inscribed in all being means that the body is already an order of reason and truth, which is saturated with meaning for man and his destiny.

This also means that the relationship between the body and the rest of

---

Christ attaches himself to "all flesh," which is said to include the entire cosmos. Cf. also Adrian J. Walker, "'Sown Psychic, Raised Spiritual': The Lived Body as the Organ of Theology," *Communio: International Catholic Review* 33 (2006): 203-215.

44. Hence, Schindler tells us, we must "recuperate a cosmology rooted in an ontology of giftedness, and physics and biology integrated by and into such a cosmology; [and] recuperate simultaneously an anthropology likewise rooted in an ontology of giftedness, and a politics, and economics, an academy, and a science, medicine, and technology integrated by and into such an anthropology" ("Significance of World and Culture," 135).

45. "Significance of World and Culture," 126.

46. Ratzinger, *Introduction to Christianity*, trans. J. R. Foster (San Francisco: Ignatius Press, 1990 [orig. German ed., 1968]), 31-32.

the cosmos, in a way that is analogous to that of the body and soul, entails mutuality (but again, "asymmetrically" — man is the culmination of God's creative act, while at the same time man completes the cosmos). The body makes visible not only the soul as form, but also the person who exists and indeed recapitulates the world as a whole. If man is the summit of creation, the body makes visible not only the soul but also, in a real way, the world in its destiny. The body, in other words, relates not only the soul to the world, but also the world to the soul. Or, to make the point from a different direction, Mary's embodied fiat, which is expressed in her virginity as readiness to receive the Christ child, is a fiat not only on behalf of all of human nature, as St. Thomas tells us *("consensus virginis loco totius humanae naturae"),*[47] but also, as John Paul II suggests, on behalf of the entire cosmos.

My point, then, is twofold: (1) embodiedness implies an order and as such "contributes to the meaning of the soul qua soul" as, in a real sense, "obedient" to a cosmological order which both serves and anticipates it; (2) this order is not simply biological in a reductive sense but, as an order, is already meaningful as a "logos" of the *Creator Spiritus.* These points place the body at the center, as it were, of the anthropological-cosmological reality of creation. We might say that the body articulates in the grammar of physicality the spiritual and free soul that both is part of and transcends the world, thereby revealing the interior ordination of both man and his world. This centrality of the body, at the crossroads between the world and the soul in their destiny, then, serves to make that destiny manifest — or, in other words, to be its "sign."[48]

4. But does this twofold conclusion raise more questions than it answers? How can the body's visible structure or meaning help constitute freedom? Are we back to square one? If the body represents an order that itself shapes freedom, how is this not an external limitation of freedom by what, in the final analysis, is not itself free? While it is clear that inclination, which is in part rooted in the body, is interior to freedom as its dynamic force, it is more difficult to see how the body as a visible expression of order is not an imposition on freedom, as a kind of *lex naturalis* that gives "form" to freedom only insofar as it also externally limits it. Again, the bodily order we are speaking of here is not that of a methodologically

---

47. Aquinas, *Summa Theologiae,* III, q. 30, a. 1.

48. Cf. John Paul II, *Man and Woman He Created Them: A Theology of the Body,* 203; *Veritatis Splendor,* 48.

David S. Crawford

reductive empiricism. Thus, to speak of a form given to freedom is also not to engage in the "biologism" that is the *bête noire* of modern ethics. Here, it seems to me, it is necessary to recuperate the constitutive character of desire or inclination, only now from within the objective "sign" character of the body. The body as a sign is also an order that communicates the actual meaning of the desire that animates freedom. Thus, the body co-constitutes freedom not only as a partial source of the inclinations of the embodied person, but also insofar as the body is capable of revealing the identity and destiny of the person in love. The truth of the body and the cosmic order is, in a real sense, not simply the truth of an external law to which freedom would have to conform, but the truth of human desire itself. In telling us who we are, *it also tells us what we really desire*. The body makes visible what is otherwise invisible and represents for man a sign of his true vocation. As John Paul II puts it:

> In man, created in the image of God, the very sacramentality of creation, the sacramentality of the world, was thus in some way revealed. In fact, through his bodiliness, his masculinity and femininity, man becomes a visible sign of the economy of Truth and Love, which has its source in God himself and was revealed already in the mystery of creation.[49]

It is, in other words, only in the experience of this "sign" character of the lived body — including in the visibility of its interior order as both personal and "cosmic" — that we can know who we are and what the world really is. The anthropological-cosmological centrality of the body means that the body is uniquely capable of serving as a "sacramental" or "real" sign (John Paul II says the *only* sign) of the person and his end in love, recapitulating the whole of the cosmos and pointing to its destiny in God. This is why it is only in and through virginity that the world is remade; or, to put it in a more paradoxical form, it is only in the enfolding space opened by the virginal womb of the Church, and its prior order, that the union of man and woman can truly remake the world from generation to generation.[50]

As distinct from the tendency of modern conceptions of freedom, precisely in their abstraction of freedom from the body, to produce an an-

49. John Paul II, *Man and Woman He Created Them: A Theology of the Body*, 203.

50. Cf. John Paul II's statement in *Redemptionis Donum* that the consecrated members of the Church are the ones who in the first instance recover the meaning of the creation on behalf of all.

drogynous culture and to shape its institutions accordingly, we have here a version of freedom that draws on and is partially constituted by the visibility of the body in its metaphysically relevant structures and their meanings for the person. The body contains the "anticipatory signs" of self-gift precisely because it bears within itself, especially but not exclusively in the sexual difference, the primordial structure of being a gift both from and for another. But this also means that the body is uniquely capable of showing us who the person is, not only with respect to his end in Triune love, but also with respect to his concrete worldly situation in a tissue of relations, a set of relations that is itself an "already-but-not-yet" anticipation of his destiny, and indeed in relation to the cosmos as a whole.

III

By way of conclusion, it seems to me that two points can be drawn from the foregoing.

First, this centrality of the body in its visible expression of order and form, and in its resultant character as sign, would seem to be demanded by the basic elements of Christian revelation. For example, it seems to be a necessary implication of what Ratzinger called the "overwhelming realism" of God's relation to the world instituted in Christ's flesh, in "the absolutely staggering alliance of *logos* and *sarx,* of meaning and a single historical figure."[51] Christ does not simply deliver God's word to man; rather, he *is* God's Word, incarnated in the "flesh" of the universe and of history. He is God's Word to man precisely in his visibility to man. Thus,

---

51. Joseph Ratzinger, *Introduction to Christianity,* trans. J. R. Foster (San Francisco: Ignatius Press, 1990 [orig. German ed., 1968]), p. 141. Ratzinger has also emphasized this "realism" in his discussion of the covenantal theology of Scripture. When Moses sprinkles the altar with blood in Exodus 24:8, he reenacts a kind of legal fiction by which a stranger is admitted into a familial relation (cf. Ratzinger, "The New Covenant: A Theology of Covenant in the New Testament," trans. Maria Shrady, *Communio: International Catholic Review* 22 [1995]: 635-651, at 641-642). By invoking this tradition in pouring out his own blood, Christ is radicalizing it. The covenant has become not only a fictitious or juridical kinship, but a covenant written in the body of Christ himself, thus intensifying it "to an overwhelming realism and simultaneously reveal[ing] a hitherto inconceivable depth. . . . For this sacramental communion of blood, which has now become possible, unites the recipient with this bodily man Jesus, and thus with his divine mystery, in a totally concrete and even physical communion" ("The New Covenant," 642).

> [w]hen Jesus speaks in his parables of the shepherd who goes after the lost sheep, of the woman who looks for the lost coin, of the father who goes to meet and embrace his prodigal son, these are not mere words: *They constitute an explanation of his very being and activity.*[52]

And, of course, Christ is also man's answer to God. One of the more recent and indeed provocative expressions of this "taking man's part" can be found in Benedict XVI's first encyclical, which tells us that man's situation elicits from God a decisive "turn . . . against himself."[53] Indeed, the whole idea of divine substitution contained in traditional notions of Christ's salvific mission expresses this very turn. Hence, the freedom Christ manifests toward the Father, as directed toward and realized in his response, is the archetype and indeed the radical source of all human freedom precisely because it is the carrying out of the *"motus"* of freedom toward its concrete fulfillment. Thus, man's response to God's call, before it can mean anything else, means participation in Christ's embodied freedom — in its visible order and form — for God.

But the constitution of this freedom as an expression of both God's freedom for man and man's freedom for God is bodily, specifically in the "visible" aspect of "sign" or "sacrament." It is the whole of Christ's Incarnation and of his actions in the "flesh" of time and space, his birth to the virgin and his obedience unto the Cross, that constitutes this responsive freedom. In a word, freedom possesses its authentic "form" only in the embodied "form" of Christ's response and "turn" to the Father. At the same time, Christ's expression of freedom in relation to the Father in the Incarnation is accomplished within the order and form of the human body; indeed, the Incarnation respects that order even as it radicalizes its meaning. What Christianity draws out of freedom, then, is the visibility of Christian "sacramental" forms — marriage, virginity, fatherhood, motherhood, sonship, and so forth — that is to say, in sacramental-liturgical action. It is these sacramental-liturgical-bodily enactments that disclose and realize the truth of freedom.

Second, as already indicated, highlighting the body as manifesting visible order is not to deny that the inclinations are themselves crucial to the constitution of human freedom. Indeed, when this question of the formal

---

52. *Deus Caritas Est,* 12; emphasis added.

53. *Deus Caritas Est,* 12: *"contra se ipsum vertat Deum"; "contra se vertit Deus."* See also my "The Covenantal Character of Love: Reflections on *Deus Caritas Est,*" in *The Way of Love: Reflections on Pope Benedict XVI's Encyclical* Deus Caritas Est, ed. Livio Melina and Carl Anderson (San Francisco: Ignatius Press, 2006), 227-239.

and sacramental character of the body is taken fully into account, the meaning of human inclination itself is shifted. The inclinations can be seen as part of the symbolic meaning of the body, revealing the very underlying desire of the person for his perfect good. The "abyss" of human desire as such and quotidian desires are not simply parallel "types" possessing only a tenuous or even a merely verbal relationship. Again, the everyday desires we experience at the heart of our moral lives and as driving our individual actions are rooted in — or indeed are an expression of — desire for our end. In this sense, as a part of the sign character of the body, our everyday desires are also a sign of our deepest desire.

Of course, the body and its inclination are a sign only as a task.[54] We can see this when we think of the insatiability and frustration everyday desires entail when their connection to the purpose and meaning of human life is ignored, rejected, or unknown. In order for them really to have meaning — in order for them not to become the torture of Tantalus, or perhaps the hellish "itch" mentioned by Socrates in *Gorgias* — they must be seen as rooted in *and therefore as needing to be ordered within and on that basis as a sign of* man's underlying "restlessness." This is the point of sacramental-liturgical action, as Ratzinger reminds us:

> A demand is made of everyday life. The body is required to become "capable of resurrection," to orient itself toward the resurrection, toward the Kingdom of God, in a word: "Thy will be done on earth as it is in Heaven." . . . Surrendering ourselves to the action of God, so that we in turn may cooperate with him, that is what begins in the liturgy and is meant to unfold further beyond it. . . . The body must be trained, so to speak, for the resurrection.[55]

---

54. A close analogy will be helpful. On the one hand, to call sacramental marriage a sacrament of Christ's nuptial relationship with the Church means that it objectively both participates in and conveys the inner reality of the higher analogate. This objective signification is "just there" as "form" *(ex opere operato)*. In this sense, it is not conditional on further free acts of the spouses or their personal holiness. Marriage as such, then, offers the "form" of holiness or perfect love. Certainly, Benedict has held up this "form" as the paradigmatic case of human love (*Deus Caritas Est* 11; cf. also Scola, *The Nuptial Mystery*, 90). On the other hand, it is clearly and simultaneously the task of the spouses *(ex opere operantis)* to live out this love in such a way that its objective sign character, its symbolic meaning, takes on a vivid and concrete reality, that it becomes fully actualized. For spouses to be holy means that they need to be fully conformed to the inner form and truth of their state of life.

55. Joseph Ratzinger, *The Spirit of the Liturgy*, trans. John Saward (San Francisco: Ignatius Press, 2000), 176.

Donum Doni: An Approach to a Theology of Gift

Antonio López, F.S.C.B.

David L. Schindler's profound and thorough critique of American culture stems from the conviction that the novelty that Christ brought with himself, participation in God's divine life (John 3:16), reveals man's truth and his destiny, and thus affects and is called to transfigure all of man and with him all of the cosmos.[1] Man is therefore invited to let this eternal life give rise to a "culture of life," a "civilization of love," with all its implications.[2] To carry out this task, it is necessary to avoid the risks of both a fulfilled eschatology that steers clear of the toil of history and a gnostic dualism that, weary of the world's depravity, looks intently upward while remaining oblivious to the world's beauty and man's responsibility for it. The wish to allow Christianity to reach a full cultural expression, however, cannot lead man to distort its nature by either reducing it to his private sphere or forcing it into Pelagianism or clericalism.[3] In the face of these alternatives, Schindler's contention is that the Church will carry out her mission in today's Western world, and in American culture in particular, only through an anthropology able to rediscover that man's identity, and hence his liberation, cannot be the fruit of a fatherless existence.[4] Rather, as Christ him-

---

1. Irenaeus, *Against Heresies*, IV.34.1. See Schindler, "Toward a Culture of Life," 679-690; "Trinity, Creation, and the Academy," 406-428; "The Meaning of the Human," 80-103; and "Whitehead's Challenge to Thomism on the Problem of God: The Metaphysical Issues," *International Philosophical Quarterly* (September 1979): 285-299.

2. John Paul II, *Evangelium Vitae*, 19-23; HW.

3. Relativism and practical atheism are the best exponents of these approaches. See HW, 43-87, 189-202; "Modernity and Atheism," 563-579; "Truth, Freedom, and Relativism," 669-681; Joseph Ratzinger, *Truth and Tolerance* (San Francisco: Ignatius Press, 2004).

4. It is here that one needs to see Schindler's continuous insistence on an ontology of

self revealed, man's personhood stems from the fact that he is given to be and to be himself in a dramatic relation with the Triune mystery of love.[5]

Schindler's anthropology's claim to cogency is undergirded by an ontology of creatureliness that perceives being in terms of gift. His metaphysics of charity, however, goes beyond the simple retrieval of creation *ex nihilo* in that, on the one hand, it indicates that man's *telos,* and through him that of the cosmos, is nuptial union with the eternal mystery of love freely brought to fulfillment through the Paschal mystery.[6] In this light, man's rightful autonomy and fruitful creativity reside in his obedient and grateful unity with the mystery of love.[7] On the other hand, the ontology

---

childhood, the complementarity of the masculine and the feminine, the significance of the family and of the (divine and human) *communio personarum.* Cf. HW, 237-274. See UBLC; TD, 5:61-98. Ferdinand Ulrich, *Der Mensch als Anfang. Zur philosophischen Anthropologie der Kindheit* (Freiburg: Johannes Verlag, 1970); Gustav Siewerth, *Metaphysik der Kindheit* (Freiburg: Johannes Verlag, 1957).

5. Schindler follows John Paul II in indicating that perhaps the most important passage from Vatican Council II is *Gaudium et Spes,* 22 — which the late pope quotes in every encyclical. See, among others, John Paul II, *Redemptor Hominis,* 10, and *Dives in Misericordia,* 1. See also D. C. Schindler, *Hans Urs von Balthasar and the Dramatic Structure of Truth* (New York: Fordham University Press, 2004).

6. In this light, it is fitting to see with Maximus the Confessor that "He who, by the sheer inclination of his will, established the beginning of all creation, seen and unseen, before all the ages and before that beginning of created beings, had an ineffably good plan for those creatures. The plan was for him to mingle, without change on his part, with human nature by true hypostatic union, to unite human nature to himself while remaining immutable, so that he might become a man, as he alone knew how, and so that he might deify humanity in union with himself" (*Ad Thalassium,* 22, in *On the Cosmic Mystery of Jesus Christ: Selected Writings from St. Maximus the Confessor,* trans. Paul M. Blowers and Robert L. Wilken [Crestwood, NY: St. Vladimir's Seminary Press, 2003], 115). Schindler contends that the dramatic relation between man and God calls for a reconsideration of the ontology of the person and the relation between substance and relation. See HW, 275-311; Schindler, "Norris Clarke on Person, Being, and St. Thomas," *Communio: International Catholic Review* 20 (1993): 580-592; "The Person: Philosophy, Theology, and Receptivity," *Communio: International Catholic Review* 21 (1994): 172-190; Hans Urs von Balthasar, *Love Alone* (San Francisco: Ignatius Press, 2004), 141-143. For an ontology of creatureliness see the following by Kenneth Schmitz: *Gift;* "Created Receptivity and the Philosophy of the Concrete," *The Thomist* 61 (1997): 339-371; and *The Recovery of Wonder: The New Freedom and the Asceticism of Power* (Montreal: McGill University Press, 2005).

7. The call to being one with the Godhead, however, is not a denial of the creature's integrity — a denial that would be yet another attempt at self-given divinity — only because God has revealed himself to be Triune. The unity, distinctness, and ever-greater fruitfulness of the Trinitarian *communio personarum,* which man continues to encounter through the sacramental and Marian Church, is the only place in which man can be fully himself. See

of creatureliness finds its ultimate ground in a theology that considers the Triune God to be an "event of love."[8] The event is the eternal, reciprocal, and absolute gift of the divine persons. This unfathomable, gratuitous mystery, revealed in Jesus Christ, is the ultimate ground from which man and cosmos originate and into which they are called to participate. Schindler's theological anthropology, then, illustrates that man is given to himself, he is gift, so that he can be himself in enjoying and sharing the divine communion. It cannot be overemphasized that, for Schindler, the adequacy of this anthropology and ontology of gift rests on their having been grounded in a God who is a *communio personarum*, a gift of himself to himself. God's ever-greater gratuitous life posits the finite creature and makes it be itself within himself without annihilating it. For Schindler, then, either the Christian anthropology and its consequent cultural expression rest on an ontology of creatureliness, a metaphysics of charity whose truth is revealed in the Incarnate Son of the Father, or Christianity will end up making compromises with a worldly logic that will undo it from within.[9]

Bearing in mind the Church's rich theological tradition, one may inquire whether this coalescence of God and gift that underpins Schindler's reflection is a legitimate and relevant one. One may also wonder whether, despite its claims to the contrary, this ontological and theological discourse on gift, perhaps excessively determined by a cultural milieu that exaggerates autonomy and independence, is ultimately able to go beyond the realm of the descriptive. To address these objections against the identification of God with gift requires seeing that the nature of God is absolute gratuity. To this end it must be elucidated, first, that God is absolute spirit and, second, that the Holy Spirit, as Schindler says, "precisely in his 'anonymity' — that is, as the *mutuality* of the other two persons, Father and Son — is the *person* who is simultaneously the fruit of this mutuality between Father and Son and who thereby, however paradoxically, 'transcends' this mutual-

---

HW, 15-29; "Creation and Nuptiality," 265-295; NM; Angelo Scola, Gilfredo Marengo, and Javier Prades López, *La persona umana: Antropologia teologica* (Milan: Jaca Book, 2000).

8. Benedict XVI, homily to the ecclesial movements, June 3, 2006. From the Vatican web site. For an interpretation of God as event see TD, vol. 5; and my article "Eternal Happening: God as an Event of *Love*," *Communio: International Catholic Review* 32 (2005): 214-245 [hereafter cited as GE].

9. This is the problem with the different ecclesiologies that undergird certain American proposals regarding Christian presence in the public sphere (politics), their understanding of the role of capitalism, and the academy: HW, 89-176.

ity."[10] Only if the "second difference," the spirit within the absolute spirit, is the "person gift," and if his being-gift means that he is the person who confirms God's absolute gratuity, then, as John Paul II contends, "it is possible to say that through the Holy Spirit God exists in the mode of Gift." In him we see that "the intimate life of the Triune God becomes totally gift, an exchange of mutual love between the divine Persons."[11] Without claiming to give an exhaustive answer to the objections raised, the following essay would like to show that gratuity is the nature of the divine mystery revealed in Christ by examining in what sense the person of the Holy Spirit can be seen as *donum doni*, gift of gift. He, in fact, is the one in whom God's love reveals itself to be a non-arbitrary and ever-gratuitous gift in himself and thus for us. God's unity and fecundity, witnessed by the person of the Holy Spirit, are a mysterious and ever-greater gratuity.

Schindler has dealt only on a few occasions with the person of the Holy Spirit, and has always put his pneumatological reflection at the service of his ecclesiology.[12] His analysis of the third hypostasis, then, aims at illustrating that the gift of the Holy Spirit to man is that of generating communion, a unity that does not eliminate the difference. The Church, he says, is "the earthly icon of trinitarian holiness."[13] The Holy Spirit is the one who unites men to one another and men to God, because, in God, he is "the one in whom the other two [the Father and the Son] are united," as Augustine famously put it. At the same time, the Holy Spirit is both the giver of gifts (charisms) and, as St. Irenaeus beautifully stated, *communicatio Christi;* Christ is contemporaneous to man thanks to the gift of the Holy Spirit.[14] As the Holy Spirit "blows where he will" (John 3:8) and "searches the depths of God" (1 Cor. 2:10), he is the one who witnesses to God's infinite creativity.[15] Thanks to the Holy Spirit, Schindler contends, it

10. "Institution and Charism," 258.

11. John Paul II, *Dominum et Vivificantem*, 10. As is well known, the concept of gift is one of the most fundamental concepts in the thought of John Paul II. See, among others, *Evangelium Vitae; Man and Woman He Created Them: A Theology of the Body;* John Milbank, "The Second Difference," in *The Word Made Strange* (Cambridge, MA: Blackwell Publishers, 1997), 171-193.

12. Mainly HW, and more recently with "Institution and Charism."

13. "Institution and Charism," 263.

14. Irenaeus, *Against Heresies*, III.24.1.

15. Schindler clarifies that "there is in God . . . a doubly creative infinity: a creative infinity of word (visible form) coincident with a creative infinity of love ('anonymous' movement, at once vivifying and 'dispersing'). This 'newness' or 'excess' effected by the Spirit, therefore, is not to be opposed to a (putative) lack of 'newness' in the Son or Word himself. On the con-

is possible to see that the institutional dimension, which reflects the objective presence of Christ, and the charismatic dimension, which indicates God's "excessive" fruitfulness, are coextensive.[16] Even though this essay is thought in dialogue with Schindler's "trinitarian pneumatology" and with the sources of his reflection, this essay will not consist in probing his account of the relation between ecclesiology and pneumatology.[17] Focusing instead on the person of the Holy Spirit, this essay will try to show how "gift" confirms and enriches his pneumatological elucidation of "unity" and "excess."

The essay is thus divided into four parts. Following St. Augustine, the first section illustrates that the Holy Spirit is the immanent gift within the absolute spirit, in whom the Father and the Son are united. The second illustrates, with the help of Aquinas's pneumatology, in what sense the Holy Spirit is the one who witnesses to the gratuitous nature of the unity proper to divine love. The contention that gratuity constitutes the very nature of the divine mystery requires, however, revisiting Augustine's insight of the coalescence of spirit and love and developing an understanding of divine love in terms of spirit, whose eternal rhythm of *ekstasis* and *enstasis* is best represented in terms of donation. When spirit is seen as coextensive with love and being, and not thought of as opposed to matter, then, as we shall see, gift is nothing but the spiritual way of being. The third part is thus an introduction to this ontological conception of spirit, already proposed by the late French Catholic philosopher Claude Bruaire. The fourth part offers an account of the sense in which the spirit within the absolute spirit, *donum doni*, confirms that God is the unfathomable gift of himself to himself.

---

trary, the Spirit 'exceeds' the Son only in the way in which Love 'exceeds' its own Word" ("Institution and Charism," 262).

16. "Institution and Charism" corrects Komanchak's criticism that Schindler's ecclesiology, as portrayed in HW, is deprived of any serious account of the role of the Holy Spirit, and that Mariology overtakes Pneumatology. In "Institution and Charism" Schindler shows that the creativity of the Holy Spirit is the ultimate ground for the co-extensiveness of charisms and institution and for Mary's receptive and creative listening: "she is creative in her union with and her testifying to the divine Other" (262). See Joseph A. Komanchak, "Heart of the World, Center of the Church," book review published in *Commonweal* 124, 15 (September 12, 1997). Cf. TD, 5:61-109, and TL, vol. 3. See also John Paul II, *Redemptor Hominis, Dives in Misericordia*, and *Donum et Vivificantem*.

17. "Institution and Charism," 263.

I. *Donum donatoris et donator doni*

Any theological reflection on gift needs to elucidate two distinct but insep-arable issues, which shed light on each other but always resist a higher syn-thesis: God's essence and the person of the Holy Spirit. At the same time, to avoid a superficial juxtaposition, the theological reflection must emerge from the center of revelation and allow itself to be guided into the imma-nent Trinity by the form of Christ. Only when theological discourse is con-ducted in faithfulness to the economy does it contribute to deepening man's intelligence of faith.[18] Augustine's reflection meets these require-ments and thus represents a fundamental starting point for looking into a theology and a pneumatology of "gift."[19]

One fundamental aspect of God that Christian revelation offers, the discovery of which was crucial for Augustine's conversion, is that God's be-

18. It is a fundamental presupposition of this essay that any discourse on the immanent Trinity is grounded in the economy. See Karl Rahner, *The Trinity,* trans. Joseph Donceel (New York: Crossroad, 1997), 22; Luis F. Ladaria, *La Trinità: misterio di comunione,* trans. Marco Zappella (Milan: Paoline, 2004), 13-86; TL, 2:25-62, 171-218; Javier Prades, "'From the Economic to the Immanent Trinity': Remarks on a Principle of Renewal in Trinitarian The-ology (part 1)," *Communio: International Catholic Review* 27 (2000): 240-261; "'From the Economic to the Immanent Trinity': Remarks on a Principle of Renewal in Trinitarian The-ology (part 2)," *Communio: International Catholic Review* 27 (2000): 562-593. See my GE, 220-225.

19. The Cappadocian Fathers clearly affirmed the full divinity of the Holy Spirit and, as Athanasius did with the person of the Son, indicated that his personal properties needed to be found in the relation he has to the other two divine hypostases and not in the mission of sanctification he has in the economy of salvation. Nevertheless, drawn by their keen aware-ness of God's greatness and the limitedness of man's reason, they "resolve[d] to be done with images and shadows" and circumscribed their pneumatological reflection to the defense of the full divinity of the Holy Spirit and his role in history. See Gregory of Nazianzus, *Oration Concerning the Holy Spirit,* 31.3-4.9; St. Basil, *Letters,* 38, n. 4; St. Basil, *On the Holy Spirit* (Crestwood, NY: St. Vladimir's Seminary Press, 2001), 9, 23; St. Augustine, *The Trinity,* trans. Stephen McKenna (Washington, DC: CUA Press, 1963); St. Augustine, *On the Spirit and the Letter,* in *Nicene and Post-Nicene Fathers,* series 1, vol. 5: *Saint Augustine: Pelagian Writings,* ed. Philip Schaff (Peabody, MA: Hendrickson, 1994), 197-251; St. Augustine, *Homilies on St. John's Gospel,* in *Nicene and Post-Nicene Fathers,* series 1, vol. 7: *Augustine: Homilies on the Gospel of John, Homilies on the First Epistle of John, Soliloquies,* ed. Philip Schaff (Peabody, MA: Hendrickson, 1994), 4-591; Yves Congar, *Je crois en l'Esprit Saint,* 2nd ed. (Paris: Du Cerf, 1997); Joseph Ratzinger, "The Holy Spirit as *Communio:* Concerning the Relationship of Pneumatology and Spirituality in Augustine," *Communio: International Catholic Review* 25 (1998): 324-339; Marc Ouellet, "The Spirit in the Life of the Trinity," *Communio: Interna-tional Catholic Review* 25 (1998): 199-213.

ing is spirit, that is, he is other than the finite world, immaterial although not opposed to matter. God must be conceived, then, "as good without quality, great without quantity, a creator though He lack nothing, ruling but from no position . . . eternal without time" (*De Trinitate,* V.1.2).[20] Spirit's otherness, however, is not remote self-enclosedness. It is proper to the nature of "spirit" to speak, freely to reveal itself, and, in the case of the absolute spirit, to do so without deception.[21] God's revelation unveils another fundamental aspect of the one who alone is, the absolute spirit (Exod. 3:14). In Christ, God presents himself as charity: "it is said thus, 'God is love' [1 John 4:16; Rom. 8:32], as it is said, 'God is a Spirit' [John 4:24]" (DT, XV.17.27).[22] This divine love, however, is the indication of God's essence and only secondarily of his dealings with mankind. Furthermore, in Christ, the charity that constitutes absolute spirit's nature has revealed himself to be Father, Son, and Holy Spirit, a love that wants to give itself to us (John 4:10). To say that God is love, then, requires us to acknowledge that spirit is love and that love is also "from God" (1 John 4:7-16; Rom. 5:5). Within the absolute spirit, says Augustine, following Scripture, the Holy Spirit is the person who himself is love and who pours God's love into man's heart (DT, XV.17.31). The man of faith knows this from his own experience: "God's love has been poured into our hearts through the Holy Spirit which has been given to us" (Rom. 5:5; DT, XV.19.37).[23] Thus, with Augustine, one can see that being, spirit, and love name one reality, the divine essence, that absolute Triune fullness in which there is no trace of change, movement, or accident.

To see what is distinct in this "love within love" requires explaining in what sense "love" — as with "spirit" and "holy" — is both a common, absolute name, applicable to God's essence, and a personal name, proper to the Holy Spirit. Since God, absolute spirit, is an immutable essence in which there cannot be any accidents, Augustine finds no better way to describe

20. St. Augustine, *Confessions,* VII-IX, in *Nicene and Post-Nicene Fathers,* series 1, vol. 1: *The Confessions and Letters of Augustine with a Sketch of His Life and Work,* ed. Philip Schaff (Peabody, MA: Hendrickson, 1994), 37-302; St. Augustine, *Sermon 52.*

21. For a consideration of truth as unfolding and fidelity, see TL, vol. 1.

22. Christ, Augustine tells us, brings to fulfillment the revelation of God's name (Exod. 3:14; John 8:58). See *Homilies on St. John's Gospel,* XLIII.8.17-18; LII.12.11-12; DT, VII.3.6. Augustine is thus the first to bring to theological reflection the Scriptural affirmation that God is love, something foreign to the Eastern Fathers.

23. Along with Acts 8:20 and John 4:7, this is the most oft-quoted passage in Augustine when he talks about the Holy Spirit. See Augustine, *On the Spirit and the Letter.*

the hypostases than as relative *(relative, ad aliquid)* and immutable properties of the substance, not as accidents (DT, VII.4.8).[24] Thus, just as the Father and the Son do not indicate either substance or accident but their being relative to each other, the "love within absolute love" indicates the being-relative to the other hypostases rather than the divine essence itself (DT, V.5.6). What is relative in the term "love" when appropriated to the third hypostasis, Augustine tells us, appears in all its strength with the term "gift."[25] "Gift," in fact, indicates a giver, a receiver, and something given. Scripture witnesses on numerous occasions that the Holy Spirit is the "gift of God" (DT, XV.19.35). Yet, Augustine contends, it is only because the Holy Spirit is gift in God from all eternity that he is able to be given to mankind. The Holy Spirit, love from love, is the gift that calls for the presence of the giver and those who are to receive it (DT, XV.19.36).

The affirmation that the Holy Spirit is "gift" could suggest that the *relative* specific to the third person consists in that he is the "gift" the Father and the Son give to each other. The speculative effort, however, should not allow itself to be misled by the imagination here. In fact, Augustine clarifies that the fact that the Father gives does not make him "Father of the gift" (DT, V.12.13). The relation between the Father and the Holy Spirit is unlike that between the Father and the Son. While the Father remains the principle from which the Spirit proceeds, the latter is not generated *(natus),* but given *(datus),* and thus he is not Son, but Holy Spirit (DT, V.15.16). Furthermore, even though the Son gives, his "giving" the Holy Spirit is to be thought of as in unity with the "giving" of the Father and not so much as a giving "to" him — the Father and Son are one principle in the generation of the Holy Spirit. Although the Holy Spirit proceeds eternally and thus is not chronologically subsequent to the generation of the Son, it is also not possible to say "Son of the gift" because the Spirit does not play a role in the generation of the Son, as the Father does (DT, XV.17.27).[26] To

24. It is important to notice that, for fear of tritheism, Augustine prefers the use of the adjective *(relative)* to the noun.

25. Augustine also knows that love speaks of a lover, a love, and a beloved. Yet, on the one hand, whereas it is easy to perceive the lover and the beloved as two persons, to speak of "love" as a third person could seem to be an unwanted leap. On the other hand, the close relation that this imagery maintains with human love, with all its existential fragility and lack of essential unity, discourages him from using it (DT, VIII.10). Here it is possible to see the ascendancy that Augustine had on Richard of St. Victor's *De Trinitate.*

26. For the thesis that the generation of the Son takes place in the Holy Spirit see François-Xavier Durrwell in his *Le Père: Dieu en son mystère* (Paris: Du Cerf, 1987); *Jésus,*

speak of the Holy Spirit in terms of gift while respecting the Trinitarian taxis presented in Scripture requires one to say "the giver of the gift" and the "gift of the giver." This is a more adequate way to unearth the relative aspect of the relation of the three hypostases and to avoid confusing the generation of the Son with the procession of the Holy Spirit.

This understanding of gift requires seeing with Augustine that "gift" stands for a person and not for an "object" that the Father and the Son would exchange, e.g., the divine essence understood as love.[27] The "subjective," that is, personal nature of the Holy Spirit, the person-gift, can be perceived by referring to the circularity between love and gift. If, as we saw, gift reveals the relational aspect of love in the immanent Trinity, love discloses the meaning of gift, because the Holy Spirit is called gift "on account of love" (*dilectionem;* DT, XV.18.32). In the light of love, gift does not indicate a mere "inclination" of the Father toward the Son, but, more radically, the person "in whom the other two are united" (DT, VI.5.7). "What, then, is love," Augustine asks, "except a certain life which couples or seeks to couple together some two things, namely, him that loves, and that which is loved?" (DT, VIII.10.14). The Holy Spirit, then, is the "absolute love which joins together Father and Son, and joins us also from beneath" (DT, VII.3.6), a "certain ineffable communion of the Father and the Son" (DT, V.11.12), a communion that "may fitly be called friendship" (DT, VI.5.7). Thus, to say that the spirit within the absolute spirit is gift illustrates that, in theology, the Holy Spirit is the one who brings the Father and the Son to each other and, in the economy, mankind to God (DT, XV.18.32). The Holy Spirit is the gift who reveals that he is the one in whom God is an "ineffable communion."

If we want to take full advantage of the circularity of love and gift, we need to indicate something that Augustine mentions but does not develop: whereas "love" reveals that gift is unity, joining the two together — and thus speaking of the Father and the Son always requires the presence of the

---

Fils de Dieu dans l'Esprit Saint (Paris: Desclée, 1997); Thomas G. Weinandy, *The Father's Spirit of Sonship: Reconceiving the Trinity* (Edinburgh: T&T Clark, 1995). For a balanced critique of this position see Luis Ladaria, *La Trinità. Mistero di Comunione* (Milan: Paoline Editoriale, 2004), 272-319.

27. The Holy Spirit, in fact, is not only given by the Father and the Son; he also gives himself (DT, XV.19.36). In this regard we need to quote, with Augustine, John 3:8, "The wind blows where it wills," and add 1 Corinthians 2:10: "The Spirit searches everything, even the depths of God." See also Basil, *On the Holy Spirit,* 16, 37; Aquinas, *Summa Theologiae,* I, q. 38, a. 1.

Spirit — "gift" shows that God's substantial unity is gratuitous love. Without making the Holy Spirit the person-principle in which the Father and the Son are, it is possible to say that the Holy Spirit is the one thanks to whom unity, i.e., indwelling, takes place — first in God, and, thanks to his unfathomable love, then in the believer (DT, XV.17.31; XV.19.37). That unity in God can be seen as a gift does not mean either that in the Father's generation of the Son there is something incomplete that is supplemented by the spiration of the Holy Spirit or that the Father and the Son are spatially brought together by the Holy Spirit.[28] It is also not the case that God's unity is a gift because it is given by something above and beyond God or because it could have happened otherwise. That God's unity is a gift means, on the one hand, that the abiding of one divine hypostasis in the other is of such a nature that this indwelling *(caritas)* is not some*thing* that happens to the Father and the Son but some*one* distinct from them, a person without a name. On the other hand, as Augustine's reflection seems to suggest, the giftedness of God's unity that the Holy Spirit confirms is an absolute love that is both necessary and utterly "uncalled-for," nothing but utter gratuity in himself and thus *quoad nos.*

St. Augustine helps us to see both that God's being is spirit and love and that the Holy Spirit is the person-love, the person-gift, the hypostasis in whom God is one. Gift, as a personal property of the Holy Spirit, unveils the relational and unitive aspects of love. Nevertheless, despite the coalescence of being, love, and spirit — which he clearly sees — Augustine seems unable to take full advantage of the potentiality of the term "gift." His disinclination to ascribe a substantial weight to the hypostases for fear of tritheism prevents him from seeing in what sense the being relative *(ad aliquid)* of the Father, Son, and Holy Spirit constitutes the persons and thus from speaking more clearly about the fact that God's love is a threefold hypostatic gift.[29] In this regard, Augustine's acknowledged perplexi-

---

28. Balthasar notes that the inverse relation is the correct one; that is, time and space find their ultimate explanation in the Trinitarian processions. See TD, 5:91-95; "Time in Eternity," 53-68; and my "Restoration of Sonship: Reflections on Time and Eternity," *Communio: International Catholic Review* 32 (2005): 682-704.

29. Augustine's perplexities, clearly expressed in the famous *De Trinitate,* VII.4, stem also from the insight that the name "person" cannot hold together what is unavailable to human thought; that is to say, it is not given to man to have one name able to signify simultaneously what is common, i.e., divine essence, and what is proper and incommunicable to each person. "Person," in fact, is not a super-concept that could bring together the difference and the identity of the three hypostases.

ties in distinguishing between generation and spiration indicate that, although "gift" implies otherness (a third one), it is not sufficiently clear to him how this term distinguishes the coming forth of the Holy Spirit from the Father and the Son the generation of the Son (DT, XV.27.48-49).[30] At the same time, although his theology leaves room for it, Augustine's understanding of the relation between the divine essence and the hypostases does not allow him fully to consider the aspect of gratuity, freedom, and being-uncalled-for inherent in gift, in the Spirit's "joining together" of the other two persons.[31] For these reasons, it does not seem far-fetched to state that, while Augustine cogently shows that the name "gift" is rightly appropriated to the Holy Spirit and that this appropriation does not collapse the immanent into the economic Trinity, for him the primary use of this concept is reserved for the economy (DT, XV.19.36). If divine Triune love is to be absolute gratuity that is capable of positing a finite spirit other than itself in order to call it to union with itself, one needs to see not only that the Holy Spirit is gift and the giver of gifts to mankind, but also in what sense God can be properly called gift in himself.

II. God's Gift

Aquinas's Trinitarian theology, highly indebted to Augustine's, as is well known, sheds a decisive light on these difficulties by offering both a more precise elucidation of the relation between the persons and the divine essence and a clearer rationale to distinguish, in the unity of their being-given, the Son and the Holy Spirit.[32] Like Augustine, Aquinas also perceives that, from a certain point of view, the three divine persons are really identical with the divine essence: the Father is God, the Son is God, and

---

30. It is important not to forget that even if the Son is *natus* and not *datus,* to "be born" is the primordial form of being-given.

31. Augustine is aware of the possibility of the coexistence of nature and freedom: see Augustine, *The City of God Against the Pagans,* ed. and trans. R. W. Dyson (Cambridge: Cambridge University Press, 1998), IV.10. We shall return to this issue later.

32. See A. Malet, *Personne et amour dans la théologie trinitaire de Saint Thomas d'Aquin* (Paris: Vrin, 1956); Gilles Emery, O.P., *Trinity in Aquinas* (Ypsilanti, MI: Sapientia Press of Ave Maria College, 2003); Ghislain Lafont, *Peut-on connaître Dieu en Jésus-Christ? Problématique* (Paris: Les Éditions du Cerf, 1969); Juan José Pérez-Soba, *"Amor es nombre de persona": Estudio de la interpersonalidad en el amor en Santo Tomás de Aquino* (Rome: PUL, Mursia, 2000).

the Holy Spirit is God. Yet, the identity between the divine essence and the three hypostases does not make them three separate gods, as Augustine feared. At the same time, the indistinguishability of the essence from the persons does not indicate that the divine substance is a "fourth" deity that determines itself at a second moment in the three divine hypostases. The divine essence, *ipsum esse,* is, as the person of the Holy Spirit witnesses, spirit; and, as such, it is characterized by a certain "movement" that is called "procession," an immanent operation or "emanation" according to which the Son is begotten and the Holy Spirit spirated.[33] This "operation" or "movement" does not refer to any sort of change from potency to act. Rather, the ever-greater mystery that remains always ungraspable consists precisely in the fact that the pure, absolute act that God is *(ipsum esse)* is so only inasmuch as it is the Father's generation of the Son and their common spiration of the Holy Spirit.[34]

Although identical with the divine essence, the divine persons are really distinct from each other by means of relations of opposition.[35] Aquinas clarifies that relations are "subsisting" by distinguishing between the *esse* and the *ratio* in the concept of "relation." Since the *esse* is that of the divine essence, relations are nothing but God himself. What makes the hypostases distinct, then, is the *ratio,* that is, their referentiality, their being *ad aliquid;* and what constitutes them as real persons is their identity with the divine essence.[36] Given the fact that in God there are no accidents, relations of opposition constitute the divine persons but only inasmuch as the relation is identical with the divine essence.[37] The relation of opposition, then, cannot be attributed to the divine essence, since God's being is the same for the three persons. It is important to grasp that, for Aquinas, relation of opposition indicates the distinction between the persons determined by their different ways of "proceeding" from the origin — understood both as noun (source or principle) and as verb (originating).

---

33. Aquinas, *Summa Theologiae,* I, q. 27, a. 1. "For the name spirit in things corporeal seems to signify impulse and motion; for we call the breath and the wind by the term spirit. Now it is a property of love to move and impel the will of the lover towards the object loved" (*De Potentia,* 10.1). Aquinas, however, while acknowledging the understanding of God as spirit, does not develop it.

34. See Aquinas, *Expositio super librum Boethii De Trinitate,* prol.; I.10.1.2.

35. Aquinas, *Summa Theologiae,* I, q. 39, a. 1; I, q. 28, a. 2, et passim.

36. In this way Aquinas manages to unravel Augustine's perplexities regarding the term "person." See Aquinas, *Summa Theologiae,* I, q. 29; *De Potentia Dei,* 10.1-2.

37. Aquinas, *De Potentia Dei,* 10.3.

Antonio López, F.S.C.B.

With this concept of person in mind, Aquinas is able to revisit the personal names of "love" and "gift" proper to the Holy Spirit and to show in what sense love can be said essentially or notionally to indicate the person of the Holy Spirit. As an essential name, "love" (amore, dilectionem) speaks of the relation between the one who loves and the impression of the object loved in the one who loves — i.e., God loves himself.[38] When, following Scripture, one understands love notionally and thus says that the Holy Spirit is love, Aquinas contends that, on the one hand, if we refer to the noun "love" we intend "love proceeding," and if we indicate the verb "to love" we mean "spiration of the love proceeding."[39] Although both the Son and the Holy Spirit proceed a Patre they do so differently: unlike the Son, the Holy Spirit proceeds from the Father and the Son. Hence, Aquinas allows us to see that the distinction between the Son and the Holy Spirit is safeguarded only by means of the Filioque.[40] On the other hand, whereas in the interpretation just given "love" (as noun and as verb) presupposes that the Father and the Son are one principle (filioque), Aquinas explains that, if "we consider the 'supposita' of the spiration, we may say that the Holy Spirit proceeds from the Father and the Son as distinct; for he proceeds from them as the unitive love of both."[41] According to this second account, the Holy Spirit can be represented as the bond of love between the Father and the Son, not because he is the "cause" of their unity,[42] but because he is the love whereby the Father and the Son love each other.[43]

38. Aquinas's elucidation of the Trinitarian processions follows, as is known, the so-called psychological model. An account of the mystery of the twofold procession in God that adequately respects his unity considers the procession of the Son in terms of a begetting of the Word, and that of the Holy Spirit in terms of the procession of the will (Summa Theologiae, I, q. 27, a. 1 and 3-5). Since love follows knowledge, this methodology has the advantage of reinforcing Aquinas's defense of the procession of the Holy Spirit from the Father and the Son.

39. Aquinas, Summa Theologiae, I, q. 37, a. 1.

40. Aquinas, Summa Theologiae, I, q. 36, a. 1-2; De Potentia Dei, 10.5. Aquinas gives three reasons to justify the filioque: relations between the persons, mode of origin, and essential attributes (reason and will). This last one is subordinate to the principle here of the relations of origin distinguished by means of opposition. See Emery, Trinity in Aquinas, 209-269.

41. Summa Theologiae, I, q. 37, a. 4 ad 1.

42. Summa Theologiae, I, q. 37, a. 2 respondeo and ad 3.

43. Aquinas, De Potentia Dei, 10.4 ad 10. Although St. Thomas does not follow Augustine's pneumatology in considering the perspective of mutual love as the key to explaining the personhood of the third hypostasis, as De Potentia Dei shows, when he has to give an account of the distinction between the Son and the Holy Spirit he makes abundant use of Augustine's interpretation as well as that of Richard of St. Victor.

As Augustine indicated, "gift," the other name proper to the Holy Spirit, helps to clarify further the singularity proper to the third hypostasis. Just as "Word" and "image" hint at the way the second hypostasis is God, so does "gift" with respect to the Holy Spirit. Out of the rich Thomistic pneumatology, I would like to highlight just three aspects that are decisive for the question with which this essay is concerned.

First, the Holy Spirit is the person-gift in whom it may be perceived that gratuity is the very nature of the Godhead, that God himself is gift. Once the confusion between the economy and theology is corrected by indicating that the Holy Spirit is eternal gift *(donum)* and not gift in the sense of given *(datum)* — in which case he would be a creature — it is possible to state that the term "gift" simultaneously indicates without confusion the procession, the relation between the persons, and the presence of the origin in the person proceeding.[44] According to the first, the procession, the Spirit eternally proceeds from the Father and the Son *ut amor,* and thus "he is his own and can use or rather enjoy Himself."[45] According to the latter, the person of the Holy Spirit is the pure memory of the unfathomable positivity of the Trinity's origin.

For this reason, and this is the second aspect, the personal love is gift *par excellence,* not only in the sense that love (and thus unity) is both what is first given and that in which everything else is given, but in the sense that divine love is a giving without return. Gift reveals that love is an unreturnable giving *(datio irredibilis).*[46] The donation of the Holy Spirit, then, is the affirmation that God's (essential) love knows no boundaries. God's love does not seek a "recompense"; he gives liberally.[47]

Lastly, whereas the generation of the Son implies his capacity to spirate the Holy Spirit with the Father, no other one proceeds from the third person. This seeming lack of fruitfulness is only an apparent one and

44. "Donum dicitur esse alicuius per originem" (Aquinas, *Summa Theologiae,* I, q. 38, a. 1 ad 1).

45. Aquinas, *Summa Theologiae,* I, q. 38, a. 1 ad 1; *De Potentia Dei,* 10.3. In this regard the term "gift," in fact, requires both an identity and a distinction between the gift and the giver. See Aquinas, *Scriptum Super Sententiis,* lib 1.18.1.2.

46. Aquinas, *Summa Theologiae,* I, q. 38, a. 2: "Amor habet rationem primi doni, per quod omnia dona gratuita donantur."

47. "Donum enim, ut dicit philosophus, est datio irredibilis, non quae recompensari non valeat, sed illa quae recompensationem non quaerit. *Unde donum importat liberalitatem in dante.* . . . Ratio autem omnis *liberalis collationis* est amor: quod enim propter cupiditatem datur, vel propter timorem, non liberali datione datur; sed talis datio magis dicitur quaestus vel redemptio" (Aquinas, *Scriptum Super Sententiis,* lib. 1.18.1.2 corpus; emphasis is mine).

does not mean that the Holy Spirit is less God than the other two persons. On the contrary, the Spirit's fecundity, if we can so describe it, points both toward God himself and outside him. Toward God himself, it indicates the bottomlessness of divine love. Toward the outside, the Holy Spirit is given so that he can be possessed by those who receive him. Although there is a sense in which it is possible to say that "the Father gives his essence to the Son," and the "Father, Son, and Holy Spirit give themselves,"[48] this connotation of the term "gift" is essential and not notional. Its first meaning is the Holy Spirit's mission to bring God to man. Thus it indicates God's gift of himself to the rational creature in order freely to be had by it (Rom. 5:5).[49] In the economy, the Holy Spirit is the gift of God in the objective and subjective sense of the genitive: the Holy Spirit is the gift that God gives, and this gift is God himself in his threefold mysterious nature.

Bringing Augustine's thought forward, Aquinas's pneumatology reveals itself to be far richer than what one might suspect. His understanding of the Holy Spirit as the person-gift reveals God's love to be gratuitous and unwilling to demand a return. The Holy Spirit, then, is the person who witnesses to God's utter liberality, the person in whom the Father loves the Son and the Son the Father. Although Aquinas's understanding of the Holy Spirit's givenness may allow the possibility of reading processions in God in the light of gift — the defense of "the Holy Spirit" as a proper name indirectly shows that "gift" is a common name[50] — for Aquinas, God himself can be understood as gift primordially inasmuch as he can be given to be possessed and enjoyed by rational creatures.[51] Still, without introducing into God a dialectical distinction between freedom and necessity, it is important to see that the language of gift suggests seeing the unity of the Father and the Son in terms of freedom and spirit. "Gift" expresses the nature

48. Aquinas, *Scriptum Super Sententiis*, lib 1.15.3. This understanding of the processions in terms of donation, although legitimate, is not the predominant one, as we see by the spare use Aquinas makes of it. Aquinas clarifies that Hilary's affirmation that "the Father gives the Son the divine essence" uses the term "gift" only in the sense in which gift and giver are identical. See Aquinas, *Summa Theologiae*, I, q. 38, a. 1 ad 2.

49. Aquinas, *Summa Theologiae*, I, q. 38, a. 1; *Scriptum Super Sententiis*, 1.15.3.

50. This is more clearly stated in Aquinas, *Scriptum Super Sententiis*, 1.18.1.1.

51. It is important here to reiterate that this assertion does not confuse "donum" with "datum" and that the latter is rooted only in the former, as we indicated. To deepen the issue of the mission of the Holy Spirit see Javier Prades López, *Communicatio Christi. Reflexiones de Teología Sistemática* (Madrid: Studia Theologica Matritensia, 2004), 155-182; and *"Deus specialiter est in sanctis per gratiam": El misterio de la inhabitación de la Trinidad en los escritos de Santo Tomás* (Roma: PUG, 1993).

of the unity proper to God's being-love, but it does so by indicating the utter gratuity of both the gift that the Holy Spirit is (spiration) and of the relation between the Father and the Son.

Taking advantage of Augustine's and Aquinas's Trinitarian theology, I would like now to show that to consider "gift" as an essential and proper name requires integrating a revisited notion of spirit with that of being *(ipsum esse)* and gift.

III. Absolute Spirit

To discover the richness of the integration of the concepts of spirit and love suggested by divine revelation — something that especially Augustine, but also Aquinas, already saw but did not develop fully — we first need to see in what sense thinking of God in terms of spirit helps an understanding of God in terms of gift. In light of C. Bruaire's reflection, then, I would like to illustrate in what sense God can and should be conceived as spirit. This will allow us to see in the next section what it means to say that the Holy Spirit is the person who makes God exist in the mode of gift.

Since the concept of spirit has had a troubled history and has fallen into an oblivion perhaps greater than the one Heidegger claimed for being, I would like to begin by proposing to conceive of spirit, as Bruaire suggested, in terms of inner dynamic principle *(Geist)* and not only as that which is opposed to matter, or body.[52] The meaning of spirit is to be found in the spirit itself and not in its relation over against another — "same" and "other" are not here the ultimate reference. Spirit, Bruaire reminds us, translates the two Greek terms of *pneuma* and *nous.* Understood as *pneuma,* spirit indicates life as characterized by a twofold and inverse movement of expression of self. Divine life, before any dealings with creation, is itself a movement of *ekstasis* and *enstasis,* expression and reflection, inspiration and expiration, secret and manifestation. In this regard, God is himself only inasmuch as he is that movement of interiority and exteriority. As *nous* (intelligence), spirit is that unlimited truth that follows

---

52. See the following by C. Bruaire: EE; *Pour la métaphysique* (Paris: Fayard, 1980); "L'être de l'esprit," in *L'univers philosophique,* ed. André Jacob (Paris: PUF, 1987), 34-38; "The Being of the Spirit and the Holy Spirit," *Communio: International Catholic Review* 13 (1986): 118-124. For a more detailed presentation and critique, see my *Spirit's Gift: The Metaphysical Insight of Claude Bruaire* (Washington, DC: The Catholic University of America Press, 2006).

the rhythm proper to the life *(pneuma)* that spirit is. According to this connotation, it is possible to perceive that the movement is that of expression of self (the Father's Word) and of knowing his own depths (Holy Spirit).[53]

To correct the obvious objection that understanding God in terms of spirit implies historicizing the divine essence, one needs to see that the concept of spirit requires the co-presence of the two terms of its dynamic movement because they are ordered one to the other. "The expression," Bruaire illustrates, "retains within itself the reflection from which it emanated while the reflection is hollowed out of the manifestation that it preforms."[54] The movement proper to the absolute spirit is not a disintegration of unity or the exaltation of the category of relation over that of substance. Spirit indicates being in its subsistence because spirit includes the *unitive* potency within itself — and this is for both finite and infinite spirit. Only that which can be one with itself really is. Regarding the finite, spirit is that which preserves being from being lost in the multiplicity of its appearances. Spirit is the unity between the phenomenon and the noumenon, the depth and the form, in that it shows that this movement is circular. Spirit holds beings in their unity of essence and distinction of interiority and form.[55] Consequently, spirit is being-of-spirit and vice versa. Regarding infinite spirit, it suffices now to remember what was mentioned earlier regarding the unitive virtue of the Holy Spirit in Augustine's and Aquinas's pneumatology: the Holy Spirit, the one who joins the Father and the Son, is the one who does not add anything to God, is the one, that is, who accounts for God's unity. It is the spirit within the spirit who makes God one, the one who makes God "be," because being is there only where there is unity.[56]

53. Here we can only mention that the inseparability of *pneuma* and *nous* affords the possibility of illustrating why a theology of gift does not do away with but, on the contrary, includes "wisdom" and "knowledge" within itself.

54. EE, 35.

55. Bruaire comments that the invaluable Aristotelian hylemorphic theory, according to which beings are accounted for by means of the interplay of the two principles of matter and form, spirit and nature, was bisected by Kant's *Critique of Pure Reason* into the irreconcilable poles of phenomenon and noumenon. Blinded by an anthropological lordship over creation as conceived by Descartes, idealism's subsequent development discarded the noumenon and reduced beings to their phenomenality. As K. Schmitz shows, the outcome of this reduction was that modernity found itself before nothing more than quantifiable "data," good only for man's technological manipulation. See EE, 35-37; *Gift*, 34-63.

56. In this regard, any discourse on the ontological difference, claims Bruaire, has to be rooted in this theological difference. See EE, 95-107.

Along with the unitive and ontological aspects of the rhythm proper to spirit, it is crucial to perceive that this rhythm reveals that spirit is free. The coalescence of spirit, being, and freedom indicates further that freedom must be conceived ontologically. For example, to say that the spirit is free does not mean that although it is able to utter the word, the reflection keeps it to itself and does not speak. Rather, to say that the spirit is free reveals that the movement of reflection and expression is one of donation. Spirit's rhythm is the freedom that manifests itself without giving away its secret.[57] Briefly thinking of language and of affective knowledge can help us to illustrate further this decisive issue. First, language itself, while not impermeable to man's appropriation of it, precedes him. Concepts, or words, are not simply created by man; they are the way man is allowed to enter into being-of-spirit's intelligibility.[58] Man is born into and to language. Second, as the relation between the mother and her child witnesses, knowing a person requires that he allow himself to be known by another, that is to say, that he give himself to the other. Man's somatic and spiritual structure epitomizes what seems to be a common denominator of being itself: there is no knowledge without giving oneself to be known. The manifestation of a being-of-spirit is always free.[59] To think of God in terms of spirit, then, invites the contemplation of these three things: first, that the absolute is a movement of expression and reflection; second, since the two elements of this movement are ordered to each other, spirit preserves the unity of interiority and form; lastly, that this movement is a giving of itself that can be described as love. Thus, that God is spirit means not only that he is one but also that the rhythm of the being-of-spirit that characterizes him is best described in terms of love, that is, a free self-expression, a giving of himself to himself.[60]

57. This, along with the different anthropology, is one of the differences between Hegel's and Bruaire's understanding of spirit.

58. See Martin Heidegger, "What Calls for Thinking?" in *Basic Writings,* trans. Fred D. Wieck and J. Glenn Gray (San Francisco: Harper, 1993), 369-391; Bruaire, "Réminiscence du concept et mémoire de la révélation," in *Pour une philosophie chrétienne* (Namur: Lethielleux, 1983), 137-153. Learning a new language, in fact, is far more than appropriating different grammatical rules and different terms to name the same objects; it is the acceptance of entering into a perception of reality.

59. In this regard, the epistemological account of the process of abstraction thanks to which concepts are naturally obtained by human reason presupposes a concept of truth as *alētheia* and *emeth,* a free and undeceitful unveiling and offering of oneself. See TL, 1:35-43; GL, 5:613-634.

60. If this is true, then conceiving God as absolute spirit opens up a way to uphold that the meaning of God's being lies in love. See TL, vol. 1; "Is Truth Ugly?" 701-728.

To respond adequately to the lingering objection that persists in reading the movement of the absolute spirit in terms of process theology, one needs to see that the movement of the absolute spirit is "triggered" by utter positivity and not by the spirit's necessity to determine itself by denying itself. This contention can be thought philosophically, but it has its roots in Christian revelation. In fact, the incarnate Logos discloses that which by itself is not accessible to man's reason, at least with the clarity and precision that knowledge itself would like. God, absolute spirit, is unfathomable, overabundant positivity.[61] Absolute spirit does not become itself. It is utter fullness from all eternity. Its "movement," however, is required by the absolute's spiritual nature.[62]

The exact opposite of this reading is Hegel's contention that the spirit's movement is a self-constitutive process in which final positivity, promised by the utterly void starting point, is reached only by means of the power of the spirit that denies itself in order to determine and affirm itself.[63] Bruaire cogently illustrates, however, that the absolute spirit's movement is not negation of the negation, as Hegel's Lutheran understanding of the Paschal Mystery claims, but donation, reddition, and confirmation of self.[64] One of the main reasons behind Hegel's account of the movement of the absolute spirit in terms of absolute negativity is that his system rests on an anthropological understanding of freedom as independence that seeks self-determination, namely, a freedom whose first word is a No (in-dependence) and not a (creative and filial) Yes.[65] This negative anthropology is overcome only because God in Christ reveals himself as Triune love, whose freedom is powerful

---

61. In fact, left to his own devices, man's perception of being-of-spirit as love would have been unable to move beyond the Platonic contention that the higher the perfection of a being, the more it tends to communicate itself, or the Aristotelian insight that the unmoved mover moves the cosmos by means of love without caring itself for this desire. See Aristotle, *Metaphysics,* trans. G. Cyril Armstrong (Cambridge, MA: Harvard University Press, 1990), bk. XII.

62. This is why, for instance, Plotinus has three hypostases, although he places two of them outside the one. See Plotinus, *The Enneads,* trans. A. H. Armstrong (Cambridge, MA: Harvard University Press, 1994), V.1-4.

63. See Georg W. F. Hegel, *Lectures on the Philosophy of Religion,* vol. 2: *The Consummate Religion,* trans. R. F. Brown et al. (Berkeley: University of California Press, 1995).

64. EE, 169-179; Bruaire, *Logique et religion chrétienne dans la philosophie de Hegel* (Paris: Seuil, 1964).

65. We could say that, for this anthropology, the human being is not a child, but an orphan who finds himself in a dialectical or an equivocal relation with others in order to affirm himself.

enough to create a finite spirit for its own sake and not because God's self-determining processes require it in order for him to become himself. In the light of Christ it is possible to see that the negation entailed in man's independence is the rejection of not-being, or, in other terms, the affirmation of being with another.[66] The creative act of love discloses the positivity of man's existence even though he is not God because, in Christ, it is revealed that the utterly free movement of the absolute being of spirit is a Triune Yes, an affirmation, a gift.[67] To affirm that God is absolute spirit and love, and thus that within him there is a movement of donation of himself to himself, prevents the characterization of the Trinitarian processions as an ontological and historical development without relinquishing the fact that, as Aquinas indicated, the processions are some "sort of a production." Love, or gift, expresses, then, the coalescence of spirit, being, and freedom. Gift is being's spiritual way of being because spirit is what makes being be one in the free and positive movement of *ekstasis* and *enstasis,* reflection and expression, donation and reddition.

To fully grasp this conception of God in terms of absolute spirit, it is fundamental to see that the Holy Spirit, the spirit within absolute spirit, is the one who confirms God as absolute gift, the one who witnesses to the mysterious fact that God's nature is absolute gratuity. Otherwise one could reduce the movement of spirit to two elements — the giver and the gift, for instance — and fail to see the presence of a third. Since Balthasar's Trinitarian theology is the reflection that most closely captures the coextensiveness of love (gift) with the absolute being-of-spirit described here, I will refer to his work in order to give an account of the movement of donation proper to the absolute spirit.[68]

66. This is only one of the several meanings of creation *ex nihilo,* which must be seen in concert with the others. See, for example, Aquinas, *Summa Theologiae,* I, qq. 45-49.

67. John Paul II, *Redemptor Hominis,* 10.

68. Balthasar offers an understanding of God similar to the one outlined here. I wanted to present God in terms of spirit and not event, as Balthasar does, however, because I think that the former includes the latter and has certain advantages over it: spirit requires the idea of procession, is able to preserve the unity of the spirit's movement while indicating its ontological nature, and illustrates the (ontological) role that freedom plays in the absolute spirit. See TL, vol. 3; Balthasar, "The Unknown Lying Beyond the Word," in *Explorations in Theology,* vol. 3: *Creator Spirit,* trans. Brian McNeil, C.R.V. (San Francisco: Ignatius Press, 1993), 105-116; "The Holy Spirit as Love," in *Explorations in Theology,* vol. 3: *Creator Spirit,* 117-134; Aidan Nichols, *Say It Is Pentecost: A Guide Through Balthasar's Logic* (Washington, DC: The Catholic University of America Press, 2001); John R. Sachs, "Deus Semper Major — Ad

Antonio López, F.S.C.B.

IV. The Spirit within Absolute Spirit

If the reflection on the divine mystery takes its starting point from the economy, then absolute spirit is to be seen in terms of love — as Augustine indicated. Indeed, as Balthasar clarifies further, both processions are to be understood in terms of love, not only the second — as with Aquinas and Augustine. If this is the case, then, to see in what sense the Holy Spirit is *donum doni*, the gift of the gift, and what it could mean to ascribe gratuity to the divine nature, we first need to look at how the begetting of the Son and his relation with the Father are accounted for in the light of a theology of gift.[69]

While not losing sight for one instant of the equal rank of the hypostases, one must hold firmly to the fact that the origin of all of the divinity is not an abstract essence, but the Father, who generates the Son, and who, in union with him and through him, spirates the Holy Spirit.[70] According to Balthasar, the beginning without beginning of the absolute spirit is a Father whose divinity is possessed by him only as completely given away.[71] Balthasar then describes the divine "procession" in terms of donation: the Father's generation of the Son is an absolute gift of himself *(Hingabe, Übereignung)*, a kenosis not so much because there is a negativity that needs to be overcome but because Christ reveals that divine richness is to be understood as giving all of itself to another.[72] The Father's

---

Majorem Dei Gloriam: The Pneumatology and Spirituality of Hans Urs von Balthasar," *Gregorianum* 74 (1993): 631-657; Kossi K. Joseph Tossou, *Streben nach Vollendung. Zur Pneumatologie im Werk Hans Urs von Balthasars* (Freiburg: Herder, 1983).

69. It is important to notice that we do not propose a concept of gift whose meaning and characteristics are derived from a speculative Trinitarian reflection. The full meaning of gift is found in Christ's revelation of God. This, in turn, sheds light upon and clarifies the other common characteristics that gift has in everyday parlance.

70. See DS, 490.

71. See DS, 528.

72. On this point Balthasar follows Ferdinand Ulrich and Adrienne von Speyr very closely. The latter clarifies that "the poverty and need that are at the source of our striving are altogether foreign to eternal life. Life for us is an anxious affair, and we snatch what we can, whereas eternal life is free and open, all giving and receiving, accepting and granting, and undisturbed flow of riches; eternal life is love" (Adrienne von Speyr, *The Word Becomes Flesh: Meditations on John 1-5*, trans. Sr. Lucia Wiedenhöver, O.C.D., and Alexander Dru [San Francisco: Ignatius Press, 1994], 39). And further, she continues: "in another sense both life and death are images of God. Of course, one cannot say that death, as an end, is in any sense in God, since his eternal life is unending. But if death is understood to mean the sacrifice of life, then the original image of that sacrifice is in God as the gift of life flowing be-

divinity is seen precisely in the fact that, in the total gift of himself, he remains himself.[73] The Father "is and remains Father as he renounces any (Arian) being-for-himself-alone."[74] This means, of course, that the Father is also (circumincessively) present in the Son. The *perichoresis*, however, does not undo the gift, because gift is *spirit* and thus its transitive character is not intrusive. That the origin is present in the gift — or, in Aquinas's words already familiar to us, that the gift means "something belonging to another through its origin"[75] — also presupposes the distinction between the giver and the gift. The gift that is given *(esse)* carries within itself the giver *(circumincessio),* yet it is other than it (another person).

For a gift to be completely given, it has to be gratuitously given, that is, it has to be given without the claim of a return — *datio irredibilis,* as Aquinas mentioned in his account of the Holy Spirit. This lack of a return means, first of all, that the giving of the gift is the positing of otherness; in order for the gift to be real, it has to be given to *itself.* If this were not the case, we would not have grasped the *ontological* dimension of gift that the concept of spirit entails, and we would still be thinking of "gift" as something that is had. Instead, for man (creation) and eminently so for God himself (generation, spiration), gift is what defines being.[76] Hence, the ab-

---

tween the Father and the Son in the Spirit. For the Father gives his whole life to the Son, the Son gives it back to the Father, and the Spirit is the outflowing gift of life" (42-43). See also Ferdinand Ulrich, *Leben in der Einheit von Leben und Tod* (Freiburg: Johannes Verlag, 1999); *Homo Abyssus. Das Wagnis der Seinsfrage* (Freiburg: Johannes Verlag, 1998); *Gabe und Vergebung. Ein Beitrag zur biblischen Ontologie* (Freiburg: Johannes Verlag, 2006).

73. See DS, 805.

74. TL 3:225.

75. Aquinas, *Summa Theologiae,* I, q. 38, a. 1 ad 1.

76. Normally, renditions of the dynamics of donation tend to be associated with an economical logic according to which a purported inseparability of giving and losing is only temporarily overcome by the seeming necessity to repay the debt contracted by the receiver when he willingly or unwillingly accepts the gift. In this way, by fruitlessly seeking to construct a dynamics of gift in which gratuity is prevented from soliciting the receiver's free reciprocation, these accounts are further unable to justify the unsurmountable relation between the gift and the need for a return — consequently condemning ethics to an extrinsic coercion. Instead, as R. Brague clarifies, gift does not form part of the alternative between winning and losing, keeping and letting go. To think of the absolute spirit in terms of gift requires moving beyond the realm of having — according to which things need to be owned in order to be given later on — by means of the concept of spirit. Spirit, in fact, enables us to discover the ontological nature of gift, because gift is the spiritual mode of being. See Marcel Mauss, *Sociologie et anthropologie* (Paris: Quadrige/PUF, 1999), 145-279; Jacques Derrida, *La fausse monnaie,* vol. 1 of *Donner le temps* (Paris: Galilée, 1991); *La question de l'esprit* (Paris:

solute gift and the positing of ipseity can never be separated: the first donation is the positing of the Son *(natus)*; the generation of the Word, as the
second, is the positing of the Holy Spirit.[77] If subsistence is of one piece
with donation, then the divine persons can be adequately understood as
relations of donation.[78] The divine essence, Balthasar contends, is indeed
"coextensive with the event of the eternal processions," but it is also "con-
comitantly determined by the unrepeatably unique participation of Father,
Son, and Spirit in this event and so would never exist except as fatherly,
sonly, or spirit-ually." The identification of person with donation allows us
to see the role of the persons in the movement of the absolute spirit without breaking the divine godhead into three. Hence, "the Father," says
Balthasar, "generates the Son as God, that is, out of his substance, but precisely as Father, not as substance."[79] In so doing, the Father's original donation does not set in motion a historical process. The fullness of the origin
is that proper to the spirit, and thus it is itself only inasmuch as it is the gift
of all of itself to the Son who is eternally simultaneous to the Father.

The affirmation that donation "constitutes" the person — the Son and
the Spirit are given to themselves — not only requires that the gift be given
to itself but also that it be so given without claiming anything back. The
gift is, moreover, not truly given to itself if the "self" does not welcome it
and answer the expectation of a response with a gratuitous reciprocation.
The expectation of a return does not indicate that the paternal giving was
not complete or gratuitous. On the contrary, the return is determined by
the nature of the gift itself: gratuity generates its own response, but since
the latter also has the form of the gift, it is free, gratuitous. The movement
of the donation of the absolute spirit is indeed gratuitous both in its giving

---

Galilée, 1987); "Donner la mort," in *L'éthique du don. Jacques Derrida et la pensée du don,* ed.
Jean-Michel Rabaté and Michael Wetzel (Paris: Métailié-Transition, 1992), 11-108; Jean-Luc
Marion, *L'idole et la distance* (Paris: Grasset, 1977); *Réduction et donation: Recherches sur
Hegel, Heidegger et la phénoménologie* (Paris: PUF, 1989); *Étant donné: Essai d'une phénoménologie de la donation* (Paris: PUF, 1998); *De surcroît* (Paris: PUF, 2001); "L'événement, le
phénomène et le révélé," *Transversalités* 70 (1999): 4-25; Rémi Brague, "Dieu ne se donne pas
sans confession," in C. Bruaire, *La Confession de la foi* (Paris: Fayard, 1977), 305-316.

77. Aquinas, *De Potentia Dei,* 10.3; TL, 2:125-134.

78. Thinking of the generation of the Son in terms of a donation that posits the second
hypostasis indicates Balthasar's agreement with Aquinas, for whom the concept of divine relation is notionally multiple and thus can be understood in itself, as relation, and as it constitutes a person; but it also indicates Balthasar's preference for the second connotation of relation. See Aquinas, *De Potentia Dei,* 10.3; TL, 2:130.

79. TL 2:137.

and in its response.[80] In this regard, the first response is the Son's acceptance of the gift, i.e., of his own sonship. Balthasar contends that one needs
to hold both of these affirmations simultaneously: the Son is begotten
from all eternity, and he "gives his antecedent consent to be begotten."[81]
Along with the acceptance of his own sonship, the gift gratuitously given
wishes to be returned gratuitously. The Father's "unsurpassable expectation is being continually surpassed [by the Son] in its fulfillment, even
though the expectation itself was unsurpassable."[82] The one who is loved,
in fact, wants to reciprocate to the beloved. This return of the gift is accomplished by the Son's being what he is, the perfect image of the Father.

The Son's absolute gift of himself to the Father, both free (personal)
and necessary *(esse-donum)*, is never a balancing out of the original donation of the Father. This is because, if donation is the positing of a self —
and in this regard, the person of the Son, although fully God, is God in an
absolutely different way from that of the Father — then donation, to be
real, is more than itself. The Son images the Father in that the Son
"coexecutes the movement of groundlessly loving self-expression, and
does so together with the ground that produces the Logos."[83] The Son's
loving response is not only a conversion to the paternal origin; it is further
giving to yet another. In fact, the Son's loving response to the Father's gift
moves "in two directions." The first follows the same direction of the Father, that is, outside of himself toward another, the Holy Spirit, "a totality
that could only be described as absolute love *per se*."[84] The other direction

---

80. These two are to be kept together: the gift given does not impose a response, and, at
the same time, the gift is reciprocated. In the event of love, the lover wants a response, but he
seeks only a free one. Love elicits its own response, but it does not predetermine it. The ultimate reason for this apparent contradiction is that if love and being are coextensive, the self
is itself only within a communion and not self-referentially.

81. TD 5:86.

82. TD 5:75-81. This eternal overcoming of the inherent waiting in the gift of the Father
and the Son, coming from God's ever-greatness, is what invites Balthasar to talk about wonder in God. See my GE, 236-242.

83. TL 2:152.

84. We saw that Augustine's perplexities in explaining the difference between generation and procession were addressed by Aquinas, who proposed the criterion of opposing relation of origin to shed some light on this mystery. The account of the personhood of the
third hypostasis in this elucidation of God understood as spirit and gift takes advantage of
the distinction between the Son and the Holy Spirit proposed by Aquinas inasmuch as "gift"
indicates procession, origin, and self. Nevertheless, instead of presenting the distinction in
terms of relations of opposition or the psychological image, Balthasar portrays the third

is toward the Father inasmuch as his very substance "subjectively" coincides completely with that of the Father.[85] Thus, there is never a moment in which the Son's being "from" the Father does not have a "toward" the Holy Spirit, and vice versa.[86]

The Holy Spirit is thus seen as the superabundance, the excess of love that, as is proper to God's spiritual essence, "always wills to, indeed, must give more, in excess of every 'proportionate' measure."[87] Gift, in order to be truly given, has to be more than itself. As Schindler rightly indicated, this overabundance proper to God is not a matter of quantity.[88] If this were the case, the spiration of the Holy Spirit would take place because the Father had not given everything to the Son, or because the Holy Spirit needed to undo a purported balancing off of the gift of the Father and the response of the Son, or it would simply be an unnecessary appendix to an already complete donation — in which case the "gratuity" of the absolute spirit would simply mean arbitrariness and would be foreign to the infinity proper to love. Nor is the overabundance proper to the absolute spirit a matter of speculative deduction. One cannot deduce the third person from a loving donation between the Father and Son simply by means of necessary reasons and without any substantial reference to God's revelation in history. It is divine revelation that shows that the absolute donation of the Father with the Son and through the Son is so overabundant that it posits another: if the Son is the gift of the Father (*natus*), the Holy Spirit is the gift

---

hypostasis in terms of overabundance and excess of love. Balthasar, in fact, wonders whether the precedence given to reason over will as one of the means Aquinas offers to explain the difference between procession and generation "is not in the end merely read off of the created *imago* and then elevated to a metaphysical principle." Balthasar proposes to follow Bonaventure in explaining the procession of the Holy Spirit *per modum liberalitatis* (TL 2:164).

85. TL 2:153.

86. I would like to indicate that understanding the Trinitarian processions in the light of gift opens a road for discovering that gift also discloses the spiritual truth of causality, understood as communication of act. The Father gives all of himself: *omne agens agit inquantum est actu.* The similarity between the gift and the giver can be seen in the distinct way in which the gift given by the Father and the receiver are identical: *omne agens agit sibi simile.* At the same time, the generation and the spiration indicate that in God it is good for the other to be. The "telos," then, is the existence of the one, in communion, with the others. This is why the purpose of creation is for man to be in union with God (*omne agens agit propter finem*).

87. TL 3:163; "Institution and Charism," 258.

88. "Institution and Charism," 255, 262.

of that donation which is the relation between the Father and the Son, *donum doni*.[89] Thus, any thinking of the Father and the Son in terms of donation is always incomplete unless one sees that the gift is greater than itself, *semper maior*. The loving exchange between the Father and the Son is real, thanks to the ever-greater nature of the gift. For this reason, Balthasar likes to present the Holy Spirit both as the objective bond of the love of the Father and the Son, and as the subjective fruit of the love who searches even the depths of God.[90] He is the one in whom the Father and the Son are united, and the fruit of their love, the person-gift. Balthasar aptly calls the Holy Spirit "fruit," not in the sense that he proceeds from the Father and the Son like a child from his parents, but in the sense that the giving of the gift confirms and witnesses to the overabundant and gratuitous nature of the love of the absolute spirit.[91] The Holy Spirit *(datus)* can be distinguished from the Son *(natus),* not only because the former is the "excess of love," but also because when the Father gives with the Son (spirates), says Balthasar, quoting Bonaventure, he gives in every way he can give. In the person of the Holy Spirit, God's nature presents itself as a "love that cannot be anticipated by thought," as an absolute spirit whose nature is sheer gratuity that exists in the eternal rhythm of overabundant donation of itself to itself.[92]

It is at this point that we are enabled to grasp more thoroughly Schindler's claim regarding ecclesiology that was mentioned earlier, namely, that an echo of this infinite fruitfulness can be seen in the ever-new unity of the Church. The Church is continuously liberated from the resilient dangers of clericalism and Joachinism by the unexpected irruption of the gifts and charisms of the Holy Spirit. The Holy Spirit generates abiding, indwelling,

89. The economy verifies this: Christ's complete gift of himself *(consummatum est)* is, at the same time, to give more than himself: "and he gave up the spirit" (John 19:30). The epistle to the Romans shows how, after the rejection of his first donation to man (creation), God responds with a donation that is overabundant (Rom. 5:20).

90. Upon this interpretation of the Holy Spirit Balthasar builds the other connotations of witness: the one who brings us into the whole truth, and the charismatic and pneumatological aspect of the Church. See TL 3:251-411.

91. Balthasar writes that "he in God whom we call 'Father' is the 'fruit' of his self-giving to the one we call 'Son'; he exists as this self-giving, and the Son exists as receptivity, gratitude, and giving-in-return. Again, this giving in-return does not close the Two in on themselves but opens them to the fullness of the 'with' (the 'co-' of 'communion'), which is made absolute in the Spirit who is common to both" ("God Is Being With," in *You Crown the Year with Your Goodness,* trans. Graham Harrison [San Francisco: Ignatius Press, 1989], 144).

92. TL 2:35-138.

and continually prevents this love from crystallizing in a doctrine detached from the form of revelation by the ever-surprising bestowal of new forms of holiness, through the presence of which the light of divine beauty shines forth and reconstitutes what was thought to be lost.[93]

I would like to bring this reflection to a close by opening it up to an important implication of the understanding of gift delineated here, whose full elucidation is beyond the scope of this essay. If the foregoing theological rendition of the Triune God and the Holy Spirit in terms of gift is adequate, then it may be possible to perceive that divine gratuity beckons us onward toward the mystery of freedom proper to the absolute spirit. In fact, if the economic Trinity is the immanent Trinity, then the revealed divine freedom, identical to and yet different for each person, must say something about the freedom proper to the absolute spirit — without making of the three hypostases three different and independent centers of operation.[94] Thus, the contention that the Holy Spirit, *donum doni,* witnesses to the gratuitous unity of the Triune God suggests that the Trinitarian processions are both utterly free *and* not arbitrary.

It was noted earlier that the movement of the absolute spirit always entails freedom — to give, to receive, and to express itself — and that this rhythm of donation is both natural and non-mechanical. We also saw that donation is always absolute, that is, freely given, given to itself without demanding a return while awaiting a gratuitous and overabundant answer, and greater than itself. What should not be overlooked here is that the freedom to give is not simply a condition that allows a gift to be given — that is, although it could remain in silence, spirit gives itself over to be known. Rather, freedom is the very nature of the gift. Spirit's gift is free not

---

93. "Institution and Charism," 265-273; GL 1:407-417.

94. This understanding of freedom in God builds upon Aquinas and Augustine, who knew full well that the economy speaks of God's freedom: the "spirit blows where it will" (John 3:8) and that "creation is the Father's free act, and redemption is the Son's free act" (John 10:18) (TL 3:236). Aquinas's understanding of person as having the capacity to determine oneself to action *(dominium sui actus),* or, as we saw with the Holy Spirit, to give oneself, is not a crypto-tritheism, because the giving of himself and enjoying himself proper to the Holy Spirit is his inasmuch as he eternally proceeds from the Father and the Son. Aquinas, *Summa Theologiae,* I, qq. 29, 38, a. 1. For an interesting account of the way in which freedom can be predicated of the different hypostases, see Michael Waldstein, "The Analogy of Mission and Obedience: A Central Point in the Relation between *Theologia* and *Oikonomia* in St. Thomas Aquinas's *Commentary on John,*" in *Reading John with St. Thomas Aquinas: Theological Exegesis and Speculative Theology,* ed. Michael Dauphinais and Matthew Levering (Washington, DC: The Catholic University of America Press, 2005), 92-112.

because it is created or arbitrary, or because it is able to give or not to give. The freedom of the absolute spirit does not reside in its capacity to be what it is or to determine itself to be something altogether different. In this sense, an account of the intra-Trinitarian processions in the light of gift does not mean either that the Father generates the Son because he so wills it, or that their spiration of the Holy Spirit could have happened otherwise. The coalescence of "donation," "procession," and "relation" does not place God beyond being, in the realm of unreasonable arbitrariness. Instead, the gift that constitutes the unity of the absolute spirit is utterly free precisely because it gives, and because it gives itself with complete gratuity — both in the giving and in the receiving of the gift.[95] It is this freedom, then, that lies at the roots of what human speech about the Triune God perceives as necessary. Thus understood, divine gratuity, being's shared secret, is the ground and the form of logical and ontological necessity, and not vice versa. God cannot be otherwise than what he is, because the absolute spirit cannot but be the overabundant gift of himself to himself.[96] In this sense it can be said, with Balthasar, that "the [Holy] Spirit's perfect freedom to

95. Theological and philosophical reflection are so accustomed to thinking of freedom in terms of independence and self-determination that, as we saw, although Augustine's and Aquinas's rendition of the divine processions leaves some room for the account of the Holy Spirit in terms of *liberalitas*, and thus of freedom in God, they are very clear in showing that the second procession is not arbitrary.

96. This understanding of absolute gift in terms of freedom allows us to have a better grasp of the meaning of freedom of choice and to see what it means that the latter is grounded in the former. Freedom of choice rests on an ontological sense of freedom according to which the primordial movement of the spirit is to give itself of itself. Anthropologically speaking, the true aspect of the oft-proclaimed freedom of choice to do what one determines is that it still affirms that the primary meaning of freedom is not "choosing" but fulfillment of one's own *telos*. The fallacy in an exaggerated freedom of choice consists in man's claim to obtain his fulfillment, final beatitude, by his own means, that is, forgetting that his fulfillment has to respect the form of gift that man's being has. Man's freedom, in fact, does not have to do with a solipsistic independence determining itself to action from itself, but rather with "reaching one's own fulfillment." Freedom, then, more than choice, is the "capacity to possess" the meaning of one's own existence, that is, a Father who does not spare his own Son in order for man to be himself (Rom. 8:32); hence, a free possession within a free and gratuitous being-possessed and awaited. It is through man's freedom that the end, the *telos*, final beatitude — that is, God himself — can be man's. The great mystery of God's creative act is not so much that he allows man the possibility to choose him or to run away from him, but rather that God desires to be man's. Man, being made *capax Dei*, becomes himself in accepting the gift that God makes of himself to man. See Luigi Giussani, *The Religious Sense* (Montreal: McGill University Press, 1997), 80-93, 120-124.

blow whither he will" arises from the fact that the Father and Son are themselves only in the absolute gift of one to the other *(Hingabe).*[97] At the same time, the freedom of the Holy Spirit to search the depths of God (1 Cor. 2:10) is the confirmation that the unity of the absolute spirit exists in the absolute gift of himself to himself. The Holy Spirit witnesses that the necessity proper to the absolute spirit is a gratuitous and infinitely fruitful love. Without ever exhausting it, the "gift of gift" reveals the mystery that the freedom of the absolute spirit, the Triune God, is nothing other than an indwelling whose form is that of a gratuitous and eternal giving of oneself.

97. TL 3:241.

The Marian Dimension of Existence

Stratford Caldecott

> *Mary is totally dependent upon God and completely directed towards him, and at the side of her Son, she is the most perfect image of freedom and of the liberation of humanity and of the universe.*
>
> John Paul II, *Redemptoris Mater*, 37,
> quoting from Congregation for the Doctrine of the Faith,
> Instruction on Christian Freedom and Liberation, 97

As David Schindler writes in his seminal essay, "Catholic Theology, Gender, and the Future of Western Civilization" (chapter 9 in *Heart of the World, Center of the Church*), "gender implicates not only the main teachings of Christianity (theology), but also our basic view of the world (ontology), and indeed our entire way of life (spirituality)."[1] So, of course, does Mariology, because for Catholics the Blessed Virgin Mary is the supreme, concrete embodiment of the feminine — the most perfect woman, in fact the most perfect human person (since her Son is a human being but not a human person) — and therefore, in conjunction with her Son, anchors and enshrines the Catholic understanding of gender. It is only when we discover this Marian center of Schindler's thought, which is the key to his understanding of gender, that the whole matrix of his theological and philosophical work becomes evident.

In order to convey a sense of the gestalt, I will need to touch upon a number of disparate themes, without treating any of them in great detail (they are in any case covered by other authors in this collection). It is the

---

1. HW, 327.

radiant center on which they converge, or from which they emerge, that interests me here. I intend to explore the Schindlerian vision of Mary under three headings given to us in my quotation from *Heart of the World,* namely (1) theology, (2) ontology, and (3) spirituality.[2] In a brief conclusion I will touch on the implications of this vision for the evangelization of America.

I. Theology

The "main teachings of Christianity" that are implicated in Mariology are these. First, the Incarnation: the sending of the Son through the hypostatic union of divine and human nature in the womb of Mary. Second, the Redemption: the Son's self-sacrifice as the source of all grace for the salvation of the world. Third, the Trinity: the origin of all spousal and familial bonds in the relations of God with himself. Thus a Mariology implies a Christology, for Mother and Son cannot be separated except to be reunited. You could say Mariology *shadows* Christology: the Catholic doctrines about Mary, such as her virginal motherhood, her cooperation in the redemption, her immaculate conception, her spousal relationship with the Holy Spirit, and her motherhood of the Church, are attached to the corresponding doctrines about her divine Son and depend upon them. The Assumption, in the same sense, "shadows" our Lord's ascension into heaven.

Let me unpack that paragraph slightly, before moving on to show how Mariology also carries with it an implied ecclesiology, and how both imply a Christian anthropology (which will lead us into the section on ontology). In this way we shall obtain a glimpse of the internal coherence of Catholic belief that is a particular hallmark of David Schindler's writing. Few if any other modern authors have shown such a keen and sustained awareness of the interrelationship of all Christian doctrines, arising as it were from a single principle, the impact of an event. That event is our encounter with the living Christ, and working out what follows from it is the essence of theology.

The Incarnation begins in time with the annunciation, or more pre-

2. Schindler has not as yet written a systematic Mariology, though a devotion to Mary permeates his work and leaves nothing unaffected. My approach will build on the relevant formulations found in Schindler's book, filling out the outline this provides with thoughts that I believe to be in the same spirit. I will not attempt to trace all the influences on Schindler's thought, much less engage with his intellectual opponents and interlocutors.

cisely with God's response to Mary's fiat, her willing acceptance of the mystery she is offered. By virtue of this "letting be" on her part, the divine will is realized in the assumption of a human nature (miraculously from the mother alone) by the second divine person, making Mary the *Theotokos,* the God-bearer or Mother of God. The precondition of Mary's motherhood is the fiat, because God would not force himself upon anyone, and the precondition of her fiat is the immaculate conception, which gives her the freedom to say "yes" without reservation. Being preserved, precisely in view of her mission, from the damage to our wills normally transmitted from one generation to the next does not *determine* her to say "yes" but enables her to do so perfectly.[3] It is still her own created will that must assent to the annunciation, no matter that God has foreseen (or rather, eternally sees) her assent, and prepares his plans accordingly.

Schindler's Mariology, which centers on the fiat viewed as inseparable from the various Marian dogmas, is just as inseparable from the dogma of the Incarnation, of which it forms (as it were) simply the other side of the coin. For in order to assume, and thereby heal, the human nature once fallen in Adam, it was necessary for God to take that nature from a human being rather than create it from scratch. In order for him to take it, it must have been given freely, for God is nothing if not love. (And, as we have seen, in order for it to have been given perfectly freely, the mother must have been immaculate.) Furthermore — and this is also crucial to the Mariology we are discussing — the free act by which Mary gives herself to God is no mere historical condition for the Incarnation to take place (albeit a necessary one) but a *continuing structural element* in the salvation being wrought. For Schindler, this is to be interpreted ontologically. The Christian does not leave the fiat behind, for the assent of all other human beings to the saving grace God offers them is a participation (to use Platonic language) in Mary's fiat as well as being contingent upon it. This is not to say that their assent is inevitable, or determined by that of Mary, only that it is enfolded within it. Each of us must make Mary's fiat our own.

That implies, as Schindler comes close to saying (but carefully, without calling for a new dogma!), that Mary can in a way be called "co-redemptrix." He uses that term in the first *(Communio)* version of the essay

---

3. The question of whether God might have chosen to sanctify Mary later than at the moment of her conception, say in the womb or during childhood, would take too long here to explore. At the very least we can say it was "fitting" that at least one human person, and that person she from whom Christ's human nature was derived, should be as pure in her whole existence as the first Eve before the Fall.

under discussion, but corrects it to *mediatrix* in the book, giving a footnote reference to Balthasar's nuanced discussion of these terms in *Theo-Drama*, volume 3. Mary's unconditional maternal receptivity to the Word extends to the Cross, for it enfolds the entire existence of the Incarnate One from his conception up to and beyond his bodily death. Only a consciously offered receptivity without conditions or limits is able to welcome all the grace that God wishes to give mankind in his Son. Thus Mary welcomes the Son as an embryo, as a child, as a teenager, and as a grown man. For this reason she is "full of grace" — as full as a human being can be.

Her cooperation in the redemption consists in this: that she is the human being who feels most deeply and accepts most perfectly the Son's gift of his death of the Cross. Her agony is secondary to his, but inseparable from it (because caused by it). Her fiat is the foundation and deepest reality of the Church, because it receives on behalf of all who will come afterward the gift of the Lord's body and blood.

Our own fiat depends on hers, because the Incarnation depends on it. But Mary's fiat paradoxically depends on that of her Son, in whom it pre-exists. "[T]he Son of God, already 'feminine' (bearing a 'receptive womb') within himself, in turn generates the feminine in the created order, thus making possible his Incarnation!"[4] This brings us to the Trinitarian core of David Schindler's Mariology. Picking up on Balthasar's treatment of the Trinity in *Theo-Drama*, and seemingly not afraid to emphasize its more controversial elements, Schindler speaks of a "super-femininity" in God in a way that links to the ontology of gift we will be touching upon later. Theologically, he builds on the Thomistic understanding that the divine persons are constituted as "relations" and not as substances. These relations are precisely the form of love (that is, the *actus purus* which God is), because in them the self or divine nature of God is completely given and received: it is this giving and receiving characteristic of love in its highest sense that we call by names such as "generation," "procession," and "spiration." God as self-giving love in three substantial relations supplies the archetypal model — both the formal and final cause — of all loving relationships, indeed of all relationships, in the created order. The closest resemblance to this model is present in the hypostatic union of divine and human natures in Christ, and then the union of God and man in the mystery of the Church.

Mariology is bound up with ecclesiology, as the Council signaled by

---

4. "Catholic Theology, Gender, and the Future of Western Civilization," *Communio: International Catholic Review* 20 (1993): 251.

situating its treatment of Mary within its document on the Church. The Church is simply the extension of the Incarnation, or of the human nature of the Son. In Mary the full reality of the Church is concentrated, and every human being who is joined to the Church becomes through the Holy Spirit an adopted child of Mary. Ecclesiology in its complex ramifications unfolds from this point. One step outward from Mary herself, we find gathered around her at Pentecost the apostles and disciples, to whom she mediates the presence of her Son and his Spirit. The "constellation" of saints around "the Woman" itself has a structure, a form, in which John and Peter hold a privileged position (representing all subsequent saints and office-holders within the Church, the complementary charisms of love and of authority).[5] As Schindler writes, "Feminine receptivity both is at the origin and is the end of masculine priestliness: there is and can be no male priesthood in the Church except on the basis of the always prior *fiat* of Mary, and the initiative of the male priesthood would come to rest on barren ground but for the receptivity of the *fiat*. The seed of grace takes root and grows only within the receptive womb of the Woman."[6]

As for the Eucharist, this is not merely the human nature of Christ but the Lord himself, in both his human and divine nature, present in the Church sacramentally. Specifically we are asked to identify the Eucharist with the act of oblation on the Cross, anticipated at the Last Supper. This is Jesus giving himself to his disciples. We can think of the Blessed Sacrament as both the center of the Church and the heart of the world. This is the final lynchpin of the *communio* ecclesiology, which integrates de Lubac's insight into nature and grace with a doctrine of the Church and therefore Church with cosmos. Schindler writes: "the whole world, in and through the Church, is destined for a transfiguring espousal with Jesus Christ" — an espousal, he explains, that will include society, economy, and cosmos as

---

5. Thus around Mary in this constellation are three male figures apart from her Son: Joseph, John, and Peter. It is almost as though the feminine "womb" of Mary contains along with the Lord a male triad representing the three aspects of the Lord manifest in the Church: Joseph here taking the place of the Father, John the Son, and Peter the Holy Spirit. The triangle of the Holy Family (Mary–Jesus–Joseph) is mirrored in a second, entirely human triangle that shares one corner with it (Joseph–Peter–John). Much more could be said of this Trinitarian "hall of mirrors," but not here. It is important to note, however, the importance Schindler often attributes to the fact that in *Mulieris Dignitatem* Pope John Paul II quotes Balthasar — at that time still living — concerning the primacy of the Marian over the Petrine principle in the Church.

6. HW, 254.

well. "This marriage," he goes on, "is understood in the radical and comprehensive sense as a Eucharistic exchange intended to leave not even the smallest particle of the cosmos unwed. The terms of the offer of marriage are established by Trinitarian and Christic love, and the marriage is made actual only though the Marian fiat."[7] It is made actual through the fiat, from which the entire Incarnation follows, and its consummation takes place on the Cross. It takes place for each member of the Church in the Eucharist, where, already indwelt by the Holy Spirit through baptism, the Christian in a state of grace is able to unite himself with the sacrifice of Christ, as Mary did.

If the first analogy to the Trinity is found in the hypostatic union, so that Mariology is entwined with Christology, and the second analogy, as we have seen, is found in the Church, so that Mariology cannot be separated from ecclesiology, the third is the resemblance that we find in the sacrament of marriage, where man and woman become "one flesh" for the procreation and education of children (Eph. 5:31).

The Holy Family is thus an image of the divine Trinity, and it is from the relationship of the genders made for marriage that we draw the analogical language of "femininity" and "masculinity," of spiritual "motherhood" and "fatherhood," which Balthasar (following the precedent of mystical writers such as Anselm of Bec and Julian of Norwich) applies to God. It is here, too, that we find the basis of the concept of the "nuptial body" developed by John Paul II, the human "aptness for marriage," which is so central to the personalism of the John Paul II Institute for Studies in Marriage and the Family. It is a mark of the Trinity in human beings that determines human nature to subsist in complementary genders for the procreation of children, making the fruition of love dependent on the giving of self to another. This nuptial reality is expressed in the relation of Jesus to Mary, in the sense that all other gender relations are subsumed by the most intimate relation of all — that of Mother and Child. (The marriage of Mary and Joseph and the giving of John to Mary at the foot of the Cross both take place within that prior relation of New Adam to New Eve.) Thus theology for Schindler cannot be separated from anthropology, as these much-repeated sentences of *Gaudium et Spes*, 22, suggest:

> The truth is that only in the mystery of the incarnate Word does the mystery of man take on light. For Adam, the first man, was a figure of

7. HW, 21-23.

him who was to come, namely Christ the Lord. Christ, the final Adam, by the revelation of the mystery of the Father and his love, fully reveals man to man himself and makes his supreme calling clear.

Another line from the same document takes us to the heart of the matter: man can "fully discover his true self only in a sincere giving of himself" (24).

This is the self-giving love, Trinitarian (open, asymmetrical, fruitful) in form, that through the Incarnation and on the Cross reveals man to himself. This is also the nature of that pure act of being *(esse subsistens)* by which the sun and the other stars are moved.

II. Ontology

For Schindler, there is a reciprocal relationship, amounting almost to a "union-coincident-with-distinct-identity,"[8] between the fields of theology and philosophy. Philosophical reason has its own "legitimate autonomy" (a favorite phrase borrowed from the Second Vatican Council), but its symbiosis with theology is such that its own deepest concerns are illuminated and its ability to address those concerns is strengthened by the assistance of theology. Theology, in turn, involves the use of reason in the service of revelation, and therefore is both dependent on and superior to philosophical reason. Schindler sometimes likens this relationship to the "mutual submission" of marriage, in John Paul II's innovative interpretation of the Letter to the Ephesians. As in marriage, each partner remains distinct from the other even in union with the other; indeed, the deeper the union between the two, the more distinct each becomes — for the more we love another person *for himself,* rather than for our own benefit and use, the more we set that person free to be himself within the relationship. John Paul II himself, in *Fides et Ratio,* famously likens faith and reason to the two wings of a single bird flying in search of the truth.

Nowhere are this symbiosis and mutual support more evident than in the study of being (ontology), where metaphysical philosophy overlaps with fundamental theology. The revelation of the Trinity, received in faith, provides a key to understanding the structure and dynamic nature of being that could not have been anticipated by the Greeks and necessitated a

8. HW, 19.

transformation in their categories of thought. "[T]he sole dominion of thinking in terms of substance is ended; relation is discovered as an equally valid primordial mode of reality."[9] Accordingly, being has to be re-interpreted as a participation in Trinitarian love. Nevertheless, the doctrine of the Trinity required philosophical sophistication even to be formulated, let alone meditated upon. These deep matters are studied in other essays in this volume. Here it is important only to note one aspect of the relationship of theology and philosophy, namely, the close connection between ontology and Mariology.

Mary, who is entirely creature (as distinct from her Son, who is both God and man) yet full of grace, represents and is the *creation re-made,* or the beginning and form of that re-making. In her assumption and coronation we see an icon of our own longed-for *theosis* and final end. She becomes the Church, the fruit of the redemption and the mother of all Christians in the order of grace, starting with John at the foot of the Cross. In her we see the proper relationship of nature and grace, undistorted by human sin. And the relationship is one of *active receptivity.*

In the annunciation, we are shown Mary in the act of accepting the Lord's statement (mediated by the angel), "You shall bear a son. . . ." It might seem that her role here is entirely passive, but the account makes it clear that she is no pushover. "How can this be, since I am a virgin?" she asks. Far from punishing her for seeming to doubt his word, as he punishes Zechariah, the Lord answers her question, knowing that in her case there is no sin lurking behind it. She merely wants to make the decision her own, and to understand as best she can what is being said to her — such an attitude is entirely right and proper. Mary is actively engaged in this decision, not merely bowing to authority. Her agreement will be motivated by love, not fear.

Mary's fiat is a "letting be done" that recalls the more reluctant fiat of Jesus in the garden of Gethsemane ("Nevertheless let your will, not mine, be done"), as well as the fiat of God in the creation of the world ("Let there be light"). For Schindler, this must imply that Mary's "letting be" — conventionally described as obedience or submission — can be traced back all the way to the Trinity itself. This involves a significant revision of the Aristotelian-Thomistic tradition, for which the condition of receptivity or passivity, let alone obedience and submission, could never be a perfection

9. Joseph Ratzinger, *Introduction to Christianity* (San Francisco: Ignatius Press, 2004), 184. This book by the future Pope Benedict XVI is undoubtedly a favorite of Schindler.

appropriate to God, who is *actus purus* and supreme Lord over all. For Schindler, it is a "defect" in classical metaphysics to regard receptivity as merely a deficiency.[10] The capacity to receive is a necessary complement to self-communication in and between the divine persons. Thus one might say, perhaps, that the fiat of Jesus does not merely show him as receptive in his human nature to the divine will, but expresses a quality in the divine nature itself. (Jesus is not simply obedient to *his own* divine will, but precisely as Son is obedient to the will *of the Father*.) Thus what is introduced here is a distinction, unknown to Aristotle, between passivity and receptivity, or a distinction *within pure act* between active activity, let us say, and active receptivity, or "between the *'aktive actio'* proper to giving and the *'passive actio'* proper to receiving."[11] Only the fact of the Trinitarian relations makes such a distinction at all conceivable.

Self-subsistent *esse*, then, which is the pure act of existence identical with its own essence or "whatness," possesses this Trinitarian form. It is love, and therefore an act both of giving and of receiving. Crucial to Schindler's gift-ontology is the fact that created being, too, has a triadic structure because it participates in this Trinitarian form — it is "from," "in," and "for" (or "toward")[12] — with receptivity fundamental to its nature as gift. The "constitutive relation from and toward God *(Esse)* establishes in the creature . . . an intrinsic relation also from and toward all that participates in *Esse*" in and through Jesus Christ.[13] Mary, as pure creature divinized by grace, manifests this receptivity, which in God may be called divine maternity or spiritual motherhood. Her active role in the annuncia-

---

10. HW, 282. In this chapter, which discusses the Thomism of Norris Clarke, Schindler unfolds Balthasar's notion of receptivity as a perfection. The Son is a "child" because eternally *from* the Father, "even as the Son remains equal to the Father in this eternal difference as receptive" (283) — and creatures constitutively image God first in this sense, as Son not Father, and so as children in the Child (albeit without the equality that is proper to the divine nature alone). Among human persons it is Mary who recapitulates this receptivity, and so her fiat is "the most perfect image of freedom and of the liberation of humanity" (277).

11. HW, 241, citing Balthasar and Adrienne von Speyr. On the same page Schindler cites Balthasar on receptivity as a perfection as follows: "Receiving *(Empfangen)* and letting be *(Geschehenlassen)* are as essential for the concept of absolute love as giving *(Geben)* which, without the receptive letting be — and everything else which belongs to love: the grateful owing of oneself and the turning back of oneself to the giver — would have no capacity to give at all."

12. HW, 296-297. We must, of course, make due allowance for the *maior dissimilitudo*. Schindler is always very clear on the analogical distinction.

13. HW, 290-291.

tion — the activity by which, cooperating with grace, she exercises her human freedom to the full in accepting the divine will — therefore has its deepest root in God himself. It is an aspect of the divine image and likeness in her, not a falling away from likeness. At one and the same time, it reveals the perfection of grace and the perfection of nature. In the very dependence of the creature we see the "from another" character of divine personhood. Respecting the analogy of being, one would say that her receptivity participates in the mutual loving submission and devotion of the three divine persons, precisely as the creature intended by God to receive the gift of his Son, who is the fullness of grace.

Our "view of the world," then, and of the *being* of the world (*esse commune* existing only in the multiplicity of creatures, but rooted in the subsistent *esse* of God), or ontology, is bound up with our view of Mary's role in the annunciation — and the whole Incarnation that unfolds from that moment — and with our view of gender as an intrinsic part of the identity of all created persons made in the image and likeness of God, beginning with Adam and Eve and all over again (at a new level) with the new Adam and the new Eve. Mary reveals the meaning of being as love. She is the archetypal "mother's smile" that awakens this intuition in her children.

III. Spirituality

The Christian way of life is understood in the Catholic tradition as being exemplified in Mary, as the first and closest of all Christ's disciples and his most perfect creation. Thus Catholic spirituality — even masculine spirituality — is Marian in form, albeit suitably differentiated according to function and charism within the Body of Christ. This does not mean, as some have alleged, that Catholic sanctity is overbalanced toward the feminine. It means, rather, that it *derives* from the feminine, in the sense that all creaturely existence, and especially sanctified existence, is primarily receptive in order to be active. The capacity to be truly active, to be responsible and free, depends on the reception of existence and essence from God in humility, reverence, and gratitude.

Knowledge itself is nuptial, contemplative. To know something we must be open to it; we must be capable of receiving it into ourselves and giving ourselves to it. "In short, what we learn from the Marian *fiat* is not only that the meaning of being is love, but that, in order fully to see this, *we must ourselves be in love.*"[14] This, however, runs completely counter to the analytic and reductive method of knowing that Western culture has inherited from Galileo and Descartes. It aims to see the whole in the fragments, not the fragments in the whole, and it does so by discerning the *form* that radiates through the surface appearances of things. Only faith, hope, and love can open these eyes in us.

In a chapter called "Sanctity and the Intellectual Life," Schindler applies these insights to life in the academy. With Balthasar, he wishes to overcome the separation of theology and spirituality. The call to holiness "is a task which comprehends the intelligence."[15] The various disciplines may possess their own autonomy, but every subject bears an intrinsic relation to the Creator God. For every subject concerns one or another aspect or dimension of created being, whose Trinitarian form is revealed in Jesus, Mary, and the Church. In fact, any attempt to exclude God *a priori* will ensure that we will fail to grasp anything in its ontological depth.

More generally, Marian spirituality is a spirituality of childhood. We can say, in fact, that the authentic Christian *never grows up.* "Only the Christian religion, which in its essence is communicated by the eternal child of God, keeps alive in its believers the lifelong awareness of their being children, and therefore of having to ask and give thanks for things."[16] It is only sin that causes us to become old (in an other-than-physical sense). Bernanos was perfectly correct, then, in describing Mary as "younger than sin." The saint lives in an eternal spring, because her existence is always being received, celebrated, and appreciated (that is, shared and given back) instead of snatched, hoarded, and taken for granted. Motherhood and childhood are very much alike in some ways, since it is necessary for the mother to understand the child and for the child to feel understood by the mother. But the childlike aspect of motherhood is also present in genuine fatherhood, and Joseph's readiness to take the child and his mother to Egypt and back in response to a dream exemplifies this, even as it demonstrates an adult sense of responsibility and ability to get things done. Only a pure soul, uncorrupted by cynicism, could have received such a dream and listened to it. It is through spiritual childhood that spiritual fatherhood is derived from spiritual motherhood.

The spirituality I am attributing to Joseph here is Marian, and yet at

14. HW, 201.
15. HW, 215.
16. UBLC, 49.

the same time perfectly masculine. It is Marian in the sense of being primarily receptive — to Mary herself, to the mysterious child, and to the messages of angels in the night. It is by contemplating Mary that we see the beauty of the natural world perfected — brought to fruition — by grace, in both men and women. Even in the weakness and humiliation, the poverty and death, which mar the surface of things, the light is not overthrown. We see the life of God in man, Jesus the child of Mary and Son of God. Spirituality is rooted in ontology, and the secret design of all creaturely being, revealed in Jesus through Mary, is love.

Conclusion

Elsewhere in this volume, David L. Schindler's critique of American culture, Catholic neo-conservatism, and liberalism has been examined in depth. This has clearly been one of the preeminent themes of his life and work. But it, too, rotates around the Marian center. We can bring some of the threads of this chapter together by relating Mariology to the concern for an evangelization of Western civilization — otherwise put (by Popes Paul VI and John Paul II), the creation of a civilization of love and a culture of life. For the conclusion of a (Marian) theology, ontology, and spirituality must be more than a dry theory of Catholic life. It must itself be life-giving. Evangelization correctly understood is the transmission of life to a culture.

Schindler does not oppose democracy or even "capitalism," but identifies a radical distortion in the logic of democratic capitalism in Western (and particularly American) civilization due to its prior commitment to a certain false notion of freedom. He traces this back historically to a breakdown in the correct relationship between nature and grace at the time of the Reformation and Counter-Reformation. Building on Henri de Lubac's analysis, he argues that both the Reformed and to some extent the Catholic intellectual tradition (from Ockham through Suarez down to John Courtney Murray) forgot or misrepresented the "natural desire for God" recognized in the Patristic writers down to St. Thomas. Nature (in man) can achieve self-fulfillment in God only through a grace to which it has no natural "right." This paradox is an expression of the theology and ontology outlined above. Created being receives itself as gift. It is "from," "in," and "for," and as such its end is achieved only by going out of itself to another in God. If our nature is primarily gift, we express ourselves most authentically by giving rather than taking, and the fundamental human choice is not *what do we take?* but *to whom do we give?* True human freedom is not "creative," in the sense that it originates with us (taking), but "responsive," and therefore interiorly related to all others and to God. But mainstream economic and political theory assumes the opposite.

This is why Schindler proposes that

> liberalism of *any* stripe — including the liberalism of "open" capitalism — remains unacceptable insofar as its freedom remains conceived as primarily creative — or rather, insofar as its creativity is not conceived as anteriorly receptive. Indeed, here we discover the basic definition of a liberalism which, at its deepest level, threatens the integrity of Christianity, because it poisons at its source the meaning of autonomy. In overlooking receptivity in favor of creativity as primary in the basic human act, such a liberalism overlooks the implications of the relation that is constitutive of the human being *as creature*. At stake is the nature of the solidarity characteristic of a "civilization of love" — and thus the nature of the "new order" which we are to propose to the world.[17]

By which he means, of course, a "Marian" order. The question, he says, is whether we can have a spirituality wherein "being" is prior to "doing" or "having"; where contemplation–immanent activity is an anterior condition for all action-transitive/transcendent activity; and where the interiority of the former activity therefore keeps the latter activity from sliding off into extroversion and simple externality.[18]

American culture, Schindler believes, has done precisely this: it has become extroverted from the outset, by founding itself on an individualism that carries within it an implicit rejection of the Marian fiat forged in the fires of the Reformation. The distortion of the culture is essentially a masculinization, and to overcome or heal this imbalance we need to look not simply to Woman, or even to Mary, but to Mary-Christ and thus to the (extended) Holy Family, in which the masculine is reintegrated with the feminine by participation in the life of the Holy Trinity and the mission of the Spirit in the world. (The John Paul II Institute for Studies in Marriage and the Family comes in precisely here.) In response to the criticism that his critique lacks a sufficiently pragmatic edge, Schindler points to ecclesial movements such as Focolare and Communion and Liberation, whose impressive creativity in the realm of culture, and even economics, is

17. HW, 119-120.
18. HW, 103.

founded on an anterior (ontological and spiritual) receptivity to an objective order of the true and the good, expressed in their devotion to Mary and the Marian/Petrine Church.

Masculinization, in the above sense, is associated also in Schindler's view with mechanization, and the rise of liberalism is paralleled in his thought with the rise of modern science. But again, he does not condemn science or technology as such, only the distortion caused by its rejection of the Marian ontology. This he traces back through Newton to Galileo and Descartes, in whom nature is reduced to sheer externality. Interior relatedness to the whole and to God is lost in the attempt to measure and control every piece of the cosmic puzzle, and Bacon's expression "knowledge is power" becomes the banner of a brave new world.[19]

Enough has been said to suggest that Schindler's profound sensitivity to the assumptions of our culture has revealed the degree to which Mariology can contribute to its evangelization. The "homelessness" of the modern soul reflects the lack of a maternal rootedness in being. The Marian fiat in which we can participate to the degree we ourselves become holy is the source of all spiritual maternity. It is this maternity to which we must look for a civilization of love and a culture of life.

19. See, for example, HW, 193.

Works by David L. Schindler

I. Books Authored

Heart of the World, Center of the Church: Communio *Ecclesiology, Liberalism, and Liberation.* Grand Rapids: Eerdmans, 1996.
Ordering Love. Grand Rapids: Eerdmans, 2011.

II. Works Edited

General Editor of the Series. *Ressourcement: Retrieval and Renewal in Catholic Thought.* Grand Rapids: Eerdmans.
Editor. Communio: International Catholic Review.
With G. McLean, F. Ellrod, and J. Mann. *Act and Agent: Philosophical Foundations of Moral Education.* Washington, DC: The University Press of America, 1986.
Beyond Mechanism: The Universe in Recent Physics and Catholic Thought. Washington, DC: The University Press of America, 1986.
Catholicism and Secularization in America: Essays on Nature, Grace, and Culture. Huntington, IN: Our Sunday Visitor, 1990.
Hans Urs von Balthasar: His Life and Work. San Francisco: Ignatius Press, 1991.
With Doug Bandow. *Wealth, Poverty, and Human Destiny.* Wilmington, DE: ISI Books, 2003.
Love Alone Is Credible: Hans Urs von Balthasar as Interpreter of the Catholic Tradition, vol. 1. Grand Rapids: Eerdmans, 2008.

III. Articles and Contributions to Books

"Creativity as Ultimate: Reflections on Actuality in Whitehead, Aristotle, and Aquinas." *International Philosophical Quarterly* 13 (1973): 161-171.

Works by David L. Schindler

"History, Objectivity, and Moral Conversion." *The Thomist* 38 (1973): 569-588.

"On the Critical Study of Religion: Positivism, the First Amendment, and the Roemer Case." *Communio: International Catholic Review* 3 (1976): 301-317.

"Theology and the Historical-Critical Claims of Modernity: On the Need for Metaphysics." *Communio: International Catholic Review* 6 (1979): 73-94.

"Whitehead's Challenge to Thomism on the Problem of God: The Metaphysical Issues." *International Philosophical Quarterly* 19 (1979): 285-299.

"Metaphysics and the Problem of Historicism in Contemporary Theology." In *Historicism and Faith,* ed. Paul L. Williams, 87-101. Scranton, PA: Northeast Books, 1980.

"David Bohm on Contemporary Physics and the Overcoming of Fragmentation." *International Philosophical Quarterly* 22 (1982): 315-327.

"Can a Roman Catholic Be a Historian? A Response to Philip Devenish." *Journal of Ecumenical Studies* 20 (1983): 86-108.

"Whitehead's Inability to Affirm a Universe of Value." *Process Studies* 13 (1983): 117-131.

"Beyond Mechanism: Physics and Catholic Theology." *Communio: International Catholic Review* 11 (1984): 186-192.

"Toward a Christian Culture." *Communio: International Catholic Review* 11 (1984): 414-417.

"On the Foundations of Moral Judgment." In *Act and Agent: Philosophical Foundations of Moral Education.* Committee for Research in Values and Philosophy, 1986.

"On the Integrity of Morality in Relation to Religion." In *Act and Agent: Philosophical Foundations of Moral Education.* Committee for Research in Values and Philosophy, 1986.

"On Being Catholic in America." *Communio: International Catholic Review* 14 (1987): 213-214.

"Is America Bourgeois?" *Communio: International Catholic Review* 14 (1987): 262-290.

"Catholicity and the State of Contemporary Theology: The Need for an Onto-Logic of Holiness." *Communio: International Catholic Review* 14 (1987): 426-450.

"Once Again: George Weigel, Catholicism and American Culture." *Communio: International Catholic Review* 15 (1988): 92-120.

"Catholicism, Public Theology, and Postmodernity: On Richard John Neuhaus's 'Catholic Moment.'" *The Thomist* 53 (1989): 107-143.

"Grace and the Form of Nature and Culture." In *Catholicism and Secularization in America,* ed. David L. Schindler. Huntington, IN: Our Sunday Visitor, 1990.

"On Meaning and the Death of God in the Academy." *Communio: International Catholic Review* 17 (1990): 192-206.

"Time in Eternity, Eternity in Time: On the Contemplative-Active Life." *Communio: International Catholic Review* 18 (1991): 53-68.

"The Church's 'Worldly' Mission: Neoconservatism and American Culture." *Communio: International Catholic Review* 18 (1991): 365-397.

"Response to Mark Lowery." *Communio: International Catholic Review* 18 (1991): 450-472.

"Christology, Public Theology, and Thomism: De Lubac, Balthasar, and Murray." In *The Future of Thomism,* ed. Deal W. Hudson and Dennis W. Moran, 247-264. Mishawaka, IN: American Maritain Association; Notre Dame: University of Notre Dame Press, 1992.

"Christology and the Church's 'Worldly' Mission: Response to Michael Novak." *Communio: International Catholic Review* 19 (1992): 164-178.

"Towards a Eucharistic Evangelization." *Communio: International Catholic Review* 19 (1992): 549-575.

"On Catholicism and American Culture." *Desert Call* (1993): 16-21.

"Catholic Theology, Gender, and the Future of Western Civilization." *Communio: International Catholic Review* 20 (1993): 200-239.

"Norris Clark on Person, Being, and St. Thomas." *Communio: International Catholic Review* 20 (1993): 580-592.

"Sanctity and the Intellectual Life." *Communio: International Catholic Review* 20 (1993): 652-672.

"Religious Freedom, Truth, and American Liberalism: Another Look at John Courtney Murray." *Communio: International Catholic Review* 21 (1994): 696-741.

"'Civilization of Love': On Catholicism, Neoconservatism, and American Culture." *Catholic World Report* (1994): 42-49.

"Review of: 'The Immutability of God in the Theology of Hans Urs von Balthasar,' by Gerard F. O'Hanlon." *The Thomist* 58 (1994): 335-342.

"The Person: Philosophy, Theology, and Receptivity." *Communio: International Catholic Review* 21 (1994): 172-190.

"Economics and the Civilization of Love." *The Chesterton Review* (1994): 189-211.

"A Civilization of Love: The Pope's Call to the West." *Communio: International Catholic Review* 21 (1994): 497-499.

"Christological Aesthetics and *Evangelium Vitae:* Toward a Definition of Liberalism." *Communio: International Catholic Review* 22 (1995): 193-224.

"Christology and the *Imago Dei:* Interpreting *Gaudium et Spes.*" *Communio: International Catholic Review* 23 (1996): 156-184.

"At the Heart of the World, from the Center of the Church: Communio Ecclesiology and 'Worldly' Liberation." *Pro Ecclesia* 5 (1996): 314-333.

"On the Catholic Common Ground Project: The Christological Foundations of Dialogue." *Communio: International Catholic Review* 23 (1996): 823-851.

"Modernity, Postmodernity, and the Problem of Atheism." *Communio: International Catholic Review* 24 (1997): 563-579.

"Be Not Afraid: A *Crisis* Symposium on the Legacy of John Paul II." *Crisis* 15 (1997): 15-36.

"Reorienting the Church on the Eve of the Millennium: John Paul II's 'New Evangelization.'" *Communio: International Catholic Review* 24 (1997): 728-779.

"Introduction to the 1998 Edition." In *The Mystery of the Supernatural* by Henri de Lubac, xi-xxxi. New York: Crossroad, 1998.

"Going to the Heart: An Interview with Dr. David L. Schindler." In *A Compendium for*

Catholic Higher Education Officials: Called to Continuous Renewal Both as "Universities" and as "Catholic" (1998): 35-41.

"Luigi Giussani on the 'Religious Sense' and the Cultural Situation of Our Time." *Communio: International Catholic Review* 25 (1998): 141-150.

"Institution and Charism: The Missions of the Son and the Spirit in Church and World." *Communio: International Catholic Review* 25 (1998): 253-273.

"The Pneumatological Foundations of Dialogue: Response to Imbelli, Tekippe, and Culpepper." *Communio: International Catholic Review* 25 (1998): 366-376.

"*Communio* Ecclesiology and Liberalism" (Symposium with Michael Baxter and Michael Novak on *Heart of the World, Center of the Church*). *The Review of Politics* 60 (1998): 775-786.

"'The Religious Sense' and American Culture." *Communio: International Catholic Review* 25 (1998): 679-699.

"The Meaning of the Human in a Technological Age: *Homo faber, Homo sapiens, Homo amans.*" *Communio: International Catholic Review* 26 (1999): 80-103.

"God and the End of Intelligence: Knowledge as Relationship." *Communio: International Catholic Review* 26 (1999): 510-540.

"The Catholic Academy and the Order of Intelligence: The Dying of the Light." *Communio: International Catholic Review* 26 (1999): 722-745.

"Beauty, Transcendence, and the Face of the Other: Religion and Culture in America." *Communio: International Catholic Review* 26 (1999): 916-921.

"Homelessness and the Modern Condition: The Family, Community, and the Global Economy." *Communio: International Catholic Review* 27 (2000): 411-430.

"Is Truth Ugly? Moralism and the Convertibility of Being and Love." *Communio: International Catholic Review* 27 (2000): 701-728.

"Creation and Nuptiality: A Reflection on Feminism in Light of Schmemann's Liturgical Theology." *Communio: International Catholic Review* 28 (2001): 265-295.

"Trinity, Creation, and the Order of Intelligence in the Modern Academy." *Communio: International Catholic Review* 28 (2001): 406-428.

"Introduction to Schmemann's *Journals.*" *Communio: International Catholic Review* 29 (2002): 606-610.

"Toward a Culture of Life: The Eucharist, the 'Restoration' of Creation, and the 'Worldly' Task of the Laity in Liberal Societies." *Communio: International Catholic Review* 29 (2002): 679-690.

"Religion and Secularity in a Culture of Abstraction: On the Integrity of Space, Time, Matter, and Motion." In *The Strange New World of the Gospel,* ed. Carl E. Braaten and Robert W. Jenson, 32-54. Grand Rapids: Eerdmans, 2002; *Pro Ecclesia* 11 (2002): 76-94.

"For the Life of the World: Hans Urs von Balthasar on the Church as Eucharist." In *The Cambridge Companion to Hans Urs von Balthasar,* ed. Edward T. Oakes and David Moss, 51-63. Cambridge: Cambridge University Press, 2004.

"The Significance of World and Culture for Moral Theology: *Veritatis Splendor* and the

'Nuptial-Sacramental' Nature of the Body." *Communio: International Catholic Review* 31 (2004): 111-143.

"Biotechnology and the Givenness of the Good: Posing Properly the Moral Question Regarding Human Dignity." *Communio: International Catholic Review* 31 (2004): 612-644.

"The Significance of Hans Urs von Balthasar in the Contemporary Cultural Situation." In *Glory, Grace, and Culture: The Work of Hans Urs von Balthasar,* ed. Ed Block Jr., 16-36. Mahwah, NJ: Paulist Press, 2005.

"*Veritatis Splendor* and the Foundations of Bioethics: Notes Toward an Assessment of Altered Nuclear Transfer (ANT) and Embryonic (Pluripotent) Stem Cell Research." *Communio: International Catholic Review* 32 (2005): 195-201.

"A Response to the Joint Statement, 'Production of Pluripotent Stem Cells by Oocyte Assisted Reprogramming.'" *Communio: International Catholic Review* 32 (2005): 369-380.

"Truth, Freedom, and Relativism in Western Democracies: Pope Benedict XVI's Contributions to *Without Roots.*" *Communio: International Catholic Review* 32 (2005): 669-681.

"*Agere sequitur esse:* What Does It Mean? A Reply to Father Austriaco." *Communio: International Catholic Review* 32 (2005): 795-824.

"The Dramatic Nature of Life in the Light of Love: Liberal Societies and the Foundations of Human Dignity." *Communio: International Catholic Review* 33 (2006): 183-202.

"Charity, Justice, and the Church's Activity in the World." *Communio: International Catholic Review* 33 (2006): 346-367.

"Liberalism and the Memory of God: The Religious Sense in America." *Communio: International Catholic Review* 34 (2007): 482-487.

"'Keeping the World Awake to God': Benedict XVI and America." *Communio: International Catholic Review* 35 (2008): 107-114.

"In memoriam: Patricia Buckley Bozell." *Communio: International Catholic Review* 35 (2008): 167-170.

"Homelessness and the Modern Condition: Family, Community, and Global Economy." *Journal of Law, Philosophy and Culture* 2, no. 1 (2008): 149-168.

"The Embodied Person as Gift and the Cultural Task in America: *Status Quaestionis.*" *Communio: International Catholic Review* 35 (2008): 397-431.

"Editorial: President Obama, Notre Dame, and a Dialogue That Witnesses: A Question for Father Jenkins." *Communio: International Catholic Review* 36 (2009): 7-12.

"Regarding Legal Recognition of Same-Sex Unions." *Communio: International Catholic Review* 37 (2010): 149-152.

"Living and Thinking Reality in Its Integrity: Originary Experience, God, and the Task of Education." *Communio: International Catholic Review* 37 (2010): 167-185.

Contributors

Stratford Caldecott is G. K. Chesterton Research Fellow at St. Benet's Hall and the editor of *Second Spring*. Formerly a Senior Editor at Routledge, Harper Collins, and T&T Clark, he has written and edited books on J. R. R. Tolkien, sacramental theology, the historian Christopher Dawson, and liturgical reform in the Catholic Church. He is the author of *Beauty for Truth's Sake: On the Re-enchantment of Education* (Brazos Press).

Peter J. Casarella is Professor of Catholic Studies at DePaul University. He is the founding Director of DePaul's Center for World Catholicism and Intercultural Theology. He has served with David Schindler as co-organizer of the annual meeting of the Hans Urs von Balthasar Society at the Catholic Theological Society of America. He has published in the areas of theological aesthetics, Nicholas of Cusa, medieval Christian thought, and Hispanic/Latino theology.

Larry S. Chapp is Professor of Systematic Theology at DeSales University. He is the author of *The God Who Speaks: Hans Urs von Balthasar's Theology of Revelation* (International Scholars Publications) and *The God of Covenant and Creation: Scientific Naturalism and Its Challenge to the Christian Faith* (T&T Clark).

David S. Crawford is Associate Professor of Moral Theology and Family Law at the John Paul II Institute for Studies on Marriage and Family. He is the author of *Marriage and the Sequela Christi* (Lateran University Press).

Michael Hanby is Assistant Professor of Biotechnology and Culture at the

John Paul II Institute for Studies on Marriage and Family. He is the author of *Augustine and Modernity* (Routledge) and a forthcoming book tentatively entitled *Creation: Theology, Cosmology, and Biology* (Blackwell).

Nicholas J. Healy Jr. is Assistant Professor of Philosophy and Culture at the John Paul II Institute for Studies on Marriage and Family. He is the author of *Being in Communion: The Eschatology of Hans Urs von Balthasar* (Oxford University Press).

Rodney A. Howsare is Associate Professor of Theology at DeSales University. He is the author of *Hans Urs von Balthasar and Protestantism* (T&T Clark) and *Balthasar: A Guide of the Perplexed* (T&T Clark).

D. Stephen Long is Professor of Systematic Theology at Marquette University. He is an ordained United Methodist minister and served churches in Honduras and North Carolina. He works in the intersection between theology and ethics. His publications include *Divine Economy: Theology and the Market* (Routledge), *The Goodness of God: Theology, Church, and Social Order* (Brazos), *Speaking of God: Theology, Truth, and Language* (Eerdmans), and *Christian Ethics: A Very Short Introduction* (Oxford University Press).

Antonio López is Dean and Associate Professor of Systematic Theology at the John Paul II Institute for Studies on Marriage and Family. He is the author of *Spirit's Gift: The Metaphysical Insight of Claude Bruaire* (Catholic University of America) and a forthcoming book entitled *Gift and the Unity of Being* (Eerdmans).

Tracey Rowland is Dean and Permanent Fellow in Political Philosophy and Continental Theology of the John Paul II Institute for Marriage and Family (Melbourne) and an Adjunct Professor of the Centre for Faith, Ethics and Society at the University of Notre Dame (Sydney). She is the author of *Culture and the Thomist Tradition: After Vatican II* (Routledge) and *Ratzinger's Faith: The Theology of Pope Benedict XVI* (Oxford University Press).

D. C. Schindler, the son of David L. Schindler, is Associate Professor of Philosophy in the Humanities Department at Villanova University. He is the author of *Hans Urs von Balthasar and the Dramatic Structure of Truth*

(Fordham University Press), *Plato's Critique of Impure Reason: On Goodness and Truth in the Republic* (Catholic University of America), and a manuscript tentatively entitled *Schiller, Schelling, and Hegel on the Perfection of Freedom: Germans Between the Ancients and the Moderns.*

Adrian J. Walker is an Editor of *Communio: International Catholic Review* and a professional translator. He has published in the areas of metaphysics, philosophical anthropology, bioethics, and the thought of Maximus the Confessor.